W9-CRK-732

CASS LIBRARY OF AFRICAN STUDIES

MISSIONARY RESEARCHES AND TRAVELS

No. 5.

General Editor: ROBERT I. ROTBERG
Massachusetts Institute of Technology

TEN YEARS NORTH OF THE ORANGE RIVER

MISSIONARY RESEARCHES AND TRAVELS

No. 10. Frederick Stanley Arnot
Garenganze, Or, Seven Years' Pioneer Mission Work in Central Africa (c. 1886)
With a new introduction by Professor Robert I. Rotberg.
New Edition.

No. 11. Hope Masterman Wadell
Twenty-Nine Years in the West Indies and Central Africa. A Review of Missionary Work and Adventure 1829-1858 (1863)
With a new introduction by G. I. Jones
Second Edition.

No. 12. W. A. Elmslie
Among the Wild Ngoni. (1899)
With a new introductory note by Ian Nance
New Impression.

No. 13. Robert Pickering Ashe
Two Kings of Uganda. Or, Life by the shores of Victoria Nyanza. Being an account of a residence of Six Years in Eastern Equatorial Africa (1889)
With a new introduction by Professor John Rowe.
Second Edition.

No. 14. A. M. Mackay
A. M. Mackay, Pioneer Missionary of the Church Missionary Society to Uganda (1890) by his sister (J. W. H.).
With a new introductory note by Professor D. A. Low.
New Impression.

No. 15. Samuel Crowther
Journal of an Expedition up the Niger and Tshadda Rivers undertaken by Macgregor Laird, Esq., in connection with the British Government in 1854 (1855)
With a new introduction by Professor J. F. A. Ajayi.
Second Edition.

No. 16. Charles New
Life, Wanderings and Labours in Eastern Africa. With an account of the First Successful Ascent of the Equatorial Snow Mountain, Kilima Njaro. And remarks upon East African Slavery (1873, 1874).
With a new introduction by Alison Smith.
Third Edition.

No. 17. Ruth H. Fisher
Twilight Tales of the Black Baganda (1911).
With a new introduction by Professor. Merrick Posnansky.
Second Edition.

No. 18. James Frederick Schön and Samuel Crowther
Journals of the Rev. James Frederick Schön and Mr. Samuel Crowther, who, with her Majesty's Government, accompanied the Expedition of the Niger in 1841, on behalf of the Church Missionary Society (1842).
With a new introduction by Professor J. F. A. Ajayi.
Second Edition.

TEN YEARS NORTH OF THE ORANGE RIVER

A STORY OF EVERYDAY LIFE AND WORK AMONG THE SOUTH AFRICAN TRIBES

FROM

1859—1869

BY

JOHN MACKENZIE

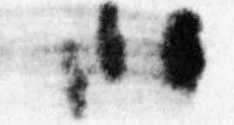

SECOND EDITION

With a New Introduction by

CECIL NORTHCOTT

FRANK CASS & CO. LTD.

Published by
FRANK CASS AND COMPANY LIMITED
67 Great Russell Street, London WC1B 3BT

Distributed in the United States by
International Scholarly Book Services, Inc.
Beaverton, Oregon 97005

Library of Congress Catalog Card No. 76–169805

ISBN 0 7146 1875 6

First edition	1871
Second edition	1971

PRINTED IN GREAT BRITAIN BY
STEPHEN AUSTIN AND SONS LTD., HERTFORD, ENGLAND

GENERAL EDITOR'S PREFACE

During the critical years of the nineteenth century when the Ngwato of Botswana, under their great chief Khama, were beginning to accept the Christian Gospel and the practical degree of Westernization that such a radical shift of allegiances implied, John Mackenzie was in attendance. Indeed, Mackenzie not only assisted in the evangelization of the Ngwato, he was one of Khama's primary sources of external support in the young chief's struggle against his non-Christian and pro-Afrikaner opponents. Mackenzie was instrumental in bringing about the "protection" of what became Bechuanaland (now Botswana) by Great Britain, a move which was directed against Afrikaners (from the Republic of the Transvaal) and other, more vaguely-defined enemies of the Ngwato and their neighbours.

As a result of his unique involvement in the creation of Bechuanaland and the furtherance of the presumed interests of the Ngwato, Mackenzie's observations form an especially valuable historical record. More than his *Austral Africa, Losing It or Ruling It* (London, 1887), the book here reprinted in its entirety for the first time since its original publication in 1871, includes a reasonably complete and, given Mackenzie's own involvement, candid appraisal of Botswana at the onset of colonial rule. Mackenzie served the London Missionary Society, to which organization in Botswana Robert Moffat and David Livingstone were also affiliated. But he was a man of independent mind, and his book was written for an audience wider than that usually associated with nineteenth-century missionary literature.

Ten Years North of the Orange River is introduced by Dr. Cecil Northcott, sometime home secretary of the London Missionary Society and now senior editor of the Lutterworth Press. Dr. Northcott has written the standard biography of Robert Moffat, *Robert Moffat, Pioneer in Africa* (London, 1961), a popular history of the London Missionary Society, *Livingstone in Africa* (London, 1957) and *Christianity in Africa* (London, 1963).

September 1970 R.I.R.

INTRODUCTION TO THE SECOND EDITION

John Mackenzie most correctly describes his book with its sub-title, " a story of everyday life and work among the South African tribes from 1859 to 1869 ". During those years Mackenzie was a young missionary, reaching the age of 34 in 1869 in Bechuanaland. He was an eye witness of the life of the Tswana tribes, particularly as they reacted to the presence of white men in the persons of Boer farmers, missionaries, and traders. He also observed the customs and traditions of the Tswana and the Ndebele (Matabele), whose internal organisation he describes in some detail in chapter seventeen. The book has been described as an " important source book on Ngwato history and culture "[1] and this fact alone gives it a place in southern African history. Mackenzie was aware of the shifting boundaries both of geography and culture in the vast area of southern Africa stretching from the Orange to the Zambezi Rivers. He understood the political importance of Bechuanaland, and raised the question of British responsibility, for which he campaigned with such vigour in his later years.

From the moment that he landed at Cape Town in

July, 1858, Mackenzie was alert to the African scene, its people and its problems, and he could write engagingly about them. His description, for instance, of his first journey northwards into Bechuanaland, with its vignettes of the Dutch farmer at home,[2] and of the sociological influence of the *Nachtmaal*,[3] are memorably done. Mackenzie wrote with British readers in mind, and especially those committed to the support of Christian missions, but he is always objective and never propagandist, and his book has rightly taken its place as one of the minor classics of southern African history.

Like many other men of the London Missionary Society who were sent to southern Africa in the first half of the nineteenth century, John Mackenzie was a Scot, born at Knockando on August 30, 1835. Coming from the ranks of the " godly poor ", as did Robert Moffat and David Livingstone, his famous predecessors in Africa, Mackenzie left school at thirteen and was apprenticed to the printing trade in Elgin. His religious awakening appears to have come from association with the Independent, or Congregational, Chapel in Elgin, and his spiritual diary for the years 1854 and 1855 shows an extremely introspective young man struggling to reconcile his " worldly engagements " with the " holy work of the service of the Gospel ".[4] He made two applications to the London Missionary Society, and, in 1855 at the age of twenty, was accepted for missionary service " on probation ", and sent to Bedford to study under two local Congregational ministers who conducted a small academy for the training of prospective missionaries. A Bible-based curriculum, with special emphasis on the making of sermons, was Mackenzie's chief preparation for his missionary vocation.

> Everything except Greek had to be thrown aside to complete my sermon, and after all I had barely time for it. I have not had more than seven hours sleep, nor less than six during past week. I am really quite lazy; it requires effort to rise on a freezing morning while your companion is soundly sleeping. I have a watch now—a very fine one; and I must be regular in this matter now. Next week I shall always be in bed by eleven and up at five—for a trial. I shall encourage meditation and soul communion with God in the house and by the way, so I shall be moulded. I have done nothing besides Greek this week and that sermon. It was too long.[5]

While on holiday in Scotland in 1857 he met and became engaged to Ellen Douglas, daughter of William Douglas of Portobello, and, eight days after his ordination, on April 19, 1858, in the Queen Street Hall, Edinburgh, they were married.[6]

Douglas Mackenzie in his biography of his father describes him as:

> Six feet in height, broad shouldered but lithe and active, with his fair hair thrown back from a massive forehead, with a ruddy beard encircling his strong features, with those deep-set light blue eyes, that could with amusement, or flash ' sunbeams like swords ' in a moment of moral indignation. Long afterwards an observant man who met him said, ' I shook hands with him and he looked right through me '.[7]

The Tswana called John Mackenzie, *Mohibudi*, the Red One.

The mission party of which Mackenzie was a member was intended to be a powerful reinforcement for the London Mission's stations in southern Africa, and to carry the Christian faith to the Zambezi among the Makololo and the Ndebele. This northward thrust had been prepared for by the pioneers—David Livingstone among the Makololo and Robert Moffat among the Ndebele. The time had now come to test the possibility of making a permanent Christian settlement among these tribes, and the planning in London had been conducted in the atmosphere of concern for Africa generated by Livingstone's presence in Britain, and especially by his famous Senate House speech in Cambridge on December 4, 1857. Mackenzie was destined to be in the Makololo party and his immediate colleagues were Roger Price (1834–1900), also a new recruit, and Holloway Helmore (1815–1860), the leader, who had already spent nineteen years with the Bechuana mission. The Ndebele group consisted of two recruits: William Sykes (1829–1887), and Thomas Morgan Thomas (1828–1884), with John Smith Moffat (1835–1918), Robert Moffat's eldest son, in the role of an " independent missionary ", supported by his brother-in-law, David Livingstone, and ready to serve in either party.

The expedition left Cape Town on the 600-mile ox-wagon trek to Kuruman, in three sections. The first, led by the veteran Robert Moffat and Mrs. Moffat and composed of four wagons, was an all-Moffat group including his son John and his newly married wife Emily Unwin of Brighton, and his daughters Mrs. David Livingstone and Jane Moffat. Oxen were hard and expensive to obtain in Cape Town so Jane Moffat tried a dozen donkeys on her wagon but gave up after two days and used mules.[8] Then came the Helmores, Prices, Sykeses, and Thomases, and finally, in September, the Mackenzies—delayed by the onset of Mrs. Mackenzie's pregnancy. Each missionary was allowed £150 for travelling expenses, as well as £10 for books; £100 worth of medicines was provided for the expedition. They were expected to live off the country as they went along and to procure supplies by payment or barter.

Looking back on the journey from Kuruman, where he arrived on January 1, 1859, Mackenzie describes it as "disastrous and protracted and therefore expensive and unpleasant".[9] It had been dominated by all of the miseries of unfit and exhausted oxen and the attitude of white drivers who refused to share the same fire with "their black brethren of the whip".[10] But there were happy, idyllic moments, too, on the long road when John and Ellen Mackenzie gathered flowers to decorate their wagon, laughed at the baboons who came to gaze at them and enjoyed cooking the evening meal under the stars. They named their wagon "Patience Lodge".[11]

Mackenzie was soon involved in discussions on the strategy of the two proposed new missions.[12] The Makololo plan, largely the product of Livingstone's contention that the Makololo could be persuaded to move north of the Zambezi from the unhealthy Linyanti area, hinged upon Livingstone's meeting the expedition at Linyanti after battling his way up the Zambezi.

Mackenzie realised the grave risks in taking a party of missionaries, wives, and children into the Linyanti area and proposed a "bachelor expedition" to explore the ground. But the enthusiastic Helmore was prepared to take his wife and four children and the Prices were ready to go too. Mackenzie was unable to join them, owing to Mrs. Mackenzie's confinement at Fauresmith, where their son was born eight days after the Helmore expedition set out for Linyanti on July 8, 1859. The Mackenzies followed in May 1860 with four wagons, thirteen people, seventy oxen, and three horses—a compact, well organised expedition of nine months duration during which, Mackenzie claimed, "no one travelling in our company ever endured a day's hunger or thirst".[13]

Mackenzie was twenty-four and the vivid impressions of his first northward journey, although written ten years later, are conveyed to the reader in chapters seven to twelve of this book. At Shoshong, the then capital of the Ngwato—to be his home for twelve years—he met Robert Moffat in July 1860 on his way back to Kuruman after the successful planting of the Matabele Mission at Inyati. There was no firm news of the Helmore expedition until September, when Mackenzie met Roger Price dramatically at a ford on the Zouga River, and from one glance at his emaciated condition knew that the worst had happened.[14]

Mackenzie was the first to hear and record a consecutive account of the disaster that befell the Helmore expedition. During its four months at Linyanti, the lives of Helmore, his wife and two children, and Mrs. Price and her infant daughter were lost. Roger Price,[15] who related his tale to Mackenzie in emotional stress at Chief Lechulatebe's at Lake Ngami, was convinced that Chief Sekeletu of the Makololo had poisoned the party, but Mackenzie believed that the symptoms that Price described all pointed to "African fever",[16] and his belief has been borne out by most subsequent investigations of the Makololo disaster.[17] But it has to be remembered that Sekeletu and his Makololo were then at the last low ebb of their life as an independent tribe, and had deteriorated in conduct since the days of their great chief Sebituane—Livingstone's friend—who had given them the vision of an empire north of the Zambezi and had then led them back again to Linyanti sadly reduced by disease and warfare. Treachery and poison for the mission party therefore, cannot be ruled out. Livingstone, when he heard of the disaster, was particularly acid in his comment to his brother-in-law, John Smith Moffat—" a precious mull they made of it ".[18] The tragedy was all the more inexplicable to Livingstone because when he arrived in Linyanti in August, 1860, five months after the deaths, he found his old wagon still safely in the care of Sekeletu. It stood with its medicine chest intact only a few hundred yards from the graves.[19]

With the Makololo tragedy weighing heavily on him, there was nothing else that Mackenzie could advise the stricken Price but to turn back to Kuruman, which they did in the September 1860, taking the journey in leisurely fashion, and staying for two months at Shoshong. They arrived at Kuruman in February 1861, having been met on the road by Robert Moffat, who had been stirred by rumours of the disaster, to organise a relief party.

Mackenzie's mind had already begun to consider the future of missions in the north, and, in a letter to Dr. Arthur Tidman, Secretary of the London Missionary Society, he showed his capacity to think of the broad issues:

> Altho' the mission to the Makololo has proved so disastrous, there is a teeming population to the eastward, in that district recently discovered by Dr. Livingstone. . . . It seems to me that there is a greater prospect of success in a mission to some of these tribes approachable from the sea-coast than there ever was in connection with the mission to the Makololo. Should the Directors resolve to continue their efforts for the evangelisation of Central Africa, I am quite

> willing to devote myself to the work. I think the mission to the north of the Zambesi has hardly received a fair trial, there being high, all but insurmountable, obstacles in connection with the Makololo . . . it might take some time to establish such a mission on a permanent basis; but if an agent or two were directed to visit the country and to feel their way quietly, it is not improbable that success might ultimately attend their efforts.[20]

But the eastward approach was not favoured in London and, in 1862, Mackenzie was sent northwards to Shoshong still with an eye on resurrecting the mission to the luckless Makololo. In June 1862 Mackenzie, Price, and John Smith Moffat met at Shoshong to plan their next moves, and to write a joint letter to Sekeletu[21] telling him of their intention to cross the Zambezi and select a suitable site for a mission station. The letter[22] is an excellent example of the mission approach to an African chief with its mixture of respect, narrative, and straightforward speech. While the letter is in the names of the three men, it was evidently signed by John Smith Moffat as a son of the great Moshete:

> To Sekeletu, son of Sebetwane, King of the Makololo. We write to you Sekeletu. We are three. First I am Price, whom you have seen at Seodi, where the teachers died. After I left your country I went to the white people and took the children of Helmore to their friends. Now I hope to return to you to do the work for which I am sent, namely to teach you and your people respecting God and Jesus Christ His Son. Second I am Mackenzie. I also am a teacher. I started from Kuruman to come to you, but I met Price and the children of Helmore on the way and we all returned.
>
> Third I am John the son of Moshete. You heard about me from the Doctor[23] when he visited you last year, and told you that I was amongst the Matebele

teaching them the word of God. Now I am travelling. I am going to Kuruman to see my father and mother, that is Moshete and MaMeri.[24]

We three write to you, Sekeletu. We wish to tell you that which is in our hearts. Sebegwe, the son of Sebobi will carry our letter.[25] Our hearts weep. They weep for our friends who died at Seodi. Moreover we weep for them because they suffered much, being made to suffer by you Sekeletu and by your people. But still we love you, Sekeletu. God has commanded us to love all men, and to do well by them. We hope to start next year and to draw near to your country. We will come to you where you are because we do not wish to place ourselves in the district which has fever. We shall direct our course lower down so as to fall in with the great river at Mosioatunya,[26] because we are informed by the Doctor that this road leads to the healthy district on the other side, a high land which has no fever. When we reach this place we shall have an opportunity to talk to you Sekeletu, and to hear how we are to live with the Makololo. Now we seek your answer. Sebegwe will read you this letter[27] and we shall expect your answer by him. We shall hear by Sebegwe whether you are willing to receive us and to let us live in the district of which we have spoken.

Also I, the son of Moshete, speak concerning myself and say: I am still on my way to my father, to ask his permission to come. It is he who took me to the Matebele, and now I shall ask him to send me to you. But, if he consents, I shall return to the Matebele, because I promised them to do so and if I perceive that they speak words of peace and allow me to leave in a friendly manner I will come to you with the rest, namely Mackenzie and Price with our wives.

And now Sekeletu, mark well that we are all teachers. We wish to teach you and your people. We wish to proclaim among you the great love with which God has loved men. God bless you Sekeletu and keep you. Farewell.

Sekeletu's reply came in December 1862 and was favourable provided the missionaries went first to the Victoria Falls.[28] The ailing chief[29] was still seeking a missionary shield against the powerful Ndebele, but Mackenzie, in a final message of June 1863, warned him against relying on this shield, and well he might for, in March 1863, the Ndebele swooped on Shoshong itself, in spite of its being a mission stronghold, in a devastating raid during which the young Khama, the Chief's son, showed a resourceful generalship. Mackenzie's vivid narrative of the raid (Chapter 14) gives a description of Ndebele tactics, and also of the power of a few firearms in this sort of warfare. Mackenzie had the courage to conduct divine service in his house with a congregation under arms and also proposed to visit the Ndebele camp.[30] Since the Ndebele were clearly capable of swift raids, the attack on Shoshong put the finishing touch to any hope of a mission among the Makololo north of the Zambezi and, after Sekeletu's death, the Makololo hugged the remote country between Linyanti and Lake Ngami and finally perished as a tribal force through the treachery of Lechulatebe in Ngamiland.[31]

This experience of the Ndebele on the warpath may have persuaded Mackenzie to accept John Smith Moffat's invitation to go with him to the infant mission station at Inyati and to see Mzilikazi and the Ndebele at home. He arrived in August 1863 and left in January 1864. These five months show Mackenzie as a competent judge of local conditions and of the prospects for missions despite the military system of the Ndebele. More than the Moffats, he saw that the inner totalitarian structure of the Ndebele was unyielding and that the old chief Mzilikazi knew that to yield was to agree to his own and his people's destruction.[32] During Mackenzie's visits to the chief he always pressed for permission to teach the people, a frontal attack which ruffled his colleagues—although they would have welcomed him as a member of the mission—and Mzilikazi was keen that he should stay.

John Smith Moffat sums up the differences of outlook in his Journal for December 11, 1863:

> Mr. Mackenzie has by no means determined to stay in the country. In fact he stated yesterday that he would not remain unless the king gave express permission to any of his people to learn to read who might wish to do so. Under these circumstances to ransack the country in search of a new station seems to be very like a fool's errand, not to mention the aspect the thing might present to the king and people. Mr. Sykes and I both think that there is quite enough religious liberty to afford a reason for his remaining here. We are free to preach the gospel to every creature. This seems to me the first thing. Learning to read is very good, but it will follow soon enough. For my own part—but in this I stand alone—I object to ask the king for liberty to preach the gospel or to teach people to read the scriptures. To ask him seems to imply that he has a right to forbid it if he will. I think he has a right to say whether or no we shall live in the country and to decide all matters in respect to our civil privileges, but not when we come to the relations of men with God. . . .[33]

Mackenzie was naturally under suspicion as "Sekhomi's missionary" from the Ngwato, but he was able to convince Mzilikazi that he was no spy. As Emily Moffat points out in a letter to her father J. S. Unwin, of Brighton, on August 9, 1863:

> Even if Mackenzie should not permanently stay at the Matabele, it is a grand point to have gained the entrance of another teacher, and also a principle is

established that teachers have nothing to do with wars of the different tribes.[34]

Emily Moffat, not always over-charitable in her judgment of others, and convinced that no one but a Moffat could handle the Ndebele (Matabele), says of Mackenzie:

> Oh, this Matabele yoke is a galling one. Mackenzie is not quite so used to it as we now are, and he kicks at it. And no marvel! But he would get on well with the Matabele I think. He can be cool and will talk over a thing long and this suits them.[35]

Mackenzie had now gone as far north in Africa as he was to go throughout all of his career, and he had evidently made up his mind that there was more chance for his mission among the Tswana than among the Ndebele. So he returned to Shoshong, the Ngwato capital, and rejoined Roger Price as a resident missionary. Then the largest African town south of the Zambezi, with a population of about 20,000, Shoshong lay on a high plateau 3,350 feet above sea-level, and the town itself spread along the mouth of a ravine with its precipitous walls of black rocks. On either side of the ravine Mackenzie and Price built their little two-roomed cottages of wattle and daub. The site was bare of trees and the ground was so stony that gardening proved impossible. The wind whistled through the ravine and, in summer, the rocks radiated the heat and made the place like a furnace. In 1865 Mackenzie started to build a more permanent brick house, making his own burnt bricks of clay, dragging in timber from the forest, and teaching two of his congregation to use a pit-saw. From this house of 38 feet by 23 feet, with five rooms and kitchen and pantry, Mackenzie conducted his mission, and recorded the observations of tribal life that make his book so valuable a source for this period of Tswana history.[36]

In Chapter eighteen he deals with the internal civil disruption of the Ngwato, and the new pressures which Christianity was putting upon the traditional customs of the people. Mackenzie describes the arrival of Macheng, the rightful heir, from captivity among the Ndebele through the good offices of Robert Moffat,[37] his ultimate exile, the disputes between Sekhomi and his two sons Khama and Khamane, and the gradual emergence of Khama as the chief. Khama, who had been baptised by the Hermannsburg missionaries during their temporary stay in Shoshong, was steadfast in his opposition to the tribal customs of initiation and circumcision and the mysteries of the rain maker, and, while Khama was naturally the " missionary's man ", Mackenzie skilfully managed to keep a friendship with Sekhomi, his wily old " heathen " father, and the feckless young Macheng. When in 1867 Mackenzie built a church, he managed to invite Macheng (then in the ascendancy) as well as Khama and Khamane, to dinner in his house, and when Sekhomi was fleeing for his life it was to Mackenzie's house that he fled.[38]

While the quarrel was still unresolved, news arrived that gold had been discovered in the Tati area in the north of the Ngwato country, and Mackenzie immediately helped Macheng to draft a statement for presentation to the Governor of the Cape Colony, asking for his protection. He also asked the Governor to " govern the gold-diggers, in the name of the Queen of England ".[39] The Tati gold rush did not mature, but Mackenzie's policy for Bechuanaland had been enunciated in its simplest terms. He began to see that whether it was gold-diggers, or Boer farmers seeking minerals or farmlands, Bechuanaland was wide open to them. There was only one power capable of securing the lands of the Tswana in peace and safety and that, he believed, was Britain.

Mackenzie's chapters 19 to 23 are an important contribution to the inner history of the Ngwato. In many ways they represent a new tradition in missionary writing. For, unlike Robert Moffat, Mackenzie did not dismiss tribal customs and practices as being unworthy of attention because they were "heathen". He was against them as wholeheartedly as was Moffat, but he realised that a sure way into the heart of the Ngwato was to understand what the practices meant and why it was that the people were so attached to them. Mackenzie had respect for the office of a chief who united in himself the persons of "king, supreme judge, commander-in-chief, high priest and sorcerer",[40] and realised that the gospel he preached meant the erosion of the chief's multifarious authority.

This was the reason for the often treacherous conduct of Chief Sekhomi, who was bewildered and humiliated when, in April, 1865, he was deserted by his sons at the *boguera*, or initiation ceremonies. While most Ngwato fathers marched off with their sons to the initiation camp, Sekhomi's sons were at Mackenzie's school, and in church on Sundays.[41] The idea that the teaching of "the teachers" could ever interfere with the public and private life of the tribe had never entered Sekhomi's head, and he failed to adjust himself to the internal revolution in the tribal life that Christianity had created.

Mackenzie's chapters contain a first-hand account of the civil war between Sekhomi and his sons, and of the intrigues of Macheng on his restoration to the Ngwato chieftainship, and of the part that Sechele of the Bakwena played in them. It is a complicated story and Mackenzie's account of Macheng's history differs from that given by Robert Moffat in his *Matabele Journals*. But they both agree that Macheng was undoubtedly the son of the principal wife of Khari, the great Ngwato chief, while Sekhomi was the son of a secondary wife. Macheng, as a child of nine or ten had been in the guardianship of Sechele of the Kwena and had been carried off by a marauding gang of Ndebele. For twenty years he had lived with the Ndebele and had received the training of an Ndebele warrior. His restoration to the Ngwato chieftainship came through the intervention of Robert Moffat who, on his fourth journey to Mzilikazi in 1857/8, persuaded that monarch to allow the young man to go home to his own people. Moffat describes Macheng as "good looking, a mild countenance and a fine fellow about twenty-six years of age or less. I have been very much pleased with his unassuming disposition."[42] Moffat's optimistic judgment was not fulfilled, for there followed eighteen years of tribal strife which, during Mackenzie's first period at Shoshong (1864–1869), developed into a triangular struggle between Sekhomi, his sons Khama and Khamane, and Macheng. Mackenzie was trusted by all sides, but there is no doubt that he, and later his colleague, J. D. Hepburn, who joined him at Shoshong in 1871, were personally on the side of the young chief Khama and saw in him the best hope of stability in the Ngwato chieftainship.[43]

In his father's life Douglas Mackenzie quotes a description written by Mackenzie of the way in which he secured the identification of Khama, the "Christian

Chief", with the new "Christian way" in tribal custom:[44]

> I suggested to Khama that he should begin a new thing in the country, and issue his "letsemma"[45] as a Christian Chief in a Christian way. Inasmuch as every Chief has the right to choose the nation from whom his son shall receive his doctors or priests, Sekhomi had only exercised that right in choosing for his sons a missionary instead of a priest. The teaching of the missionary was therefore entitled to at least as much public respect as that of any native doctor. By publicly acknowledging his firm adherence to Christianity at the outset of his career, I hoped also that Khama would escape molestation from the heathen party in the future.

The proceedings at which Mackenzie made his speech were not in church but in the *khotla*, or public courtyard. Khama also made a speech declaring his unwavering loyalty to the Christian faith, and asking the people to regard the act of public worship which Mackenzie was leading as their *letsemma*, after which they might dig as they pleased. The worship consisted of Psalms 100, 33, and 65, and prayers.

Then Mackenzie spoke:

> The points which I aimed at establishing were the suitability of Christianity as a "custom" or religion; that, therefore, under Khama's sway, they were not to anticipate calamity through having given up the public recognition of the old customs; it was a religion which had come to them from no mean nation, but one whose skill and prowess were patent to them; it was not for one nation but for all; and it had made their young chiefs truthful, kindhearted and brave—their praise was in every tribe. Let no one therefore hinder them or molest them in God's service in the future; but rather let all learn how to love and to trust the

God of Khama and Khamane . . . thus ended Khama's public and solemn recognition of God and of Christianity among the Ngwato people.[46]

This event marked the height of Mackenzie's influence at Shoshong. By his speech he had skilfully identified the tribe and its chief with the Christian faith and the church. The Christian God was the God of Khama and Khamane, and to worship him was henceforth almost a tribal duty. A kind of "church-state" relationship developed between the tribe and the church with the missionary as a political as well as a spiritual adviser. The note of "imperialism" in Mackenzie's speech was also typical of his whole approach to the problems of Bechuanaland. What was good for Britain was good, he thought, for the Tswana and, on these grounds alone, the Christian religion had a lot to be said for it.

This event came in Mackenzie's second term at Shoshong, which began in 1871 after a furlough in Britain (1869–1871) during which he wrote this book. He was then joined by Hepburn and began to give most of his time to the development of a teacher-training school, which was transferred in 1876 to the newly built Moffat Institution at Kuruman, with himself as principal. This move brought Mackenzie into southern Bechuanaland and nearer the developing political, racial, and economic movements which were to occupy the major part of his time for the next fifteen years.

The "Mackenzie Policy" of British control from London of what he called "Austral-Africa", developed later in his *Austral Africa: Losing It or Ruling It*,[47] was already uppermost in his mind before he left Shoshong for, in 1875, he had spoken thus to his fellow missionaries at Kuruman:

> England has a great and incumbent duty to perform. It is within her power to cause that the European population of South Africa shall be as loyal and attached as in Australia or Canada. On the other hand it is quite possible for her to see growing up beside her Cape Colony, states whose bitter dislike of her government shall equal, if not exceed, any such feeling entertained now or at bygone times, by the people of the United States. . . . Let England then come forward and avowedly take charge of and direct the northward progress of Europeans in South Africa.[48]

In May 1876 he wrote a long letter to Sir Henry Barkley, the British High Commissioner in Southern Africa, which showed his grasp of the intricacies of the situation as the Afrikaner farmers trekked northwards:

> As I write there are over 40 ox-wagons lying on the Limpopo River—about two days from this place—the owners of which were until recently burghers of the Transvaal and inhabitants chiefly of the district of Magaliesburg . . . I hear they declare they are going to march on Mashonaland lying to the east of Matabeleland. . . . If the Dutch settle in Mashonaland as an independent people, there will never be one united South African Government. On the other hand, there will speedily grow up a large community or communities, richer and more powerful than the countries under the English Crown, agreeing in one thing if not in others—in dislike of their English neighbours . . . surely your duty to England and to the various English colonies in South Africa calls upon you to prevent if possible the addition to its territory by the Transvaal, of a country fairer and even more frutiful than the South African Republic itself. The Dutch can be checkmated and the outrages of the Matabele gradually put down, by the prompt appearance, in the interior, of a British Commissioner or Resident. . . . If the English power once got fairly to the north of the Dutch they would be forced to settle down and till the

soil . . . the Dutch would probably become in South Africa what they are in the United States.[49]

Mackenzie had had a thorough grounding in African affairs, and his vision of a British-controlled Southern African Commonwealth grew out of his concern that the indigenous peoples should have a fair and honourable position in it. But as this book shows, he was equally capable of thinking of the place of the white man in southern Africa and of his need for land and labour—a theme expanded in his later book *Austral Africa*. While always a missionary " to the heathen ", Mackenzie saw the need for strong political and economic government, and he firmly advocated the provision of it by Britain. During his brief period of authority in 1884 as the British Deputy Commissioner in Bechuanaland, he acted on this belief. He was an " imperialist " as much as Cecil Rhodes, but with a difference. Rhodes believed that the unification of southern Africa had to be the achievement of the government from Cape Town, while Mackenzie saw it as a British responsibility from London, for only in this way could he be sure of a fair deal for the African peoples and of the protection of Bechuanaland. Although he was defeated in his major concern for direct British control from the Cape to the Zambezi, he did triumph in securing British protection over Bechuanaland (1885), which led to the Bechuanaland Protectorate (1895), and to the independent Republic of Botswana (1966). Mackenzie has every right to be regarded as one of the " fathers" of modern Botswana.

One other aspect of Mackenzie's book shows him in the pioneer role of anthropologist and ethnographer. The appendix to the present book—" The Races of Southern Africa "—was quite a new venture in books of this kind, and Mackenzie's skilful discussion of languages, dress, and customs, with a further note on the contact of Europeans with Africans, was a forerunner of the many larger volumes of African scientific studies which have appeared since his time.

The book itself appeared in Edinburgh in the spring of 1871 and was " received with remarkable favour by reviewers of all types ". His son describes Mackenzie's style as having " no pretensions [being] . . . characterised by clearness and force ".[50]

Eleven years later, in 1883, Mackenzie wrote a children's version of *Ten Years* at the request of the London Missionary Society, with the title *Day Dawn in Dark Places*[51] for presentation to children who collected money for the support of the missions. This book shows Mackenzie's ability to write simply, and in narrative form.

In 1887, three years after he had resigned his brief appointment as Deputy Commissioner in Bechuanaland, Mackenzie published his large two-volumed work *Austral Africa*: *Losing It or Ruling It* in which, in over a thousand pages, he marshalled all of his experiences in southern Africa in a great effort to convince the British Government and British public opinion that what Britain had done so successfully in Canada and Australia could be done in southern Africa if only the British Government had the necessary resolution. Mackenzie believed that Britain had an " imperial duty " in southern Africa, from the Cape to the Zambezi, and that the test of her good intentions and ability to carry them out was to be seen in Bechuanaland. He knew that the extension northward and westward of the Transvaal frontier with its stark inequalities between black and white, the dispossession of native landowners and the Boer system of pass laws and employment, would be disastrous for the Tswana people. The only power capable of ruling the frontier was, he believed, British power controlled from London, and this was at the heart of Mackenzie's political philosophy.

Mackenzie's policy was defeated by a combination of Cape colonial politics, the frontier mining and land interests organised by Cecil Rhodes, and the irresolution of the British Government. Rhodes was triumphant with the establishment of the British South Africa Company (1889) and Mackenzie had to be content with the promise of direct British protection of the Tswana tribes north of the Molopo River, an assurance that was gravely threatened in 1895 when the Tswana chiefs went personally to London to re-affirm their desire for British protection.

In 1891 Mackenzie accepted the offer of the London Missionary Society to become the superintendent of the Hankey Settlement, fifty miles west of Port Elizabeth in the valley of the Gamtoos River. Hankey, named after a former Governor of Cape Colony, was one of a group of agricultural settlements under the management of the London Missionary Society in the Cape Colony where African tenant farmers could lease land at favourable rents. The estate, of over four thousand acres, had become an almost unworkable proposition on a tenant farming basis, and Mackenzie's task was to bring some central direction to the estate while at the same time encouraging individual initiative and the growth of self-reliant citizenship. In his eight years at Hankey, Mackenzie succeeded in bringing a new spirit into the administration, and prepared the way for the eventual large scale fruit farming which developed on the estate after its mission ownership had ceased. In 1893 he was elected chairman of the Congregational Union of South Africa, and his chairman's address, which fills twenty-two pages of the Union's year book for 1894, was on "The Christian Outlook in Cape Colony ". Mackenzie died at his son's home in Kimberley on March 23, 1899.

September 1970 CECIL NORTHCOTT

NOTES

[1] Isaac Schapera, *The Tswana, An Ethnographic Survey* (London, 1953) 70

[2] Below, 13ff.

[3] Below, 18, 19

[4] Douglas Mackenzie, *John Mackenzie* (London, 1902) 10–17

[5] Ibid 26

[6] Mrs. Mackenzie survived her husband and died in Bulawayo, July 14, 1925, aged 90

[7] Ibid 41

[8] The donkeys were intended by Sir George Grey, Governor of the Cape Colony, to establish a postal service between Kuruman and the Zambezi River, but they defeated even Robert Moffat's patience.

[9] Mackenzie, *John Mackenzie*, 54

[10] Ibid 54

[11] Ibid 50, 51

[12] Below, 32

[13] Below, 221

[14] Below, 18

[15] Below, 186

[16] Below, 188

[17] Edwin Smith, *Great Lion of Bechuanaland* (London, 1953), 411–425. This life of Roger Price contains the most detailed study of the expedition and disaster.

[18] J. P. R. Wallis (ed.) *Matabele Mission of J. S. and E. Moffat* (London, 1945), 160

[19] George Seaver, *David Livingstone: His Life and Letters* (London, 1957), 374

[20] Mackenzie, *John Mackenzie,* 70, quoting a letter from Mackenzie to the L.M.S. February 29, 1861

[21] Below, 239

[22] Smith, *Great Lion of Bechuanaland*, 127

[23] Livingstone

[24] J. S. Moffat and his wife Emily were on their way south from their station at Inyati in Matabeleland

[25] Sebobi was the trusted teacher at Kanye among the Ngwaketse

[26] The Victoria Falls

[27] Written in Sechuana

[28] Below, 240

[29] Sekeletu died of leprosy in August, 1863

[30] Below, 279, 281

[31] Below, 243–248

[32] Below, 336

[33] *The Matabele Mission*, 214

[34] Ibid 223

[35] Ibid 222

[36] Below, 355ff.

[37] Moffat (ed. J. P. R. Wallis), *Matabele Journals II*, London, 1945, 135ff.

[38] Below, 449

[39] Below, 453ff.

[40] Below, 371

[41] Below, 411

[42] Moffat, *Matabele Journals II*, 142

[43] J. D. Hepburn, *Twenty Years in Khama's Country* (London, 1895) to be reprinted by Frank Cass, 1970, with a new introduction by Dr. C. Northcott; see Chapter 6

[44] Mackenzie, *John Mackenzie* 143–144. No date but from internal evidence it must have been in the spring of 1872

[45] *letsemma*=the inauguration of seed-time

[46] Ibid 145

[47] (London, 1887) 2 vols

[48] Mackenzie, *John Mackenzie*, 171, 172

[49] Ibid 176

[50] Ibid 131

[51] London: Cassell & Co. Ltd., 1883

Orange River, near Aliwal North.

TEN YEARS

NORTH OF THE ORANGE RIVER

A STORY OF EVERYDAY LIFE AND WORK AMONG THE SOUTH AFRICAN TRIBES

FROM 1859 TO 1869

BY JOHN MACKENZIE
OF THE LONDON MISSIONARY SOCIETY

EDINBURGH
EDMONSTON AND DOUGLAS
1871.

PREFACE.

I OFFER this work to the public as a humble contribution to our literature on Southern Africa.

The reader is first introduced to the rural and village life of the Cape Colony. Sketches of social and religious life in the Free State and Transvaal Republic are followed by a description of long-established mission stations. Several chapters are devoted to the Makololo Mission, which was inaugurated so auspiciously and ended so fatally. Narrating events as they took place, I have left their lessons to be drawn by others. My journey to Matebele-land enables me to describe the hideous form of society in a purely military tribe. Our residence at Shoshong, and the experiences of the Mission there, are given in the concluding chapters. The Appendix contains what may be read with advantage as an introduction to the present work. I would specially direct attention to that part of it which describes the results of the past contact of Europeans with South Africans.

Every Christian believes in the spread and final triumph of Christianity. Various opinions are held as to the methods of securing this end, and different views have been expressed as to the capacity for improvement of certain races. I return to my work in Africa, cherishing the hope that the present volume will furnish some information for the discussion of this important subject.

I beg to thank my friend Mr. Samuel Edmonston for the carefully executed and faithful Illustrations which enliven the following pages.

I am under obligation to the Rev. Dr. Mullens for access to documents in the Mission House, and for his kind assistance with the Map. I am also indebted to the Rev. R. Moffat, Rev. W. B. Philip, Rev. Dr. Brown, late Colonial Botanist at the Cape; to F. W. Reid, Esq., T. Elliot, Esq., and other friends, for photographs or sketches of African subjects.

PORTOBELLO, NEAR EDINBURGH,
23d February 1871.

CONTENTS.

INTRODUCTION.

PAGE

Arrival of Dr. Livingstone in England in 1856—Proposal to form new missions—Mission to the Makololo—Dr. Livingstone resigns connection with London Missionary Society—Rev. H. Helmore appointed in his stead to be the leader of the mission to the Makololo—Departure of the missionaries from England, 1-4

CHAPTER I.

THE CAPE COLONY.

Arrival at Cape Town—The young missionary and his work—South African Dutch: first attempt to speak it—A Dutch store at mid-day—"Baas Slaap!"—Ascent of Table Mountain—Introduction to the Governor of the colony—Environs of Cape Town—Rifle practice—Arrival of Mr. and Mrs. Helmore—Preparations for waggon journey—Description of our camp—The Karroo—Failure of draught oxen—A pious drover helping the "good cause"—Beaufort West—Victoria—Hope Town—Sketches of rural life in the Cape Colony—The farm-house: its occupants, their daily habits, their hospitality—Evening worship in a Dutch farmer's family—The Dutch colonists and Romanism—The colonial village rises round the church—Nachtmaal—Business and religion—The Boy and Bible—Candidates for "aanneming" and for matrimony—The colonial Churches—The London Missionary Society directing chief attention to the tribes in the interior. 5-27

CHAPTER II.

FIRST YEAR IN BECHUANA LAND.

Crossing the Orange and Vaal rivers—Waggon upset—Griqua Town—Rumours of war—Arrival at Kuruman at the end of 1858—

PAGE

Discussions as to the interior missions—Proposed bachelor expedition to Linyanti—Objections on the part of the Dutchmen of the Transvaal to the new missions—Impending attack on the Batlaping, and occupation of Kuruman—Postponement of departure for the interior—Death of Mrs. Ashton and of Mrs. Sykes—Dispersion of the mission party at Kuruman—Fauresmith—Remonstrance of Sir George Grey with Transvaal Government—Abandonment of hostilities by the latter—Hasty visit to Kuruman from the Free State, with Rev. W. B. Philip—"Kom binnen!"—Departure of Messrs. Helmore and Price for Makololo country—Residence at Kuruman—Learning Sechuana—Sechuana literature—Medical studies: introduction to practice—Bechuana gratitude—"'Naea thipa, 'ra!" 28-45

CHAPTER III.

THE ORANGE FREE STATE AND TRANSVAAL REPUBLIC.

Northward movement of European population in South Africa—"Emigrant Boers" and "trekking"—The Orange River Free State, its extent and products—The Transvaal, its boundaries undefined—Natural products—Comparative legislative and administrative talent in the "independent" States—Feudal Bechuanas—Griqua field cornets—Dutch farmer on the Landdrost's bench: "te veel uitlanders in de dorp"—Religious life and opinions of the Dutch: the "Doppers," Liberaalen, and Orthodox—The Dutchmen and Canaan: "Could one go there in his waggon?"—Ignorance and superstition in remote districts: Sechuana idioms creeping into use among the Dutch—The "large bag" of the Sechuana interpreter: result of the mistake—The white skin passport—Questions concerning the future government of the country: are there to be many small independent states, or one large republic bordering on our Cape possessions, or are the boundaries of the English possessions to be extended farther north? 46-55

CHAPTER IV.

GRIQUAS OR HALF-CASTE HOTTENTOTS.

Mr. Anderson and his nomadic charge—Learn to live a settled life—Christian instruction—Agriculture—The "dorps" of Griqua Town and Philippolis—The Griquas protect northern frontier of the colony—Bergenaars and Mantatees—Beneficial result of Christian teaching—Waterboer, a pure Bushman, elected chief at Griqua Town—Progress of the work of Christian

PAGE

instruction—The out-stations of Griqua Town—Drying up of the fountain and consequent dispersion of the people—Philippolis in 1859: intelligence of some of the people—Colonists' charge of idleness and pride—Imitation of the Dutch in the every-day habits of the Griqua men and women—Drunkenness the besetting sin of Griquas and Hottentots—The brandy waggon—Griquas "trek" to No Man's Land—"Menschen," "volk," and "schepsels," 56-66

CHAPTER V.

KURUMAN, FORMERLY LATTAKOO MISSION.

Bechuanas first described by Messrs. Truter and Somerville, who visited Lattakoo in 1801—Lichtenstein and Burchell—Visit of Mr. John Campbell in 1812—Messrs. Evans and Hamilton attempt to establish a mission in 1815—Mr. Campbell returns with Mr. Moffat in 1820—Purchase of a tract of land from the chief—Building of church and dwelling-houses—Impressions of the people in 1859—Irrigation now practised—The influence on the people of an inadequate supply of food—"Lo yang?" "What are you eating?"—Sunday morning at Kuruman—Estimate of Bechuana Christians—Catechumens—The inquirer at the waggon—Influence of those who introduce Christianity among a people—"The nearer the kirk the farther frae grace"—Too much teaching—Best Christians not on stations with European missionaries—Native teachers in 1842 and 1866—Proposed seminary for training native ministers—The heathen who resist the gospel—Backsliders—The future of the Bechuanas—"God is merciful, and the ages are long," . . 67-83

CHAPTER VI.

BATLAPING MISSIONS AT TAUNG AND LIKATLONG.

Taung.

Batlaping tribe leave Kuruman—In 1842 Dr. Livingstone and Mr. Ross join Bechuana mission—Mr. Ross proceeds to Taung, the residence of the Batlaping—Removal of tribe to Mamusa—Sketch of Mr. Ross's life—His labours as an evangelist—His death—The war between the Dutch and the Batlaping in 1857-8—The Christians kept clear of the raids which led to the war—The native newspaper at Kuruman and the war—A Sunday at Taung in 1862—Former enemies unite in celebrating the Lord's Supper—Masse, and his attempts to irrigate the land.

PAGE

LIKATLONG, THE DIAMOND COUNTRY.

Likatlong originally an out-station of Griqua mission—Mr. Helmore takes over the station in 1840—Christianity interferes with the reconstruction of the model heathen town—The Batlaping scattered under the head men of the tribe—Jantje, the Christian chief of Likatlong—Mr. Ashton joins Kuruman mission in 1842—Removes to Likatlong in 1864—The native Church and brandy-drinking—Discovery of diamonds in 1867—Surprise of the natives—Rush to the "diggings"—Description of diamond-seeking—Canvas towns—Claimants for the ownership of the country—Jantje addresses the English Governor—Necessity for a strong government, ... 84-97

CHAPTER VII.

JOURNEY INTO THE INTERIOR.

Leave Kuruman in May 1860—My travelling companions—Joined by a hunting party—A Sunday at Maritsane river—"Auld lang syne"—Detention at Kanye—A colonial blacksmith and his health—Visit to the Barolongs—Ruins of Dr. Livingstone's station at Kolobeng—New belt of vegetation—More genial country—Sechele, chief of the Bakwena—A sketch of his career and character—Dutch mode of treating African fever—An eland shot—Arrival at Shoshong—Meet Mr. Moffat—The Bamangwato remember Mr. Helmore's address in their court-yard—Mrs. Helmore and her projected home north of the Zambese—Arrangements for entering the desert—Purchase calabashes for the men—"At the jar again!"—Furu and his wallet—Roualeyn Gordon Cumming—The desert—Nkowane wells—Arrival at Lotlakane—Traces of Messrs. Helmore and Price—Extract from a letter of Mrs. Helmore written from Lotlakane, ... 98-127

CHAPTER VIII.

BUSHMAN LAND.

The system of vassalage among the Bechuanas—The Bakalahari formerly independent Bechuanas—The mode of raising tribute from them—The Bushmen have less in common with their masters—Assist in hunting—The reason for chiefs' reluctance to opening of the country—Vassalage and Christianity—The wretched condition of vassals in time of war—The evangelist in the desert—The Bushmen at our camp on Sunday—The Bushmen very superstitious—Fetichism—Sleeping at the Bushmen's fire—Hunting for a guide at Nchokotsa—A Sunday at Kube—

PAGE

Vassals with and without Christianity—"Norval" hunting on Sunday—Ntwetwe—First baobab—Waggon-mending under difficulties—A horse killed by a lion—Tall Bushmen—A strike—Reach Maila—The Makalaka an agricultural people—Narrow escape—The "boy with the beard"—Fear of mentioning the lion's name at night—Account of disastrous end of Messrs. Reader and Burgess's expedition, ... 128-155

CHAPTER IX.

BUSHMAN GUIDANCE.

Makalaka refugees—Matebele outrage—Putse's joke—Preserving the water for the oxen by keeping off the herds of game—The news of the old Bushman from Mababe: "Sekeletu had killed the missionaries, and seized upon their property"—The story discredited—The Bushmen decline to accompany me to the north of Maila, and narrate the sufferings of Messrs. Helmore and Price in that country—Extract from the last letter received from Mrs. Helmore—Accept the offer of the Makalaka to show a route to the east, leading to Victoria Falls—The dilemma—The Bushmen and the Makalaka meet and discuss the route to Linyanti—Recommend a new road to the west—Leave Maila with two Bushmen guides—The Bushmen and the compass—Deserted by our guides—Ruse to bring them back—Bechuana oxen endure thirst best—Opening up the fountain—Scarcity of water—Proceed with one waggon and open up a path to the Zouga or Botletle at More oa Maotu—Meet Batowana boatmen on their way to the Lake—Story of the death of our friends at Linyanti repeated—Still incredulous, refuse to turn aside to visit their town—Folly of paying for guides before starting—"Making hay while the sun shines"—Reiterated statements of the calamity at Linyanti—The waggons stopped—The party of men from the Lake—"The white man in the boat"—Suspense—Meeting with Mr. Price—Relieving the Makololo mission—An "express" from Kuruman—Bushman guidance and Bushman kindness, ... 156-185

CHAPTER X.

LINYANTI.

Messrs. Helmore and Price reach Linyanti in February 1860—Hospitably received by Sekeletu—The chief refuses to remove to Tabacheu—Unhealthy season—Sekeletu refuses permission to the missionaries to remove to Sesheke—The party stricken with fever—Suspicion of poisoning—Death of Malatsi—Death of three little children—The guardian mother—Mrs. Helmore's death—Mr. Helmore resolves not to leave Linyanti till Dr.

PAGE

Livingstone arrives—He has a relapse of fever, and dies—Death of Tabe and Setloke—Fever accompanied by acute physical pain—Mahuse the tempter—Sekeletu robs Mr. Price and the orphan children—Hospitality among natives—Its breach by Sekeletu—His endeavour to explain away his crime—Death of Mrs. Price on the Mababe plain—Mr. Price led into the tsetse—Arrives at Lake Ngami, ... 186-203

CHAPTER XI.

RETURN JOURNEY FROM LAKE NGAMI.

Cross the Zouga at Khame's ford—Effects of tsetse bite—Boating on the Zouga—The Batowana lords and their vassals—The Makoba fisherman's proposal, "Come in and conquer the Bechuanas"—Makoba belief in a future state—Lechulatebe's town—Delight of Mr. Helmore's children on our arrival—Lechulatebe complains that no missionary came to him—Lake district and native evangelists—Mistake in selling a horse—Powder must be in a bag—Death of Dr. Holden—Game-pits—Bechuana sportsmen—Reluctantly resolve to return to Kuruman—Case of African fever—Effect of the air of the desert on fever—Our sweet-tempered goat-herd—Shoshong—Meet Mr. Moffat—Sympathy of friends at the Cape—Reach Kuruman—Illness of Mrs. Mackenzie—African fever, different types—Livingstone's prescription a specific—Visit to Fauresmith, . . 204-225

CHAPTER XII.

THE LAST OF THE MAKOLOLO.

Appointment to Shoshong—Visit to Montsiwe's town—Moleme's story—Steadfastness of the believers—Montsiwe's daughter—Her father's persecution—Night travelling—Boatlanama—Sleeping while walking—A lion in the way—Follows the waggons and kills an ox—The Bushman's portion—Pool of Selinye—Meet Mr. John Moffat and Mr. Price at Shoshong—Project for again attempting a mission to the north of the Zambese—The scheme entirely fails—Death of Sekeletu—Feuds among the Makololo—Insurrection of the vassals—Betrayal and assassination of Makololo by Lechulatebe—The tribe extinct—Native interpretation of these events, ... 226-248

CHAPTER XIII.

FIRST YEAR AT SHOSHONG.

Temporary hut—Co-operation with Hanoverian missionary—Smallpox—Its past ravages in Southern Africa—Its slow progress into

PAGE

the interior—Its ravages at Shoshong—Inoculation in the forehead and knee—Prowling hyenas and their habits—A few days in the open country—A misadventure—The Bushman's fire—Mr. Price kills two giraffes—The oryx or gemsbuck at bay—Horse-sickness—Attempts to cure it—"Salted" horses—Gradual acclimatization of horses in Southern Africa—Woman stoned by boys—Brought to mission-house for protection—African features—Bewildering effect of colour—Departure of German missionary—Knowledge of medicine of great consequence to the missionary—The old man and the colourless eye-lotion, . 249-266

CHAPTER XIV.

THE MATEBELE RAID.

The native wars always in summer, the Dutch always in winter—The dust-covered messengers—The war-cry in Shoshong—Assembly of the men—A native review—Women and children hasten to the mountain—A lonely night—Visit from the young chiefs—Prayer in the moonlight—Refuge on the mountain—Engagement with the Matebele—The war-cry in the night—Incidents in the fight—Sunday: an armed congregation—"Love your enemies"—Proposal to visit the Matebele camp—The Matebele give up the attack and return to their own country—Cruel death of a Matebele soldier—Khame and the lesson of Sunday morning—The Bamangwato raid on the Matebele, 267-285

CHAPTER XV.

JOURNEY TO MATEBELE LAND.

Return of Messrs. Price and J. S. Moffat to Shoshong in June 1863—Death of Mrs. Thomas from fever—Temporary reinforcement of Matebele mission—Leave Shoshong—Country to the northeast drained by the Ouri or Limpopo river—A buffalo shoots a Dutchman—Accident in the Seribe river—Perils of elephant-hunting—Arrive at Mahuku's town—African Glencoe—The massacre of the Batalowta by the Matebele—Announce our approach to Moselekatse—Pass through the beautiful Makalaka country—Monyame's town—A rhinoceros cow and calf killed—Moselekatse refuses to see Sekhome's missionary—Explanations—A Sunday at Tlapa Baloi—First impressions of the Matebele—The camp of Moselekatse—Our reception—Arrival at Inyate—Mrs. Thomas and the Matebele, . . . 286-306

CHAPTER XVI.

MOSELEKATSE.

PAGE

Early history of this chief—Deserts from Tshaka, leading with him all his regiment—Scatters the Bechuana tribes and occupies their country—Visited by Mr. Moffat and Dr. Smith—His ideas of the English—Attacked by Griquas, by Zulus, and by Dutchmen from the colony—He removes northward—Rebellion and death of one of his sons—Takes up his residence in Mashona country—Massacres Makalaka women—Followed by Dutchmen, who are unsuccessful—Mr. Moffat twice visits him in his present country—Arrival of mission party in 1859—Waggons pulled by soldiers—Early difficulties of the mission—The missionaries distrusted as spies—Explanation of this feeling—A change takes place in the treatment of the missionaries—They are invited to settle at Inyate—Preaching through interpreters before Moselekatse—The chief's emendations—Village preaching begun—Killing game for the congregation—A native history of the planting of Christianity—Moselekatse's chief officer conducting the white man's dance, or religious service—The etiquette of Moselekatse's court—Sitting on a stool—The missionaries rank as "sons of Moselekatse"—Dining at court in Matebele-land, . . 307-323

CHAPTER XVII.

A MILITARY TRIBE AND CHRISTIANITY.

Matebele tribe exhibits a complete military despotism—Society exists for the chief—All the people and all the property belong to him—The head men: their precarious life, their habits—The "chief's knife"—Death of Monyebe—The common soldiers—Law of celibacy—The career of the captive boy to Matebele manhood—Incentives to leave the restraints of Matebele barracks for the license of the war-party—The Zulus despise the captives; the latter have little or no religion—The missionary among such a people—The "strong man armed"—Impatience for results—The Spirit of God all-powerful—The condition of the Matebele without a parallel in New Testament—Dawnings of good impressions—Conversation with Moselekatse—His cunning reply—Experiment to show Matebele head men the power of letters—Law of celibacy relaxed through influence of missionaries—Decrease of bloodthirstiness among the Matebele—Various theories concerning barbarous tribes—Christianity effete—French polish—Christianity and civilisation united at a mission station—The old heathen life impossible to the natives through the destruction of game—Trade followed Christianity

PAGE

into Matebele-land—Soldiers begin to acquire private property—Ideas as to dress—Mistaken identity—Taking leave of Moselekatse: the old chief pleads for medicine—My waggon pulled out of a river by soldiers—A scramble—Mr. and Mrs. Sykes accompany us to Monyame's—A night scene at Shashane river—"Nero" and the lion—Arrive at Shoshong—Discovery of gold in Mashona-land by Mr. Mauch—Matebele object to exploration of the country—Death of Moselekatse in 1868—Romantic story of a son and successor in Natal—The tribe divides on the subject—Lobingole, the victor, declared chief—The mission station at Inyate a place of refuge for the wounded of both parties, ... 324-354

CHAPTER XVIII.

A CHAPTER OF BAMANGWATO HISTORY.

Bamangwato tradition preserves names of seven chiefs—The Bahurutse take the first rank in North Bechuana-land—The Bangwaketse, the Bakwena, and the Bamangwato, originally one tribe—Division of the Bamangwato in the days of Matipi—Affecting story of this chief: broken-hearted in his old age he commits suicide—Khari, the favourite of Bamangwato story—His death in the battle-field—The Bamangwato scattered—The Makololo and Matebele pass northward—Moselekatse's cruelties—Heroic speech of one of the Bamangwato—They rescue their cattle from the Matebele—Sekhome kills the Matebele tax-gatherers—The history of Macheng—Complications at Shoshong—Sechele plays at chief-making—The "child of cattle"—The Bamangwato are fond of their hills—Possible explanation of fondness of mountaineers for their native land—The town of Shoshong—The Machwapong—The Basilika—The laying out of a Bechuana town—The cattle-posts and hunting stations, and their relation to the town—No purchase of land—No boundary lines between tribes, ... 355-370

CHAPTER XIX.

RELIGION AND POLITY OF THE BAMANGWATO.

Offices of the Bechuana chief—As *chief*—Public assemblies—Their uses—As *judge*—Ideas of property—Head men the assessors—Advocates and their speeches—Modes of procedure—Justice often miscarries—Irritation of Europeans, and unreasonable expectations—Theory and practice of law—Fine, maiming, death—As *commander-in-chief of the men*—Circumcision—The lesson of endurance—Not sparing the rod—The steps to Bechuana

PAGE

manhood—Regiments enrolled according to age—Early missionaries and circumcision—"Boyali"—Introduction to Bechuana womanhood—The lesson to endure well learnt,—also a Christian lesson—As *ngaka or priest*—The medical profession at Shoshong—Entrance fee—"Teaching to dig"—Baboon-skin head-dress and hyena skin mat—A consultation of doctors—Attending a stingy patient—Public duties of lingaka—Preparation of lipeku or town-charms—Rain-making—Cutting the sacred hack-thorn—Widows and widowers unclean—Cleansing the hearths—Sacred fire—Sacrificing, and praying to ancestors—"The rain has fallen"—Ngaka and moloi—The wizard mounted on the hyena—Driving away rain—Sekhome bewitching Sechele's cornfields—Punishment of the wizards—"Given over" to a buffalo—Worship on high places and in groves—Prayer before a large tree—Superstitious fears—The sacred animal, the owl, the goat, and the cow, which "transgress"—Ceremonies somewhat similar to Levitical code—Morimo (God)—Two plurals—Only one singular, ... 371-395

CHAPTER XX.

THE LEAVEN OF THE GOSPEL.

Feigning ignorance—Bechuana "caste" the barrier to the speedy reception of the gospel—Work in the schools—Capacities of Bechuanas—Opinions of Rev. H. Calderwood—Rev. Dr. Wilson of Bombay—Dr. Livingstone—Retentive memory of the people—Bechuana diplomacy—The plea Not Guilty fully taken advantage of by Bechuanas—Beautiful appearance of the town in summer—Suicide of a Matebele refugee—Bamangwato attacked by Bakwena—Rumoured attack by Matebele—Perplexity of Sekhome—His evening visits to my house—"The heart of the white man straight, the heart of the black man crooked"—Sekhome's conception of becoming a Christian, . . 396-409

CHAPTER XXI.

THE TRIAL OF FAITH.

Polygamy the cause of feuds—The ceremony of "boguera"—Attempt on the part of Sekhome to compel his sons to attend—By his entreaties and threats he persuades two to give up attending church and school—Steadfastness of Khame and other two sons—Beginning of persecution—Build a new house—The chief seeks a quarrel with the missionaries—Hostility of the head men to Tshukuru—This is mixed up with the opposition to the

PAGE

Word of God—Khame commanded to take home a heathen woman as his head wife—His refusal—Khamane's wife does not attend the "boyali" before marriage—The town in arms—Sekhome's men desert him—His flight—Forbearance of his sons—Settlement of the strife—The baloi bewitching the young chief's house, ... 410-422

CHAPTER XXII.

THE FATHER AGAINST THE SON.

Mr. and Mrs. Price leave Shoshong—Their labours at Sechele's town—Ideas of church-membership—Khame warned of a new plot against him—Driven from the town—Attitude of the people—Firing begins at dawn—Position of some English traders—A strange "neutral" position—Missionary's premises respected—A congregation on the mountain—The property of absent Englishmen handed to the missionary by both parties—"Blood drawn by an Englishman"—A "black watch"—Invisible attendants—Sekhome's secret council—His mother's speech—Hooted on the streets—The scene in the kotla—Cause of the irritation—The wizard shot—The people's temper improves, ... 423-440

CHAPTER XXIII.

FLIGHT OF SEKHOME.

Khame besieged on the mountain—The missionary acts as messenger—Terms of agreement—Flight of Tshukuru—His death at Sechele's town—The death-wail—Arrival of Macheng—Khame's speech—The two brothers—Macheng recognised chief—Confession of Sekhome—Final effort of Sekhome to overcome his enemies—Failure of the scheme—Sekhome's trust in the missionary—His flight from Shoshong—Fact and fiction—Opinion of Dr. Fritsch, ... 441-452

CHAPTER XXIV.

DISCOVERY OF GOLD—BUILDING OF THE CHURCH.

Gold discovered at Tatie river in 1867 by Mr. Mauch, and afterwards in Mashona-land—The mines had been previously worked—Proposal by the Transvaal Government to native chiefs—Its reception—Sweeping measure of Transvaal Executive—Public assembly at Shoshong—Macheng's offer to the Governor at the

PAGE

Cape—The Cape Parliament and the Colonial Executive—Mashona-land suitable for a colony—Necessity for a seaport on the east coast—Anticipated beneficial result on natives and Dutch frontier men—Building of the church at Shoshong—Macheng assists me with two regiments of men to hew timber, and women to cut grass for thatch—Opening of the church—Fears of the heathen—Public service—A breakfast-party—The head man's share of the entertainment—Good feeling produced—District meetings, ... 453-465

CHAPTER XXV.

"BY LITTLE AND LITTLE."

Ancient and modern missions—The life of the mission family attainable—A Sunday at Shoshong—Bible class and morning service in church—Afternoon service in public court-yard—Impressing on the heathen mind the leading truths of revelation—English service in the mission-house—The missionary the servant of all classes—Delay in organizing a native church—Circles of hearers—The mission has left some mark on the whole community—Conclusion—The evangelization of the heathen appeals to the highest Christian thought and feeling—The Church has been slow to realize the aggressive and expansive aim of her Head—Rallying-cries of the Church—High type of Christianity appears for a time—Proposed chair or lectureship—Influence of parents—The youthful reverie, ... 466-482

APPENDIX.

The Races of Southern Africa—Section 1 : Antiquities and traditions—Stereotyping tendency of South African superstition. Section 2 : Division of natives of Southern Africa into two families. (*a.*) Language—Bushman and Hottentot languages—Connection with northern nations—"Tones" as in Chinese—The Ba-ntu family of languages—African and Oceanic sections—Construction—A sentence in Hottentot—In Sechuana and Samoan—Pronouns—Numerals—Classes of nouns—The Sechuana verb. (*b.*) Physical appearance—Resemblance of first family to Chinese—The second family approach the Arabs in the Zulus and Kaffirs, and the negro type in the Makoba and Damara. (*c.*) Religious and social customs—Mode of building houses and laying out towns. (*d.*) Dress and weapons of war Section 3 : Possible physical effects of climate and food on Bushmen and other tribes, ... 483-508

PAGE

The contact of Europeans with natives of Southern Africa.—Bushmen: The enemies of the pastoral and agricultural tribes—The Dutch shoot them down—The death-rate under the English and under the Dutch—Why Bushes-men have been shot down—Their position not peculiar to themselves—Fulfilling the Divine decrees. *Hottentots:* decrease under the Dutch—Increase under the English Government, and with Christian instruction—Census of 1865—Physical change slowly taking place. *Kaffirs:* early position of Kaffirs, Hottentots, and Dutch—Kaffirs moving towards south-east, Dutch north-west—Disappearance of Gonaqua Hottentots as a tribe—Kaffir wars—Their real cause—Kaffir soothsayers—The killing of the cattle in 1857—Gradual dispersion in the colony, and decay of feudal power. *Bechuanas:* breaking up of large tribes in Bechuana-land—The people have not died away, but are in the Cape Colony working for wages—A strong Government needed on the frontier—Sir C. W. Dilke on the Red Indians—Solution, in Southern Africa, of the interesting problem of the settlement together, in one community, of various races, ... 509-523

LIST OF ILLUSTRATIONS.

PLATES.

ORANGE RIVER, ... *Frontispiece.*

POTCHEFSTROOM, ... *fronting page* 50

SUNDAY MORNING AT KURUMAN, . . „ 72

ON THE ZOUGA, ... „ 173

FEVER-STRICKEN AT LINYANTI, . . „ 188

REFUGE ON THE MOUNTAIN, . . . „ 274

TRIBAL ARCHITECTURE, ... „ 499

TRIBAL WEAPONS, ... „ 503

WOODCUTS.

WOODEN PILLOW, ... *page* 248

MATEBELE HERD-BOYS, ... „ 328

MATEBELE SOLDIERS, ... „ 330

MASHONA MUSICAL INSTRUMENT, . . . „ 354

GOURD SNUFF-BOX, ... „ 369

WATER-POT AND GOURD, ... „ 378

INTRODUCTION.

IN 1856, after a period of such anxious waiting as is now being endured in 1870, the friends of Dr. Livingstone had the happiness of welcoming him to his native country, and of congratulating him upon the success of his exploratory journey across the African continent. And while the public admired the patience and indomitable perseverance of this Christian missionary and explorer, it was felt on all hands that his discoveries widened the range of our sympathies and of our responsibilities. Christian Churches took for their text a sentiment uttered by Dr. Livingstone: "The end of the geographical feat is but the beginning of the missionary enterprise." The two English Universities organized a mission, which they placed under the care of the lamented Bishop Mackenzie. The Free Church of Scotland, embodying in this instance caution as well as enterprise, sent out the Rev. James Stewart[1] to report upon the practicability of commencing missionary operations in the newly-explored territory. The London Missionary Society, under whose auspices the explorations had been effected, took steps to carry into execution a scheme suggested by Dr. Livingstone, and which had been conditionally announced by him to the people for whose benefit it was intended. The Makololo tribe, originally from Basutoland in the south, were found by Dr. Living-

[1] Now Rev. Dr. Stewart of Lovedale Seminary, Cape Colony.

stone occupying the country between the Chobe and the Sesheke, and exercising supremacy over the Barotse, the Bashubea, the Bashukulompo, and other tribes of the interior. The Doctor paid several visits to Linyanti, the chief town of the Makololo, and possessed great influence with the chief. Members of the tribe had been his faithful companions to Loanda on the west and to Quilimane on the east coast. The Makololo had expressed a desire that a missionary should reside with them; and had given the Doctor to understand that they were willing to remove with their "teacher" from the deadly swamps of Linyanti to a healthier locality on the north bank of the Zambese. They had indeed some misgivings about returning to a country which they had evacuated through fear of their sworn enemies the Matebele Zulus. But it was hoped that the presence of a missionary among the Makololo would be a "shield" or protection to them from Moselekatse; and to complete the scheme it was resolved to establish a second mission among the Matebele, with a view not only to the enlightenment of that tribe, but in order to insure the success of the mission to the Makololo. The Rev. Robert Moffat of Kuruman, an old friend of Moselekatse, the chief of the Matebele, was commissioned to superintend the establishment of the southern mission, while the northern one was to be under the care of his son-in-law, Dr. Livingstone. This enterprise excited considerable attention, and received liberal support.

But the interest in the recent explorations extended beyond the supporters of missionary societies. The information which had been received as to the configuration and the capabilities of the country only whetted the appetite for more. Special stress was laid upon the possibility of raising cotton in the newly discovered region. The Government only gave expression to the general feeling of the public by organizing and fitting out an expedition, of which Dr. Livingstone agreed to take the leadership. Hoping to find a suitable port at the mouth of the Zambese or elsewhere, the Doctor threw his energies into a scheme which had for its object the benefit of the African as well as the advantage of England. It matters little to a good soldier in what regiment he fights. The Doctor had been an explorer whilst a missionary, and when he became an explorer no one who knew him imagined that he ceased to be a missionary.

The loss, however, of the experience and guidance of Dr. Livingstone, at the outset of their new enterprise, was one which the Missionary Society could not adequately supply. The local knowledge and the personal influence which he possessed could only be acquired by others after years of contact with the natives, and would probably never be so great as that of their first "white man," the friend of their beloved chief Sebituane. In the Rev. Holloway Helmore, who was appointed to fill his place as leader of the Makololo Mission, the Society obtained the services of one of the most amiable, single-hearted, and steadfast of men. But although he had been for seventeen years a hard-working and successful missionary at Likatlong, in the southern part of Bechuana-land, the country to the north had not been visited by him; and he was a perfect stranger to the Makololo people. It was however announced by the officers of the Missionary Society that Dr. Livingstone had agreed to meet their agents at Linyanti, that he would introduce them to the chief and people, and assist in the negotiations concerning the removal of the tribe from that unhealthy region.

The young missionaries who were selected for these distant and somewhat difficult missions were Messrs. Sykes, Thomas, and John Moffat, for the Matebele, under Mr.

Moffat; and Mr. Price and myself for the Makololo, under Mr. Helmore. And when we embarked at Southampton in June 1858, we were accompanied by gentle and true-hearted wives, who had left happy homes for our sakes, and who, sharing our desire to carry the gospel to the heathen, ventured to hope that they could go where Mrs. Livingstone had been, and reside where their husbands resided.

CHAPTER I.

THE CAPE COLONY.

We sighted Table Mountain early on the morning of the 13th July 1858, after a pleasant voyage of some thirty-eight days. Kind friends who were expecting us speedily boarded our vessel, and gave us a very hearty welcome to Africa. One of the first of these was the Rev. Robert Moffat; and we were delighted to meet a missionary whose writings and whose life had been familiar to us from childhood. Nor were we alone in these feelings.

"Please to introduce me to Mr. Moffat," said a fellow-passenger to me—a young officer proceeding to join his regiment. "My mother would be so pleased to hear that I had met him."

And so we bade farewell to the good ship 'Athens,' on the conclusion of this its first voyage to the Cape.[1] Proceeding towards the shore, our attention was attracted by the number of flat-roofed houses; the straight streets, the "squareness" and regularity of which contrasted strongly with the rugged and irregular mountain in the background. As we approached the pier our friends informed us that in the groups which we saw there would be found the

[1] In the same bay, some years after, during one of those dreadful storms which periodically visit those shores, the 'Athens' was wrecked, and all on board perished. Although the vessel was no longer in charge of the same captain, we felt a peculiar regret when in the interior we read an account of the disaster.

Malay, the Hottentot, the Kaffir, the Mozambique negro, half-castes of all shades of colour, besides Europeans and Americans. Cape Town is indeed in a wider sense than its first founders could have anticipated a place of refreshment for passing vessels; and if modern navigation renders this less necessary than it was two hundred years ago, the wants of modern society at the Cape require the services of many vessels, and from all parts of the world: for the trade is no longer confined to brass wire and beads, in exchange for cattle and sheep, as in the days of Jan van Riebeek, the founder of Cape Town.

We were guided by the Rev. William Thompson to his house, which was our home for about six weeks. This building was then the property of the Missionary Society, of which Mr. Thompson is the local agent; and as Cape Town is a house of call for "refreshment of passing vessels," so was this mission-house a temporary home for missionary voyagers, whether outward or homeward bound. We were a large and very happy family. Indeed, I feel sure that nowhere in all the dwellings of Cape Town or its suburbs were there to be found a more gracious host and hostess, and nowhere more happy and joyous guests than in the quiet mission-house overlooking Table Bay. As for ourselves, the life which we had chosen had begun to open up before us. The past with its crowding memories did not on the whole lead us to despond as to the future. The class-room had been now exchanged for the pulpit; drill and review for actual warfare. And if a young man is enthusiastic on the reception of an appointment which in a certain number of years will enable him to enjoy independence, so were we all enthusiastic about our appointment to the work of evangelist. Our office and our work linked us to historical Christianity. In God's providence His gospel was to be introduced into certain Pagan regions by us. Those who in one age had been martyred, and in another canonized, at first persecuted, and afterwards endowed with lands and with titles, were our historical predecessors in this great work. Above all, in our quiet moments, when our minds were calmed and our souls hushed, a Presence stole upon us, and a Voice addressed us. They seemed as of One who had appeared in Palestine, and who spoke to us through the long ages of the past; but anon His words thrilled our hearts as fresh and real utterances of the present: "Preach the gospel to every creature; lo, I am with you alway. And I, if I be lifted up from the earth, will draw all men unto me."

We had been learning Dutch on board ship, and some of us were anxious to have a little practice. Finding myself alone one day in Cape Town, I resolved to make a commencement, and carefully arranging my words went up to a "person of colour," and fired off my question, which was about some street or place. To my disgust the man stared at me in silence. He might be deaf; I raised my voice, and repeated the question. After some delay, and in a patronizing tone, my dusky friend condescended to address me in English, and gave me the information I desired. When I got home I stated my case, and was not a little reassured when my kind host informed me that I had made no mistake as to words, while in pronunciation I had followed only too strictly the rules given in the Grammar, from which South African Dutch has considerably departed, especially as spoken in distant localities. Dutchmen fresh from Holland are sometimes misunderstood, and their language mistaken for German. We were told that some preachers accommodate themselves to this South African dialect, which is in use even in the wealthiest families. We found afterwards that the children of English people living in the midst of a Dutch population learn the colloquial Dutch from their nurses and from other children—as Scotch is acquired by children north of the Tweed, no matter how particular some mothers may be that young Sandy should learn nothing but pure English.

In making preparations for our journey into the interior, we had frequent occasion to visit various shops and places of business in Cape Town. It was then the custom for the Cape Town storekeepers, at any rate those of the old school, to indulge in a siesta after dinner, which they usually take about noon. I made my appearance one day at a shop at this sacred hour, to complete some purchases, and was astonished to find everything shut, except one-half of the adjoining house-door, at which stood a little black girl. In answer to my demand for the shopkeeper, this sentinel said, in a low tone, "Baas slaap"—"The master is asleep!" I thought what would be the result to this easy-going man of business were he borne by genii, while asleep, and laid gently down and left to awake on London Bridge or Cheapside!

At the invitation of some newly-formed friends, we devoted a day to the ascent of Table Mountain. A pleasant party of some twelve or fourteen sat down to "tiffin," or luncheon on the table-land at the top, and beside a stream of water. It was thought by certain of our number that water at such an altitude needed modifying by the application of what is not called "mountain dew" in South Africa, but "Cape smoke." It was here, and from a respected Professor's flask, that I drank my first and last "soepje," or dram of Cape brandy. I do not at all recommend it. The view from the top of Table Mountain is one which will abundantly repay the fatigue of the ascent. There was the town itself below us, with its miniature streets and scarcely visible inhabitants. The noble bay, with ships approaching or leaving the harbour, the rugged rock-bound coast on the left, the wide plain on the right, bounded by blue mountains in the distance, gave us our first impressions of African scenery.

We were able also to make acquaintance with the environs of Cape Town, which we found to be very beautiful. At Green Point there are many delightful marine residences, while on the road to Simon's Bay there are villas and villages of surpassing beauty. At the time of our visit, gentlemen in business usually rode or drove into town from these places; but more recently the first South African railway passes through the villages in question, extending through the wine-producing district as far as the town of Wellington. In his suburban residence, embowered in trees, with its vineyard, its orchard, and its garden, the Cape merchant lives amidst beauty and luxuriance unequalled in England.

Preparations for our journey and excursions into the country were interspersed with exercises of another description. Intending to reside in a country where the man would be best served who could help himself, we had all more or less given attention to various useful arts in England. Knowing also that our future residence would be surrounded by wild beasts, some of us had given a little attention to the use of fire-arms; but none of our party could boast of much knowledge of such carnal weapons as guns and rifles. We were anxious to remove this defect in our training; and when we had an hour to spare in Cape Town resorted to the beach for practice. Now, it is well known to crack-shots, but not much thought of by beginners, that loading well is necessary to shooting well.

"Pray don't put in so much powder at once, Mr. ——," said the son of our host, then a lad of eighteen, to one of our number, who was loading his gun. His only answer was a stern look of superior wisdom, upon which the friendly adviser prudently withdrew to some distance. Hearing a report, he turned round, and beheld Mr. —— standing with nothing in his hand but a bit of the stock of his gun! Happily he escaped unhurt, which fact only added to his bewilderment, as he thought of the rest of the stock, the lock, and the barrel, which had all joined the powder and the shot in their sudden departure! This striking lesson was not in vain. Mr. —— afterwards became a good shot, and in the ordinary discharge of his work as a missionary, has brought down many an antelope with his rifle.

Our party had the honour of being presented to Sir George Grey, then Governor at the Cape, himself a traveller and explorer. He expressed himself as interested in our undertaking, and cheered us when taking leave by saying that it was not at all impossible, if the country were fully opened up from the east coast, by the efforts of Dr. Livingstone and his companions, that he might yet see us at our own stations on the Zambese. His Excellency was kind enough to grant a number of asses, to be used by the missionaries in the transmission of letters, etc., through the habitat of the tsetse-fly. Since 1858 a small sum has also been annually voted by the Cape Parliament for the carriage of letters between the frontier colonial town and Kuruman, which is a great boon, not only to missionaries, but to traders, travellers, and hunters.

Our departure was hastened by the arrival of Mr. and Mrs. Helmore by the steamer which had followed us. The oxen having been purchased, servants hired, and waggons made ready, Mr. Moffat and his family left first. About a week after, the young missionaries started under the guidance of Mr. Helmore.

I shall not attempt to describe my first experiences of waggon life. I congratulated myself that, with the assistance of my Hottentot driver Jan Sandveld, and my Kaffir leader William Brown, I had made everything comfortable for my wife's reception, especially as she was then in indifferent health. But a waggon at rest and a waggon in motion are widely different things. This fact was soon deeply impressed on my mind as I beheld a leg of mutton, just provided by our kind hostess, leave the place where I had put it, and with a loaf of bread, some oranges, and sundry other articles, join my astonished wife on the kartel or waggon couch. The whip cracked, driver and leader shouted, and away we went, jolting and shaking, on our way to the Zambese!

Our encampment was itself a small village. The six waggons, when "outspanned" for the night, were drawn near to each other. The men having finished their day's duties, assembled at one of the fires, when a violin was produced, to the music or at least scraping of which dancing was kept up till past midnight. We sometimes sat outside our waggons enjoying the bright African moonlight, and noticing the uncouth motions of the men, upon whose grotesque forms the large camp-fire cast its light. Or when the night was cold and cheerless, and nothing greeted the ear but the distant barking of the farm-dogs, we fastened down the sails at both ends of our waggon, adjusted our little table, which was suspended from the side of the waggon-tent, and lighting our candle, spent the evening in reading or in conversation.

Our first halting-place after leaving Cape Town was at Stickland, which had been a military post under Sir James Craig, the first English governor of the colony. We then passed through the picturesque town of Paarl, where we formed the acquaintance of the Rev. Mr. Kolbe, a missionary of our Society, and pastor of a large and self-supporting coloured congregation. As we proceeded northward, the wild mountain scenery to which we were introduced at Bain's Pass gave place to the dreary treeless and grassless Karroo. This arid region is not however devoid of interest. Its bushes are more valuable to the sheep-farmer than grass, and two of them supply an alkali which is used extensively in colonial soap-making. Many bright-coloured flowers enlivened the dreary plain—the design in the construction of which the flowers themselves revealed to us; for some, with succulent and fleshy stem and leaves, preserved their beauty and freshness for some seven or eight days, in the heat of our waggon-tent, and without any external application of water.

The expedition was brought to a standstill in this desert through the failure of our draught-oxen. One of the cattle-dealers from whom the troop had been purchased professed to be a religious man, and those who bargained with him trusted to his religious reputation, and rejoiced that the Missionary Society had found a friend among the drovers and cattle-dealers. The joy was premature. Some of the high-priced oxen were not able to walk a few miles to the missionary camp, but died on the road from weakness or disease, and, although paid for, were never really "delivered" to their owners. Others died after a few days' march, and seven were re-sold to a farmer at 20s. per head, which was better than nothing. The Jews were forbidden to offer the sickly or the poor to God in sacrifice, but this exemplary Christian sold the lame and the dying to the missionaries, and all "to help on the good cause."

At Beaufort West we were able to re-equip ourselves for the remaining part of our journey. We received a Highland welcome from the Rev. Colin Fraser, the respected minister of the Dutch Church. At Victoria West, where we halted for some days to rest our oxen, and at Hope Town, which is on the northern frontier of the Colony, and which we reached in the end of November, we were received with unexpected hospitality by our own countrymen and by others, who bade us also God-speed in the great object of our journey. Before crossing the Orange River, and leaving Her Majesty's dominions, it may not be uninteresting to give a few sketches of rural and village life in the Cape Colony.

The house or "plaats" of the Dutch farmer is usually built close to his garden, and as the latter must necessarily be a tract of ground at a lower elevation than the neighbouring fountain, in order to its irrigation, the site is frequently to be admired neither for its beauty nor its healthiness. One cannot help thinking that a good deal of the fever and rheumatism of which the Dutch complain are traceable to the low-lying situation of their houses. In the Eastern Province farm-houses are to be seen built at a great elevation, combining strength in time of war, a healthful atmosphere, and a commanding prospect. As to architecture, the best houses of Dutch farmers are seldom more than one storey in height, and when they are, the upper part is often used as a lumber-loft.

Proximity to a colonial farm in the Western Districts is usually announced to three senses some time before your arrival. The whitewashed premises in a flat and bare country can often be seen at a great distance; then the wind, if in the right direction, brings to your ears the loud barking of some half-a-dozen fierce watch-dogs; and brings also to your unaccustomed nostrils the smell of the cow-dung fires, which are here used in villages and on farms as the only fuel. Visitors being comparatively rare in certain districts, the approach of waggons is evidently an object of interest to the farmer and his family, all of whom in turn make their observations as you approach. It is said that on one occasion the sharp eyes of a farmer's little son discovered a horseman at a considerable distance, on reporting which to his father the following conversation took place :—

"Who is it, my son?" said the Dutchman, still inside the house.

"I don't know, pa," was the reply.

"Is het een mensch?" (Is it a man—*i.e.*, a Dutchman?) inquired Mynheer.

"No, pa," said the keen-sighted youth.

"Perhaps it's a Hottentot?" suggested the farmer.

"No, pa," again replied the son.

"Then it must be an Englishman, my child," said the Dutchman, as he appeared himself at the door to take an observation.

The plan of farm-house which obtains almost everywhere is a very simple one. On entering at the front door you find yourself in the "voor-huis" or front room. In front of you, if the house is a first-class one, is the "eet-kamer" or dining-room; and beyond that the kitchen, etc. On each side of you are the bedrooms, which are usually half the size of the parlour. Such houses are the property of farmers who have considerable means, and who are not content with the clay house or the hartebeest hut which many others inhabit. There is yet another class, who are called "trek-boers," wandering farmers, who live in their waggon and tent, and shift about from place to place with their flocks and herds. Many of these people never possess houses, but pass their whole life in this nomadic manner.

Our own intercourse with the Dutch farmers in the colony was invariably of a pleasant description. We were usually met by a portly heavy-visaged man, the master of the house, who silenced the dogs and extended his hand in greeting. As we no longer wore any article of dress that could be styled clerical, we were often taken for "smouses," or travelling dealers. It was amusing to see the evident disappointment when it was known that we were missionaries, not pedlars; and that the visions of showy prints and ribbons, of moleskin and "laken," or black cloth, had been prematurely indulged. However, interest was at once renewed when we expressed the wish to buy a sheep or goat, bread, eggs, etc. Cut tobacco for immediate use was then offered by the master; tea or coffee soon followed from the mistress. The whole family is innocent of stockings; the young ones of shoes also. But the old grandmother, who is rather feeble, and sits in the corner with snuffbox and handkerchief in hand, and the good lady of the house, who pours out your tea, make up for the want of stockings by having each a perforated footstool which contains a vessel filled with live charcoal. In the cold winter mornings this appliance is no doubt, as one of our number suggested, extremely comfortable. Coming from Scotland, the thought certainly did occur to me that a very little trouble would suffice to put some of the farmer's wool upon the feet of his household in the shape of worsted stockings. I fancy, however, Jufvrouw would prefer the charcoal "komfoor" to a spinning-wheel.

But it is when you arrive at a Dutch farm on horseback, and are requested to "off-saddle," and stay over night, that you can see Dutch hospitality and manners to perfection. The Dutchman speaks about his farm and his stock; the lady inquires your age, how long you have been married, and how many children you have.

"But is England really as beautiful as this?" said a good Dutch housemother, as surrounded by her daughters, we stood gazing upon one of the most dreary of colonial scenes. When I had exhausted my Dutch in describing the rivers, streams, and fountains, the enclosed fields, the numerous farmhouses of England, I am afraid my picture was regarded as overdrawn.

The washing of the hands of the whole company by a servant girl is still kept up in most households. Then comes supper, which is just a second edition of breakfast, these being the only meals in ordinary Dutch households. Stewed meat cut into small pieces is served in a large dish, out of which each person helps himself. Very seldom have I seen vegetables served with meat; the latter is usually eaten alone, or occasionally with bread or rice. Soup with flour-dumplings sometimes follows the meat. The Dutch farmers do not usually eat potatoes; I have heard "potato-eater" employed by them as a contemptuous term for an Englishman!

After supper, in a respectable household, and before separating for the night, the house-father asks for "the books." Accordingly a very large Bible and copies of the Dutch metrical Psalms and Hymns are produced and laid on the table. They have the peculiar custom of singing a single verse of several psalms or hymns, rather than several verses of one psalm. Then a chapter of sacred Scripture is read, and afterwards

> "The saint, the father, and the husband prays."

There is no phase of colonial character on which I would so willingly linger, as there is none which so excites my admiration, as this simple family worship offered daily in many a secluded glen and isolated homestead throughout the Cape Colony. Such reverent worship moulds the thoughts and feelings of the young who grow up to take part in it; and if the Dutch colonist has not himself been able to teach his children many of those branches which are elsewhere regarded as indispensable to a rudimentary education, he impresses on their mind the all but exclusive importance of the knowledge of the Word of God.

Despite the wide difference in the character and genius

of the two peoples, I confess that these acts of family devotion brought vividly to my mind similar gatherings in Scotland, which are happily more characteristic of that country now than when Burns penned his "Cottar's Saturday Night." But there is one point of difference which at once strikes the stranger. In the colonial farmhouse no servant is ever present at worship. The Dutchman confines the thanksgiving and the praying to his own family and white visitors; the servants who at the hour of prayer throng the large kitchen or parlour of a God-fearing English or Scottish farmer, are nowhere to be found here at family worship. If the poor creatures do listen to the Divine words, and hear also the earnest prayer, it is necessarily at a distance.

I hope that in some cases this prejudice is breaking down. It is of importance not only to the coloured people, but to the Dutchmen themselves, whose Christianity is disfigured by this unworthy feeling. By establishing a mission of their own among the heathen in the interior, as well as by their liberal aid to village missions throughout the Colony, the members of the Dutch Church already give evidence of entertaining such opinions and feelings as shall infallibly lead, in the course of time, to happier and worthier relations between themselves and their dependants in their own households. In distant and secluded districts it is at present the custom for the farmers to meet for worship on Sunday in the house of an office-bearer of the church, who has the spiritual oversight of his neighbours intrusted to him. Were these worthy elders to have a second service for the servants of all colours who reside on their farms, a home mission work of a very important kind might be carried on throughout the Colony—the ramifications of which would reach its most secluded glen.

Reverencing the whole Bible, the Dutch colonist is especially familiar with the Old Testament. He is indeed partial to the Book of Revelation, because he inherits from his forefathers a horror of Roman Catholicism, which is fed by perusing, in the last book of Scripture, the visions of the deeds and the doom of Antichrist. I was surprised not to meet with a translation of some of Dr. Cumming's works in Dutch families. His writings on Popery would nowhere meet with more sympathetic readers than among the Dutch colonists at the Cape!

The colonial villages or towns—as some of them may now be properly termed—have usually grown up round the Dutch Church as a nucleus; and it has been remarked that these church or town sites had been chosen with great skill by the Dutch colonists. I have come into contact with those who had seen the growth of considerable villages from the solitary farm-house of the first owner. As soon as the church is built, there is no doubt as to a certain amount of business being done where it stands. The "Nachtmaal," or celebration of the Lord's Supper, by the Dutch Church, takes place several times in a year, and brings to the church almost the whole population of the surrounding district. Irreverent men draw attention to certain points of resemblance between the Nachtmaal in South Africa and the Scottish scene which has been described, or perhaps caricatured, by Burns in his "Holy Fair." The Nachtmaal is looked forward to with equal interest by the inhabitants of both town and country. In the former, the shops are overhauled, and goods long ago ordered are anxiously looked for. Clerks and shopmen are bustling on the coast; waggons are journeying day and night along the road; and everybody, down to the little bush-boy who leads the oxen, would give as the reason of all this anxiety, that it is "Nachtmaal" at a certain date in their village; and their waggons must be forthcoming before that time. In the country the excitement is of a varied description, and reaches every household. The good man rejoices that he will soon be called upon to go up to the house of the Lord with the multitude that keep holy day. Nor is he forgetful of debts which fall due to him during the Nachtmaal week; while he has a whole load of farm-produce prepared to clear up his own account with the storekeeper. His partner in life has her own responsibilities at this time. In one family there may be children for baptism; children for "aanneming," or admission to church-membership, and children who are now men and women who are going to be married. The family leave the farm early on the week preceding the Nachtmaal Sunday, on their way to the village. The waggon may be a smartly-painted one kept for the purpose, and drawn by ten horses, the reins of which are held by one man, whilst a whip is wielded when necessary by another seated beside him. But if the family is poorer, their journey is performed at the slower pace of oxen. Each waggon has a fabulous number of occupants; but once in the village, wealthy farmers repair at once to their "town house;" whilst poorer men pitch their tents beside their waggons. When all is done, however, the accommodation, as might be expected, is somewhat scanty for the large and promiscuous gathering. But as no genuine Dutch colonist ever thinks of undressing before going to bed,[1] he is in no way incommoded by his overflowing household. Temporal and spiritual engagements now fully occupy general attention. The farmer reverently appears in his place in church; and in the store also he

[1] I have heard a Dutch hunter describe a new arrival from Europe as still having much to learn,—"for," said he, "the fellow undresses every night in his waggon!"

negotiates concerning corn or wool, or skins or leather, with perhaps a few ostrich feathers, which he has brought for sale. His wife has brought butter, soap, and cheese. He is persuaded that he needs a new hat, and selects one with enormous brim; Sunday clothes are next bought, of a cut and texture which the dealer is careful to have on hand. Then pieces of coarser material for every-day wear are selected, to be made on the farm by his wife and daughters, according to a fashion which seems never to change. Scented snuff must not be forgotten; and a keg of strong waters is also quietly conveyed to the waggon—frequently a present from the storekeeper on receiving payment of the farmer's account. Then the ladies, young and old, who have baptism and marriage and churching before them, require very many things, which they find the careful storekeeper has provided; and of course both wives and husbands buy twice as much as they intended.

"Any fool," said an outspoken storekeeper to his assistants, "can sell these people what they want; our aim is to make them buy also what they don't want."

Accordingly new fashions in harness, fire-arms, horse-carts, household furniture, etc., are shown and extolled by the dealer; and, it is said, the farmer on reaching home after the Nachtmaal frequently finds articles in his possession of the proper use of which he has not the slightest idea. There is a peculiar trait of character brought out in connection with Dutch colonial shopping at these Nachtmaal times, which I have been repeatedly assured is not confined to one village or to one state. And as this foible is well known to the storekeepers, so is its peculiar treatment invariably the same. It would seem that one of the injunctions which a shopman newly arrived from Europe receives from his master, as Nachtmaal-time approaches, is to keep a sharp look-out on little articles lying about the counter, "which are apt," says the owner of the shop, "to find their way into the pockets of customers without the formality of purchase."

"Leave me alone to pounce on them," says the uninitiated European; "I'm up to all that sort of thing; I guarantee that not one shall escape me. I shall march them off to the station as fast as they attempt anything of the sort where I am."

"Not so fast," answers his instructor; "we don't do things in that way here. My customers don't steal; you must never use the word; they merely put things away without ascertaining their price. This is not kleptomania either; it is a purely South African phenomenon, and to be met in a South African manner."

"And pray how is that?"

"When you discover that one of your customers has thus appropriated a certain article, do not appear to take any notice whatever of the transaction; but at the first opportunity add the article abstracted to the orders in that customer's account."

"But will he pay it?" asks the astonished assistant.

"Of course he will. I never had any difficulty myself on this score; and I never heard that elsewhere this plan had been unsuccessful. At the same time, I am not aware that the custom is given up by those who are thus dealt with."

And behind the counter of the colonial store, business is sometimes conducted in disregard of what are accepted as first principles elsewhere. If Cape wool is inferior to Australian in the English market, commercial men of a certain class are content that it should be so. It is a fact that an enterprising English sheep-farmer in the Cape Colony was recently discouraged from washing his wool by the nearest village dealer, who candidly told him that he was not in a position to go beyond the current price, however well his bales might be got up. The easy-going Dutchmen, who do not read newspapers, take no thought about being outstripped by Australia in the supply of wool for the English market. Accustomed but a few years before to the large-tailed African breed of sheep, which was of no value except for slaughter, the Dutchman is generally pleased to shear his sheep, and pack the wool into bales as best he can, and take it to the "dorp" for sale. As most of the price would be "taken out" in merchandise, the storekeeper humours the wool-seller by giving him a nominally high price for his wool, which is again neutralized by the proportionately high prices of his merchandise. In this way, the nominal price of wool in frontier districts is sometimes higher than at the sea-coast! Dimly surmising that there was something unsound in the dealings of the village storekeeper with whom they for years transacted business, it occurred recently to some farmers in the interior of the colony that they might themselves convey their own wool to the sea-coast, where, of course, the highest price ought to be obtained—accompanied with the cheapest merchandise. This journey is not attended with much expense, and the farmer can take his family with him, who have never seen the sea, and who venture on board a ship as a most daring feat. When he is some miles from the sea-port town, he unyokes to make all due preparation. When about to proceed on his journey next morning, an incident occurs which the farmer is at first inclined to regard as one of the most fortunate events in his life. A neatly-dressed young man rides up to his encampment, and after the most cordial salutations makes it known that being out for an early ride for the benefit of his health, he saw the wool-waggons, and as his employer is a large purchaser of wool, he thought he could be of real service to a stranger, and guide him at once through the confusing streets to a commodious yard which had every convenience, and where he might stay as long as he liked, and regard himself as at home. This seems equally wonderful and acceptable; but whilst the farmer is profusely thanking his generous friend, he perceives several horsemen approaching his waggon, who are apparently running a race. They dismount, one after the other; and never were more hospitable and disinterested offers made than each now tenders to the bewildered countryman. The explanation is, that in the "wool season" many of the wool-dealers in the sea-port towns appoint one of their assistants, who, besides other acquirements, must be a good horseman, to "look after" all wool-waggons and bring them, if possible, to his master's yard. Once there, it is supposed to be more than likely that his host will be able to buy the farmer's wool. It is said that one visit has been enough for some of these farmers. Others, again, persevere in what is certainly the practical carrying out of a commercial axiom—to sell in the dearest market and buy in the cheapest. But the farmers' children, who know the English language and have received a fair education, are likely to conduct wool-selling in a somewhat different manner from their fathers. When the Cape wool-grower is no longer ignorant and careless, certain nondescript methods of business will cease to pay. Cape wool is likely to rise in the market with the education of the Cape colonists.

But to return to the inland village during Nachtmaal-time. The village, which has all the appearance of a fair during the week, decently puts up its shutters on the Sunday, and is supposed to be at church. Those who are not remarkable for a church-going habit join the crowd on the Nachtmaal Sunday. Some time ago, a little black boy was seen bending his way toward a certain village church, carrying on his shoulder or head an enormously large Dutch Bible, flaring with gilding and showy binding. Behind him slowly walked a certain dealer, whose face bore an expression of real or assumed solemnity. Meeting an acquaintance, these mysterious features were for a moment relaxed; and, eyeing his Boy and Bible before him, he whispered, "Wat zal een mensch niet voor geld doen?" which may be freely rendered in English, "All in the way of business."

On entering a Dutch church you are struck with the portly frames, the large heads, and open countenances of your fellow-worshippers. And if you do not come in a captious spirit, you cannot but be impressed with the deep reverence and apparently true devotion of the worshippers. They listen with close attention to the instructive discourse, the earnest appeal, the solemn warning, the tender invitation addressed to them by the able ministers who lead their devotions. And then they pledge themselves to be the Lord's at His table, after the impressive order of their church. The children look on with awe-struck gaze, and with bated breath. The Saviour is indeed "remembered" by many of the young and old at those Nachtmaal services.

In Dutch families it is customary for the young people to be publicly received (aangenomen) into the church before marriage. So far as I can understand, the course to matrimony runs very smoothly and with great regularity in those regions. The volcanoes of feeling, the black depths of despair, the wasting away of man or woman disappointed or neglected in love, are things beyond the conception of the young men and maidens of South Africa. They are firm believers in the adage that "there are as good fish in the sea as ever came out of it." And as to remaining unmarried, on any account, the thing is unknown, from the sea-coast to the most inland Dutch district. Young

Dutchmen get wives with the same regularity as they get their wisdom-teeth; and they usually have the former, with several children, before the latter make their appearance. After the consent of old and young has been obtained there is still, however, one obstacle between the youth and the consummation of his domestic happiness. It would not be "the correct thing" to marry before being "aangenomen," and in order to this he must pass an examination before the predikant or minister. It will be readily perceived that motives of a mingled character stimulate the youthful mind to diligence at this interesting and critical period of his life. The ordeal itself, indeed, is one which very small boys at a Scottish parish school would think lightly of. But our South African candidate for church-fellowship and for matrimony looks upon this examination as a great bugbear. Sometimes, indeed, candidates are rejected, which one would think must be very trying to the young lady who has not been won, and to the thick-headed young man himself, who perhaps too often saw wandering over the pages of his catechism his betrothed in bridal array, followed by the flock of sheep which was to be her dowry. Those whose parents can afford the paltry salary secure the services of a "meester," or family tutor, who, on closer acquaintance, turns out to be an old pensioner, or a disabled Scotch mason, or a German, who speaks confidentially of having seen better days. While teaching all the children with regularity, special care is of course given and expected in the case of those who may be about to apply for admission to the church, and who are already betrothed. When mentioning a teacher's qualifications, a Dutchman will never fail to give prominence to his success in "coaching" for this critical occasion. "He is a capital teacher; not one of his pupils was ever rejected by the predikant."

Being ourselves agents of a Society whose fundamental principle is simply to evangelize and not to inculcate any form of church-government, and whose agents themselves, in point of fact, belong to different Churches—we were pleased to be invited to mingle with different religious communities in the Cape Colony. Instead of passing harsh and hasty judgment on what we saw, we endeavoured to derive instruction from a study of the different modes of accomplishing the same end, the different names for virtually the same office or person, the different phases of Christian life among the calm and reticent as well as the demonstrative and outspoken. The true evangelist is the broadest churchman, the most generous and charitable critic. These views have only been deepened and strengthened by eleven years' work. It is a source of much gratification to look upon the energetic and successful efforts of these colonial Churches.

The Dutch Reformed Church, with her able ministers and attached congregations of wealthy and influential colonists, if she be only true to herself, is destined to take the lead in every Christian work in South Africa. The Episcopal Church, under the spirited and far-reaching oversight of Bishop Gray, has recently extended its influence throughout the colony, and beyond it. With its recently organized local synod to aid the bishops or overseers in the administration of the church's affairs, and with its hold upon the affection of many Englishmen throughout the colony, the South African Episcopal Church, like its American and Australian sisters, is entering upon a noble and useful career. The Wesleyans are the same everywhere. No denomination occupies fresh ground in colonial villages with such promptness as the Methodists. Their well-organized staff of local preachers do not confine their efforts to their own countrymen. Much of the Christian life of the Eastern Province is connected with Methodism, which is indeed the predominating church in that important district. An Evangelical Union has recently been formed in the colony, consisting of Presbyterian and Congregational ministers. Hitherto this Union has answered its purpose, and is perhaps destined to teach the churches of the same order in England and Scotland the wonderfully weighty lesson, that it is possible for a church with three classes of office-bearers to be associated with a neighbouring church which has only two. The London Missionary Society, rejoicing in the energetic action of those colonial churches, resolves in the meantime to direct her chief attention to the pagan "regions beyond." The churches in the colony will carry on and extend as a Home Mission work what Christian people in England have for years sustained as a mission to the heathen abroad.

CHAPTER II.

FIRST YEAR IN BECHUANA LAND.

As the rainy season had set in towards the east, where the Orange and Vaal rivers have their sources, we were recommended at Hope Town to proceed westward before crossing, until we had passed the point of their confluence. We were assured that although we might cross the Orange river at Hope Town with little trouble, we were likely to be detained by the sudden filling of the Vaal. The most expeditious plan therefore was to cross both rivers at once, although we should have not only to unload our waggons, but to take them to pieces in order to place the parts in the small ferry-boat. It was well we acted on this advice, for Mr. Helmore, who had crossed the Orange river at Hope Town, and made direct for his station of Likatlong, was detained in sight of his own house for more than a month before the swollen Vaal subsided so as to permit the passage of his waggons. Being a good swimmer, Mr. Helmore was able to cross regularly for the purpose of conducting Divine service; but this detention was an unwelcome prolongation of camp life to Mrs. Helmore and the children.

The proprietor of the boat by which Mr. Price and I crossed the Orange river was a Dutch farmer, whose house was in the neighbourhood. It took nearly the whole day to ferry over the pieces of the two waggons with their loads, the river being here more than 300 yards broad, and flowing very rapidly. Mrs. Price and Mrs. Mackenzie were deprived for the day of the shelter of their waggons, and had to make the most of the shade of some willow and thorn trees, which abound on the banks of the river. The sun was setting when everything was again in its place, and the oxen were brought to pull the waggons to a safer place of encampment, which would also be suitable for the approaching day of rest. But the work of that Saturday was not yet over. Although the Dutchman had given minute directions to my driver as to the course he ought to take in ascending the bank of the river, I had not sufficient confidence in the position of affairs to consent to my wife's reoccupying the waggon until we had ascended to level ground. I noticed with some uneasiness that the river was constantly rising, and that the waters now reached the place where my waggon stood. The oxen were yoked, and the word was given by the driver to go on. What was my dismay to see that as soon as the waggon moved forward the wheels next the river sunk deeper and deeper in the moist sand, and before any change of course could be suggested the waggon and its contents had fallen over into the river! It was no time for speculation. We stripped at once, and by dint of great exertion had emptied the waggon of its contents in ten minutes, and placed the articles high and dry on the bank. We succeeded also in raising the waggon on its wheels again. Thoroughly exhausted with the labours of the day, as well as our recent exertions in the water, we now improvised a place of rest for the night. Next morning we found that one side of the waggon tent had been broken by the fall, that some provisions were slightly damaged, and that a few of our books had also been reached by the water. Our property had been saved from further damage by the promptness with which it had been removed from the water. The ferryman paid us a visit in the course of Sunday forenoon; and it was edifying to witness the volubility and apparent earnestness with which he scolded my driver for taking the course which he himself had recommended the night before!

After travelling over a stony and uninteresting tract of country, we came to Griqua Town, a station usually supplied with two missionaries, but then under the care of Mr. Hughes[1] of the London Missionary Society.

We had heard in the colony of a war between the Dutch inhabitants of the Transvaal Republic and the Batlaping tribe inhabiting the country in which Kuruman is situated. At Hope Town and Griqua Town we were told that the Dutch were about to follow up the advantage which they had gained, and occupy Kuruman. My fellow-traveller Mr. Price, and myself, resolved to test the truth of those reports, and accordingly started for Kuruman on horseback, the distance being about 100 miles. We reached Daniel's Kuil the first night, where we were hospitably entertained by the two chief men of the hamlet. The next day being Sunday, we attended the service, which was conducted in Dutch by the deacon or village schoolmaster, who, by the way, was the son of a former missionary at Griqua Town, who had married a Griqua. It was late on Monday night before we reached Kuruman; but we were delighted with the appearance of the country in the bright moonlight—the thorn-trees on both sides of the road near Kuruman reminding us of the grounds of a country-house in England. On approaching the station we found everything in profoundest stillness; the little village was asleep. Our

[1] After forty-seven years' diligent and uninterrupted service, latterly as the overseer of several native churches, this admirable missionary died at his post in 1870.

knocking however soon roused Mr. Moffat, who gave his unexpected visitors a joyous welcome to his South African home, which was repeated by his family, and, in the morning, by Mr. Ashton, his colleague. The latter gentleman had been resident at Kuruman during the disturbance between the Dutchmen and Batlaping, and had visited the scene of the fight after it took place, with a view to mitigate the sufferings of the wounded. Both Mr. Moffat and Mr. Ashton expected that the Dutchmen would renew the attack; and both were quite sure that hostilities would not be resumed before May. This was explained to us to be on account of a deadly disease which prevails in the summer months among the horses, and causes their removal to certain elevated regions, where experience has shown they can live in safety. As a Dutchman never goes to war on foot, it was held certain that no resumption of hostilities would take place until May, when the horses might with safety be brought down into the lowlands. Satisfied with the result of our visit, we returned to Griqua Town for our waggons. Our weary journey from Cape Town to Kuruman ended with the year 1858; and the new year brought with it new scenes and new duties.

When we contemplated the last stage of our journey —from Kuruman to the Zambese—we could not help feeling that it was encompassed with grave and peculiar difficulties. We had made up our minds to the performance of a journey over a country insufficiently supplied with water. But how were we to accomplish the great object of our journey—the removal of the Makololo to the north bank of the Zambese, and the establishment of a mission among them in that healthy region? We could not look for immediate success in this matter except through the intervention of Dr. Livingstone; and it was encouraging to us to learn that Mrs. Livingstone, who had come as far as Kuruman, intended to proceed with the Makololo mission party, with the view of meeting her husband on the Zambese. After giving the whole subject my own most serious thoughts, I communicated to my fellow-missionaries the course of action which I deemed best under the circumstances. In a letter addressed by me to Dr. Tidman, the Foreign Secretary of the Missionary Society, under date Kuruman, 1st March 1859, I thus described my proposed "bachelor expedition:"—

"Mr. Helmore having lately visited Kuruman, the brethren connected with the new missions met together to consider plans for the future. In the course of the deliberations, I took occasion to propose the following plan in connection with the mission to the Makololo, which commends itself strongly to my judgment as being the best which we could adopt in present circumstances. Instead of committing ourselves entirely to the undertaking at the outset, on the ground of those probabilities of success which are now ascertained, I suggested that the 'Makololo brethren' should, in the first place, make a bachelor-expedition to Linyanti, and negotiate the removal of the tribe to some healthy locality on the north bank of the Zambese. Of course you are aware that it is neither an easy nor a speedy matter to induce a native tribe to 'shift its quarters' without force, even after some of the people have promised to do so. The difficulty is increased if they are asked to return (as will be the case with the Makololo) to a country from which they have been driven by their enemies. . . . Supposing however that the difficulties were all removed—that the tribe agreed to receive missionaries and to remove to the north bank of the river—the plan suggested that the three brethren should proceed with them, and open up (if that were possible) a waggon-road to the new station. Arrived at the spot which they and the people agreed in preferring, the missionaries could build temporary huts for themselves and their goods. Their way thus opened up, and a beginning made in the work of instructing the people, Paul, the native teacher, who has agreed to accompany the mission, could be left in charge of the station, while the brethren retraced their steps for their wives and for the remaining portion of their property. The native teacher and our goods left in their midst would in the meantime form a sufficient assurance to the people that we were not deceiving them. When all this should be accomplished, our position in commencing our second journey for the interior would nearly resemble that of the Matebele mission at present. A great deal of time would, no doubt, be spent in accomplishing this plan; but then it has to be proved that the same amount of work could be accomplished in less time by any other; and besides, this objection must be balanced against others connected with bringing females and children into that country, in the present uncertain state of things."

This proposition was not received with favour by some of those whose age and experience entitled their judgment to great respect. It was, of course, very unpopular with the ladies. And in point of fact the prospect of being left for more than a year in an unsettled country, and with little protection, was not an inviting one to those who were only newly married, and quite unaccustomed to such a life. However, both Mrs. Mackenzie and Mrs. Price agreed to it "under protest;" they reluctantly consented to what they believed would be the best. Mr. Price fully approved of the plan. Mr. Helmore, who had been on a visit to Kuruman, promised to inform us of his decision after his return to his family at Likatlong. When his letter came, it announced his intention to take with him at once his wife and four children to the Makololo country; and Mrs.

Helmore at the same time wrote in a tone of quiet determination which showed that she also had carefully considered the matter, and had fully counted the cost. When the news of the disasters at Linyanti reached England, grave charges were brought against the missionaries in the public papers of the day for heedlessly and heartlessly leading women and children into such calamitous circumstances. With the limited information before the writers, it was perhaps inevitable that this complaint should have been made. But I must be excused for expressing the hope that this sketch of the history of the mission will now testify to the anxious deliberation and forethought which were exercised by the gentlemen connected with it, before the last and decisive steps were taken. And although my own ideas were not eventually adopted, I have never ceased to respect the judgment and to admire the heroism which dictated what seemed to me at the time a more hasty and hazardous course.

Our thoughts and our movements as missionaries to the interior came to be largely affected by other events transpiring at this time. Soon after our arrival at Kuruman, a letter was received by Mr. Moffat, signed by two officers of the Government of the Transvaal Republic, warning him not to proceed to the establishment of missions in the interior until he had received the sanction of the President of the Republic. As both the Matebele and Makololo countries were far beyond the territories of the Transvaal, and the road thither did not lead through any part of the Republic, Mr. Moffat regarded this as an unreasonable demand, with which he could not comply. Greater uneasiness, however, was produced in the minds of the missionary circle at Kuruman, by the news, which no one doubted, of the intended resumption of hostilities between the Transvaal Republic and the Batlaping tribe, in whose country Kuruman is situated. While no one had any reason to fear personal violence at the hands of the Dutchmen, the spoliation of Dr. Livingstone's station at Kolobeng taught us all that our equipment for the interior would probably be regarded as a fair prize, and the forcible seizure of it looked upon as no sacrilege by the "Christen menschen" of the Transvaal. It was therefore thought unadvisable to bring in supplies which were lying at Hope Town. A meeting of the missionaries then residing at Kuruman, or visiting it for a few days, was held there on the 4th of May, for prayer and deliberation regarding the threatening aspect of affairs. Those present, who were seven in number, embodied their views in three resolutions, which were transmitted to the directors of the Society. The following is the second resolution :—"That in consequence of the disturbed state of the country, and the advanced period of the season, it is exceedingly improbable that the Makololo, or even the Matebele mission will be able to proceed this year." Soon after this meeting, the large party, which had now spent some months together at Kuruman, was suddenly broken up. Mrs. Livingstone relinquished the idea of meeting her husband by way of the Makololo country, and returned to Cape Town. Death also had its share in this breaking up. Mrs. Ashton, who had for some seventeen years lightened the dwelling and shared the labours and joys and sorrows of her husband, who had been for that period one of the missionaries at Kuruman, was suddenly called away. After a fortnight's absence at Griqua Town, on missionary business, I found on my return a fresh grave in the quiet Kuruman churchyard, and motherless children still weeping in the first bitterness of their grief. Soon after this, Mrs. Sykes, one of our own companions, received the same summons; only she was called upon to endure severe and protracted suffering before her release. The genuine meekness and resignation which she exhibited were long spoken of by those who witnessed her last days. At the threshold of her life in Africa, she was summoned to receive the reward of the humble and truly devoted Christian. Although far from the English home which she had so recently left, all was done for her that the experience and hospitality, and watchful care of Mr. Moffat and his family could accomplish; and although the sufferer's hour had come, the sweet acts which eased the restless pillow, and lighted up the fading features, were not performed in vain. We looked upon both events in the light of family bereavements, for our intercourse had been of that pleasant and unreserved character. It is some satisfaction to be able to record that in neither of these cases was death caused by anything connected with the climate of Africa.

Whilst we were unanimous in passing the resolution already quoted, as well as others which had reference to the imminence of the advance of the Dutchmen, and the advisability of temporarily removing missionary outfit and supplies to places of safety, individual judgment was brought into requisition in carrying out these ideas. Thus articles which were intrinsically valuable to interior missions, or were prized by mission families at Kuruman, were removed to Hope Town, to Griqua Town, or to the Free State, as it seemed best to their owners. Mrs. Mackenzie was not at that time in a state of health in which I could consent to expose her to the uncertainties and disorder of war, so I judged it best to remove to the village nearest to Kuruman, where, with medical attendance, I could obtain a peaceful home for the next few weeks. We left Kuruman in May for Fauresmith, in the Free State, which possessed to us the additional attraction of being the residence of some members of one of the mission families. Our hurried leave-taking of our friends at Kuruman was in some cases to be a final farewell on earth. We reached Fauresmith on the 7th of June, and met with a warm welcome from the English residents, who had built a little church, but had no minister. I endeavoured to supply this want as long as I was in the village. In the house of Mr. Dickson we found a very pleasant home.

Mr. and Mrs. Helmore, whom I had hoped to meet at Likatlong, arrived by another road at Kuruman a few days after my departure. Their hearts were bent on proceeding at once to the Makololo country. Mr. Helmore himself proceeded to Hope Town for the necessary outfit for the journey, which all had hesitated to bring in sooner. His earnest confidence and unquestioning devotion infected others. What had been hastily removed was now more hastily brought back, and preparations were at once begun for speedy departure into the interior. And then as the season advanced all fear of hostilities on the part of the Transvaal Dutchmen was removed; and the news was heard that the men who had been "commandeered," or called out, had been again disbanded. This sudden change in the tactics of the Republic was to be ascribed to a timely remonstrance on the subject of the threatened attack on Kuruman, addressed to President Pretorius by Sir George Grey, Her Majesty's representative at the Cape. In his reply the President showed no opposition to the missionaries, and almost re-echoed every sentiment of the Governor's letter—expressing his admiration of the evangelistic labours which had been carried on at Kuruman, etc. Danger from this quarter was thus at an end, at least for a time. I received at Fauresmith the first intimation of the change of plan on the part of the missionaries from some natives who had met Mr. Helmore on his way to Hope Town for supplies. Leaving my wife in charge of her newly-found friends, I proceeded at once to Kuruman in a horse-cart kindly furnished by Mr. W. B. Philip, then minister to the Griquas at Philippolis, who also accompanied me on the journey. The speed of the horses was an agreeable change from the slow lumbering ox-waggon. It is usually reckoned in South Africa that the horse goes exactly twice as fast as the ox. Mr. Philip and I left Fauresmith on the 29th June, and reached Kuruman on the 4th July, having spent the intervening Sunday at the station of Likatlong, which we found in charge of Mr. Ross, as Mr. Helmore's successor. I was thus able to visit Kuruman and return to Fauresmith by way of Griqua Town and Campbell by the 14th of July, little more time being spent in travelling than would have been required to reach Kuruman by ox-waggon. It being winter, the weather was pleasant during the day, but bitterly cold at night. Mr. Philip's cart, which was our quarters by night and by day on the road, was just long enough for us to lie down comfortably in it, and broad enough to hold Philip and myself, provided the one who went in first turned on his side, when he was joined by his companion, and the cart-sail was shut from the outside by the servant. The luxury of undressing was reserved for more favourable circumstances. Wishing on one occasion to start at an unusually early hour, we had given the two "boys" or servants orders the night before to call us if they awoke first. Accordingly, a tap came to the side of our cart at early dawn. Half awake, and doubtless fancying himself in his study at Philippolis, Philip shouted out "Kom binnen!"—"Come in!"—awaking both himself and me with the earnestness of his hospitality. The impossibilities connected with any immediate acceptance of this invitation appeared with great force to the boys outside, who gave unrestrained expression to their amusement. And we who were wedged inside the cart certainly never felt so straitened in circumstances as when contemplating Mr. Philip's invitation to a third to "kom binnen" and join us.

Arrived at Kuruman, I found that, by dint of great exertion, Messrs. Helmore and Price had nearly completed their preparations, and were soon to commence their long journey. In deliberating upon the future, it was arranged that I should follow my friends early next travelling season, with provisions and other necessaries. Aware that I was disappointed at not being able to accompany the rest of the party, Mr. Helmore very generously remarked that my detention for a season would probably be the best disposition of the members of the mission—as it would secure those supplies to the whole party, which would certainly be needed in the course of twelve months. It was evident to me during this visit that Mr. Helmore felt deeply the responsibility of his position as leader of the Makololo mission, and was anxious to realize the expectations of its supporters in England. The first part of the journey having been disastrous and expensive, it was his earnest desire to perform the remainder with no waste of either time or money. Above all, his great thought was to be at Linyanti in time to meet Dr. Livingstone there. He knew enough of the natives to be aware that a stranger would not be likely suddenly to acquire such influence with the chief and people as would be necessary to induce them to change their residence. Hence the importance of being introduced to the tribe by Dr. Livingstone as his friend. On no account must the Doctor reach Linyanti, and find that Helmore had not arrived. These feelings were fully shared by Mrs. Helmore, and also by Mr. and Mrs. Price. Mr. Helmore's little children, having no anxious thought about the future, were delighted with the prospect of another long waggon journey, with its constant change of scene and variety of incident. It was under such circumstances that on Thursday the 7th July I bade my friends God-speed, and returned southward. On the following day Messrs. Helmore and Price left Kuruman for the country of the Makololo.

During this visit I arranged with Mr. Moffat to return as soon as possible to Kuruman, as that station, owing to Mr. Ashton's absence, would be without a missionary whenever Mr. Moffat left with his party for the Matebele. As a novice in the work, I looked forward with eager pleasure to the quiet months at Kuruman, and was glad to learn that Paul the native teacher had been engaged to assist in the public services, as his knowledge of Dutch would be useful to me in my study of Sechuana. If this hurried visit to Kuruman was opportune, just enabling me to consult with my friends before their departure for the interior, my return to Fauresmith was equally so; for not two days after, domestic anxieties and fears gave place to grateful joy in the birth of our first child. I take the liberty to mention this event, because it led us away from the rest of the mission party at a crisis in its history. Our son, however, was only a fictitious addition to the population of the Free State; for as soon as possible after his advent we left the little congregation at Fauresmith, and our kind and hospitable friends, amid many expressions of goodwill, and returned to mission work at Kuruman.

As a dialect of Sechuana was spoken by the Makololo, I had a twofold inducement to its study: the discharge of duties now devolving on me, and the qualifying of myself to speak to the more ignorant people on the Zambese. Before our departure from Kuruman, most of the young missionaries had preached short sermons in Sechuana. We had been assisted in our study of the language by Mr. Ashton. At that time there was no printed vocabulary, and practically no grammar on the language. We had copied part of one grammar which was exhibited in a public museum or library in Cape Town, and I managed, as a favour, to procure, for the purpose of copying, another grammar which had been printed for private circulation. For a dictionary we had the Sechuana Bible and Cruden's Concordance. So we were compelled to stick to language employed in Scripture at the outset, and it was seldom we were at a loss for the word we wanted. Of course these were immense advantages compared with the position of those who had first committed the language to writing, and had done so in a disturbed country, and with much manual labour to perform. Mingling with the people, and picking up words and phrases as uttered by them, I believe none of us had found the acquisition of a smattering of the language to be difficult. On my sitting down to the composition of a sermon every week, I found gradually my store of words increasing, and some of the idioms and finer shades of meaning becoming plain. It was my custom to read over what I had written in the hearing of Paul, the native teacher, who stopped me when I used a wrong word or expression. At first I troubled the good man sadly by asking him in my ignorance why it was as he said, and not as I had rendered it. This seemed to him an unnecessary question. It simply was so—that was all he knew. After a little time and care I came to see for myself the rules or laws of the language concerning which my instructor knew nothing whatever, although daily observing them in practice. For a long time every word which I uttered in the pulpit in Sechuana was scrupulously written down. A facility in acquiring languages is a great recommendation to a person intending to be a missionary; but I am persuaded that it is a great mistake to discourage young men of average ability from devoting themselves to this work, because they have not particularly distinguished themselves in classical studies. Such a person, if thrown amongst the people whose language he is to speak, will infallibly acquire it. He may take longer time to do so than another man. But slowness and sureness often go together. In order, however, to speak a foreign language correctly, giving every consonant and vowel its sound and its quantity, it is necessary that one should have what is called a good musical ear. Without this no one will speak "like a native;" but at the same time it ought to be understood that without this a man can fully master the language, in everything except this delicacy of pronunciation, and may prove himself a useful and successful missionary.

To those accustomed to the immense number and variety of books in the English language, it is strange to be shown on a single small shelf the entire literature of a people. The Bechuanas have not a "voluminous literature," and what they have has arisen in a single generation, and is the production of foreigners. They have first and best of all, the Bible. The New Testament was translated by Mr. Moffat, and printed in London during his visit to England in 1838-42. The Old Testament was afterwards translated by Mr. Moffat, now assisted by his colleague Mr. Ashton, who joined the Kuruman mission in 1843, and for many years had charge of the mission press there. A selection of passages of Scripture for the use of schools, recommended by the British and Foreign School Society; a hymn-book, and the Shorter Catechism, had been composed or translated by Mr. Moffat, and printed in London; while the Pilgrim's Progress, a supplemental hymn-book, and Brown's Catechism, were prepared by him and printed at Kuruman. "Line upon line" was translated and printed by Mr. Ashton, and has passed through two editions. A number of religious tracts had been translated and printed at Kuruman by Mr. Edwards during his connection with the mission. At the time of our arrival at Kuruman a small monthly paper was issued by Mr. Ashton, which was called the *Bechuana News Teller*, and was occasionally contributed to by natives.

The time which was not required for the study of the language I gave to works on medical subjects. This period of reading at Kuruman, with what attention I had snatched from other studies and given to medicine in England, helped me afterwards to alleviate much pain; and with God's blessing to effect many cures after native doctors had deserted the cases as hopeless. I believe a young practi tioner in this country is much the better of a strikingly successful case upon his first settlement in a district. One of my first cases at Kuruman was sufficiently striking, and very successful. In consequence of it I found on the following travelling season that my fame had preceded me into the interior, and all sorts of cases were brought, some for delicate surgical operations—all of which I declined—telling the people that I was a teacher and not a doctor, but that I was willing to help them as far as I could. But now for the case itself, which was the bite of the South African tiger or tiger-cat. Two men belonging to the Batlaro Town, which is some twelve miles from Kuruman, were returning home after a day's hunt. They had been unsuccessful, having expended all their ammunition without killing anything. The hunters were passing through some dense bush when a tiger sprang on one of them, seizing him by the cheek with his teeth, and scratching his body with his claws. Having inflicted what it considered a deadly wound, the tiger let the man go and retreated into the bush—for this animal does not immediately devour its prey, although it is said often at once to suck the blood. The wounded man's friend now returned, and carried him home. His face was in a dreadful state, the jaw being damaged, the cheek torn and perforated, and even the poor fellow's tongue injured. The man who had carried him home now walked to Kuruman to ask help; confessing to me, however, that he did not think his friend could survive. I gave him the wherewithal to make a poultice for the whole side of the face, and sent also some medicine to strengthen and support the man. Many a time that faithful friend walked the twelve miles to report the progress of the cure. At length his visits became less frequent; and I was wondering what had become of him; when one day a stranger walked into the mission-house where I was living. It was my patient, come to exhibit the cure, and, I thought, to make at least a touching speech expressing his indebtedness to me. He sat down, and narrated the whole thing over again, mentioning the various medicines which had been given, etc. He then said—"My mouth is not exactly where it used to be" (which was quite true, the damaged cheek having shrunk), "but the wound is quite whole. Everybody said I should die, but your herbs cured me. You are now my white man. 'Naea thipa tle, Ra,'—Please to give me a knife!"

I could not believe my own ears, and asked, "What do you say?"

"I haven't got a knife; please to give me a knife. You see," he added, as I wondered what reply I should make, "you are now my own white man, and I shall always come and beg of you!" This seemed to me a most wonderful transposition of relationship; and I began to think the man's mouth was not the only oblique thing about him.

I mildly suggested that he might at least thank me for my medicines.

He interrupted me, "Why, am I not doing so? Have

I not said that you are now my white man, and do I not now beg a knife from you?"

I gave the man up as a very wonderful specimen of jumbled ideas; but after all there was an explanation to his conduct which subsequent intercourse with heathen people enabled me to discover. The man's position, which was so mysterious to me at the time, was this. Here is a person who has cured me. I am come to do him honour. How shall I do so? By begging from him! To be begged from is one of the marks of chieftainship among Bechuanas. A stranger will say that his chief is a great man; people come from all quarters to beg from him!

Before proceeding farther north with our narrative, I wish to describe the two Dutch-speaking republics, both of which I have more than once visited. I shall also give here the impression produced on my mind by my visits to the old-established missions among the Griquas and Bechuanas.

CHAPTER III.

THE ORANGE FREE STATE AND TRANSVAAL REPUBLIC.

EVER since 1652, when Riebeek built his fort at the Cape, the Europeans in South Africa have been slowly travelling northward. This movement has been more than once hastened by social and political changes taking place within the colony. The complete disenthralment of the Hottentots from serfdom in 1829 was followed, in 1833, by the emancipation of the slaves throughout the British dominions. These movements were distasteful to the colonists at the Cape, as emancipation was to the West India planters. But the latter at least received the compensation-money granted by the English Government, which was not payable in the different colonies, but in London only. The Dutch slaveholders assert that little of this money ever reached them, through the dishonesty of the agents whom they employed. Their discontent reached its height after the settlement of the Kaffir war in 1835; and many families removed beyond the boundary of the colony, some seeking a new country in what is now called the Free State, others in the direction of Natal, and in what is now the Transvaal Republic.

It is not my intention to follow the exciting history of these movements. At first the English Government regarded these "Emigrant Boers," as they were called, as British subjects; not preventing them from "trekking" or removing out of the colony, but following them to Natal and to the Orange River Sovereignty, and in both countries assuming supremacy over them. Natal still remains a British colony under a Lieutenant-Governor; but some six years after the government of the Orange River Sovereignty had been assumed by England, the country was again abandoned to the local government of its inhabitants. This took place in 1854. In 1852 a convention was entered into by Commissioners appointed by the British Government and the "Emigrant Boers" under Pretorius, in which the independence of the latter was recognised, in the country which has been since known as the Transvaal Republic. It was promised by the Dutchmen that they would not practise slavery in the new country; and on the part of England that she would not permit the sale of guns and ammunition to any native tribe, while the trade in these articles in the colony, was to be free to the Dutchmen.

The Orange Free State, formerly called the Orange River Sovereignty, contains perhaps the finest sheep-runs in Southern Africa. It is a flat and uninteresting country, and ill-supplied with timber. The Likwa spruit and the Vaal river divide this state on the north and west from the Transvaal and from Bechuana Land; on the north-east it is bounded by Natal, and on the east by the newly acquired British territory of Basuto Land; on the south it is bounded by the Orange river. It contains an area of about 50,000 square miles.

The Transvaal Republic is not such a fine sheep-country as the Free State, but its products are more varied, as its scenery is more interesting. Near the Vaal river, where Potchefstroom, the capital of the Republic, is situated, the landscape retains the bare appearance of the Free State, but in the districts of Rustenburg and Marikwe the traveller finds himself in a fine agricultural region, with strong fountains and running streams; and the mountains are said to yield lead, copper, and iron, while coal has also been discovered in the country. It is much larger than the Free State—being estimated at some 80,000 square miles. On the north its territory reaches as far as the Limpopo river; but both its eastern and its western boundaries are not easily defined, and indeed are constantly widening. Its southern boundary is the Vaal river. Its population has been estimated at some 40,000 whites. Both these States are governed by a President, Executive Council, and Volksraad.

In the Government of the Free State there are Europeans and Colonial men with a liberal education. But in the more distant Transvaal Republic, some of the offices are occasionally filled by men whose qualifications would not be readily recognised south of the Orange river. Indeed, some who have held offices in this distant region are men whose career in the Cape Colony is said to have been more marked by cleverness than by high character, and whose exit therefrom was somewhat sudden. But the fact is, education is the great qualification here—with, of course, fluency in Dutch. The comparative legislative and administrative talents of the various "independent" states and governments north of the Orange river, is an interesting subject. The purely feudal Bechuanas take an offender before their chief, who is capable of deciding in simple matters. But when the quarrel is about something written or printed on a bit of paper—the chief is fairly nonplussed. He wonders why white men will foolishly quarrel about such little things. The Griquas divide their country into Cornetcies—here as in other things following a Dutch model. The Griqua Field Cornet will attempt to adjudicate on all cases that may come before him; and give at least Border justice. In the "Free

States," the Dutch farmer raised to the office of field-cornet, will perhaps be able to understand a little more than his Griqua neighbour, about civil and criminal cases, and how to dispose of them. But when he comes to fill the office of Landdrost or magistrate in a village, he is painfully out of his element—just as any hill-side farmer in Scotland would be were he elevated to a similar position. As the village grows and its business increases, the perplexities of the magistrate multiply also, until it is resolved that Mynheer Suikerlippen, who has long acted as clerk and general prompter behind the scenes, should now be installed as Landdrost. "Ya, oom," exclaims old Landdrost Dikkop to a friend, as he descends from the bench into private life, "een fatsoenlijk mensch kan niet daar langer zitten; daar's nu te veel uitlanders in de dorp"—"A decent man cannot sit there longer. There are now too many foreigners in the town." So ignorance and incapability stand aside, whether with black or white exterior, and education gradually comes to take the lead. He who mounts the bench may not be really so "decent" a man as the person who descends from it; but, at least, he knows about the business of these "foreigners."

A few years ago, religious strife and party-spirit ran high in the Transvaal country; and on more than one occasion the opposing forces took the field. They kept, however, at long range from one another, and happily not much blood was shed. A description of the causes of the combats would take us back more than two hundred years in the history of our own country. The "Doppers," as they are called, occupy the position of dissenters from the Established Dutch Church in South Africa; although they do not object to receive aid from the State. The only difference between them and their opponents which an elder of the Dutch Church could mention to me, was first that (like the Cameronians in Scotland), they sing only the Psalms of David in public worship; all other sacred hymns being "carnal." Then there was a certain cloth or covering used by the Doppers in public worship and at the Table of the Lord, different from that used in the Church. Beyond these two points in "religion" my informant could not go; although the difference had been the cause of bloodshed. He went on to say that in their own dress the Doppers, like the Quakers, do not approve of the changes of fashion. Their costume is usually a hat of the very largest dimensions; a short jacket, part of the cloth for which would seem to have gone to make the trousers, which are very roomy; a large vest, buttoned to the chin; and the usual "veld-schoen." My informant admitted that the Doppers were very good people, although he thought they would be improved by "conforming" both as to the singing of hymns and the wearing of longer coats. The remaining portion of the Dutch community is divided ecclesiastically into Orthodox and "Liberaalen" or Rationalists, as they are called in English. In Potchefstroom these three sections had separate congregations—all consisting of Dutch-speaking people. It was perhaps better that they should differ and even fight about a hymn or a vestment than remain in the torpid routine of formalism. The existence of the Orthodox, Liberaalen, and Doppers, in the Transvaal and also in the Cape Colony, is an evidence of increasing life and thought among the people.

The frontier Dutchman prefers the Old to the New Testament. He is at home among the wars of the Israelites with the doomed inhabitants of the Promised Land. And no one who has freely and for years mingled with this people can doubt that they have persuaded themselves by some wonderful mental process that they are God's chosen people, and that the blacks are the wicked and condemned

Potchefstroom, Transvaal Republic.

Canaanites over whose heads the Divine anger lowers continually. Accordingly, in their wars with the natives, the question of religion is at once brought into continual and prominent mention. Dutchmen will tell you that in a certain engagement the "heathen" loss was so many, and there were so many Christians *murdered.* Worship is conducted in the laager or camp by some official of the church, who probably exercises military rule as well. In their prayers the language of the heroes of the Old Testament is freely appropriated: they are God's people, and their enemies are His enemies. And here a geographical question presents itself to their minds. If they are the chosen people, they must be either in or out of the promised land. The latter is the received opinion:

"Man never is, but always to be, blest."

In their journeys northward they would seem to have cherished the hope of speedily reaching the land of Canaan. A map of the world drawn by a Dutch colonist would be a curiosity. At a certain mission station some Dutchmen laughed to scorn the idea that the earth was round. A Dutch clergyman declared it would be as much as his influence and position were worth to announce publicly that *he* believed the earth to be round! Those therefore whose cosmos is what they have seen on horseback, or heard described by "travelled" neighbours, are to be excused if their ideas of the distance between Southern Africa and Palestine are peculiar to themselves. I have been often privately questioned on this point by some grave housefather. "Was Canaan near?" "Where was Egypt?" "Could one go there in his waggon?" In this connection it is somewhat affecting as well as amusing to know that the farms in some of the most northerly districts inhabited by the Dutch, have names given to them indicating the longing of the farmers to reach the land of promise and of rest.

The faith and the simplicity of the devout and humble Dutch colonist are changed into fanaticism and superstition in the case of those who have only the "form of godliness," without loyally submitting themselves to its "power." What they want in their own life and character they strive to make up by wonderful "experiences," of which they themselves are the only witnesses. I have listened a whole evening, in a company of Dutchmen, to the recital by one and another of anecdotes of Divine interpositions and warnings; of people who were told, as in Old Testament times, that they would get better of some sickness, how long they would live, etc.—the event always tallying with the prediction. It is a fact that many Dutch hunters resort to the use of dice before going out to the day's sport, a native diviner being called upon to declare by this means in which direction game is to be found that day. A Dutchman in the border districts will often submit to the charms and necromancy of a heathen priest and doctor, under the delusion—which the native of course encourages—that he has been bewitched. Not long ago a native doctor was liberally rewarded by a Dutchman, who had been long without an heir, because through the said doctor's charms and spells the farmer's wife had at length brought forth a son! Ignorance has thus been gradually lowering the tone of the people, especially in the case of those coming into close contact with the natives. The remark which I have often heard made by Englishmen who had long resided among the frontier Dutch, might no doubt have been made with equal justice for several generations—that "the young Dutchmen are seldom such fine men on the whole as their fathers." This of course does not apply to those who have come under European influence, but to those who have fled from it.

The farther the Dutch-speaking population is removed from centres of civilisation, from churches and from schools, the ruder are their manners and the more uncouth the dialect which they speak. Their fellow-countrymen to the south affect great contempt for their restless connections on the frontier, and sometimes call them "Vaalpensen," which is the Dutch for Bakalahari, the ill-favoured and lean vassals of the Bechuanas. I have observed that many young Dutchmen, surrounded from their youth by Bechuana servants, introduce certain Sechuana idioms into their own language in ordinary conversation. For instance, the Bechuanas have a hyperbolical way of speaking about pain or sickness, which is ridiculous when reproduced in Dutch. If a Bechuana man has a headache, the idiom of his language requires him to say, "I am killed by my head;" if he has a sore finger, "I am killed by my finger." This is now in constant use in Dutch in certain districts. Again, when a Bechuana wishes to rouse or to hasten his servant, he will say, although it should be before sunrise, "Make haste: the sun has set." The Dutchmen on the frontier are learning to say the same thing, not only to their servants, but to one another.[1]

[1] A singular instance of the introduction of a new phrase into a language is supplied by the early history of the Kuruman mission. The Dutch language, which was at first the vehicle of communication there, has *zaak*, a matter or affair, and *zak*, a sack or bag. Mr. Moffat, in his work, mentions the mistake which the interpreter made in retaining "bag" as an equivalent for both these words. It may interest some to know that the phrase thus introduced by mistake has passed into the language of the people of that place. The missionaries told them day after day that their spiritual well-being was "eene groote zaak"—an important matter. The interpreter, understanding them to say "een groot zak," rendered it accordingly, "khetse e e kholu"—a large bag. Salvation was a large bag: it was the bag of old and young to attend to the Word of God, etc. Now, hearing this phrase constantly recurring, and from the variety of expression and of illustration being at no loss to find out *what was meant* by it, the people came to the conclusion that the Dutch idiom for an "important matter" was "great bag;" and began to use amongst themselves in Sechuana the same expression. And at the present time the people of Kuruman usually say "khetse e e kholu" (large bag) for "an important matter;" and also "ga se khetse ea me"—"it is not my bag," when they mean "it is not my affair." Elsewhere in Bechuana-land this expression is never

The hospitality of the Dutchmen residing in the remoter districts may be said to be wonderful, and is a most worthy trait in their character. No person, black or white, leaves a frontier farm without having partaken of food. Natives travelling through these districts count upon such entertainment along with the farm servants; and Europeans know that they may quite reckon upon a place at the farmer's own table. On much frequented roads this habit is gradually changing; and a "bondel-drager," a person on foot, who carries his all in a bundle, is not very welcome at farm-houses, and for sufficient reasons. In the Transvaal, when gold-diggers in large numbers were expected to pass through the country, I had an opportunity of observing the high place which hospitality occupies in the mind of the Dutch householder. Not wishing to invite suspicious characters to his house, a farmer whom I knew proposed to build on his premises a little "house of entertainment," where he intended to supply food and a night's lodging to passing strangers. "The bad character of the people must not cause us to fail in what is our duty," said this Dutchman; and I believe he gave utterance to the feelings of many of his neighbours. But the white-skin passport to the Dutchman's table sometimes leads to amusing incidents. For instance, a gentleman living in a certain distant village rode out one day to visit a Dutch neighbour. To his surprise, when all had assembled for dinner, he found his own coachman among the guests. He had obtained leave of absence that morning, and, not knowing his master's intentions, was paying a visit here on his own account!

used. In other cases we have the copying of characteristic sounds. For instance, although there is no "click" in Sechuana, I have heard Batlaping, residing close to the Korannas, occasionally introduce them into their own language. In the same way the Basutos have now in constant use in a few words "clicks" which they have borrowed from the Korannas and the Kaffirs, by whom they were once surrounded. And some assert that the "clicks" in Kaffir were originally borrowed from the Hottentots.

The question seems to be settled as to the northward progress of the European population in South Africa. Stringent enactments that colonists should not pass a certain boundary for any purpose whatever, were always a dead letter. Intercourse with Europeans has been welcomed by all the tribes. But when large numbers of Europeans appear in a certain district, the ignorant uniformly yield up the government, with, or even without, a struggle, to the men of force and resource. How is this advancing emigration to go on? Are our frontiers to be left to decide their own quarrels? Because men are ignorant, are their rights of property to be ignored? Are "filibustering" expeditions to characterize our frontier policy in South Africa. Or does England act worthily when she virtuously washes her hands of all such questions, and says, I have "abandoned" the frontier men in my South African possessions to govern themselves, and to deal with the natives, as they choose? Is it best that the Europeans in South Africa should be divided into small "independent" and antagonistic States; or are we to have in a few years an important and jealous republic bordering on our South African possessions, and extending from the Orange river to the Zambese, with its sea-ports on both the east and west coasts? Would it not be better that there should be one large and powerful European community in Southern Africa, and that the energetic Border-men should be held in wholesome check by the inhabitants of the more settled localities? And if English subjects and the English language are steadily spreading northwards in this continent, from generation to generation, might not all the provinces be united in one general Federation and Parliament, under the Queen of England as its head?

CHAPTER IV.

GRIQUAS, OR HALF-CASTE HOTTENTOTS.

THE mission to the Griquas was the first which was established north of the Orange River. It was commenced in the year 1800 by Mr. Anderson, who was also connected with the Colonial Government. The Griquas, or "Bastaards," as the Dutch call them (many of them being half-castes), had crossed the boundary of the colony in considerable numbers, and at different times, and taken up their abode in what was then the country of the Bushmen and the Korannas. The new-comers lived in the same manner as the Korannas, to whom, and to the Hottentots, they chiefly belonged on the maternal side. The missionaries who first resided with them had to exercise fortitude, forbearance, and patience, being at times in great personal danger, and having to remove with their people when the latter shifted for the sake of pasture. Agriculture was entirely unknown among these tribes. But the influence of Christian teaching and example gradually effected a change in the habits of the people. Many professed faith in Christ, and were baptized. Education made progress. They began to give up their nomadic mode of life; agriculture was introduced; and at length a "dorp," or village, after the colonial example, was projected at Klaar Water, and named Griqua Town. Settlements of a similar character were afterwards established to the westward —one at a fountain, named Campbell, after the missionary traveller, and another called Philippolis, after Dr. Philip, who was for many years the energetic superintendent of the missions of the London Missionary Society in South Africa.

At first these centres of Christianity and civilisation suffered from the attacks of the Bushmen, who had their abode in the fastnesses of the neighbouring mountains. Nor were these the only enemy with whom they had to contend; for some of their own people, who did not choose the quiet life of the Christian village, assumed instead that of bandits or freebooters,—attacking indiscriminately, and for the sake of plunder, the farm of the colonist, the cattle-post of the Griquas, and the missionary station. These lawless characters were called Bergenaars or mountaineers, and are not to be confounded with the Bushmen or other natives living under the influence of Christian missionaries. And it is only fair to assert that but for the example and teaching of these missionaries all the Griquas would, without doubt, have followed the disorderly and dishonest manner of life of the Bergenaars. Instead of this, the Christian Griquas were able, by vigorous action, to preserve peace and order on the northern border of the Cape Colony, in a country which they gradually occupied as their own, and which began to assume many of the signs of civilisation. It is well known that the inhabitants of Griqua Town and Campbell drove back an invasion of Mantatees, afterwards known as Makololo, whom they met in the neighbourhood of Kuruman, and whose appearance in the colony must have led to the most disastrous results. Many of the Griquas professing Christianity made a sort of compromise between the somewhat monotonous life of the village or farmhouse and the nomadic life of their fathers by occasionally undertaking an elephant-hunt in Bechuana-land. When missionaries first went to reside at Griqua Town and Philippolis, large game was still abundant in the immediate neighbourhood. But every year, as they decreased, the Griqua hunters pierced farther to the north; and Lake Ngami and the river Zouga were visited by them some years before Dr. Livingstone brought that district to the knowledge of the civilized world. Adam Kok, the chief at Philippolis, and Kornelis Kok of Campbell, were half-castes; while Andries Waterboer, elected to be chief at Griqua Town, was a Bushman. He was filling the office of village schoolmaster when chosen to be chief; and all are agreed that his administration was characterized by wisdom and energy. On his death he was succeeded by his son Nicholas Waterboer, to whom we were introduced as chief of Griqua-land. Although not possessing the energy of his father, we were assured that he was an upright and estimable Christian man.

Perhaps the most prosperous period in the history of the Griqua Town mission was between the years 1831-40. Not only among the Griquas but from the Bechuanas were numerous converts obtained. The Batlaping tribe had been broken up, and were scattered over the country under "head-men;" the power of the supreme chief being considerably in abeyance. Hundreds were added to the churches in those years. Men and women who had been living together came in rows of fifty couples at a time to have their union solemnized in church. One whole village —with the exception of its old chief and two or three of his councillors—professed themselves disciples of the new faith. Basuto refugees, who had fled during the commotions which preceded the consolidation of the power of Moshesh, gave attention to the preaching of the missionaries; and when, at the request of Moshesh, Waterboer allowed all who chose to do so to return peacefully to their own country, some of them had already been baptized.

Both the Bechuanas and the Basutos who preferred to remain in Griqua-land were protected in the enjoyment of their property on the payment of the same "opgaaf" or tax which was paid by the other inhabitants of the country.

But some years before my first visit, the once prosperous villages of Griqua Town and Campbell had been ruined by the drying up of the fountains—the apparent strength of which had been the chief reason for their selection as sites for villages. At Griqua Town everything bore the evidence of former prosperity. But the gardens and fields were now parched up and quite uncultivated, while many of the houses were deserted and in ruins. The impression produced on our minds was one of sadness and disappointment. But when we had visited some of the neighbouring homesteads, and saw the manner in which the people were living, our feelings were considerably changed. Both in Griqua Town district and Philippolis we found some of the people in possession of houses, waggons, and clothing quite equal to those of many Dutch farmers. For several years they had had good central schools, while rudimentary instruction was given in the villages by schoolmasters, who were usually office-bearers in the church. And the church-books told of a community whose breaches of morality were not lightly passed over, but brought under rigorous discipline. It was very interesting to young missionaries to hear the congregations addressed by their ministers both in Dutch and in Sechuana. When I first visited Philippolis in 1859, I was surprised at the intelligence and apparent respectability of many of the people. Even from a local or caste standpoint, their only fault was their features. Some showed considerable enterprise in farming and in rearing sheep. It was here I first saw a flour-mill driven by water in possession of a native. The chief, Adam Kok, who succeeded his father of the same name, enjoyed the confidence of Mr. Philip, the missionary, as a Christian man, and showed considerable ability in conducting public affairs. At this time they supported their own minister and also paid a good salary to a schoolmaster.

I was aware that a certain charge was usually brought against missionary stations, and especially missionary "institutions," in the colony. They were said to be nests of idleness and pride. But if such was their character in the colony, where the people were surrounded by the excessively stimulating influences of colonial society, I argued that beyond its boundaries the idleness and the pride would be very marked indeed. So I kept my eyes open. I cannot say, however, that the Griquas and Hottentots at those stations appeared to me to be sinners above some of the other inhabitants of the country. As to idleness, for instance,—having built their "hartebeest house," and their "kraals" for cattle and sheep, what remained for them to do but to light their pipes, fold their hands, and enjoy that ease with dignity, which is so sweet to most of the inhabitants of Southern Africa? I of course remembered that these people had passed over from the hard-working to the easy-going class in society. I did not therefore compare their habits with those of English navvies; nor even with their own countrymen in colonial service. They were sheep and cattle farmers; and I recollected having come across some of a higher caste in South African society, who were "indisposed" to lead out a very good stream of water which was on their farm, finding it easier to purchase flour with some of the increase of their flocks and herds. The fact is, there is a certain steady, deliberate current,—or rather placid lake,—of action in South Africa, which is disturbed only by the newly arrived European. Whether he is farmer, merchant, or artisan, he is sure to be at first shocked with the "slow" ways of the inhabitants. But, owing either to the atmosphere, or to the African mutton, or to some other occult cause—in a year or two the bustling "uitlander" or foreigner himself succumbs. Beginning, then, with the active "new arrival," there are no doubt many interesting phases of this South African "indisposition" before we come to the Koranna, described by early missionaries as almost too lazy to get up to allay his hunger with a drink of milk or to light his pipe. The assertion, however, that Hottentots and Griquas at mission stations are most subject to this malady is not borne out by my own observation; and I am persuaded its truth could only be established after a very wide and careful induction.

As to being "parmantig" or conceited, I believe we must bring the Griqua and Hottentot in as guilty, at any rate from a caste standpoint. In 1862 I certainly saw Griquas in Philippolis standing at their doors in the morning attired in showy dressing-gowns and smoking their pipes. Now some might wonder what the world was coming to, when they gazed on such a spectacle. The explanation, however, was simple. The people were selling their farms at the time, and had too much money in their pockets. They bought the dressing-gowns, and a good many other things, to please the eloquent storekeepers. The fact is, the class of people whom we are now considering, speaking the Dutch language, seemed to me to have all chosen the Dutch colonists as their model in social life and manners, although most of their missionaries have been Englishmen. Now this ought to be a gratifying circumstance to the Dutchman when viewed by itself. That his mode of dress, of salutation, and of sitting on horseback, should be the high models after which the Griqua seeks to comport himself, instead of being regarded as manifestations of consummate impudence, ought rather to be viewed as gratifying proofs of the discrimination of these intelligent people. In the same way it would seem to be a mistake on the part of the wife of the Dutch colonist to set down to pride the desire of the Griqua and Hottentot women to imitate her own dress and domestic manners and customs. Her taste as to colours and shapes in kapjes, handkerchiefs, and dresses; her use of herbs and medicaments, as well as numerous little observances resorted to in sickness and in times of maternal anxiety; even her gait and mode of addressing domestics, are faithfully copied. I have never had the pleasure of seeing a Dutch lady on horseback, and therefore cannot affirm that the Griqua horsewoman's posture is a copy therefrom; but it is certainly widely different from the attitude adopted by English ladies. Now, I submit that it ought to be a great pleasure to the wives of the Dutch colonists, not merely to see that they are leading the fashion at the neighbouring Griqua or Hottentot village, but also to learn that their less favoured sisters are copying from them in the detail of the management of their households.

The besetting sin of the Griquas, as of the Hottentots in the colony, is fondness for brandy. Wretched Europeans, who have lost self-respect, and who have ceased to inquire into the moral qualities of actions, loading up brandy in large casks in the colony, cross over into Griqua-land for the purpose of exchanging the destructive drink for the cattle, sheep, and goats of Griqua or Koranna. A brandy-waggon is to me a most hateful sight. Its European owner, all dirty and ragged, burned with the sun, and bloated with brandy, hangs his head or turns away his eye when you salute him, and for the moment perhaps wishes he filled a less disgusting position. Here are no flaring sign-boards or misleading announcements; no glare of gilding and gas-light. There is but a rotten and rickety waggon, whose tent is broken and its sail torn; and the huge casks containing the brandy. As the vultures crowd overhead to feast on carrion and offal, so do poor wretches make their appearance as soon as such a waggon arrives, leading or driving their live stock for barter. Below the waggon, and beneath the neighbouring trees, are men and women in different stages of drunkenness. When they partially bestir themselves, it is only to put to their heads the black bottles which lie beside them. There is of course a good deal of fighting, and drink and remorse drive some to desperation. It is counted a master-stroke on the part of the brandy-seller if he can escape from a place when it gets too hot for him, by leaving all who have a grudge against him dead drunk on the ground. Both Waterboer and Adam Kok enacted that no brandy-waggon should be permitted to enter their territory. This enactment, which was occasionally evaded, was productive of much good to such of his subjects as had not the power to resist the craving for raw brandy. On one occasion a large cask was seized in Philippolis by order of the chief, its end stove in, and the drink poured on the ground. It is said that whilst the officer was obeying the commands of Adam Kok, there were several people with lips at the ground trying to catch a little of the fluid before it sank into the earth! And we learned that eau de Cologne was extensively bought by Griquas, who had given way to intemperance, and was drunk by them in evasion of the law, which forbade the sale of brandy. In the absence of anything stronger, those who have the acutest "tickling" in their palates seek to allay it with tea or coffee. I have been often asked first for a "soepje" or dram by Griquas whose "places" I was passing; and when my driver whispered that I was a missionary, nothing daunted, the beggar would then substitute the request for a "treksel" or "single infusion" of tea or coffee.

Previous to my visit to Philippolis in 1862, the Griquas under Adam Kok had resolved to remove from that district. A party among them advocated a "trek" or removal to a district in Namaqualand; but the chief and the majority preferred a country then known as No Man's Land, to the south-west of Natal. Accordingly the sanction of Sir George Grey, as Her Majesty's High Commissioner, had been obtained, and at the time of my visit everybody was making preparations for the journey. "Trekking" is quite a South African institution. The immense extent of territory renders this possible. The fact that the land which you sell will bring twice or perhaps ten times its purchase-price, and that the farm which you hope to occupy in some frontier district will cost little or nothing, has considerable influence with those who trek. Then all who are fond of hunting get impatient with the restraints of trespass and game laws. Again, to people of a certain disposition there is a degree of civilisation, and a certain number of "new ways," which they can bear; but, beyond that, society becomes intolerable, and they "trek." In the case of the Griquas there was added the strong caste feeling, or prejudice on account of their colour. They might be good, intelligent, and wealthy; they were only "bastaards and Hottentots" after all. This had not been so manifest in the early years of their contact with the Dutch in the district of Philippolis. It was then not unusual for a Dutchman to give his hand in greeting to a Griqua, and call him "oom" (uncle), or "neef" (nephew)—in short, to treat him as an equal; but as the colonists increased in number their clannish feelings returned. The same feeling is manifest in the history of the Cape Colony. We find that after the Dutch had obtained a footing in some inland districts, the word "inhabitant" came to stand in the letters and despatches of the period, not for Bushmen or Hottentots as one might suppose, but for the Dutchmen themselves. They were "the inhabitants" of the country. The same feeling has modified the use of certain Dutch words; for instance "menschen" is used by Dutch colonists of themselves, to the exclusion not only of black people, but of Europeans also; "volk" is used by them of all coloured people, and never of white persons; although, of course, no such usage obtains in Holland or in the Dutch Bible.

As some colonists preferred a country where there would be fine fountains, plenty of game, and numerous "volk" in the surrounding villages, with only just enough Europeans to supply them with ammunition, moleskin, prints, and a little coffee and sugar, so the Griquas sought a place where they might again become "menschen," and cease to be "volk" and "schepsels" (creatures). They were selling, it was true, some of the finest sheep-runs in South Africa; but they were getting hard cash in return; and there was no sentiment binding them to the country, which was not "the land of their sires," except such of them as happened to be Bushmen. The Christian man hopes for the time when this caste feeling shall have died away before the influence of true religion and wise legislation. It is of importance for those at a distance to notice the reasons for those "treks" or removals—which have no claim to be regarded as "national" or "patriotic," but simply as dictated by sympathy in taste or sameness of colour. The Dutch word for Griquas (Bastaards) would seem to strike at the root of all nationality among them. Half-an-hour's study of a list of the names of Dutch colonists leads to the same conclusion with reference to them.

I learn that in No Man's Land, or New Griqua-land, as it is now called, a fair amount of prosperity is enjoyed by the new "inhabitants." They encountered great suffering on their first occupancy of the country; and their mode of life in a grain country will not be so easy as in the pastoral district which they left. One of their own number has been recently ordained as minister of the gospel among them.

CHAPTER V.

KURUMAN, FORMERLY LATTAKOO, MISSION.

THE town of Lattakoo, then the residence of the Batlaping, a tribe or clan of the Bechuanas, was first visited by Europeans in 1801. The Cape Government had despatched an expedition to the interior for the purchase of cattle from the natives; and Messrs. Truter and Somerville, who were at its head, were the first to describe the Bechuanas to the civilized world. Having been formerly accustomed only to the wild Bushmen, the Hottentot serfs, or the savage Kaffirs, the travellers were favourably impressed with the higher social life and character of the Bechuanas. They reported that "they may in every respect be considered to have passed the boundary which divides the savage from the civilized state of society."[1] Dr. Lichtenstein carried his explorations as far as this region in 1805, and was followed by Burchell in 1812. During the latter year Mr. John Campbell visited the missions in South Africa, and pierced into the interior as far as Lattakoo. Mr. Campbell is to be regarded as the pioneer of the Bechuana missions. It is true that before his arrival two persons had resided on the Kuruman river, who were known in the colony as missionaries. Among the Batlaping, however, they were known only as traders. Mothibe, the chief of the town, expressed to Mr. Campbell his willingness to receive missionaries; and accordingly in 1815 Messrs. Evans and Hamilton,

[1] Account of a Journey in 1801-2 to the Booshuana nation, appended to a Voyage to Cochin China. By Sir John Barrow. London, 1806.

accompanied by some Christian Hottentots, proceeded northwards through the colony to establish the new mission. This was then regarded as a formidable enterprise, for Lattakoo was at a considerable distance from Graaff Reinet, which was the nearest colonial town. The difficulty, however, was materially lightened by the fact that Griqua Town was within a week's journey of the contemplated station; and its inhabitants had been at that time accustomed to missionaries for fifteen years. Messrs. Evans and Hamilton proceeded with great caution, leaving their wives at Griqua Town, "according to the wish of the Directors," as Mr. Hamilton explains in his journal. They paid two visits to Lattakoo in 1816, but were not favourably received. Forgetting the promise made to Mr. Campbell, the people declared "the teaching" should not come to them. They feared that the missionaries would change their old customs. It would be with them as with the people of Griqua Town, "who," they said, "once wore a 'kaross,' but now wear clothes; once had two wives, but now only one." At this time Mr. Evans gave up the mission, but Mr. Read took his place, and, proceeding to Lattakoo, met with a favourable reception. In 1820 Mr. Campbell again visited the country, accompanied by Mr. and Mrs. Moffat, whose names have been since connected with the Lattakoo or Kuruman mission, and with Bechuana-land generally.[1] Mr. Read returned with Mr. Campbell to the colony; and for many years Messrs. Hamilton and Moffat shared between them the labours and anxieties of

[1] Mr. Moffat's eloquent account of his connection with the mission in Namaqualand, and the history of his missionary life in Bechuana-land, have long been before the public in the volume entitled *Missionary Labours and Scenes in Southern Africa*—a work which has reached its thirtieth thousand. Mr. Hamilton died in 1851, after a lengthened and honourable career. In 1870, Mr. Moffat, now aged and in feeble health, returned to England, retiring with reluctance from a work which he commenced in 1815, and in which he has been pre-eminently distinguished.

this frontier station. Their difficulties were considerably increased by the unsettled condition of the country. There was no peace in the land. Cattle-lifting expeditions were constantly on the move; and in these engagements the Batlaping were not always the victors. They had removed from Lattakoo to Kuruman after one of these reverses, and were found there by Mr. Moffat. The present station, however, was not commenced till 1824. A tract of about two miles of the country was bought by the missionaries from Mothibe, and paid for with articles which Mr. Moffat had brought from Cape Town. Here were raised a large and substantial church, and two good dwelling-houses, all of stone. I am about to speak of the higher moral and spiritual structure which has been reared in this district; but having myself made some acquaintance with the house-builder's tools in Africa, I feel bound to mention with respect the solid stone walls and the well-constructed roof of the Kuruman church. The station was laid out by Mr. Moffat, who to his services as land-surveyor and architect added with equal diligence the humbler but no less necessary and arduous callings of quarrier of stones and hewer of timber for the church. The walls were built by well-qualified stone-masons, Millen and Hume. The roof was the work of the Rev. R. Edwards, for more than ten years connected with the Kuruman mission, afterwards resident at one of the stations broken up by the Dutchmen of the Transvaal, and now missionary at Port Elizabeth. These buildings were completed in 1839. The Kuruman station is one of those "marks" in the country which would remain to testify to the skill and power as well as Christian perseverance of its founders, were the white men all expelled from the country, and driven back into the sea, according to the dreams of Kaffir soothsayers. Let us hope that as long as it stands it shall ever be the house of God, supplied amid the fluctations of African society by devout men for its ministers, and filled with humble and earnest Christian worshippers.

I found that most of the people living at Kuruman have considerable knowledge of agriculture and the ordinary management of a garden. The hoe has largely given place to the plough, and in such cases the work of the garden ceases to belong to the women, and is performed by the men. Here are the best-kept native gardens in Bechuana-land; but even here the "straight line" in fence and furrow is not always what it ought to be. As the land at this station belongs to the Missionary Society, the apportionment of the gardens rests with the missionaries, and is perhaps not the most pleasant of their offices. It is required that the occupant be a well-conducted man, and the "husband of one wife." These irrigable gardens at Kuruman are, however, comparatively few in number and limited in extent; and the country being unfavourable to cattle, great distress frequently prevails. The game has been long since killed or driven to a distance, and it is only the most skilful and persevering huntsman who, after hours of stalking, succeeds in bringing home a steen-buck, a duiker, or a springbuck. In times of scarcity the women and children spend hours every day in digging up, drying in the sun, and grinding into coarse flour the root of the motlopi-tree, of which they make porridge. This root is also extensively used by the frontier colonists as coffee. The berries of the moretlwa bushes are also very welcome when their season comes round. Should disease or accident put an end to one of your cattle, it is soon surrounded by hungry claimants, to whom it is very welcome. The constant uncertainty of obtaining a supply of the necessaries of life would seem to have impressed itself on the mind and language and features of the people. In districts often visited by scarcity, there is a certain restless, anxious, greedy expression to be observed on the people's faces. And just as the energetic and enterprising Englishman says, "How do you do?" as a form of salutation, the Bechuanas, who in times of scarcity are in the habit of cooking a little food during the silence of the night, lest their neighbours should beg from them—make it their first question when they meet on the street next day,—"Lo yang?"—"What are you eating?" "Nothing whatever" is the conventional answer. This has passed into daily use as a mere form of greeting, and is used in times of plenty as well as scarcity. It is evident that missionaries labouring in such districts have much to discourage them in connection with the outward circumstances of the people. "What's the use o' speakin' aboot releegion when there's nae meal in the house?" demanded an eccentric character in the north, of some one who had been proffering ghostly counsel. And sometimes the missionary in South Bechuana-land would as soon give some of his people a dinner as a sermon—if it were possible to do so.

After Christianity had made some progress in the country, the wealthier natives, following the example of the Griquas in the south, began to purchase waggons, guns, and ammunition, and every winter to engage in hunting. Now, in itself considered, this is a miserably unsettled kind of life. The Griqua missionaries complained loudly that their people came back deteriorated from "the hunt." The Bechuana missionaries also came to understand that members of their churches did not always give the best impression of Christianity in the remoter regions which they visited. But after all the hunt was better than the cattle-lifting raid; and it seemed to the natives, as it does to many Europeans, to be the readiest way of procuring money. Then as Europeans increased in number in the country, occupation was offered the poorer natives as drivers, leaders, and guides. For my own part, it is only just to say that I could not expect better service or greater trustworthiness than I have experienced from Bechuana men. By and bye it came to be observed that as the game receded to a distance, and longer time was consumed on the journey to the hunting-field, the people who had remained at home, and attended carefully to their gardens and their stock, were better off at the end of the year than the hunters, although there might be less display about their industrious mode of life. The missionaries encourage their people to stay at home when it is possible for them to do so. And everywhere fountains are being put to account in order to raise from the thirsty ground abundant food for their families.

If you wish to see Kuruman to advantage, you must come to church on Sunday morning. I do not mean to the prayer-meeting at sunrise, but during the hour before service, when the people assemble in groups outside the church, in the grateful shade of the syringa trees. Some read the Scriptures; others are going over the spelling-book; acquaintances are greeting each other; while occasional strangers from the interior stand in the background in their karosses, and gaze with mute wonder on the scene. Inside the church and school-room the children are singing hymns and listening to the instructions of their teachers. You see many people who are respectably dressed. Most of the men belonging to the station wear European clothing; the trousers, however, are frequently of skin, tanned and made by themselves. The Bechuanas are skilful in patching; and one sees coats and gowns of many colours, and wide-awake hats so operated upon that you cannot well describe either their shape or colour. Most of

Scott & Ferguson Photo

SUNDAY MORNING AT KURUMAN.

the women wear a handkerchief (or two) tied tightly round the head; and it is counted rather elegant to have one coloured, while the other is black silk. Ladies' hats were patronized by a few; and there seemed to be a division of opinion as to whether the hat ought to be worn on the bare head or over a handkerchief rather ingeniously folded so as to imitate long hair in a net. Shoes are now neatly enough made, somewhat after the fashion of "brogues" in Scotland; but stockings are regarded as equally superfluous with gloves. You observe that a good many have brought with them a pretty large bag, while some also carry a chair on their shoulder. The bag contains the Sechuana Bible, which is in three volumes, and the hymn-book, which, here as elsewhere, is a great favourite. The chairs are brought chiefly by the aristocracy of the village, the reason being, as you see on entering the church, that the congregation sit on benches or forms without backs, which is not the most comfortable position in which to hear a sermon. The bell rings for service, and the people hasten into the church. The mothers who have little children remain on forms near the doors, so that in case of a squall they can readily make their exit.

The minister of the day ascends the pulpit; and as the London Missionary Society is a very "broad" institution, and takes no notice whatever of clerical dress and appointments, black cloth seldom extended farther than the coat; while pulpit-gowns and bands, and even white neckties, were nowhere; and it was not unusual for one of the ministers to make his appearance in smoking-cap and wrought slippers! The cap was off in church, and the slippers were not seen in the pulpit; and when both were seen outside, instead of shocking any of the congregation, they seemed to be much admired. The singing at Kuruman in 1859 was equalled only by that of a Dutch frontier congregation. The latter would bear off the palm on account of the strength of the voices and lungs of the Dutch people. Every one seemed to me to improvise a tune as he went on, only looking out that he was not more than two notes behind or before the rest. The leader always stopped a note or two before the end of a verse, apparently to take breath, and before all had finished struck up a new one. The effect was wonderful, although difficult to describe. But at Kuruman a great improvement took place in the singing in a very short time. Lessons in church psalmody were given by the Misses Moffat, assisted by an excellent harmonium, kindly sent out for the use of the station by some Christian ladies in London. The singing is now as good as in an English or Scotch village church. Many of the Bechuanas showed themselves possessed of a fine musical ear, although in this respect they are perhaps excelled by the Griquas and Hottentots. Instead of thumping the dusty earth the whole weary night long, to a monotonous recitative, as in the olden time, the villagers in South Bechuana-land now collect in little parties round a neighbour's fire, and sing hymn after hymn till a late hour. At present all music is sacred among the Bechuanas; the love ditty and the comic song are unknown; and several song airs are used in public worship, being known to the people only as psalm-tunes. Thus "Jock o' Hazeldean," usually sung at a marriage service, suggests nothing of elopement or letting the "tear doun fa'" for an absent lover; but all its associations in Bechuana-land are connected with a match approved by the parents and ratified by the church.

The service now proceeds with the reading and exposition of Scripture, succeeded by solemn prayer. A sermon or lecture follows, in which the preacher strives to reproduce some incident in the sacred narrative,—some parable or doctrine, so as to impress its lesson on the minds of his audience. In 1859 there were three such services at Kuruman on the Sunday—the evening one being attended chiefly by the cattle-herds, bird-frighteners at the gardens, and others who were prevented from coming to church during the day. The church was lighted with tallow candles, one of which was on each side of the reading-desk, and in the middle of the church a chandelier was suspended from the roof. An hour-glass is beside the snuffers in the pulpit—articles not usually found in pulpits now-a-days. There is an officer for the general snuffing of candles, who operates several times during the service. In the course of the week there is one public evening service conducted by one of the missionaries, and another entirely in the hands of the natives.

In speaking of the religious attainments of the Christian Bechuanas, their former manner of life must never be forgotten, if we would do justice to the people and to their spiritual instructors. Their present condition must be studied in connection with their past history. It is not to be expected that a loquacious news-telling people, unaccustomed to solitude and to consecutive thought or study, should on their conversion to Christianity become at once remarkable for their elevated spirituality, and for delighting in protracted seasons of prayer, meditation, and communion with God. Godliness is the highest state of being on earth. He was godly who sang of "Holy Light" in Paradise Lost; and he who in our own time meekly and trustfully pleads—

> "Lead, kindly Light, amid the encircling gloom,
> Lead Thou me on."

This Light is kindly, and it is very lovely; but it is bright, and man's spiritual eye is weak. But if not attaining, so far as I have known, to a life of closely-sustained spiritual meditation, the minds of many are deeply impressed with the truths of religion. If not godly in the highest sense, they are sincerely religious. They believe in God, and their faces and hearts are turned towards Him. I have been struck with the touching manner in which some, in leading the prayers of the congregation, have besought the help of God's good Spirit to assist them in their struggle with temper, habits, and passions which were formerly unrestrained, but are now "kept under" as becometh Christians. The name "Yesu" is a very sacred and precious one amongst these people. I have never heard it lightly used. Few prayers are offered by Bechuanas in which the scripture is not introduced,—"God so loved the world that he gave his only begotten Son, that whosoever believeth in him might not perish, but have everlasting life." Even the most ignorant of the members of the church, those who have become Christians in advanced years, have got fast hold of a few leading truths. God loves them. Christ died for them. God will help them if they cry to Him. They are like lean scraggy oxen that have grown up unaccustomed to the yoke. But at all events they will put that yoke on their necks, and if they cannot pull much, they will at least walk with the rest in the team; and they hope that when the journey is over "Yesu" will allow them to go with the rest to the green pastures and beside the still waters of the heavenly land.

There is usually at a mission station of some years' standing a class of catechumens or inquirers who come to the missionary once a week for instruction. And here latitude is given to individual missionaries as to the method they will pursue in this important and interesting department. The Westminster Shorter Catechism is used by some at these meetings; certain answers are committed to memory; and these form the ground-work of the lesson of that day. Another missionary, or the same one, if the number at the time is not great, will prefer to take the inquirers one by one, that he may give them the greater attention. During my stay at Kuruman, and often when travelling, and spending the night at some village or cattle-post in South Bechuana-land, has a person come, usually, like Nicodemus, in the dusk of the evening, and taking me aside, made known his thoughts on the most momentous subjects, his hopes and his fears. At an old-established station I have known some to come because it was expected of them ; but I have also met with others whose whole attitude was expressed in the words, "Sir, we would see Jesus." I have seen men very deeply moved during those interviews. Although they are taught to suppress such demonstrations, the unbidden tear would sometimes fall silently but not unseen by Him of whom we spoke. When I was travelling, such interviews usually took place at the side of the waggon—the children being now inside and the sail shut, while the servants were seated round the camp fire, the light of which dimly shone on us. One or two of my dogs, if not barking at the prowling jackal or hyena, would nestle close to my feet, mute witnesses of the highest service to God and to men which man can undertake in this world—the divine work of the evangelist.

Those who introduce Christianity into a certain region occupy a most influential position. Their type of piety, their mode of thought and administration, will be copied by their disciples. So long as the original Christian spirit is present in the copy there is nothing to reprehend. But the slavish following out of the letter when the spirit has fled would seem to explain many of the abuses which have been perpetuated in the Christian Church. The class of catechumens, originally pervaded by deep spirituality, may degenerate into a mere formal examination, by means of which so much knowledge will command a certain position in the church. And by continually lowering its standard a church may come to be so constituted that every citizen is potentially a member. Again, the first preachers, in a simple and natural manner, retire into privacy with the individual inquirer, and direct him to the Lord Jesus Christ, praying with him and for him. But in the history of that church the humble elder or presbyter may come to be succeeded by the priest and father-confessor, who teach the inquirer to trust, not in Christ, but in the Church as represented by its ministers, and who profess to hold in their hands the destinies of the living and the dead. Baptism, originally administered to converts and their children, may come to be administered to every child who is born in a certain country, and "christening" be looked upon by many as not more sacred than vaccination.

There is a circumstance of a very striking character connected with the Christian life of the Bechuanas which I must not forget to mention, inasmuch as it would seem to teach an important lesson for future guidance. There is an old Scotch saying which I have always regarded as singularly bold and somewhat inexplicable :—"The nearer the kirk, the farther frae grace." Under whatever circumstances this saying originated, a somewhat analogous statement might be made with reference to Bechuana-land at the present time. Excluding heathen men altogether, and confining our observation to professing Christians, the best specimens are not to be found on the station of the European missionary, but at out-stations occasionally visited by him. On the mission-station, the learning, the skill, the higher civilisation of the Europeans become overwhelming, almost repelling, to the native Christian. An attitude of reverent wonder and ready assent becomes habitual to him. The question with him comes to be, not so much what does the Bible say, as what does the teacher say; he does not seek to think for himself: the missionary thinks for him.

And in listening to the public preaching, as well as in reading the words of Scripture, the attitude is exactly that which Bishop Butler describes in his preface to his Sermons:—"People habituate themselves to let things pass through their minds, as one may speak, rather than to think of them. Thus by use they become satisfied merely with seeing what is said, without going any further. Review and attention, and even forming a judgment, becomes fatigue; and to lay anything before them that requires it, is putting them quite out of their way." Of course all this very much depends upon the personal character and disposition of the missionaries. Where there is a very strong will and great resource and determination, as well as genuine benevolence on the part of the spiritual guide, the dependence of the people will sometimes be carried to a great extreme. On the other hand, where there are a few Christians under the care of a native schoolmaster, more independent thought is begotten. The Bible is the court of appeal. It is studied with some amount of intelligence. From its armoury they obtain weapons for defence against the snares of surrounding heathenism. The office of native teacher in these circumstances is no sinecure. The man must know his Bible at least so as to explain it to his little flock. And after he has done his best, his explanation is sometimes not satisfactory; so a journey is undertaken by him or by some of his flock to the neighbouring European mission station to obtain a solution of the knotty points under discussion. The fact of the undoubted superiority of Bechuana Christians, not directly under European influence, is quite opposed to the idea that the success of European missionaries is to be accounted for by the influence of a superior over an inferior race. From what I have seen I am deeply convinced that it is the power of Jesus Christ in His gospel which overcomes men; and that by standing as it were in the way of this specific agency, the European missionary may even retard and deteriorate the work.

And here we have suggested the importance of trained native agency, which, considering the number of years it has been established, is perhaps the weak point of the Bechuana mission. The success of the Griqua mission is largely to be ascribed to the diligence and tact with which the energies of the more promising natives were thus guided. As early as 1834 two natives were employed at Kuruman, and others were subsequently appointed to surrounding districts. In 1842 a missionary then newly arrived in Bechuana-land thus writes on this subject:—"At present the state of the mission here is very promising regarding native agents employed in teaching and addressing. Six such men are now connected with the Kuruman. It is truly delightful to observe the fervent zeal of these godly men. It is the imperative duty of all of us to raise up and instruct such men as far as possible."

All the schoolmasters mentioned were trained by Mr. Moffat at Kuruman, and some of them continue to do worthy service in the country. But they would seem to have had few or no successors; and a seminary for native preachers in Bechuana-land, although often projected, was never fairly established. And so in 1868 we have not such an encouraging view as in 1842. In 1868 a missionary writes from a station in South Bechuana-land:—"The educational department of the mission has been kept in the background. The youth have sunk back for want of a continued course opened up to them. The village schoolmasters, uneducated themselves, and mostly unpaid, make but a feeble impression." The Directors of the Society are about to establish a seminary for training native youths in Bechuana-land; and if, with higher training, they will only imitate some of the present teachers as to diligence and zeal, the result will be all that could be desired.

On every mission station there are some who refuse the gospel; and occasionally others who, having made a profession of religion, sink back into evil ways. Thus the old opposing elements of "the church" and "the world" are to be found everywhere. Now it is certain, the more you teach a bad person without his character becoming changed, the more powerful you make him for evil; and the knowledge obtained on a mission station is occasionally thus abused. I have once or twice heard the remark, "The servants from such and such a station are the worst in the country; they are much worse than heathen." Upon inquiry you find the remark is made in connection with somebody who, in his own little village, is a "thorn in the flesh" to the Christian community, and who is surely not to be taken as in any way representing them. The character of men and of communities is ever changing; and Christianity, while she offers her blessings to all, sets her *imprimatur* only on those who obey her precepts. In order to find out the value of Christianity, the comparison must be instituted not only between the members of the church and the heathen in a distant part of the country, but between them and their neighbours who refuse the gospel. There are certain villages in Bechuana-land where the gospel has been seldom preached, and where the people are bitterly opposed to it. At the same time the influences of civilisation and commerce by themselves have been fully felt in these places; and here, as on the mission station, the old power of the chiefs has been greatly diminished. What is the character of these villages? They are in the country what the opposing and reprobate man is on a mission station. There is one especially on the highway to the interior where the inhabitants practise the only approach to highway robbery of which I have heard in Bechuana-land; and travellers are heartily glad when they have passed this place without losing any oxen. The village to which I now refer is within sight of a mission station; but its inhabitants, or perhaps rather its chiefs, have strenuously resisted the often-proffered services of Christian evangelists.

I was standing one Sunday at the door of a church in Bechuana-land after the service was over, following with my eye the people as they wended their way to their homes. Musing on the change which had already taken place in them, the great difference in the world of thought and idea in which they were now living as compared with their forefathers, I went on to think of the littleness of one man's life when viewed alongside any of God's great processes. How many ages had revolved before the gospel had reached them! My meditations were interrupted by the approach of an English trader, whose lumbering waggon had just unyoked in the quiet village. After the usual salutations, and following my eye, which was still upon the retreating people, Mr. —— remarked—

"I'm afraid this is slow work, Mr. Mackenzie."

"Well, in one sense you are quite right," I replied. "The history of our own native land leads us to expect that." Glancing at his handsome face, and the beard which he was then caressing, I added, "Say that you and I are near to perfection, 'finished specimens' of what civilisation and refinement, as well as religion, can accomplish, we must remember two things: that 'good people' are still proverbially scarce in our own country, and that it has taken a long time to bring humanity to the elevated position which Englishmen occupy! But come; how long will you give these people, through Christianity, and the commingling of races, and the aid of peaceful commerce, with perhaps the sterner discipline of war—how long will you give these Bechuanas of the discipline by which the Almighty educates nations, before they will produce our equals?"

"But will they not die out in the process?"

"Not they. During the first shock of the revolution in their habits there may be many lives lost. But these people are not like the Red Indians: they will change with changing times, and live."

"Well, they might get on, perhaps," replied my companion, "were it not for their colour and ungainly features."

"They will get on in spite of the colour. They are sharp enough, as every one knows who has been in the country. And who knows the future colour of South Africans? Even at present you are aware that many of our fellow-countrymen, whatever they may say in English society to the contrary, do not find colour so very repulsive. And we have not yet fairly tried the effect of shelter from the weather, with good food, industrious habits, and a pure Christian heart, upon even the features of the people."

"Well, sir, you are very sanguine," said my friend, bidding me good-evening.

"God is merciful, and the ages are long," I replied, as we parted.

I was now alone. The evening sun scattered its brilliant rays over village and country-side, and by and bye seemed to come down and kiss the mountain range before me. So let Thy gospel, O God, come to all races of people in the land, and bind them together in kindliness and fellow-feeling!

CHAPTER VI.

BATLAPING MISSIONS AT TAUNG AND LIKATLONG.

TAUNG.

THE Batlaping tribe of Bechuanas, among whom the Lattakoo mission was commenced, removed from Kuruman a few years after the establishment of the mission there, leaving behind at that station a few members of a subject tribe called Bachwene, whose numbers were increased by occasional stragglers from other tribes. The Batlaping were for many years without a resident missionary—those under Mothibe at Likatlong and along the bank of the Vaal river being visited by the missionaries of Griqua Town; while the other divisions of the tribe were connected with Kuruman as out-stations. At length, in 1843, the spiritual oversight of the Batlaping residing at Taung was undertaken by Mr. Ross, who joined the Bechuana mission at the same time as Dr. Livingstone. He then undertook what has proved a most arduous and trying mission. The same difficulties which were encountered in earlier times at Lattakoo, in connection with the opposition of the chief and head men, were now met with by Mr. Ross. When the tribe removed from Taung to Mamusa, their missionary patiently accompanied them, beginning over again the labour of raising another church and dwelling-house. But when it pleased the fickle chief Mahure, after a few years residence, to return to the neighbourhood of Taung, Mr. Ross, now considerably advanced in years, took up his residence first at Griqua Town, and afterwards at Likatlong, while he regularly itinerated among his former charge. After the departure of Mr. Helmore for England, and again for the Makololo country, Mr. Ross, who now resided at Likatlong as a head station, carried on his itinerancies throughout the united districts of Likatlong and Taung. The unwearied labours of this evangelist and pastor were brought to a close by death in 1863. His last illness was protracted, but the ruling passion of his life was strong even in death; and to the last he encouraged and exhorted those about him to put their confidence in the Saviour. The career of Mr. Ross affords great encouragement to Christian young men in humble life. If David Livingstone was a cotton-spinner, William Ross, his companion in the voyage and journey to Bechuana-land in 1842, once followed the plough in the Carse of Gowrie, and afterwards served an apprenticeship as a house-carpenter. As the cotton-spinner qualified himself at Glasgow University to pass his examinations and to take his diploma as a doctor of medicine, so the ploughman and carpenter, aided by a kindly and genial-minded parish minister, who is still alive, passed his university course at St. Andrews, and afterwards his theological curriculum in Edinburgh. Possessed of a liberal education, and occupying the position of a licentiate of one of the Presbyterian Churches in Scotland, he offered himself to the London Missionary Society, having been, in point of fact, with others "enlisted" for the Bechuana mission by the eloquent and earnest appeals of Mr. Moffat, when on a visit to Scotland. While Mr. Ross's name and career are comparatively unknown in England, both are familiar in every hamlet of the extensive district where he laboured.

It having been represented to the Directors of the Society that Mr. Ross's successor should if possible be a man of experience and sound judgment, they requested Mr. Ashton to remove from Kuruman, where he had laboured for more than twenty years, and to take the oversight of these frontier stations. This wide field has been again subdivided, and Mr. Brown, who joined the Bechuana mission in 1865, has the oversight of the Taung district, while that of Likatlong remains in charge of Mr. Ashton.

In 1857-8 the Batlaping were involved in war with the Free State and Transvaal Republic. On this occasion the natives were clearly the aggressors. While the Free State was at war with Moshesh, Kousop, the chief of a small Bushman village within the boundary of the Free State, taking advantage of the unprotected condition of the homesteads of the Dutch farmers in his neighbourhood, attacked several dwellings, killing women and children, and stealing the personal property from the houses, as well as live stock from the fields. When he had amassed a considerable booty, Kousop crossed the Vaal into Bechuana-land, where he was allowed to reside by Gasibonwe, who was by birth paramount chief of the Batlaping. The example of Kousop was followed by Pohuetsile, the son of Gasibonwe, and by Boyong, his brother. Motlabane, chief of the Bamairi, a neighbouring tribe, also made raids into the Free State and Transvaal. Meeting with little or no opposition, these freebooters returned to their villages, after a few days' absence, mounted on fine horses, and driving live stock of all kinds. But the day of reckoning came. As soon as men could be spared for the purpose, a party of Dutchmen was sent against Kousop, who was himself killed and his tribe completely broken up. Pohuetsile, acting on the aggressive, endeavoured to surround a division of the Dutch force, but his men were scattered, and he himself was killed. Gasibonwe and Motlabane were also defeated, and the former was shot and beheaded by the Dutchmen. By this time, however, the desultory fighting had reached

Taung, the residence of Mahure, the chief of the largest division of the Batlaping tribe. Mahure had discountenanced the raids, and none of his people had joined them. But he was unable, and perhaps unwilling, to deliver up to the Dutchmen the scattered members of the guilty tribes who had taken refuge in his town. The Dutchmen, therefore, next attacked Taung, and after an engagement, in which the Batlaping were again worsted, a treaty was made between the commandants on the one hand, and the sons of Mahure, as representing their father, on the other. It was agreed, on behalf of Mahure, that within three months' time he should compel the marauding chiefs to deliver up all the stolen property of the farmers, and should also make good to them all their losses suffered on account of the war. No sum was specified in this document, but the young chiefs had no hesitation in putting their mark on the sheet of paper, and probably thought they were exhibiting consummate tact in averting imminent peril by a promise having reference to the future. When, however, President Pretorius, writing some time after in behalf of his own subjects, and those of the Free State, mentioned the amount of the indemnity which he demanded, the folly of their act became apparent. They promised to indemnify the Dutchmen; they now learned that in order to do so they must deliver to them 8000 cattle, 300 horses, 500 guns, and 10 men who had committed a certain murder. It was probably known to President Pretorius, who is familiar with the intertribal distinctions which obtain among the Bechuanas, that no Batlaping chief could compel a levy of this description. The alternative, which was that the Dutchmen should remunerate themselves by taking possession of a portion of Batlaping territory, was probably looked forward to as more desirable, and more likely to be realized, than that the fine should be paid. Indeed, it soon became evident that the Dutchmen intended next year to carry their operations as far westward as Kuruman. To give a colouring of justice to such a course it was publicly asserted that the missionaries had instigated the natives to the late disturbances, and especially that the little monthly paper, published at Kuruman, was filled with inflammatory articles. It is needless to say that these charges were wholly unfounded. On the contrary, the missionaries warned all against the example of Kousop and his followers; and the whole tone of the little newspaper would certainly be approved of by the Peace Society. But the glaring injustice of the above charges will more clearly appear when it is stated that not one of the marauding chiefs was a Christian; not one of the members of village churches followed their own heathen chiefs on these lawless raids. Jantje, the Christian chief of the Batlaping village of Likatlong, denounced from the outset the apparently successful raids of Kousop the Bushman. Unlike his heathen neighbours, he so ruled his people that not one of them became a freebooter, and not one was involved in the war at Taung. While Christian missionaries do not hold themselves responsible for the political relations of the country in which they reside, it is surely an instructive fact that, of the natives who engaged in robbery and bloodshed in the Free State and Transvaal, every one, without exception, was an opponent of Christianity in his own town or village. In these circumstances, to denounce the missionaries as being at all blameworthy is not to be accounted for in any way that is creditable to the community whose leaders and public men thus openly bore false witness against their neighbours. The timely remonstrance of Sir George Grey deterred the Dutchmen from proceeding against Kuruman in 1859; but the fine has never been paid by the Batlaping, while the promise to pay anything, as signed by the sons of Mahure, is still in the hands of the Dutchmen.

Only one of Mahure's sons has been baptized. The rest, with their father (who died in 1869) continued to cling to heathenism themselves, and of course to draw many people with them. But the life and teaching of Mr. Ross were not without encouraging results, even under those unfavourable circumstances. If the chiefs have not believed, many of the common people have done so. When I visited the station in 1863, in company with Mr. Ross, I had the great pleasure of meeting at the table of the Lord a considerable number who had been gathered by this most diligent evangelist from among the ranks of the heathen. The apparent interest which one native Christian shows in the well-being of another is a great contrast to their former indifference as heathen. More callous-hearted people than Bechuanas, to what does not affect themselves, could not well be imagined; and it is very gratifying to observe any indication that the people are learning "to look not only on their own things, but also on the things of others." I found in this neighbourhood a small town of Barolongs, who had been formerly under the care of Mr. Ludorf, a Wesleyan missionary, at a station which was broken up at the same time as Dr. Livingstone's, and for the same reasons. Thus members of tribes formerly at enmity sat down together at one table; and disciples of different societies united in "remembering" their common Lord.

After leaving the station, I passed the fountain called Lithakwaning, where Masse, the Christian son of Mahure, has a small village, and where he has commenced to irrigate a patch of land as a garden and corn-field. It is very easy to talk about the slowness, the incapacity, and the fickleness of such people; but it is surely a great change when the pursuits of agriculture and irrigation take the place of drinking sour milk and trapping game; and when from living the unrestrained life of a heathen, the man's character for purity and truthfulness is such as to satisfy the missionary and the native church. In the eyes of his fellow-countrymen such a person occupies a prominent position. He has dared to change the "customs," and yet no calamity happens to him for the breach of all that the tribe held sacred. The water does not refuse to flow in his furrow although he is a black man; and irrigation is here supposed to be a custom practised only by the whites. The white men's fruits also grow in his field. The old people may denounce him, the rain-doctor or priest may hate an innovation which sends the life-sustaining rill of water along the thirsty roots of the drooping corn and maize; but many come to regard such a man as a hero, and in their journeys into other districts do not fail to mention the deeds of him who has given himself to the Word of God and to the wisdom of the white men.

LIKATLONG, THE DIAMOND COUNTRY.

Likatlong was originally an out-station of Griqua Town; and one can imagine the extent of the influence of the Griqua Town mission on the surrounding country from the fact that when, in 1840, the station of Likatlong was handed over to Mr. Helmore, 190 church-members were committed to his care.

The people of Likatlong were a branch of the Batlaping tribe, which broke up into several sections not long after the date of the establishment of Christianity in the country. The power of the new religion soon became apparent. In the olden time one or other of these factions would have swallowed up the rest, and the successful brother or uncle, as the case might be, would have been chief of the whole tribe. And once under a single head, the clan would have again become manageable for aggressive and for defensive warfare. The separated condition of the Batlaping, which no doubt weakened them as one tribe and restrained them to a great extent from aggressive warfare, is to be regarded as one of the beneficial results of a doctrine which spoke of the love of God, which raised their estimate of human life, and pictured to their minds a day of future reckoning. Thus Christianity interfered with the reconstruction of the model heathen town; it caused even Pagan men to pause and stop short at the commission of the crimes necessary to their obtaining command over the whole people.

Jantje, the eldest son of Mothibe, but by an inferior wife, made a profession of Christianity at an early period, and has been for many years a member of the church in the town where he is also chief. He appeared to me to be a quiet, sedate, and amiable man. My first attempt at administering medicine was made in the case of one of Jantje's sons who was very ill with dysentery, when I passed through the village in May 1859. My treatment was very successful, while that of the village doctors had entirely failed. Jantje, who was described to me as a just but not very generous man, was so grateful for the restoration of his little son to health that he presented me with a sheep in acknowledgment of my services. Thus my introduction to Jantje and to the practice of "simples" among the Bechuanas was a very gratifying one. Jantje spends a good deal of his time as a farmer at a fountain called Manyering, which is about twenty miles from Kuruman.

Near Likatlong, the native gardens are usually not very successful; in a dry season especially the people have to trust to their flocks and herds, and to the unfailing motlopi for subsistence. But throughout the whole district irrigation has been introduced, not indeed in a first-class manner, but to the best of the ability of those to whom it is an entirely new custom. Impossible things are often attempted; and what is accomplished is sometimes done in a slovenly manner. The water-furrow is usually more or less of a zigzag instead of a straight line; and the gardens and arable land are laid out in a manner which offends the eye of a European. But it is a fair beginning; such gardens are a welcome sight to those who wish well to the natives.

Mr. Ashton, who has recently had charge of this mission, finding that some traders were in the habit of bringing in brandy for their own consumption, and for the purpose of "treating" the native chiefs, recently called the members of his church together, and laid the matter before them. Here was a new source of evil—a new and powerful hindrance to those who wished truly to serve the Lord Jesus Christ. White men had become accustomed to this drink; but the Batlaping had not yet learned to like it. Why should they drink it at all? It was no part of their duty as Christians to do so. Although they had received many new thoughts, and many useful and beautiful articles from the white men, evil would be found mixed up with the good, and they must be able to choose the good and resist the evil. "I am your teacher," said the missionary, "and wish to lead you into the right and safe path. We all pray, 'Lead us not into temptation;' therefore we ought not ourselves to rush into new temptations and dangers. I am willing as your leader and guide to promise not to taste the white man's drink. Who will join me, and promise also?" Every hand in the church-meeting was held up; every one promised to refuse the drink himself, and to discourage others from using or selling it. All will join in the wish that this church may be kept steadfast in the performance of this vow.

The district of Likatlong, in common with other parts of Bechuana-land, was visited annually by English traders, who exchanged European goods for ivory, ostrich-feathers, karosses, etc. In the towns of the Batlaping shops had been opened, where this trade was regularly carried on. In 1867 great excitement was created in the colony by the rumoured purchase of a diamond from a native by one of those traders; and by and bye it was announced that the gem in question had been sold for £500 to his Excellency Sir Philip Wodehouse, then Governor at the Cape. The news was at first received with suspicion. Could anything worth while be found in South Africa? It was even announced that a well-known dealer in precious stones had sent a qualified agent to report on the district in question; and that the latter had positively denied the existence of any rich diamond-field in the country. But the light of these gems could not be hid. One after another was disposed of for considerable sums. For a diamond which a Bushman had in his possession a colonist offered all the stock on his farm. The offer was accepted; the native returned home a wealthy man; and the colonist obtained in the nearest village £11,000 for this gem. A native woman, making some repairs on her premises, dug up a diamond with her "kepo" or sharp-pointed piece of wood, for which her husband obtained a waggon, oxen, and load of goods. Nothing which had taken place in their previous contact with Europeans was more wonderful to the natives than this. "Who can understand you white men?" was now the general remark. "You first clear off the elephants for the sake of the ivory, and the ostriches for their feathers; and when you have swept the country clean as to what is above ground, you then proceed to find treasures in the bowels of the earth."

There being no longer any doubt of the reality and importance of the discovery, the frontier towns were soon deserted of their floating population. Parties were formed in more distant colonial towns. Government servants obtained leave of absence; men of business deserted their offices and shops. All sorts of conveyances were placed under contribution—from the ox-waggon to the light horse-cart, which is the South African express. The contagion spread to England, and a new line of steamers is advertised at reduced fares. Meanwhile what took place in California and Australia has been enacted on the silent and solitary banks of the Vaal river. Where a few months ago there was only a scattered native population, with perhaps a dozen Europeans, there are now nearly 10,000 people.

I believe the mode of procedure at the diamond-fields is as follows:—A "claim"—that is a piece of ground—is marked off under the sanction of the provisional government. The pick and the shovel are used to loosen the soil, and to collect it into a heap. The large stones are removed at once, and the sand separated by means of a fine sieve. These processes are generally performed early in the morning, sometimes by the light of the wood fire. The residuum consists chiefly of pebbles, among which may be found rock-crystals, agates, jaspers, quartzite, garnet, spinel, peridot, and blue corundum. It being now necessary to use water in the search for the diamond, a vehicle of some kind is brought into requisition, and the pebbles are conveyed to the washing-place on the bank of the river, which is connected with the claim. A sufficient quantity of material having been removed during the imperfect light of the early morning, the most exciting work of the day commences when the bright African sun has made his appearance. The washing is performed by means of a "cradle" or a "long tom"—articles whose names are familiar to gold-diggers as well as diamond-seekers,—and which, as used by the latter, consist each of two sieves, the upper one having holes about half an inch in diameter, while the under one is made so as to detain a diamond of about half a carat. The "cradle" is used by solitary workers; the "long tom," being a larger implement, is employed by companies working a claim together. After the washing has been performed the "sorting" process begins. A rude table has been constructed upon which the pebbles are placed. The novice performs the sorting slowly and carefully; but the experienced worker, whose eye has been trained by practice, goes through the operation with great rapidity. With a small shovel or scoop he conveys a quantity of pebbles to the table. One glance, one touch with the hand, to expose all parts of the heap, and, if it is rejected, he sweeps it off at once and another heap takes its place. But if the welcome and unmistakeable gleam of the diamond is discovered by the eager eye of the seeker, it is carefully and tenderly picked out and placed in his own or the company's purse. And so hour after hour and day after day men work at this wonderful lottery, heedless alike of the cold of the winter morning and the fierce heat of the summer noon; at one time heated by wielding the pick and spade; at another shivering over the washing and sorting; for one "find" would more than repay all their toil, and might make them possessors of "a fortune."

Canvas towns have sprung up. Stores, brandy-shops, a newspaper, billiard-rooms, and other signs of "civilisation" are now to be found. Ministers of religion visit the diggings for the purpose of preaching. In one of the late colonial papers it was announced that the President of one of the neighbouring states, laying aside for the time the cares of office, had embarked in the exciting career of the diamond-seeker.[1]

Of course there is a dispute about the ownership of the country. The Korannas and the Bechuanas, the Griquas under Waterboer, the Free State under President Brand, and the Transvaal under President Pretorius, all lay claim to the district. The diggers do not care much about the politics of the country, provided they get the diamonds. But the general feeling seemed to be that England would extend the northern boundary of the colony.

As to the part of the country north of the Vaal, and near to Likatlong, Jantje, the chief, undertakes to prove that it belongs to him, and that the other inhabitants asked and obtained his permission to occupy their present position. We shall see what the event will be with reference to this now valuable tract of country—whether an upright Christian chief like Jantje of Likatlong, whose past career is without a single blot, whether judged by his English or by his Dutch neighbours, will be quietly ignored on account of the smallness of his tribe, by whatever government eventually assumes sway over this district, or whether the fact of his ownership or former occupancy of the country will be recognised. To say that he shall retain it and rule

[1] The following is a diamond-seeker's outfit, as given in a colonial paper :—"A Scotch cart ; waggon axles ; a long tom ; three sheets of iron (heavy) ; tools of all sorts, not forgetting braces and bits ; a pump (those made by S. Ford are very good for the purpose) ; 4 lbs. each of 1¼ and 2 inch screws ; 4 lbs. each of 2 and 3 inch nails ; four or five hoes (strongest make); ten 12-inch planks, 20 feet long ; English leather, about two or three feet square for making buckets for pump ; six light picks, double-pointed (Collins' make if possible) ; six 3-foot shovels, round steel blades ; 5 lbs. of tacks, commonly called clouts ; 3 lbs. of cast-steel for re-pointing picks ; crowbar ; one bolt of canvas ; three or four buckets ; three prospecting dishes. The articles are best put together at the fields, and the above materials can be best purchased in the colony."

over it would be to talk nonsense; to say that because he is too weak to compel recognition he shall receive none in any form, would be dishonourable in the extreme. Jantje himself some time ago addressed the Governor at the Cape on the subject, and there is no doubt of his preference that the government of the country should be assumed by England. Let, then, this man's rights of property be recognised in some appropriate way; let private property in land and fountains be respected throughout the district; let English justice be administered at the expense of the district by qualified English magistrates; and then let the meeting of the races go on, and their settling down together in the same country. Another hundred years' growth in Christianity and civilisation before the rush of Europeans took place would have made these Bechuanas capable of occupying a higher position than they can do at present—only one generation removed from the sleep of Paganism. But if they cannot occupy high and distinguished posts where the races commingle, they must just do that of which they are capable. It is at least gratifying to find that they can abide the shock of this social revolution.

CHAPTER VII.

JOURNEY INTO THE INTERIOR.

WE left Kuruman on our way to the Makololo country on the 25th May 1860. Some of the men who had accompanied Dr. Livingstone in his journeys to the distant interior were natives of Kuruman and its neighbourhood; and as they took care not to understate the privations which they had endured on the road we were about to take, I had at first some difficulty in hiring suitable men. Those also who had good waggons were reluctant to part with them for such a length of time. Mr. Helmore had engaged a native to follow him with a load of necessaries for the new mission; but this person had not fulfilled his engagement, and the goods were still at Kuruman. It being thus absolutely necessary that I should convey supplies to Messrs. Helmore and Price, I was compelled to avail myself of such waggons as were procurable. These were old and very rickety, and were a source of annoyance to me during the whole journey. Then in my inexperience of such wretched vehicles, and with the desire to carry in as much as I could for my friends, I so overloaded them that one actually broke down altogether, and had to be left behind. Taking warning, I lightened the others while still in the neighbourhood of Kuruman.

I had got thoroughly interested in the work of the Kuruman station, and was gratified by the good wishes which were expressed on all hands when we left. Two promising boys, then at school, put into my hand each a little note full of affection and earnestly-expressed prayers. Mrs. Moffat and her daughters kindly accompanied us as far as Klein Chwai, where we spent a peaceful and very happy Sunday together, before taking what we then thought might be a last farewell. At that time we cherished the hope that should an available port for commerce be found by Dr. Livingstone on the east coast it might be possible for us, in the course of time, to communicate with England by that route, which would be much nearer than by way of the Cape Colony.

Among the dozen men composing my party there were representatives of several races. I had Mebalwe, who was for some time Livingstone's assistant, and who shared with the Doctor the wounds and the danger in the encounter with the lion at Mabotsa. I found him a most valuable and trustworthy man, whose years and experience commanded respect from the rest of the party. Then there were several Bechuanas, one Hottentot from the Colony, one Griqua, a Kaffir woman, who was the wife of one of the men and Mrs. Mackenzie's servant. The spare oxen were driven by Furu, a Bushman, whose master or owner was the driver of my own waggon. I agreed with his master about Furu's wages, which I made higher than usual, upon condition that he should not only drive on the loose cattle, but as soon as the waggons were unyoked, collect and herd the whole troop together. By this arrangement I was saved a great deal of trouble on my northward journey; and my cattle did not stray once between Kuruman and the Botletle river. No matter at what hour the night's journey was finished, or how dense the jungle round our encampment, Furu was always at his post, collected the wearied and hungry oxen, and whistling cheerfully to them drove them in a body for an hour's grazing, after which he brought them close up to the waggons, and then himself had the luxury of joining the circle round the fire. Accustomed to this every night, the cattle became very tame, so that often when I went to have evening prayers at the fire, I could with difficulty find an open path on account of the denseness of the cattle lying close round the waggons and chewing the cud, or sleeping off the fatigues of the day. I must not omit Fama the only child of our nurse, a bright Kaffir boy of seven or eight years of age, who accompanied his parents. Resting all the time the waggons were travelling, this sprite used to jump out when we unyoked,—ready for any amount of mischief, and taking special pleasure in teasing one after another of the wearied men, as they lay under the shade of a tree. His father had a twofold office. He was engaged as cook; but having announced that he was a good shot, and fond of hunting, his office came to include providing the meat as well as cooking it. In order still further to lighten my insufficient waggons, I hired another, with two Bakwena men, and a team of oxen from the chief Sechele. I had thus with me some thirteen people, and had in charge above seventy oxen, three horses, and four waggons. At the head of this party I was to spend the next nine months.

Before we left Klein Chwai we were joined by Messrs. Reader, Lamont, and Burgess, who were also on their way to the Zambese country. Without forming one party, we were for some time close to one another on the road; and at Maritsane river we spent Sunday together. Strange to say, on comparing notes, I found that one of these hunters, when a boy, had gazed upon the same mountain whose scaurs and crags were familiar to myself in youth. Although we met in Africa as perfect strangers, the same strath had given us birth, and the hoarse music of the same rapid-flowing river had been familiar to us both. Like the world itself, the Scotch may be said to exist between a centrifugal and a centripetal force. They are never pleased till they go abroad, and when abroad are never tired of thinking and speaking of "auld lang syne;" and many are never satisfied till they find themselves back in their "ain countrie" again. That short English service was the last which my fellow-countryman was destined to attend. But little did we think so as we worshipped together at Maritsane river.

Before reaching the Bangwaketse town named Kanye, I was hurriedly called by one of the drivers, who informed me that the wheel of his waggon could not possibly go any farther. It had been already once or twice wedged, and was now beyond all repair. What was to be done? We were in the desert, nearly two days' journey from the Bangwaketse town, and one day from some wells of water on the waggon-road before us. I left Mebalwe and another man in charge of the waggon—giving them plenty of food, and, filling all their available vessels with water, promised to send them a fresh supply of the precious fluid by the Bakalahari living at the wells, a promise which I kept. To complete our misfortunes my horses strayed from their herds and were some days away, in a country infested with lions. I was very anxious about their safety, because I regarded them as indispensable on such a journey. The possession of horses reduces distance by one half, whether for the purpose of looking for water or for pursuing strayed cattle. I was therefore thankful when two were again brought to the waggons; the third had been seized by the lion. As soon as we arrived at Kanye, I despatched an empty waggon with supplies for Mebalwe, and a spare wheel, with which to bring my three-legged vehicle to be repaired. These were not so expeditiously executed as I could have wished. Although a first-rate workman, Adriaan the blacksmith had got into idle ways, and often threw down the hammer or adze the moment my back was turned. There was something seriously wrong with his constitution, according to his own account; but I noticed that it affected him most on the hottest days, and whenever I left the waggons he was sure to have a bad attack.

But our detention here was enlivened by the appearance of Mr. Sykes from the Matebele country, who told us of the welfare and success of the party of the preceding year, under Mr. Moffat. With the large town of Kanye close to us, to whose inhabitants we could now deliver the gospel message in their own language, we found ourselves sufficient employment. Through the teaching of one of the Kuruman native schoolmasters, we found that Hasiitsiwe, the chief, and one of his wives, had made some progress in learning to read. But the body of the people were wedded to their customs, although constantly exhorted and instructed by Sebube, whose zealous efforts were however somewhat interfered with by the fact, that not having a sufficient salary, he lived at a considerable distance from the town, at a fountain where he could irrigate and raise food for himself and family. The Bangwaketse were once a large and powerful tribe, and they still number perhaps six or seven thousand people. It was very difficult for me to answer their chief's question, "Why do you pass us by, and go to the distant Makololo and Matebele? Why not teach us also?" It has always been a matter of surprise to me why certain Bechuana towns have never had a missionary, although willing to receive one. But this grave error is likely soon to be remedied; and for the first time in the history of the mission, the whole country will be occupied by an adequate band of missionaries.

While detained at Kanye, Moleme, the native teacher at the neighbouring Barolong town under the chief Montsiwe, came to the waggons with the request that we should visit his congregation and administer the ordinance of baptism. Mr. Sykes and I had much pleasure in doing so. We found that the power of Christianity was evidently felt in the village. In Montsiwe and Moleme, who are brothers, we had an instance of the separations which the gospel makes in heathen lands: the one believing in Christ, the other cleaving to Paganism. The Barolong were formerly under the care of the Wesleyan Society, and their last missionary, the Rev. Mr. Ludorf, gave up his charge at Lotlakane on the dispersion of the tribe by the Transvaal Republic. We have already referred to some of this people as living in the neighbourhood of Taung, and joining with the people of that station as members of the church. But at this town, except for the occasional visit of a missionary, Moleme has the entire charge of the infant church, and he seemed to be a careful as well as zealous man. The spirit of the people was earnest and enthusiastic; another example of the strength and power of the Christianity which is fostered by independent thought and humble prayer, and not enervated by over-dependence upon the help of the European missionary.

On approaching Kanye, the large aloe-trees attract the attention of the traveller; and again on leaving the town and descending the steep mountain on the way to the Bakwena, there are other indications that he is now entering a more genial and better-watered region. The little bushes of the Karroo had given place, after we crossed the Orange river, to an extensive belt of country covered with the larger moretlwa and mohatla bushes, with here and there, at the foot of mountains and along their gorges, small forests of acacias. Now, however, the timber increases in size and variety; the mountains are wooded on their sloping sides and table-shaped summits; while even in the case of the more rugged and abrupt hills and peaks, a generous vegetation seeks to cover their yawning fissures and unshapely rocks. We pass at some distance on our right the site of Kolobeng, where Dr. Livingstone spent many years as a missionary. I afterwards visited the ruins of the mission station, now entirely uninhabited. I stood in the roofless house, every brick of which the Doctor had laid with his own hand. I went to what had been his garden, and returning to the entrance of the house, gazed upon the scenery which must have been familiar to the eyes of its former occupants—now so far scattered from one another, and from their former home. Yonder was the site of the town which the evangelist had so often visited. There the grassy plot where strangers from a distance would "outspan" when they came for medical advice, which they always received gratis. There at my feet were the rocks upon which the bottles of medicines were dashed to pieces by the men who had been cured of diseases on that very spot.[1] Missionaries lay no claim to infallibility, and they are free to admit that their position in times of turmoil and strife is a difficult one, and if they remain at their post at all their conduct is very apt to be misconceived and misunderstood. Instances have occurred on the frontiers of the Cape Colony in which charges as heavy as any ever brought against Livingstone by the Dutchmen, were preferred against missionaries by colonists, and upon equally insufficient grounds. But then there was this important difference: where British law existed, these charges, not being supported by evidence, passed away with the excitement of which they were the product. But the Transvaal Republic, within a few years after it secured its "independ-

[1] Livingstone's *Missionary Travels*, p. 39.

ence," broke up no less than five mission stations established by disinterested men, and supported by the Christian benevolence of a distant country. Therefore it is evident that frontier feuds ought not to be finally settled on the frontier.

Two days after our departure from Kanye, we reached Liteyana, which was then the residence of the Bakwena tribe under the chief Sechele. Our reception here was gratifying; the chief himself made his appearance at the waggon, and politely greeting us in English fashion, offered us also the African welcome of an ox for slaughter, which was accordingly shot on the spot. Sechele was the finest specimen of the Bechuanas which I had yet seen, being tall and well made, with a good head, an open countenance, and unusually large eyes. His dress was somewhat singular. At one time he appeared in a suit of tiger-skin clothes made in European fashion. On another broiling day he was dressed in an immense Mackintosh overcoat with huge water-boots. After a youth of romantic adventure and great hardship, Sechele found himself at the head of the Bakwena, then considerably reduced owing to recent wars and dissensions. In 1842 he was first visited by Dr. Livingstone, who was to exercise so much influence over his mind. The Doctor afterwards resided with the Bakwena, and Sechele gave himself to instruction, and proved himself an apt scholar. I should say there is no native in Bechuana-land better acquainted with the Bible than Sechele. I have heard Dutchmen describe with amazement his readiness in finding texts in both Old and New Testaments, but especially the former. After some three years' probation, Dr. Livingstone admitted Sechele into the church by baptism. So long as the encouraging and stimulating influence of his teacher was near to him, this chief's conduct would seem to have been all that could be desired. But this consistency was not kept up after the Dutchmen had attacked his town, and he was left alone to pursue his course amid the querulous taunts of his own people. He was well-nigh alone in his tribe in his profession of Christianity; and many of the people refused to see more in it than a vain desire to "make himself a white man." Then the rain-making and other customs were still carried on in the town, and at the expense of a younger brother of the chief, called Khosilintsi. But if this person paid for the rain, and otherwise performed the "orthodox" customs every year, he would, in point of fact, be the preserver of the town, and its virtual head in the public estimation. I believe Sechele's first compromise of principle was an interference to arrest what he supposed would lead to the total subversion of his power. He resolved himself to send for rain-makers, and to pay them out of his own cattle. At first this compromise was secret and unacknowledged. But it became gradually known in the country that "Sechele was now making rain." By and bye the secrecy was thrown aside, and he openly assisted in the performance of heathen ceremonies. But it must be borne in mind that all this time this singular man was most exact in the observance of private and family prayers, and stood up regularly every Sunday to preach to the Bakwena. His position seemed to be one which he has not been by any means the first to occupy—that Christianity might be engrafted upon heathen customs, and that the two could go together. For instance, he himself would go with the people in their rain-making ceremonies, but he would not neglect at the same time to pray to God. He would use charms and incantations, washings and purifyings, according to the old rule, and yet profess faith in Him whose blood cleanseth from all sin. The Bible, in short, did not require him to give up the customs of his ancestors, although it required him to believe in the Lord Jesus Christ. He could be an orthodox Mochuana and a good Christian at the same time. This was the position which he took up, and the tenor of many of his discourses. I have spent many of the hours of night with this clever chief in the earnest discussion of these points. When one after another his arguments failed him, he has said to me, "You have conquered: your idea of the Christian life is the right one, but was I not alone? What is one man against all the Bakwena?"

"How hard it is for us all, Sechele, for me as well as for you, to believe that God with us is greater than all who can be against us!"

"Monare" (Sir), he replied with feeling, "not hard for you: you are a missionary; your faith is great; but hard for me, who am chief of a heathen town."

It would have given me pleasure to chronicle greater steadfastness and spirituality of mind as characteristics of a man who occupies so prominent a position in Bechuana-land as the chief of the Bakwena. It would have been gratifying to record, that as in the case of the Batlaping residing at Likatlong and on the Vaal river, the movement towards the new religion had spread among the people as well as influenced the chief, and that the tribe had given itself to the "likualo," or books, for all blessings which they needed, instead of to the rites and ceremonies of their forefathers. But it is no part of my duty to manufacture or distort facts. However heroically Sechele set out as a Christian, separating himself from all that was connected with heathenism, instead of carrying numbers with him by the power and depth of his convictions, in the course of time his people dragged him back to them. "Was he ever a Christian at all?" says one critic. "Is he not one still?" says another. Regarded with great suspicion by men of the old school, as insincere in his return to the observance of their ceremonies, Sechele is looked upon with even greater mistrust by native Christians, as one still in the thrall and bondage of this world, and a stumbling-block to all converts. The Europeans in the country, whose standard (for black men) of morals and consistency is decidedly high, put this chief down as a clever humbug. The most charitable interpreters of a life of temptation and struggle are the missionaries, who hope that to this chequered career a brighter chapter may yet be added, and who feel that even now it does not befit them to "cast a stone" at such a life as that of Sechele.

For a few years missionaries belonging to Hermannsburg in Hanover resided with Sechele; and under their care he occupied the position of a member of the church. The circumstances under which he procured these missionaries further exemplify the character of the man. After the departure of Dr. Livingstone, one and sometimes two native teachers resided with Sechele. Mr. Moffat gave him to understand, however, that as much valuable property had been destroyed at the stations which had been broken up by the frontier farmers, it was not probable that he could soon receive another missionary from England. But Sechele was determined, as he explained to me, to show that he had power to get a missionary at once from some quarter. So, without consulting his people, and to the surprise of all the country, he actually made application to the Transvaal Government for a missionary! President Pretorius gave prompt attention to his request, and hearing that German missionaries had landed in Natal, and understanding that they were Moravians, for whom all Dutchmen profess great respect, he forwarded the Bechuana chief's petition to the Hanoverian missionaries, who had been driven back from their original destination in the Galla country, and were somewhat uncertain as to a suitable locality for their labours. The arrival of Sechele's letter in such circumstances was regarded by these devout men as an indication of the will of Providence that they should proceed into Bechuanaland. What was their surprise, on arriving at the station, to find all the detail of missionary work in full operation, under Paul, the native teacher! They had not known the previous history of this Bechuana chief; and they were for a time afraid lest the London Missionary Society should regard them as intruders in a district so long occupied by its agents. But the arrival of Mr. Moffat on his way to the Matebele put an end to all their fears on this score. He explained to them the hesitation of the London Society at once to send a successor to Dr. Livingstone at the Bakwena; and assured them that now they were in the country, he could only bid them God-speed as fellow-labourers. The missionaries once obtained, by the exercise of his own power and influence, Sechele seems gradually to have repented of the step he had taken; or, as in other things, to have bent to the will of the people, who had always a prejudice against "the missionaries, who," they said, "came from the Boers." After the lapse of some years Sechele sent a formal declaration to Natal and to England, that "he did not wish the teaching of the Germans, but one who would instruct him as Dr. Livingstone had done." It was in the end amicably arranged between the two Societies that the Hanoverian mission should direct attention more particularly to tribes residing within or near to the Transvaal, while the London Society should reoccupy the station at Sechele's. The two Societies might thus work their way northward, the one on a route slightly to the east of the other.

We were very kindly and hospitably received by Mr. Schroeder of the Hanoverian Society, who afterwards died of fever at this station. The German missionaries had not been idle since their arrival. Besides attending to the acquisition of the language, they had built a dwelling-house for themselves and another for the chief. The latter was neatly finished, and Sechele, who had been to Cape Town, and had seen the interior of many English homes, was very careful in keeping everything in order. Masebele, his wife, was well dressed, and, if not quite abreast of her husband as to politeness, was very kind, and interested herself much in making inquiries about our relatives in England. We were introduced to Sechele's family, some of whom had been to Kuruman, and had resided for a time in Mr. Moffat's house. Like the chief himself, these young people were kind, intelligent, and pleasant, but entirely lacking in decided views or strong preference as to religion. Compromise seemed the motto of all.

Two days beyond the town of Liteyana, we met a party of Transvaal Dutchmen coming out from an elephant hunt in the interior. They inquired anxiously concerning native politics; and gave us to understand that they had protracted their hunt on account of certain warlike rumours which had reached them. This delay had well-nigh proved fatal to an Englishman in their company, who was then slowly recovering from fever. As this was my first contact with a disease so prevalent in the district to which I was journeying, I got the man to describe his symptoms and the remedies which he had used. With reference to the Dutch mode of treatment in his and in other cases, all that can be said is, that the poor people do their best in the circumstances in which they are placed. Before leaving home, and when they are buying supplies of groceries, etc., for their hunt, they purchase from the storekeeper a small tin box, gaudily painted, and labelled "huis-apotheek," being an assortment of medicines for domestic use. Some have more skill than others in the use of these medicines; but I have heard the remark made, as a matter of course, concerning a protracted illness, "We tried the whole medicine-box, bottle after bottle, but without result." Like their tea and sugar, the "huis-apotheek" is usually exhausted before they have finished their hunt. It had been so in the present case; and when the unfortunate Englishman became ill the stock of medicines had become entirely exhausted. So the Dutchmen gave him what they had: pure tar, a spoonful now and then, with water; and the fat of game, applied externally and internally. Failing to produce perspiration, they actually rolled the miserable man in the burning sand as a sudorific! Their patient however did not die, as might have been expected; and change of air had made him convalescent when we met him, although his weakness and haggard looks still excited our compassion. Some years afterwards I met this person, who walked up to me as to an old friend. Failing at once to recognise him, he said almost upbraidingly, "Don't you remember the wretch for whom Mrs. Mackenzie made such delicious beef-tea at Kopong?"

Between Boatlanama and Lopepe, Khosimore, who rode one of my horses, was fortunate enough to shoot an eland. It is considered a masterly thing if you can drive the eland or the giraffe to the waggon road, or to the encampment, as the case may be, and there shoot it. So Khosimore was not a little proud that he had succeeded in bringing it close to the waggon road, where, as he said, Ma-Willie (Mrs. Mackenzie) could see it. The eland is a beautiful creature, combining great elegance with considerable size and weight of body. The meat of a fat eland is richer than the best beef. All hands were speedily at work skinning and cutting up our prize. Having secured it in the waggons, we again proceeded towards water at Lopepe.

Khosimore spoke very highly of the horse which he had used that morning; it was, he said, well trained, and evidently accustomed to hunting. I was glad to hear this, for, as I aspired to closer acquaintance with the game, I judged it fortunate that both rider and horse should not be equally inexperienced at the outset. But a night or two after this, having travelled late in the dark, and the boy who had charge of the horses being probably in a great hurry to get to the fire, tied this horse most carelessly to the waggon, with such a length of rope that during the night his legs got entangled; he threw himself over, and next morning was so crippled as hardly to be able to leave the waggon. In a few days he was dead. In the same way I have more than once lost an ox through the carelessness of the person who fastened them up at night. So true is it in such cases that, if you only give rope enough, the animals will "hang" themselves.

We arrived at Shoshong, the town of the Bamangwato, under the chief Sekhome, on the 20th July. This is perhaps the largest of all the Bechuana towns, and, indeed, one of the largest in Southern Africa. Shoshong was afterwards to be my own station and place of residence for years, but at present it was of importance to us as the last place where supplies of native corn could be purchased, and additions made to the number of the draught oxen. There had arrived here, a short time before, a Hanoverian missionary, who very kindly received us. Here also I had the pleasure of meeting Mr. Moffat, who was then on his way to Kuruman from Moselekatse's country. He brought the good news that the mission to the Matebele had been established at a place called Inyate, and that the missionaries were already preaching to the Matebele through interpreters. This news rendered us all the more desirous to ascertain the success of the Makololo branch of the new mission. But no news had reached the Matebele country from them. Nor had the Bamangwato more recent intelligence than we ourselves had received at Kuruman before starting. I found, however, that the Bamangwato had not forgotten Mr. Helmore. My future friends and coadjutors, Khame and Khamane, the sons of the chief Sekhome, who were now attending school, and who had been already baptized by Mr. Schulenborg, spoke very gratefully of a service which Mr. Helmore had held in the large "kotla," or court-yard of Sekhome, when passing northward the previous year. I have often since heard the common people among the Bamangwato refer to this service, and mention some of the preacher's remarks. It would seem that Mr. Helmore found special favour in the eyes of Sekhome, who assembled all his people on the Sunday morning as if to a native "pitsho," or assembly. When Mr. Helmore rose to conduct worship, the large court-yard was crowded with men. The remark which the Bamangwato make concerning the preacher of that day is, "Ola a itse go bua," "He knew how to speak," *i.e.*, he preached so as to impress and interest his audience.

The following extract from a letter written by Mrs. Helmore, at Shoshong, to a daughter, then at school in England, gives a vivid picture of their circumstances and feelings when at this place the previous year:—

"I intended to write to you a long letter from this place, but am afraid I shall not be able. The people crowd about our waggons and tent all day long, making the most deafening noise, so I have been obliged to leave letter-writing till candle-light. . . .

"There must now be a post for us at Kuruman, but when we shall get it I do not know. Do not be discouraged at not hearing from us regularly; trust that we are well and safe. We will commend each other to the Lord, the parents the children, and the children the parents, and then there will be no fear nor anxiety. I want to know how you spent your midsummer holidays. By the time you get this it will be Christmas again. In about three weeks we hope to reach the Zouga or Botletle, stay there a little, and then go on to Linyanti. It will be the beginning of November before we get there. When we have seen Dr. Livingstone, we shall arrange about your coming home. . . ."

So planned this Christian mother for the establishment of a "home" on the north bank of the Zambese, such as they had possessed for years on the north bank of the Vaal.

Mr. Moffat was the bearer of a message from Moselekatse to Sekhome, which he now delivered. It was to the effect that he might "sleep," as he (Moselekatse) had now no intention of going to war with any one. He had promised to Mr. Moffat, in 1854, that he would avoid everything like aggressive war, and now announced his intention to adhere to that promise. In a future chapter we shall see how much truth and sincerity were in this message from the Zulu despot. A Sunday intervening whilst we were still at Shoshong, Mr. Schulenborg requested Mr. Moffat to share with him the labours of the day. The Bamangwato assembled in considerable numbers, and Mr. Moffat discoursed to them with great solemnity on themes seldom present to the heathen mind,—death, judgment, and the world to come.

After parting with our venerable father in mission work at Shoshong, we commenced the most difficult part of our journey. But we trusted we were not unprepared to enter it. Not having many large water-vessels, I had purchased a calabash for each man, with the understanding that no one should visit the "public" water-vessels except the cook, who would give out the necessary water for cooking. I found this plan answer very well. I was never without water, and never required to interfere and give it out myself. Khosimore jealously guarded his "vatjes," or water-vessels; and when the men were thirsty they had recourse to their own calabashes. A spirit of emulation also entered amongst them, and it came to be matter of inquiry at the evening fire who had most frequently visited their supply of water during the day. It was held that such had declared themselves to be the babies of the party. The leader of my own waggon had been provided by his father at Kuruman with a stone jar to hold water for the young man's own use. "At the jar again!" was frequently heard announced from waggon to waggon, as this young traveller washed away the sand of the desert from his throat. As for Furu, the Bushman, when the waters were far apart, he was accustomed to carry his calabash on his shoulder, but rarely had recourse to it. He obtained refreshment from the roots and tubers which he was continually digging up; and in the evening his wallet contained others which needed roasting.

In 1846 it was not necessary for Roualeyn Gordon Cumming to go farther north than the Bamangwato mountains and the Limpopo river in order to meet with troops of elephants. Although a few come from the Kalahari annually in the dry season to drink at one or other of the waters between Sechele's and Sekome's, and although in the habitat of the tsetse to the east of Shoshong, they are still to be found, yet hunters who hope to fill their waggon with ivory during the hunting season are now found every year in the district of the Zambese and in the country of the Mashona, to the north-east of Moselekatse. Cumming performed most of his daring feats in the Bamangwato country, and attended by Bamangwato men. Two brothers, still living in the town, had accompanied him on his hunting excursions, and also gone with him to Grahamstown for supplies. Although first-rate shots and brave hunters have since visited the country, no one has surpassed Mohibiru, or the Red Man, as they called Cumming, in the estimation of the Bamangwato. When they describe his taking up the lion's spoor from the water to the bush which was his lair, and his going up and shooting him dead without himself receiving a scratch, it is still customary for the Bamangwato to "lay their hand on their mouth" in expression of their unceasing amazement and admiration. Whatever people may affirm at the fire-side in England, in the country which was the scene of his exploits there is no question of Cumming's skill or prowess as a hunter. The Bamangwato say they have seen as good marksmen, but they have never seen such determined, even reckless, daring as was shown by Cumming. From all I could gather, however, it would seem to have been bravery rather than recklessness; for I learned that he trusted no servant to clean his guns, or to meddle with any of his hunter's tools. When he faced great danger, therefore, it was not in recklessness of what might happen, but in full confidence of a successful issue, trusting, as he did, to a good gun, unfailing caps and powder, as well as his own coolness.

Entering the pass of Monakalongwe we watered our cattle at the beautiful fountain of Lottotshe, which rises on the north side of the Bamangwato range of mountains. Reaching Kanne, where there is a considerable town of Bakalahari, we were cautioned that in a certain direction there were numerous game-pits, into which horses belonging to Messrs. Reader and Burgess had fallen a few days before. The water is here in an old river-bed, and never fails to come, although at times it percolates very slowly through the mud and sand. We cleared out all the wells by the light of the moon, but found next morning that there would not be enough water for all the oxen; so I sent the troop, in charge of Bakalahari and some of my own men, to Loale, a water some distance to the north-east, and on the road afterwards taken by travellers visiting the Victoria Falls. Instead of one of my oxen, the Bakalahari brought its hide and part of the meat. In its eagerness to drink it had fallen into some fissure in the rock, and broken its leg.

Some days before this I had received, by a native travelling southward, a note from Mr. Burgess, expressing a hope that I should not be long detained behind them; that after spending some months among the elephants, they intended to send out to the colony one waggon with the ivory for fresh supplies of provisions, while the rest of the party was to join us at the site of the mission to the Makololo, and open up a trade with that tribe in goods of European manufacture. But no human purpose concerning this mission was to be established. We shall hear further on of the disastrous conclusion of this hunting expedition, the circumstances being such as to make it matter of thankfulness that we were not then in their company as fellow-travellers. In the meantime we heard from the Bakalahari at Kanne that they had taken the road to the east, leading to Victoria Falls.

Leaving Kanne after sunset on Thursday evening, we entered the long and dreary desert stretching northwards. After two days and two nights' hard work for all concerned, we reached Nkowane on Saturday evening a little before sunset. Soon after leaving Kanne, I was requested to come and see one of my men who had been ailing for some days, and who was now said to be dying. On examining him I found there was not the slightest reason for alarm; and so having administered some medicine to him, we went on our way. I afterwards learned that I was looked upon as very hard-hearted in taking this course, and that I was expected to go back to Kanne to wait this young man's convalescence. But their opinion changed when they saw the symptoms give way, and the patient speedily recover strength. And certainly he who would wait till some Bechuanas recover from illness, and give themselves out as quite well, would require not to be in a hurry. The nearest approach to the position which they take up on this subject is what I have noticed among men who have spent some years as common sailors. When they announce themselves to be ill, it is without any previous hint that they are ailing, and they go and lie down, and are almost as helpless as logs; until, all at once, they say they are quite well, and resume their usual duties. This habit perhaps comes from being either "on duty" or "off duty" on board ship, with no intermediate stages. Bechuanas in a convalescent state are very long before they admit that they are well; but as soon as they have said so, they get up and attend to their work.

The country through which we were now travelling was exceedingly monotonous and uninteresting. The hollows which contain pools of water in summer were now dried up, and along the "mokoko" or ancient river-bed to our left, we were told there was not a drop of water. Without a single hill in sight, we found ourselves traversing an undulating prairie, whose gently sloping ridges of sand followed one after another like the waves of the sea. The long ripe grass, of a lightish yellow colour, gave to the landscape something of the appearance of one immense harvest-field. A solitary camel-thorn, with fantastically turned branches, was here and there seen in the distance, while a variety of small shrubs and bushes was distinguishable only in our neighbourhood from the tall white grass, gently bending to the afternoon breeze, or standing droopingly in the breathless stillness and dazzling glare of noonday.

"A region of emptiness, howling and drear
Which man hath abandoned from famine and fear;
Which the snake and the lizard inhabit alone,
With the twilight bat from the yawning stone.

. . . .

A region of drought where no river glides,
No rippling brook with osier'd sides,
Where sedgy pool, nor bubbling fount,
Nor tree, nor cloud, nor misty mount,
Appears to refresh the aching eye;
But the barren earth and the burning sky,
And the blank horizon round and round
Spread—void of living sight or sound."[1]

Not a living creature was to be seen for miles; but, once outspanned, we found that even here life was not entirely extinct. More frequently than snake or lizard, we found near to our waggon a little cricket, industriously making what noise it could; and in the dreariest places we observed a little bird about the size of a lark, which, like that bird, rose from the earth to give forth its song. But its soaring and its song were of short duration. It rose only some fifteen or twenty feet from the ground, uttering meanwhile its one plaintive note, which again subsided as it descended to the ground. After a brief interval this lonesome bird would repeat its desert dirge. In the distance we sometimes descried the shy khama (hartebeest), or the kukama (gemsbuck or oryx), fleetest of the antelopes; an occasional herd of springbucks cropping the short thick grass of the hard river-bed; and once or twice we saw in the distance troops of elands and giraffes, roaming at will and without thought of water. After leaving a fountain our cattle when unyoked usually grazed well for the first twenty-four

[1] Thomas Pringle.

hours; but thirst afterwards took away inclination to eat, so that, although surrounded by the rich sweet grass of the prairie, as soon as they were out of the yoke they sought the shade of a neighbouring tree, and there remained till brought again to their place before the waggon.

I was told by the Bakalahari at Nkowane that they kept one of the wells shut because it was easy of access, and if it had water the lions would come and drink there, and infest their dwellings, and their sheep and goat pens at night. The second well was in the hollow of the limestone rock—its sides abrupt, and the water accessible only by means of a sort of ladder. There was a conveniently shaped rock near the mouth of the well, into which the water for the oxen was poured. For a small piece of tobacco each, the Bakalahari assisted us to clear away the mud from the second well; but after all our trouble I found that the supply of water from both was not sufficient to allow all my oxen to drink at once. So I separated the party on Monday, sending on in advance the two waggons which were driven by the Hottentots. The rest of the party left Nkowane on Tuesday. On Wednesday night, while toiling diligently through the deep sand, we came unexpectedly upon one of the waggons which had started a day before us. Its solitary guardian in the desert was its Hottentot driver. He explained that he had sent on his oxen with the other waggon, as they would pull no longer. Bnt he was too impatient and anxious to use his long whip to make a good driver. Finding that we had ten loose oxen that were capable of being inspanned, although some were too old and others too young for the yoke, we made up a "span" or team, and resolved to do our best to save the other oxen a double journey. So the Hottentot and I did the driving between us, he with the whip, whilst I supplied the indispensable calling of the names of the oxen, and general shouting. To the driver's astonishment the waggon which fourteen good oxen could not pull, ten very inferior animals were now pulling. But then the difference was that Hendrik was not now allowed to thrash right and left, but only such oxen as were not pulling. There is more skill required to drive a heavily laden waggon through deep sand than one would imagine. I pity the traveller who finds himself in this wilderness with either bad oxen or unskilful drivers.

At Lotlakane we found interesting traces of our friends Messrs. Helmore and Price. The news reached us at Kuruman that they had halted for the summer months at a certain locality in the interior, and that Mr. Helmore had commenced to irrigate a patch of ground for a garden. It was said they were not to leave this spot until the unhealthy season had passed. This rumour, however, was only partially correct. There had been no irrigation, and no prolonged stay. My friends had only rested here for a few weeks. Their enclosures were still standing; and the Masarwa (Bushmen) living here explained to me where the different waggons had stood. They also described to us the great sufferings of our friends from thirst in crossing the desert out of which we had now happily come. Mrs. Helmore, writing in the hut beside which my waggon stood, described those sufferings to a sister of her husband in England—in a letter from which I give the following extracts :—

"I write this in a pretty little hut, 14 feet by 12, built by your brother. The walls are of palmyra wood, and it is thatched with palmyra leaves, so it answers literally to the name we have given it—*Palmyra Lodge*, and though rough-looking on the outside it forms a delightful shelter from the scorching rays of the sun. I should tell you that it is "hartebeest" shape, and has a window at each end, with thin calico instead of glass. I only wish I were in a hut of similar description, but of larger dimensions, north of the Zambese, instead of being still 200 miles south of it, with the prospect of another six weeks' journey; but I must be patient, and leave fearing for the future to record the mercies of the past.

"The last stage of our journey has been without exception the most trying time of travelling I have experienced in Africa. We are now within the tropics, and on a journey we are more exposed than in a house; the heat during the day is intense, 102° in the shade, and often affects me with faintness and giddiness; but the early mornings are still pleasantly cool. We may expect rain this month, and are longing for it, as those only can long who have travelled through a dry and parched wilderness where no water is. Our poor oxen were at one time four, at another five, days without drink. It was quite painful to see how tame they were rendered by thirst; they crowded round the waggons, licking the water-casks, and putting their noses down to the dishes and basins, and then looked up to our faces, as if asking for water. We suffered very much ourselves from thirst, being obliged to economize the little we had in our vessels, not knowing when we should get more. We had guides, but they either could not or would not give us any information.

"Tuesday the 6th inst. was one of the most trying days I ever passed. About sunrise, the poor oxen, which had been painfully dragging the heavy waggons through the deep sand during the night, stopping now and then to draw breath, gave signs of giving up altogether. We had not gone as many miles as we had travelled hours. My husband now resolved to remain behind with one waggon and a single man, while I and the children and the rest of the people went forward with all the oxen, thinking that we should certainly reach water by night. We had had a very scanty supply the day before; the men had not tasted drink since breakfast until late in the evening. We divided a bottleful among four of them. There now remained five bottles of water; I gave my husband three, and reserved two for the children, expecting that we should get water first. It was a sorrowful parting, for we were all faint from thirst, and of course eating was out of the question; we were afraid even to do anything lest exercise should aggravate our thirst. After dragging slowly on for four hours the heat obliged us to stop.

"The poor children continually asked for water; I put them off as long as I could, and when they could be denied no longer doled the precious fluid out a spoonful at a time to each of them. Poor Selina and Henry cried bitterly. Willie bore up manfully, but his sunken eyes showed how much he suffered. Occasionally I observed a convulsive twitching of his features, showing what an effort he was making to restrain his feelings. As for dear Lizzie, she did not utter a word of complaint, nor even asked for water, but lay all the day on the ground perfectly quiet, her lips quite parched and blackened. About sunset we made another attempt, and got on about five miles. The people then proposed going on with the oxen in search of water, promising to return with a supply to the waggon, but I urged their resting a little and then making another attempt, that we might possibly get near enough to walk on to it. They yielded, tied up the poor oxen to prevent their wandering, and lay down to sleep, having tasted neither food nor drink all day. None of us could eat. I gave the children a little dried fruit, slightly acid, in the middle of the day, but thirst took away all desire to eat. Once in the course of the afternoon dear Willie, after a desperate effort not to cry, suddenly asked me if he might go and drain the bottles. Of course I consented, and presently he called out to me with much eagerness that he had 'found some.' Poor little fellow! it must have been little indeed, for his sister Selina had drained them already. Soon after he called out that he had found another bottle of water. You can imagine the disappointment when I told him it was cocoa-nut oil melted by the heat.—But this is a digression: I must go back to our outspanning about nine P.M. The water was long since gone, and, as a last resource, just before dark, I divided among the children half a teacupful of wine and water, which I had been reserving in case I should feel faint. They were revived by it, and said, 'how nice it was,' though it scarcely allayed their thirst. Henry at length cried himself to sleep, and the rest were dozing feverishly. It was a beautiful moonlight night, but the air hot and sultry. I sat in front of the waggon unable to sleep, hoping that water might arrive before the children awoke on another day. About half-past ten I saw some persons approaching: they proved to be two Bakalahari bringing a tin canteen half-full of water, and a note from Mrs. Price, saying, that having heard of the trouble we were in from the man whom we had sent forward, and being themselves not very far from the water, they had sent us all they had. The sound of water soon roused the children, who had tried in vain to sleep, and I shall not soon forget the rush they made to get a drink. There was not much, but enough for the present. I gave each of the children and men a cupful, and then drank myself. It was the first liquid that had entered my lips for twenty-four hours, and I had eaten nothing. The Bakalahari passed on, after depositing the precious treasure, saying that though they had brought me water they had none for themselves. They were merely passing travellers. I almost thought they were angels sent from Heaven. All now slept comfortably except myself; my mind had been too much excited for sleep. And now a fresh disturbance arose: the poor oxen had smelt the water, and became very troublesome; the loose cattle crowding about the waggon, licking and snuffing, and pushing their noses towards me, as if begging for water.

"At two o'clock I roused the men, telling them that if we were to make another attempt to reach water no time was to be lost. They were tired and faint, and very unwilling to move, but at last they got up, and began to unloose the oxen and drive them off without the waggon.

"I remonstrated, but in vain; they had lost all spirit, 'lipelu li shule,' as the Bechuanas say. I was obliged to let them go, but they assured me I should have water sent as quickly as possible, and the cattle should be brought back again after they had drunk. They knew no more than I did the distance to the water.

"When they left us, I felt anxious at the thought of perhaps spending another day like the past; but they had not been gone more than half-an-hour, when I saw in the bright moonlight a figure at a distance coming along the road. At first I could not make it out, it looked so tall; but on coming nearer, who should it prove to be but my servant-girl Kionecoe, eighteen years of age, carrying on her head an immense calabash of water! On hearing of our distress she volunteered to assist us. She had walked four hours. Another servant had set out with her, but as he had driven the sheep the day before a great distance, without either food or water, he became so exhausted that he lay down under a bush to rest, and on the girl came alone, in the dead of night, in a strange country infested with lions, bearing her precious burden. Oh, how grateful I felt to her! Surely *woman* is the same all the world over! She had only lived with me since June, was but an indifferent servant, and had never shown any particular attachment to the children; but this kind act revealed her heart, and seemed to draw us more closely together, for her conduct since then has been excellent. I made a bed for her beside me in the forepart of the waggon; and the children having slaked their thirst with the deliciously cool water, we all slept till six o'clock. I made coffee, and offered some to Kionecoe and her companion, who had now come up. At first they declined it, saying the water was for me and the children. I had now the happiness of seeing the children enjoy a meal of tea and biscuits; and then once more filling up my two bottles, I sent the calabash with the remainder of its contents to my husband, who by this time stood greatly in need of it. The distance was about twelve miles. I afterwards found that we were about the same from the water. Another hot day had now commenced, and I had only the two bottles of water. About noon a horseman rode up, leading a second horse with two water-casks, and a tin canteen on his back. This was a supply for your brother, sent by our kind fellow-travellers, Captain and Mrs. Thompson,[1] who had heard of our distresses from the Prices. . . . While we were preparing the coffee, up came a pack-ox sent by Mr. Price, with two water-casks for me, and soon after some Bakalahari arrived with a calabash; so we had now an abundant supply, and my heart overflowed with gratitude to our Father in heaven, who had watched over me and mine, as over Hagar of old, and sent us relief. I related that and other instances of God's care to the children the day before, and exhorted them to

1 An English lady and gentleman who, on their marriage tour, travelled from Cape Town to Walvisch Bay, *viâ* Lake Ngami.

pray to their heavenly Father, and rest assured that He would send us help; they now referred to the subject, saying, 'it was just as I had said.' . . . Captain and Mrs. Thompson rode up to the waggon in the afternoon, to see if they could be of any further assistance, and brought a little milk for the children. . . . A span of oxen passed me in the middle of the day, going to fetch my husband, and about half-past nine on Wednesday night a span arrived for us. Next morning we reached the water, where Mrs. Price had kindly prepared a substantial breakfast. My husband did not come up till the evening."

CHAPTER VIII.

BUSHMAN LAND.

We had now come into contact with the vassalage or slavery which is practised by the Bechuanas. There are two distinct races held in subjection in this country, and we now met with specimens of both at every fountain. Those called Bakalahari are Bechuanas, whose tribes have been worsted in former contests, and who, not able to preserve their own independence, "khetha" or pay tribute to a powerful neighbouring chief. Like their rulers, these vassal-Bechuanas are not all of one tribe, nor do they all speak the same dialect of Sechuana. Within the memory of those now living, tribes once independent have been reduced to the condition of Bakalahari; while others who had been long Bakalahari, have been called, through the grace of their chief, to the privileges of citizenship, and appointed a place in the town of the tribe. The other subject race is that of the Bushmen, called Barwa by the Bechuanas in the south, and Masarwa by those in the north of the country. The relationship between the Bakalahari and their masters is much more friendly than that between the same masters and their Bushmen. The helplessness of the Bakalahari excites the contempt of their owners, and they are usually spoken of with the diminutive form of the word—Bakhalahatsane; but otherwise they are regarded as "bathu hela"—"like other people." The master therefore, knowing that he can trust to instincts and traditions similar to his own in the mind of the Bakalahari, sends his flocks and sometimes his herds to be taken care of by his vassals. The children of the Bakalahari luxuriate in goats' milk, while their father imagines himself considerably elevated in society as he gazes night and morning on the cattle as they enter and leave their pen. When the owner of the stock now and then makes his appearance at the post, he speaks of the cattle as if they belonged to the Bakalahari; and when it is his intention to sell or to slaughter a certain animal he usually announces it, and sometimes even goes through the form of asking permission to do so, although all the cattle belong to himself. The pastoral instincts of the Bakalahari thus find full occupation, to the satisfaction of their lord, and to the advantage of the vassals. Then the master provides dogs for hunting —the ivory and ostrich-feathers, the furs and skins, to be his, the meat to belong to the Bakalahari. And when he visits the little settlement, it is usually with a little present of some tobacco or wild hemp for smoking, or a clasp-knife or a few beads, which he has purchased from a trader. He now receives the "tribute" of his vassals, staying with them a longer or shorter time according to his taste. As among Europeans, there are some Bechuanas who are happiest when "out of town" and in the hunting-field with their vassals. It is only at the positive command of the chief in time of disturbance that such Nimrods reluctantly return to their houses in the town.

But the Bushmen seldom secure much liking or consideration from their Bechuana masters. "Masarwa a bolotsana thata"—"Bushmen are great rascals," "Masarwa ki linoga hela"—"Bushmen are perfect snakes," are remarks often heard among the Bechuanas. The fact is, there is less in common between the two. Their allegiance is never so genuine, and while they yield tribute they hardly conceal their contempt for their masters. The Bushman is of use only in hunting. When his Bechuana master arrives he takes possession of the little huts, and receives all skins, etc., which the family have collected. And now they hunt every day in company, the Bushmen with their spears, bows and arrows, and dogs—their master with his spears, or, in recent years, with his gun. Woe betide the Bushmen should it be found out that they have hidden away part of the produce, or that, instead of keeping the skins for his master, the Bushman has ventured to make with some of them a mantle for himself or his wife! Thus Bushmen are continually on the alert for the arrival of their masters in the country; and should they cross the path and see his foot-mark on it, they are able to recognise it at once, and if possible will hasten home before him to hide that which must not meet the eye of their lord.

Looked at in this connection, it is not difficult to account for the well-known reluctance of Bechuana chiefs to allow traders and travellers to pass through their country. The attempt on the part of a certain trader some years ago to enter the Kalahari country to the west of Morokweng, from which the Barolongs are in the habit of procuring their ostrich-feathers, cost the life of the trader and that of his son. While the Bamangwato, in whose country I was travelling, participate in the advantages of the trade recently begun with Europeans, they have lost property to the value of many hundreds of pounds through the opening up of the waggon roads to the Lake and to the Zambese. Both roads lead through districts occupied by their vassals, and it is well known that the latter do not hesitate to keep back part of the produce from their masters, and barter with it themselves as soon as a European waggon makes its appearance. On the present journey I was frequently offered beautiful ostrich-feathers for a bit of tobacco or a few strings of beads. Explaining to them that trading was not my object, I directed them to Mebalwe, who, having previously passed through the country in the service of Dr. Livingstone, had made the necessary preparations for this trade before we started, and was able to purchase on his own account all that came to the waggons. It has been found impossible by the Bamangwato to stop this "contraband" trade. They began with severity, and put some of their vassals to death for daring to sell what belonged to their masters. But they found that severity did not answer their purpose, and so the masters now are in point of fact competitors with the European hunters and traders for the purchase of ivory and feathers from their own vassals. Of course they do not acknowledge that they occupy such a position, but the "presents" which they now give their vassals are every year more handsome, and the whole transaction assumes more the appearance of barter than the levying of tribute. In a few instances masters have intrusted their Bakalahari and Bushmen with guns. The latter take to this weapon at once. What with their skill in stalking, and their steady aim, they soon excel their master in its use. Public opinion is against putting such dangerous weapons into the hands of the "lower classes," as an unsafe proceeding. But as it is to the decided advantage of the masters it is increasingly practised.

It is very interesting to observe how this vassalage becomes all but impracticable, and melts away before the teachings of Christianity and the increasing intercourse which now obtains among tribes that were formerly isolated. The missionaries in the southern district of Bechuana-land did not preach directly against this system; but they taught that the love and mercy of God were toward all, and that God was no respecter of persons. It was the custom even in the olden time, and is still in heathen towns, that if a slave regarded himself as ill-used by his master, or thought that his life was in danger, he might flee to the chief, and cast himself upon his protection. If the master complained of was a favourite with the chief, he would formally reprove him, and persuade the slave to return to his service. But if a charge of cruelty was proved against a master with whom the chief had a quarrel, he would at once release the slave from his obligations to him, and provide for him another master. It can readily be seen that Christianity, finding the slave enjoying such an amount of liberty, would speedily secure for him more. Thus in the southern district, and especially where Christian churches exist, this vassalage exists in many cases more in name than in reality. In most cases, as long as the vassals remain with their masters they receive some kind of payment for their service; and when they go away, there does not seem to be any power which is able and ready to bring them back. It is one of the faults which the heathen prefer against the partially-Christianized district in the south, that there the "batlanka" or slaves are no longer under their masters' control, as in the times of undisturbed heathenism. Christianity thus quietly lets the oppressed go free, and breaks every yoke.

But while under this system of appeal to the chief, the lot of these vassals is just bearable in time of peace, it is beyond conception wretched in time of war. I do not mean war among themselves in the country; they are too poor to quarrel seriously, or for a long time: but they are deeply interested in all the political questions of the town, being part of the property of the head men,—a quarrel among whom is often followed up in the country in a way which astonishes as it shocks the Christian man. The contest for the possession of certain villages of Bakalahari or Bushmen, is a fruitful source of strife in Bechuana towns. The vassals with all their belongings are the subject of litigation and endless jealousies; and it needs all the skill of a chief to settle these matters between greedy and plausible rivals. When a decision is come to, the poor people in the country are hastily "lifted" by the successful litigant, to be brought back again should he afterwards lose his case. When rival chiefs fight for supremacy in the same tribe, the condition of the harmless vassals is wretched in the extreme. They are then scattered and peeled, driven hither and thither, and mercilessly killed, as the jealousy, caprice, or revenge of their masters may dictate. It is quite fair in such a struggle to kill all the vassals, as it would be to lift the cattle, of him who cannot be displaced from his chieftainship. And so with the varying fortunes of a "civil war," the vassals might be attacked by both parties in turn.

Again, when one Bechuana tribe attacks another, the Bushmen and Bakalahari belonging to both are placed in the same category with cattle and sheep—they are to be "lifted" or killed as opportunity offers. In such cases, therefore, all Bakalahari and Bushmen flee into wastes and inaccessible forests, and hide themselves until the commotion is past.

We found an illustration of the terror and mistrust in which these people live, when we reached the fountain of Lotlakane. A "civil war" was still going on, in an intermittent fashion, between Macheng and Sekhome, for the chieftainship of the Bamangwato tribe. It mattered little to these serfs who the chief was to be; with them the important question was, to escape both parties while the strife was going on. And so for the first night we saw nobody at Lotlakane; but in the morning my men told me that there were footmarks of Bushmen all round our camp. They had come in the night to satisfy themselves that there were no Bamangwate in my party, before they ventured to come amongst us. How they distinguished as the men lay asleep between the two Bakwena whom I had hired from Sechele and Bamangwato, I know not; but their midnight inspection was held to be satisfactory, and next day several made their appearance at our waggon. It was affecting to witness the earnestness with which they asked if the Bamangwato were still fighting among themselves.

While travelling through their country we always invited the Bakalahari and Masarwa to join us at our morning service on Sunday. The women laid aside their ostrich egg-shells; the men their weapons and the hunting-bag, without which they never travel, and joined our little congregation. Mebalwe was wont to admonish them that "they must sit still; we were going to pray, and to proclaim the Word of God." But when the singing began they usually struck up conversation with one another as long as it lasted, no doubt criticising our doings, and probably remarking that this was the white man's way to make his encampment pure and safe. Such is the explanation which I have heard given of our worship. What message has the evangelist to these children of the desert? Nowhere have I felt my heart more thrilled than when delivering to them as clearly as I could the one gospel of peace and good-will. My "sermons to Bushmen" consisted generally of a simple recapitulation of the leading truths of Revelation. I attempted to make known to them what man discovers not for himself, but what the Father of all has mercifully revealed. In order to address men on the highest subjects with effect, it is necessary that the preacher should know something of the inner life of his audience, their hopes and their fears. In the case of the Bushmen, ignorance of their language has always been a drawback to those who have come into contact with them. But careful observation of their habits, as well as seeking to draw them out in conversation, ought to lead to some knowledge of their character. I can say with truth that no class of people excited my curiosity, or engaged my attention as a traveller in their country, more than the Bushmen. Their outward degradation, their ignorance of agriculture, their prejudice against the possession of live stock,[1] must not discourage the student of their character from continuing his inquiries.

On all subjects lying within the range of the Bushman's observation you will meet with extreme shrewdness and intelligence. The Bushman has the most extensive knowledge of the *materia medica* of the country. If my own medicines were not available, I would trust myself sooner to the care of a Bushman than to any other native doctor. Nothing can exceed the skill and intelligence of the Bushman as a hunter, and an observer of the habits of the wild animals. And as to religion, if I am not greatly mistaken, the Bushmen are the most "superstitious" race in Southern Africa. The fact that they are so peculiarly dependent for subsistence upon what is beyond their control will perhaps account for this. With other natives the chief season of praying and necromancing begins when they have sown their corn, and stand in need of rain. But all seasons are the same to the Bushman. Therefore whilst he is most accomplished in everything belonging to his own way of life, and by general consent the guide and leader of every

1 The Madenassana Bushmen "bina" the common goat; that is to say, it is their sacred animal, as the "kwena" or alligator is to the Bakwena. Now just as it would be hateful and unlucky to the Bakwena to meet or gaze upon the alligator, so the common goat is the object of "religious" aversion to these Bushmen; and to look upon it would be to render the man for the time impure, as well as to cause him undefined uneasiness.

hunting party of which he is a member, he constantly seeks by charms and by spells to supply his own deficiencies. Whether the European has bent his knee in prayer or not before he springs to the saddle in the morning of a hunt, the Bushman has not failed to consult his "oracles." Approaching with mysterious and confident mien, he announces to the hunters that if they will only proceed in a given direction they will find the game they seek. In short, he has assumed the office of "seer" for the party. He has been inquiring of his dice or charms, and announces to you their verdict with confidence. If you still hesitate, he explains to you that Morimo has told him where the game is, and at the same time shakes the dice which he carries round his neck. If you smile, and say that these are merely bits of ivory or bone, he assents at once, and would readily dispose of them to you for a few beads. But then at the earliest opportunity he would repair the deficiency, and replace them by another set. The bits of bone are nothing, he will admit, but through them he "makes inquiry" of the ex-human if not super-human. No party of Bushmen would consent to take the field without these charms. Whoever fancies he is self-contained, and able in himself, without prayer, or without divining, to cope with the difficulties of human existence, the Bushman in Bechuana-land is not. I believe life to a Bushman without this professed addressing something out of and beyond himself would be complete misery.

The relics of a tribal rite are also to be found among these Bushmen. If you point to the pierced cartilage of the nose, he will explain to you that that was done when he was introduced to Bushman manhood. He here uses the word "rupa," which in Sechuana means the introductory ceremony of circumcision. This, then, is to him what circumcision is to the Bechuanas. You point to certain marks on his face, or bits of wood on his hair, or tied round his neck. These are medicines or charms to be taken in sickness, or proximity to lions, or in other circumstances of danger. This is the fetichism which is common throughout Africa at the present time, as it was in Europe in past ages, and which is not unknown in our own day in rural districts of England and Scotland.[1] If you point to the dice, the Bushman will say that they are "Lilo tsa Morimo oa me,"—"Things of my God." He will add, "Lia impulélèla mahuku,"—"They tell me news." If he does not know much Sechuana, he will point to them and say, "Se se Morimo, se,"—"This is God." As in the other cases, this explanation is to be regarded in its connection with such views of Morimo as are known to these Bushmen. The Bushman means to say that what Morimo is to the Bechuanas and to you his dice and charms are to him. To affirm from such data that the Bushmen have a definite notion of Morimo (God) would be to say too much; to say that their God is a bit of ivory or bone would be equally incorrect; while to affirm that they have no religion or superstition to distinguish them from the brutes that perish is entirely false. What the Presence is whose proximity the Bushman never questions, what the Unseen is which can always be appealed to by means of dice, is a question

[1] A friend of mine relates an anecdote which shows that fetichism is still practised in quarters where we would not expect to find it. Some years ago a company was assembled in a private house, in a certain town in England, to meet a well-known missionary from Africa. The conversation turned upon the degradation of the people of that continent, which was forcibly depicted by the missionary, who made special mention of their foolish trust in charms. This picture of spiritual darkness evoked the commiseration of all present. One kind lady was moved to tears. But what was this lady's consternation, what the scarcely-concealed horror of the company, when she inadvertently drew out of her pocket, with her embroidered handkerchief, an ugly little bit of bone, which fell on the carpet before the missionary and all the company! It was a "charm" or "spell" in which this lady devoutly trusted.

which I cannot solve. But what I strenuously affirm, after careful observation and inquiry (chiefly the former, for the latter is often misleading), is this, that although below the other tribes as to habits of civilisation and industry, the Bushman is eminently superstitious, and is a believer in an Invisible-Agency-in-human-affairs-distinct-from-man. The Bushman will tell you in Sechuana, which is to him a foreign language, that this Agency or Agent is Morimo (God). Who has a better explanation?

In sleeping at the same fire with Bushmen or Bakalahari you are sure to be roused twice in the course of the night, or oftener, by the rising of one after the other of your companions. Their first stretchings, yawnings, and gruntings over, they assume a sitting position in a row round the fire, which they replenish with fresh logs. Sometimes they fall asleep in this position, and you see them nodding over the flames. When they lie down again you take notice that it is always in the opposite position with reference to the fire from that which they last occupied. Thus if they had their backs to the fire before they got up, they now turn their faces to it. Having no blanket or covering whatever, except a little skin mantle, which just covers their shoulders, it is only by repeated "turnings" that they are able to keep up heat in their bodies during the cold winter nights. Thus their bodies are always scorched and scarred, and generally "over-done" on both sides, by the fire at night. Before the day is fairly broken you again hear the yawning and other demonstrations—now in a louder tone. As the light increases the restless eye of the Bushman scans the heavens with a close scrutiny. On the ground also, as far as the eye can reach, he seems to notice every living thing. The process of roasting meat on the live coals now commences; and as this early breakfast goes on each one parenthetically mentions what he observes.

At length one starts to his feet. What has he descried? After great effort you can just see "manong" or vultures in the distance sweeping over a certain spot. Seizing their weapons two or three men start at once in that direction; they hope to get there before the lion has finished the antelope or zebra, which has been his midnight meal. If they find the killer of the prey still at his repast, with a jackal venturing to approach the opposite end, while hyenas or younger lions bide their time at a distance—the Bushmen, who have been talking loudly as they approached, to give due notice of their arrival, now shout at the top of their voice, rattle their spears, break off decayed branches from trees, or shake their mantles, to frighten the lion and his courtiers, who retire into the adjoining thicket. Everything is now collected which is at all edible, and carried to the encampment. Should their visit be too late, and they find only bits of bone and hide and hoofs to reward them for their trouble, all these are collected and brought away; the vulture and the hyena or jackal finding little to pick up after the visit of the Bushman. Thus although Bakalahari object to lions in their vicinity, on account of the live stock which they are rearing for themselves and their masters, the Bushmen do not at all object to this proximity, for they have a good deal to gain from it, and if they only keep up a good fire at night in self-preservation they have nothing whatever to lose.

Our oxen having had several days' rest in a district well adapted for grazing, we left Lotlakane on Monday the 6th August, and reached Nchokotsa late at night. It is situated at the side of what must have been a large lake, but is now perfectly bare and dry. The water here is impregnated with salt, and its name testifies to its effects on the system—the verb "chokotsa" meaning to wash or rinse out any vessel. There are three separate wells or "eyes" to this fountain; the upper one being so unbearably nauseous that the oxen, although very thirsty, would not drink the water. The second was a little improved by percolation, and the oxen drank from it. The third well, a little farther down the slope, was cleaned out for our own use. It was the best of the three, but this "best" was very bad. We could not drink coffee made with it. I swallowed a cup of water at breakfast, as a child takes a dose of medicine, and Mrs. Mackenzie drank nothing as long as we were here.

We had now reached the point where my men's knowledge of the road failed them. Two of them had been farther, but it had been towards the west, and along the bank of the Zouga or Botletle river. As Dr. Livingstone's road, which I had determined to follow, struck out to the north here, but was entirely effaced, it was necessary for us to obtain the assistance of guides. But how was this to be done? We saw the fresh footmarks of Bushmen at the fountain; but no one ventured near our waggon. One of my Hottentots suggested that they were sure to come in the night to draw water, and volunteered to form one of two men to watch for them at the fountain. Towards evening, however, this man told me that the water had made him too ill to watch for guides, and next morning we found that no one had drawn water in the night. Leaving instructions with the men to search for Bushmen and also for waggon-tracks to the north, I went out on horseback, accompanied by one man, in the hope of finding some of these poor terrified creatures, who, we felt sure, could not be far away, although afraid to make themselves known. After making a wide circuit we at length found in a large mopane forest a well-beaten path, on which were fresh tracks. After proceeding some distance on this footpath we came upon a deserted village. Making a short circuit we found the tracks again; but as there was now no beaten path we followed them with some difficulty. We had proceeded some miles into the forest, when we came upon a recently built village, which, however, was without inhabitant. We found evidences that its occupants had only recently left it; and after careful search discovered tracks leading still farther into the depths of the forest. It was now past mid-day, and we resolved to return to the waggons in the hope that the other parties had met with greater success than ourselves. As we were returning we espied in the distance what my companion pronounced to be a Bushman, the object of our long search. He gave us a short race, but on our nearer approach coolly sat down, apparently satisfied as to our trustworthiness, and afterwards consented to accompany us to the waggons. We found that my men had been even more successful, for there were now dozens of Bushmen at the fire, and as many women in a group in front of my waggon, gazing upon the wife of a Lekoa (Englishman) with her little child. The driver of my waggon explained that he had observed a woman creeping up to the fountain, and had seized her; "when to my surprise," he added, "every bush around me produced its Bushman, although I had not seen one before." This skill in hiding himself from view with little or no cover is possessed by the Bushmen in a superlative degree. Holding a bit of bush or a bunch of grass before him, he will stalk game upon a plain entirely without cover, and get within range, the game all the while looking at him. Let a clumsier man try the same thing, and they set off at once. As soon as the Bushmen were assured that the waggons belonged to an Englishman, and that amongst all the servants there were no Bamangwato, they came to the camp without hesitation. Khosimore also informed me, with some pride, that he had discovered the waggon-track, and going with him I found proceeding northwards several faint traces of it in the sand and rubbish collected round the roots of small bushes. I learned afterwards that Messrs. Helmore and Price's waggons had taken a course to the west of this in leaving Nchokotsa, so that the track discovered by this sharp-eyed individual must have been one of an earlier date.

On Friday the 10th, we crossed the Zouga or Botletle river, which here runs nearly due east. At the ford here I found it nearly dry, and brackish. We sent our oxen and drinking-vessels some distance up the river, where there was more water in its bed, and where we found the water was quite fresh. We were here told by our guides from Nchokotsa that this was the boundary of their territory, and that if I wanted guides I must hire them from the Bakhurutse, a few of the remnants of a formerly powerful tribe, now living here in vassalage to the Bamangwato. I found in this district that territory is narrowly defined among Bushmen and other vassals. They may hunt, or dig up roots, or act as guides in their own country, but not beyond it. I was told that to cross the boundary would be to "rumola" or "pick a quarrel" with their neighbours; and such disputes might become serious, because "trespassers" not only infringe on the rights of the Bushman in the country, but upon the "vested interests" of their lord, the grandee of the town. No gamekeeper could be more exact as to the boundaries of his master's shootings than were the Bushmen of their prescriptive rights to a certain portion of this dreary part of the interior of Africa. The Bakhurutse at first refused to act as guides, unless we remained at their village during the night; but upon my refusing to do this, some of the men followed us and came up to our fire at night, laden with pumpkins and tobacco, which they offered for sale. They no doubt wished to detain us in the hope of driving a profitable trade.

On Saturday morning we reached Kube, where we resolved to spend the Sunday. We dug out the fountain, and put a thorn hedge round it, to preserve the water from the game, which was here very abundant. Mosisane, the chief of the little village, and his people, assisted in the digging, declining to use the spade which I offered them, it being "only for white people." On Sunday, as the men came up to our morning service, the dust washed off, and dressed in their best clothes, the contrast between them and Mosisane and his people was sufficiently striking. And yet socially they were people of the same standing. Most of my Kuruman men were Batshwene who were vassals of the Batlaping, and who to this day are regarded by that tribe as inferiors. Mosisane and his people were also vassals of a Bechuana tribe. But what a difference, not only in the appearance, but in the thoughts and life of the two, as they sat down together in the shade of the waggons to worship God! Some of the vassals from the south had become free indeed, through faith in Jesus Christ; and here were the same elements to work upon, only how could they "believe in him of whom they had not heard"?

The service over, my herd-boy advanced with part of the flesh of a young kukama on his shoulder. As he threw down his burden upon the heap of firewood, he told me with some pride that the kukama had been run down and killed by a very fine dog which I then possessed. Norval seemed to understand what was being said, and came up wagging his tail. I said to the boy that I hoped he had not forgotten the "great day" and his cattle at the same time, and gone hunting with the dog? "No; the dog had gone of his own accord only," was the answer. This feat on the part of Norval was the cause of my losing him. The Bushmen thought he would exactly suit them; and when I crossed the Ntwetwe salt-pan my dog was missing. I afterwards heard where he was, and sent one of my men for him; but his new master secreted him in the reeds of the Botletle; and when my man arrived he admitted that he had had the dog, but declared it had been killed while baiting a buffalo. He sent me a few jackal skins to "make my heart white" on the subject. But the dog was alive long after this, and its fame for strength and daring spread along both banks of the river. The Bushmen do not covet anything about an Englishman's waggon so much as a good dog. Their own dogs are always in good condition —a perfect contrast to those of the Bakalahari, or even the Bechuanas, which I have often seen die of hunger before their masters' eyes. No one in our party missed Norval so much as our little child, to whom his gentleness and patience knew no bounds. The little hands daily poked his eyes and played with his formidable mouth and teeth, while the party rested in the heat of noon-day. Another camp-follower, exceedingly tame before, seemed to become more so after the loss of our dog. This was a milch-goat which I had purchased at Kanye for our child's special behoof. When crossing the driest parts of the country, this useful creature never failed to give a little milk, which made the oatmeal porridge of our child very nourishing as well as palatable. We were never so destitute of water as not to have just a basinful with which to make ourselves believe that we had washed our faces. On such occasions the goat knew what was going on in the waggon, and was ready to drink up water which had already been so usefully employed.

The first night after leaving Kube we slept in the

middle of Ntwetwe, an immense plain, entirely devoid of vegetation, except here and there a sandy mound covered with a rough kind of grass. In the morning we found that on every side, as far as the eye could reach, there extended what has probably been the bed of an inland sea, but is now completely dry in winter, and gradually curtailed and intersected by the advance of vegetation. Farther north I came upon a "pan" in which this process had been completed; vegetation extended from one end of it to the other. Ntwetwe becomes impassable in the rainy season; still receiving, it would seem, a considerable quantity of water from the drainage of the surrounding country, although not nearly so much as before. I found here unmistakeable marks of the difficulties into which Mr. Helmore's waggons had got. They had sunk down in the mud; and here lay broken waggon-poles and other furniture, indicative of an ox-waggon in a "stick-fast" condition. At the north side of the pan we halted at the first mowana or baobab-tree on this road, the large trunk of which I found well covered with names. I was glad to see that of Mr. Price, the incision still looking fresh. In another part of the tree—the letters nearly closed by the growth of the bark—I saw the initials "L. and O.," with a date which I have forgotten; but no doubt commemorative of one of Livingstone and Oswell's visits to the interior. Leaving this mowana halting-place, we came in the evening to a Masarwa village—the chief of which was called Mosheu. As usual we had to procure fresh guides. On Wednesday we had no water for the oxen, although we passed small wells which supplied our own wants. This forenoon, as very often on this journey, I had to exercise my skill as waggon-mender. I had to put in a false nave in one of the wheels, which, with my materials, was a most difficult undertaking. A shoemaker or a cabinetmaker making and inserting a set of false teeth under compulsion, would be in a position somewhat analogous to mine on this occasion.

As I saw the work would take me some time, I sent on the rest of the waggons, and followed, as soon as we were ready, in the one which I had been repairing. It was long dark before we reached the other waggons; and we had no moonlight. The sand was deep, and we had some difficulty in getting the oxen to pull the waggon through it. I was heartily thankful when we reached the encampment, and the day's work was over. A few minutes after our arrival, and while drinking a refreshing cup of coffee, I heard a peculiar noise in the direction in which the cattle and horses were grazing. "That's the death-cry of something!" exclaimed one of the leaders, a very sharp lad. I ordered the cattle to be brought by the herds, and secured to the waggons. Those for which we had no fastenings were driven between the waggons, and a third fire was lighted, so as the more effectually to protect them. When the lad who herded the horses appeared, he had only one horse; that belonging to Hendrik was amissing. The boy said he had seen it a little before along with mine. As they were never known to be separate when grazing, I suspected that it was the Hottentot's horse which had given the strange cry a little before. I noticed that the oxen that were not tied up were ill at ease, and not disposed to lie down as usual. Fearing lest some sudden fright might alarm them, I sat up most of the night. But although I listened intently, I could not hear the slightest unusual sound; and troops of zebras came near to us, standing neighing and snorting, and apparently not suspecting the proximity of the lion. I roused the men in the morning, and proceeded towards the place from which we heard the "bokwalela," or death-scream, the night before. Mounting an eminence which had intercepted our view when at the waggons, we beheld, not a hundred yards from us, a large dark-maned lion raise his head from the inside of poor Hendrik's horse, in which he had been excavating. Click went one man's gun—bang went Hendrik's, who shouted, "Dat's raak!—I 've hit him!" I was for reserving our fire and going a little nearer. As soon as he saw us approaching, the lion gave up devouring; when the gun was fired he began to retreat. It was now my time to fire. My bullet threw up the dust among his feet, and caused him to change his walk into a trot; and that was all. It was as good a shot as I had often made at game; "very good for a beginner," an encouraging friend would have said; but alas! not the shot to make the lion mine, or to avenge the death of the horse. We now went up to the carcase of the horse. Hendrik, examining the spoor of the lion, said, "I told you I hit him; here is the blood on his spoor. He killed my horse; he 's sure to die." The other driver readily assented to this. I had my own private opinion that it was the horse's blood dropping from the beard and mane of the lion. A few minutes' walk on the track would have settled the question; but I had no wish to rob Hendrik of the satisfaction which his view seemed to give him.

A Bushman who came up to our fire this morning informed us that he had seen a lion's track on the waggon-road for miles, and that it came close up to the encampment. As the death of the horse took place immediately after our arrival, it would seem that the lion had been our close attendant the night before, as Hendrik and I, walking alongside the oxen, and urging them to pull,—now stumbling over a thorn-bush, and now falling into a hole,—toiled on in the darkness till we reached the camp-fire. The Bushmen informed us very gravely that the lions in this district were "bogale thata,"—very fierce or savage. They seemed fully to believe in differences of disposition among them. And they certainly ought to be the best judges, for every petty chief here had a lion-skin on his shoulders, as a mantle.

On Thursday the 16th, we reached Mokantse's village. The people in this region are called Madenassana, although the name Masarwa is also applied to them, as to the other Bushmen. I remarked the height and strength of limb of these people, and the immense quantities of meat which were hanging about their huts, cut up into stripes and left to dry in the sun. We have here Bushmen living in plenty; the exertion necessary to obtain their food being not more than sufficient to develop their physical powers. They think as little of agriculture or a pastoral life as those farther south; but they live in a milder climate, and with the means of subsistence within easy reach.

While I was sitting talking with a party of these Bushmen, my wife came to inform me that something unusual was going on among the men. Khosimore had refused to do his usual work, saying that there was to be a meeting of the men, and he wished to be present. On making my appearance among them, I found that the Hottentot whose horse had been killed was endeavouring to concoct a veritable "strike," and thus induce me to agree to pay for the horse. Thinking he had gained his point with the men, he addressed to me his ultimatum, which was to the effect, that if I did not consent to pay for his horse, which he said had died in my service, he would go back at once to Kuruman, and all the men would go with him. He said he was not a common driver; he had come with me for the sake of hunting elephants on his return. His horse was now dead. He did not care for mere driver's wages. I waited till I should hear what the rest would say, but no one spoke. I saw through Hendrik's clumsy scheme, and said plainly I did not mean to be frightened by any one to do what I did not see to be right. I had promised to herd his horse with my own, and had done so. Where was my horse when his was taken? Were they not both together, and was not the herd in their neighbourhood at the time? If Hendrik left me, I should be sorry for his own sake, as the distance was very great for one man to travel; and as to the rest leaving me because I would not do what he desired me, I had yet to hear it from their own mouth. But even if I were left alone here, or left with few men, my case was not hopeless; there was plenty of grass and water, and I should take time to consider what to do. In a few minutes Hendrik gave it up; and every one went about his work as usual. Of course no one really thought of going back; but Hendrik imagined he could get me to pay for the horse; and some of the men seemed to think that if he got me frightened it was no matter of theirs: they would countenance his scheme so far as to give him a chance of trying it. When it failed, the thing was no longer heard of. Not even Hendrik was sour-faced a day after.

On Friday the 17th, we reached the fountain called Maila, where we found a small town of Makalaka, under Putse, a tall and very dark man. We had here another illustration of the strength of hereditary prejudices or principles as to the manners and customs of a tribe. The game was here more plentiful than we had before seen it. Vast herds of buffaloes rushed past our waggon as we approached the water. Troops of zebras and gnus were to be seen in several directions. The smaller antelopes abounded; the tracks of the rhinoceros were numerous; while elands and giraffes grazed not more than two miles from our waggons. And yet these Makalaka were starving. Although they were the best agriculturists in Bechuana-land their tribal education did not include the arts of the Bushman. We found the dead body of a man in the forest, but slightly covered with brushwood, and we were told that he had died for want of food.

"What are you eating?" I asked Putse in native style.

"Nothing whatever, sir," he replied; "*he* has not killed anything lately."

A servant standing by explained that "he" meant that the lion had not brought down anything in their neighbourhood which they might share with him.

Not long after my arrival here, I walked out alone with my gun. The zebras were within sight, and as I had lately killed one, I had a sort of confidence in trying them again. I was not, however, successful on this occasion, and was wending my way to the waggons by one of the numerous beaten game-paths leading to the fountain, engrossed in thought and paying very little attention to objects around me, when something prompted me to look up at the branches of a tree under which the path was leading me. There hung at a considerable height a log of wood about four feet long and some six inches in diameter, with a large assegai at its end pointing towards the ground. A line which was attached to the upper end of this horrid weapon, came down across the path in front of me, and was so secured that any animal going along the path, by disturbing the line would receive the heavily-loaded lance from above. A few more paces and this would have been my fate. I thanked God and passed on. When I came to the fountain I expostulated with Putse, the chief, for not performing a duty which is always observed by chiefs and head men—to inform strangers of all game-pits, poisonous plants, or tsetse-fly in in their neighbourhood."

"Who would have thought of your turning up over there? Did you not start in quite another direction? I am sorry; but we are so hungry that I did not wish to take down the trap till to-morrow."

Towards the north-west this plan of killing game is extensively followed; even elephants are killed by this suspended lance, which is sometimes rendered more deadly by being rubbed over with poison like the Bushmen's arrows.

On arriving at a fountain in the interior, after the residents at the place make their appearance at the waggons, one of my men usually put the question, "Is your country 'monate,' or nice—*i.e.*, free from lions?" Or again, "Do you sleep in this country, or have you the boy with the beard, 'mosimane eo literu,' to trouble you?" The reply would be, "Naga hela, 'ra; lo ka robala,"—"The country is all right; you can sleep." Or, on the contrary, it would be to the effect that the country was a "savage" one, and that those who herded cattle in it must be men and not boys. It is considered very unlucky to refer to the lion by name, especially after nightfall. "Speak of 'tao' (the lion) and he will appear," is the African version of a remark sometimes made in English concerning one who is said in Scripture to go about "like a roaring lion, seeking whom he may devour." I have sometimes mentioned the name by mistake; the reply was always given in a whisper. Of late years the servants of hunters, and others who have taken up with the ways of white men, seem to have pleasure in shocking the more susceptible nerves of their fellow-countrymen, by talking lightly of the lion at the evening fire, and freely mentioning him by his own name.[1]

[1] The ancient Swedes had a somewhat similar superstition. They would not give its own name to anything that was of an ominous nature, lest an imprudent tongue should give offence. They therefore employed an inoffensive circumlocution; as, when they meant to say, It thunders, they used the phrase, "God-gubben aaker,"—*i.e.* "Thor drives his chariot." The same sort of superstition prevails in some of the Western Islands, particularly among the inhabitants of Lewis, when on their fishing excursions. It is absolutely unlawful to call the island of St. Kilda by its proper Irish name Hirt, but only the "high country." In some districts in Scotland, a brewer would have resented the use of the word "water," in relation to the work in which he was engaged. "Water be your part of it," was the common retort. It was supposed that the use of this word would spoil the brewing.

We found here a newly-made and commodious cattle-pen, which had been constructed by a party of hunters from the Transvaal country, who had left only a few days before our arrival. The head of this party was one of those who had signed the letter to Mr. Moffat, forbidding him to enter the interior without the consent of their government. But had I met him I should not have experienced any molestation whatever. What such a person does officially, and often at the instigation of others, is no clue to the course he will take as a private person at his own house, or on occasion of accidental meeting in the open country. These Dutch hunters afterwards proceeded some distance to the south-east of Maila. They found elephants in considerable numbers; and their camp was now within a short distance of that of my former companions on this journey, Messrs. Reader, Burgess, and Lamond. The following account of the disastrous conclusion of the expedition of the English hunters, I give from a statement kindly placed in my hands by Mr. Reader.

On the evening of the 22d of August, after having been two days hunting elephants, Messrs. Reader, Burgess, and Lamond, returned wearied and hungry to their waggons. As they were about to dine, Mr. Piet Jacobs, a well-known Dutch hunter, arrived at their camp, with the object of buying a horse. His own encampment was about eight miles distant. He was invited to stay there that night, and joined the party at dinner. The conversation turned on hunting elephants, which for many years had been Jacobs' occupation. Reader, who was also an "old hand," had killed two out of their first troop; Burgess, who was a novice, had bagged one unaided, and a rhinoceros, on his way back to the waggons; while Lamond had finished his elephant with Reader's assistance. The fire round which the party sat smoking and talking was not twenty yards from the three waggons, which were drawn up alongside each other, and about ten or twelve feet apart. The servants had another fire about fifteen yards from the waggons. With the exception of one man, who had gone to the fountain for water, they were now all asleep round this fire. Seven horses were tied to the sides of the waggons, eating grass which had been cut for them; and three were fastened to a bush about fifteen yards off. The troop of oxen lay about three hundred yards from the waggons. Piet Jacobs, declining the offer to share one of the waggons with its owner, was provided with a large tiger-skin "kaross," and stretched himself by the fire, the hunting stories still going on. At length Burgess rose, and filling his pipe with some dry and dusty tobacco, lit it at the fire, and retired to his waggon. The fire had now nearly burned out; and as Reader sat close to it with his back towards the waggons, he could without rising lay his hand on both Jacobs and Lamond, the latter of whom had his face towards the waggons. Burgess had not been gone ten minutes when Reader says he heard an explosion and saw a great light. In an instant all the three at the fire were driven from their places, and stupified with the shock. When they came to themselves, they found they were huddled together—each unwittingly grasping the other with all his might, and afraid to stir.

"What is that?" at length asked Reader.

"Burgess is gone," said Lamond. "I saw his waggon go up." Filled with terror, the three now retreated about a hundred yards from the waggons. Reader called out Burgess's name until all hope died within his heart. They were now joined by the servant who had been at the water. He said he had heard a great noise, and inquired what lights those were among the branches of the trees? These were shreds of personal clothing, and of goods for bartering with the Makololo, which had been fired by the powder, and caught in the tree. The grass which had been cut for the horses was also on fire, and the man was now directed to go and extinguish it, "lest," added his master, "it should ignite the waggons."

"Baas," shouted the Hottentot, as soon as he got to the place, "there is no waggon here; they are all gone."

Reader and the other two now returned to where the waggons had stood, and after surveying the place by the light of the burning grass found the man was right. They could see nothing remaining of the three waggons. What had become of the servants? They called them one by one. At length they answered from a considerable distance in the bush; and after receiving many assurances ventured to make their appearance. They said they had fled under the confused impression that the camp was attacked by enemies, and that the noise of the combustion was the report of a volley of musketry. As seven or eight loaded guns were in and around the waggons, all of which were blown away, there might possibly have been separate reports from them. The report of a gun was distinctly heard by Reader as if at some distance from the waggon. One of the men was hopelessly mutilated, and died after some days' sufferings. Other two were severely scorched. All being now equally destitute, a servant tore up his shirt, and tied up the mutilated leg of his comrade as well as he could in the dark. The party then lay down till morning, in order that daylight might fully clear up the horrors of their situation. In the morning a dreadful scene presented itself to them. Of the three waggons two front wheels alone remained with their axle-tree. The remains of the seven horses tied to the waggons strewed the whole place, the head of one being found two hundred yards from the camp. The head and fore-quarter of another had been dashed against a tree near the fire, and must have passed close to where Lamond sat the previous night. The three horses tied to the bush were not killed, but all were scorched. The oxen were uninjured, except one, a horn of which was snapped clean off. It was wonderful that the rest were not wounded, as bits of iron were found all over the place, twisted into a variety of shapes. The lead which lay at the bottom of the waggons was driven deep into the sand, where each waggon had stood, some of the bars being found partly fused; the cinders and ashes of bits of the waggon being found along with the lead. All who were able now searched for the remains of poor Burgess, but not much was found. This was carefully interred by his companions; and when the driver died he was buried beside the remains of his master. For days the natives came to gaze awe-struck upon the work of gunpowder.

Being disappointed in obtaining a waggon for hire as far as Shoshong from the Dutchmen, of whom there was a large party, Reader constructed, with raw hide and undressed pieces of wood, the frame-work of a rude cart, which he placed on the two remaining wheels. Upon this primitive conveyance they placed the two wounded men, who were occasionally joined by the others as they felt tired with walking, the vehicle not being large enough to allow all to ride in it at once. Arrived at Shoshong, they at once obtained the assistance which they required, and returned to the colony. Thus suddenly was this adventurous young man and promising hunter called into eternity. A spark of fire from a tobacco-pipe, carelessly placed, had no doubt found its way to the gunpowder, of which there was a considerable quantity in the waggons, and the result was a scene such as is seldom witnessed except at a siege or on the battle-field, where greater horrors, premeditated and expected, meet the eye at every turn.

CHAPTER IX.

BUSHMAN GUIDANCE.

THE Makalaka at Maila were refugees from the cruel and bloody tyranny of Moselekatse, or rather of the Matebele soldiers; for the latter were in the habit of undertaking raids unknown to their chief against the neighbouring Mashona and Makalaka villages, for the purposes of plunder and outrage. It was their custom in such an expedition, to lie in wait near the village until the earliest dawn gave light enough for their bloody work. Then rushing like furies upon the unsuspecting inhabitants, they speared every one except young women, and children who were able to walk. From such scenes of wholesale carnage had fled the Makalaka whom I now met. They themselves had been brought up in the hereditary pursuit of tilling the soil; but their corn had been left behind in their flight, and they had not yet had time to cultivate gardens at Maila. They were therefore, as we have seen, dependent upon the trapping of game, the "leavings" of the lion, the kindness of the Bushmen, and the occasional visit of a European elephant-hunter, who would shoot down a quantity of game for them to dry, and lay up in store. But their chief Putse, with all his hunger, was capable of perpetrating a joke. When I asked guides of him to go with me as far as the Zambese, he replied in a tone of affected surprise, "Why do you ask me for guides in your own country? Did not J— V— and the Boers who were here a few days ago tell me that all this land belonged to the white men, and that they would shortly come and occupy it? Why, then, do you ask for guides in what seems to be your own country?" I replied that the Queen of England had no desire to seize their territory; and that if Englishmen came into their country it would be for two objects—to teach them about God, which was my own purpose, or to hunt and to trade with them for ivory and feathers. I told them that if peace continued, waggons filled with the beautiful things of the white people would visit their country; and that he who was industrious would be able to purchase some of them with ivory, feathers, and skins, and even with the produce of their gardens. This assurance, which has been abundantly verified in succeeding years, gave great satisfaction; and Putse declared the news was good, if only the Matebele would let him "sleep."

Although the Dutch hunters had opened up the water, and we ourselves had also worked at it for hours, we found that unless we prevented the game from drinking in the night, we should not have enough for our oxen. Even while it was still daylight, on Saturday evening, we observed the thirsty zebras gradually approaching, that they might quench their thirst as soon as the sun went down. We lighted a fire at the water, but found that to be of no use. A rhinoceros and a troop of buffaloes dashed right down to the water. One of the latter paid for his temerity with his life. On Sunday evening, as I did not wish the men to lose another night's rest, we not only lighted a fire, but constructed something like the figure of a man in a prominent position. Some prophesied that our effigy would at once be destroyed by an angry buffalo, or a black rhinoceros; but no attention was paid either to it or to the fire by creatures goaded on by thirst. There was no alternative, therefore, but again to insist upon our exclusive right to the water by the argument of the gun. As soon as their determination to drink led them too near, the men guarding the water fired at them, and caused them to withdraw. Although many more must have been killed; only one zebra was found dead at the fountain, which, with part of the buffalo, I made over to Putse and his people; directing him, at the same time, to take up the blood-tracks of the wounded. We had thus the consolation of thinking that while driven by necessity to fire upon the game in the dark, such as might die of their wounds would be very welcome to the famishing Makalaka. During the night there was quite a procession round the fountain,—a vast gathering of wild creatures in separate troops, galloping, stamping, snorting, and neighing; drawn to the fountain by thirst, and kept from drinking by fear.

After hearing that we were journeying to Linyanti, Putse brought to our camp an old Bushman, who had just returned from the district of the Mababe. Putse said it was his custom to tell strangers as much as he knew concerning the country towards which they might be journeying; and for this purpose he had brought the Bushman. "Perhaps what he tells is lies, perhaps it is truth; I shall have discharged my duty when you hear his story." The Bushman now commenced his account, which was to the effect that "the Makololo at Linyanti had killed the head-man of the missionary party and his wife, with a head-man of the Batlaping who accompanied the white men; that several little children had died; that the surviving white man and his wife had left Linyanti, and were now no doubt far on their way southward. Sekeletu, the chief, had poisoned an ox, and then presented it to the missionaries for slaughter. He had also administered to them poison in the native beer. The strangers had eaten of the ox and drunk of the beer, and died. Having killed the owners, Sekeletu had next seized upon their property. He had kept the best waggon belonging to the deceased teacher, and all the 'boxes' with white men's things in them. This is the news from Mababe," concluded the Bushman. The whole story seemed to me entirely improbable. In my confidence I smiled at my informant, and told him it was impossible that Sekeletu could have poisoned the friends of Livingstone, who were there by appointment with the Doctor. I was aware that poisoning in beer was not uncommon in the country; but then how could they be poisoned by an ox which had been driven to their waggons alive and well, and which they themselves had slaughtered and cooked? Those only who believed in the power of "charms" could credit this. Mebalwe expressed a similar opinion to my own, and so did the rest of the men, who were present and heard the news. The story was so mixed up with heathen customs and ideas as to render the catastrophe impossible in our eyes as a matter of fact. In itself the picture which the Bushman gave was certainly a very dreadful one. It was a sufficiently uninviting prospect to be told that at Linyanti we should find, not our friends the missionaries, but their graves; while in the Makololo chief and people we should meet their murderers. But not one of us received the story as truth; and in a few days we had almost forgotten it. I felt it necessary to place all the "mahuku" or news on such subjects before the grown-up men of my party, lest to serious difficulties in the future there should be added their upbraidings that they had been led forward blindfold.

It was here also I heard of the extreme sufferings which

my friends, upon whose track I was proceeding, had endured in the country north of Maila and Kamakama. When I asked for guides to go with me in that direction, not a single Bushman would consent to accompany me. To go without guides I felt to be quite out of the question. Pointing northwards, they shook their heads, and exclaimed, "Yonder there is no water; nothing but sun; nothing but sun! That land causes the cattle to stray from the waggons; the men, too, who venture thither wander about in vain search for what is not, and hasten southward to the fountains which they had left. All these things," they added, "did we see last year in the case of the white men who went to the Makololo. Both they and their oxen, and we who accompanied them part of the way, had well-nigh perished with thirst. If you are determined to travel on that path you go alone." I was aware from Dr. Livingstone's description of the country still before me, that to the north there was no spring or fountain, till we came to the Mababe or the Sonta; and therefore travellers could only proceed on it in summer after rain had fallen. Instead of giving the detail of the sufferings of my friends, with which the Bushmen now supplied me, it will be more satisfactory to quote from the last letter received from Mrs. Helmore, which was addressed to one of her daughters, then at school in England:—

"NORTH OF KAMAKAMA,
Nov. 24th, 1859.

"MY DARLING OLIVE,—It is now your turn to get a letter from me; but I fear that it will be a long long time before you receive it, for there are few opportunities of sending or receiving letters. We have had none from you since the May ones which overtook us at the Matlwaring, just beyond Kuruman. . . . However, we must be patient, and the letters will perhaps be doubly sweet when they do come. Although I long to hear of you, I do not feel anxious about you, my dear girls. We daily commit you to the care of your Heavenly Father, and He never disappointed those who trust in Him. I hope that you, dear Olive, are setting the Lord always before you. As the eldest of the family, you will have a strong influence over the rest. O seek especially to guide your sisters, dear Annie and Emily, in the way of life. I look forward with delight to the time when we shall be all united again; but still I think it is your duty to remain in England as long as you can. You may never go there again.

"You see we have not yet got to our journey's end. It is a long journey indeed; but we have had so many hindrances from waggons breaking, cattle wandering, fatigue, drought, and other causes. We have been already twenty weeks on the road, and shall be three or four weeks yet. Six weeks ago, on the river Zouga, dear little Willie was taken ill with fever, and for several days we scarcely thought he would recover; fever was very high, with delirium. He is now getting well again, and to-day is playing on the bed with Selina and Henry for the first time. He is, however, still so weak in his legs that he has to be carried about like an infant. A fortnight after Willie had been taken ill, dear Lizzie was seized with fever and erysipelas in the back, but she too is getting well now; so you see, dearest Olive, you have much to be thankful for, as well as to pray for. Selina and Henry are well, and all send their love to you all. I need not tell you much about our journey, as you have papa's journal. . . . We meet with some beautiful flowers. I often wish it were possible to transport them to you. Few of them have much scent alone; but about sunset their united fragrance is delicious.

"*Monday, Nov.* 28.—Yesterday dear little Eliza Price was baptized by your papa. We had a pleasant English service. It was quite a treat in the wilderness. The Bechuanas were present as spectators, and seemed interested. Papa has service in Sechuana regularly every Sunday. . . . Our cattle, at least some of them, have been lost ever since last Monday. Four men were seeking them three days and nights, and returned with some of them—without having tasted food all that time. They lost their way, which it is very easy to do, as the country is covered with forests and thick bush. Now another party is out after the rest of them. This is their third day. We have had no road for many weeks. Some of the party have to go before, sawing down trees, and chopping bushes to make room for the waggons to pass, and after all we frequently become entangled; so it is very slow work. There are no wild beasts here except elephants, and occasionally troops of zebras. The latter we sometimes manage to shoot. They are excellent eating; so is the gnu.

"*Dec.* 26.—A happy Christmas to you, my children! It is now nearly a month since I laid down my letter to you, dear Olive; yet, strange to say, we are only *five miles* nearer to our journey's end than we were then. I told you that a party of our men had gone out in search of some of our oxen, which had been stolen by the Masarwa, or Bushmen. They returned on the fourth day with all but three; one had been left sick on the road; the other fine large hind oxen the Masarwa had killed and eaten. It was a great loss, but there was no redress for it, and as our pool of water was almost dried up, we were glad to go forward. As we proceeded we found the country more and more dry, and at last we were brought to a complete stand-still for want of water. One waggon was unpacked and sent back with all the casks, Mackintosh bags, and vessels we could find, to bring water. All the oxen and sheep and all the men, excepting two, were sent back likewise, and what little water still remained was divided amongst us who stayed. This was only enough for drinking, there was none to cook with, and before the waggon arrived, which was two days and nights, we were so weak from want of food that the children and I could scarcely walk. The weather was at the same time extremely hot, the thermometer at eight o'clock in the morning stood at 96°, and in the middle of the day at more than 105°. Papa and the two men who remained went out in the evenings in search of water, and walked about all night, but they could find none. I forgot to say that Tabe stayed with one of his men, and they too searched for water; for we were unwilling to go back if there was a possibility of getting on. However, all the pools were empty, so we were most reluctantly obliged to retrace our steps. But by this time the ponds we had left were dried up too; so after travelling a day and night, and until nine the next morning, the poor cattle were so exhausted with thirst that they could go no farther, and we were compelled to unyoke them and send them on with the sheep, and most of the men, to the nearest water. We hoped that they would return that night and take us on; but day after day and night after night passed and neither men nor oxen came, and our sufferings were again very great. I was most anxious about Lizzie, who was still weak from her recent illness. I thought she would have fainted when I had not a drop of water to give her.

"One afternoon about four o'clock papa set out with two men, taking our Mackintosh bags, and returned about half-past nine next morning with a supply of water. When they arrived they were so exhausted that they dropped on the ground unable to speak. Papa looked so ill that I was quite alarmed. They had walked thirty-eight miles, and carried the water fifteen miles. Having found water, parties were sent in succession each night to return the following one. Fancy every drop of water we had for drinking, cooking, or washing ourselves brought a distance of thirty miles going and coming![1] At length, on Sunday, December the 11th, we were aroused very early by a heavy rain. We spread out a sail and caught enough to replenish our water-vessels. This was indeed a shower from Heaven; it revived our languid spirits, and filled us with thankfulness to Him who had remembered His promise to His servants (Isaiah xli. 17). We now hoped to go on, but the clouds passed away, and the pools remained empty.

"When the oxen returned we rode back fifteen miles to the pool from which we had been obtaining water. It appeared that on leaving us with the oxen and sheep the men had set off for Kamakama, but losing their way did not get there till the following night; and our two little calves, unable to walk so far in such hot weather, were left behind to perish; and also our entire flock of twenty-four sheep and lambs were lost through the carelessness and indolence of the man who was driving them, and have not been heard of since. This is a very heavy loss indeed.

"I must now say a few words about your coming out, for there are so few opportunities of sending letters to you now that I do not like to delay writing on that subject. . . . Lizzie says I am to tell you to bring some comfits, little baskets, etc., that we may have a Christmas-tree the first Christmas you are all at home. Your sisters and brothers send warmest love; so does papa. The God

[1] This lasted for about a fortnight.

of Love be your Friend and Portion, my dear child !—Your affectionate mamma, ANNE HELMORE."

How true and deep the love of the Christian mother! Herself in circumstances of extreme privation, abstaining from food and drink for days for the sake of her children, knowing what it is to have only a single spoonful of water for each child left before relief came: in such circumstances she did not fail to think of the distant loved ones in her native land, who were happily ignorant of their mother's distress. Amid the harassing anxieties of such a journey she snatched time to write to them; and again the hope of re-union was expressed. It was Christmas-time when she wrote, although the glare and heat of the African sun had little in common with English associations. But her faithful and enduring heart was strong enough, not only to send a cheerful greeting, but to enjoy the prattle of the children sitting around her about a future Christmas, when their happy family was to be assembled in a mission-house north of the Zambese. She had courage to send the little sister's message about a Christmas-tree, which was to be decorated by a united family among the Makololo.

Into this land of drought I felt it would be madness to attempt to enter before rain fell. What then was to be done? The Makalaka offered to show me a route to the east, by which I should reach the Zambese near to the Victoria Falls in ten days. Asking them to point out the direction of the first fountain on this road, I found they pointed south-east from Maila—which was of course going back in our journey; for our course now was north-west, or nearly so. They informed me, however, that the second fountain was to the north of the first, and that the road afterwards steadily pursued that course. I called my men, and laid the matter before them. "One does not mind a round-about road," said old Mebalwe, "provided we have water on it." This being the general opinion, as well as my own, I hired a party of Makalaka, who agreed to go with me to the Zambese by this eastern route. Having settled this, preparations for starting were going forward, when Mokantse, the chief of the Bushmen, made his appearance with a party of men from his village, which was at a few miles' distance. He had come to greet me, he said, before I left. One of his men, who had acted as my guide to Maila, had hinted to me the previous evening that he knew another road to the west of that pursued by my friends of the previous year. He assured me there was plenty of water on it; and it led to the Makololo country. As the part of the Zambese to which the Makalaka offered to guide me was considerably to the east of Linyanti, I resolved to sift this matter as far as I could, while it was still in my power to make a choice. So I assembled both Bushmen and Makalaka, and explained to them fully my position. I was a missionary on my way to teach the Makololo. I was going to join the party of last year. I had got food and clothing for them in the waggons; and my request now was to be shown the best route by which I could join them. The two chiefs and their men had a long discussion together. I could not but feel that this was a critical time in my journey. In a similar dilemma, a Bushman would have sought assistance from the Unseen by divination and charms. While my native advisers were conversing together in a language which neither I nor my men could understand, I retired in my uncertainty unto Him whose eyes are in all places, and earnestly besought His guidance and blessing at this juncture. The sequel will show whether or not the prayer was answered.

Mokantse announced the decision to which they had now come. It was that we ought to give up the road to the east, and take the route to the north-west, which his man had mentioned to me. The Makalaka agreed that "that also was a road, and that it would take us to the Makololo." My men were already assembled; so I told them that whatever road we took we must enter on it heartily, and not find fault with one another when we got into difficulties. Now was the time to speak. I then made Mokantse mention the number of waters which were on the route he proposed. He counted five, and ended with the "Great River." I asked, was it the river of the Makololo? He replied in the affirmative. All my men joined in saying that this route of the Bushmen ought to be the best. Mokantse told off two men as guides, and this perplexing question was finally settled.

We left Maila on Monday the 20th August, and after proceeding for some hours on the track of last year's waggons, bore more to the west, on a footpath almost invisible to the inexperienced eye, and were now practically under the leadership of the two Bushmen. Walking in front with them, I found towards evening that we were going almost due west, and in a little after that we were turning slightly to the south. I remarked that this was not the direction of the Makololo. Seeing that I had referred to a compass, the Bushmen said, "Why does not the 'selo' (or thing) of which you 'inquire' inform you of the direction of the next pool of water as well as tell you where Linyanti is? It is quite true that the Makololo live in the direction you indicate, but we are also sure that the next pool of water is in the course we are now taking."

On Wednesday forenoon we were toiling through very deep sand, under a burning sun. The pace of the oxen was becoming very slow, and the drivers seemed to be content if they moved at all. Proceeding to the front in order to question the guides about the water, I found to my astonishment that they were not visible. "Where are the Bushmen?" I asked Mebalwe, whose waggon was first that day. He in turn asked the leader, who was wearily marching at the head of the team. "Ga ki itse"—"I don't know"—shouted the man without turning round his head. "Then in what direction are you taking us?" I asked in amazement. "When I last saw the Bushmen they seemed to be going in the direction in which I am now guiding the waggons." So here we were without path, not even a game-track to guide us, and our Bushmen vanished! It seemed useless to be dragging four heavily-loaded waggons through the sand without road and without guide. So we gave the oxen the benefit of our perplexity, and unyoked them while we considered what was to be done. While the men were drinking a cup of coffee, it struck me that whatever might have been the cause of the Bushmen's desertion, the prospect of plenty of fresh meat at the waggons would certainly bring them back, if they were still near enough to hear the report of a gun. Accordingly I fired off my gun, and waiting a few minutes, as if following a wounded animal, fired again, and then watched the result of my experiment. Some time after, the men, who were now keeping a look-out, discovered one of the Bushmen making for the waggons at the top of his speed. Nothing was said until he had taken his place among the men, when he was asked why he had "thrown us away" in the desert? He said "he was killed by the sun, *i.e.*, thirsty, and had merely gone on to drink." It no doubt seemed to him an easy thing to find out the little well still a considerable distance ahead, and which, being inaccessible to game, had therefore no "spoors" leading to it; but it was a very different matter to strangers. I gave him some meat, so that his hurried return was not entirely in vain from his own point of view. In truth he was a welcome sight to us all. Again proceeding under his guidance we reached the water in the evening. Our second guide took guilt to himself, and never again made his appearance at our waggon. After reaching the well I went with Mebalwe in the dusk of the evening to the place where he was said to be hiding, to assure him that my heart was quite "white" towards him. We heard his retreating steps in the bush, and called after him, but in vain. I next sent his comrade, with plenty of meat and tobacco, to induce him to join us again, but he refused. He said he knew he had done wrong in throwing away the waggons in the wilderness, and he believed the white man would punish him with the rhinoceros-hide whip. Where or when he had seen this implement in operation I know not, but it had evidently made a deep impression on his mind. He preferred rather to be without pay than to run the imaginary risk of the "sambok."

We found that there was barely enough of water for ourselves in the deep well to which our guides led us. It was at the side of a large salt-pan, now grown over with grass. The water was only slightly brackish. It was still about half a day's journey to the large fountain of which the Bushmen had spoken. As we had then beautiful moonlight, I sent the whole troop of oxen forward that evening in charge of a party of men, and under the guidance of the Bushman. They were to allow the cattle to drink that night, and then giving them time to graze, lead them to the water a second time at noon the following day. Next morning, looking across the vast plain at the side of which my waggon stood, I saw what I thought at first was game, but on using a glass found to be my own oxen. They had not yet reached the water; their guide having got bewildered in the night, had led them away to the left, so that now they were farther from the water than when they left the waggons the night before. This is the only instance of a Bushman wandering from his course which has come under my own observation. He was not entirely to be excused; for although the plain was without a single object to guide him, there were numerous brilliant stars in the heavens by which he could have steered.

I had previously observed a certain ox in the troop as always heading the march to the water at noon when they were going to drink. He was of European breed, being stronger and heavier than the Bechuana cattle. As the troop now passed along the plain towards the water, this ox, seeing the waggons in the distance, rushed away from the herd, and, refusing to be stopped by the men, came up to our camp in the rage and desperation of thirst. I sent a man to bale water for him out of the well; but the small quantity brought at a time seemed to tantalize the animal, which at length became exhausted and lay down on the plain. All our efforts failed to restore him, or to cause him to proceed with the rest of the cattle after their return. The poor animal was "killed by the sun," *i.e.*, by thirst, and was the only one which I lost from that cause. I have since often observed that cattle bred by Bechuanas can stand thirst better than all others which come into the country. This is accounted for by the manner in which they are reared by their owners at their cattle-posts. While colonial farmers make sure that water shall at all times be within reach of their herds, so that they can drink when they choose, the Bechuanas teach their cattle to endure a certain amount of privation as to water. In winter, no Bechuana herdsman of the old school would think of taking his charge to the water every day. In the coldest weather, it is often the second, occasionally the third, day before the water is visited; and even then the cattle drink but sparingly. Goats in the Kalahari are months without water, and thrive without it. The Bechuanas had a reason for thus training their cattle; for when assailed by tribes more powerful than themselves, it was their custom fearlessly to drive their flocks and herds for days into the Kalahari desert, into which their enemies followed them at their peril.

My men, who had gone forward with the oxen, returned with poor accounts of the "great water" spoken of by the Bushmen; the oxen had drained it completely, without having quenched their thirst. As it was a spring, however, the men hoped that it would soon refill its basin. We reached this fountain on Friday evening, and on Saturday all hands were at work the whole day clearing out the mud and stones which had accumulated round the spring, and considerably impeded its flow. A large pen was made, so that the cattle might be kept together while the water was collecting. We found it of no use to send them to graze in charge of herds. Instead of eating, or even lying down, the oxen kept wandering about first in one direction and then in another, always with the object of passing their herds and getting to the fountain where we were working. One animal, which was suffering the agonies of thirst, shutting its eyes, broke through the pen and rushed past the men who tried to stop it, upon whom it would have blindly trodden had they not given way. We had just time to "clear out" from the spring when the poor creature rushed over the ledge of rock above the fountain, falling a distance of at least twelve feet, and lighting upon the rocks and stones out of which the water sprang. No sooner had it reached the ground than, now unable to rise or to move its body, it turned round its head to one of the "eyes" of the fountain, and there drank for a long time the deliciously cool water. We all believed the animal would die from the fall; and we had to lift it out of the water when it had finished its long draught. In the course of some days, however, it recovered, and was for many years afterwards a front ox in my team. In opening up this water we came upon pieces of elephants' tusks and antelopes' horns, mixed up with the stones and mud which had been closely embedded by the feet of the game. The overhanging ledge of rock had no doubt broken off these horns and tusks, as their owners, forgetting its proximity, tossed up their heads suddenly after finishing their draught of water.

On Sunday morning, 26th August, I found that if we stayed here together, the oxen must endure great hardship on account of the scarcity of the water. Although it flowed with increasing rapidity after our labours, it was still far from sufficient. The first question thus came to be, not to find the nearest way to the Makololo, but to reach a water which would suffice for all the oxen. The Bushmen living near this fountain, pointing to the west, said that after sleeping once on the way I should on the following day reach the great river of which I had heard. For the first time on my long journey I now found it necessary to go forward on Sunday. Taking one waggon and some sixteen oxen, I gave them as much water as they could drink, and then proceeded to open up a road to the river. Being now suspicious as to the tsetse, and not knowing what to make of the conduct of Mokantse and his men in misleading us as to the number of fountains on the road, and also as to its course, I thought it would be best to go forward myself with one waggon. I could not trust any of the men to lead the way where there was no waggon road, but I could depend upon them to take care of the cattle at the fountain. I directed the Hottentots, if they did not hear from me to the contrary, to

On the Zouga.

start on Tuesday, and follow my track. Mebalwe was to bring up the rear with the other waggon, and the weakest of the oxen on Wednesday. When I left on Sunday forenoon, some of my oxen then received the first good drink of water which they had had since the forenoon of the previous Monday at Maila! By reducing the number of oxen in one place, those which remained behind found enough water in the fountain, and a serious disaster was averted. I now travelled under the guidance of Tiane, the chief of a small town of Bushmen, which we passed soon after leaving the water. On Sunday night there fell the first shower of rain which we had seen since leaving Kuruman. Our journey was at first through an open country, but on Monday morning we came to a dense forest, through which we had literally to cut our way with the axe. The oxen were also sorely tried with a small thorn bush, which tore their legs and the lower part of their body, and impeded our progress. After a hard day's work to all concerned, we were pleased in the afternoon to descend into a belt of larger timber, growing more sparsely and on firmer soil. The Bushman now assured me that I was near to the great river, and that my cattle would know no more thirst. We were some distance in front of the waggons, my office of hewer of trees having become a sinecure, when Tiane led me to a point from which I gazed on the loveliest prospect I had yet beheld in Africa. A broad river flowed at my feet, both of whose banks were richly wooded as far as the eye could reach. The bank opposite was lower than where I stood, and I had thus an extensive view of the country on the other side, studded with large trees, in the shade of which I beheld the gnu and the zebra, the red-buck, the springbuck, and an animal which I had not seen before, the lechwe or water-buck. Having pulled the waggon beneath a magnificent camel-thorn, whose spreading branches enabled us to have delicious shade at all hours of the day, we unyoked the oxen, which made at once for the river. They were not content with reaching the water, but walked up to the belly in the river, and then drank their fill. We had all accompanied them to the bank, and enjoyed the delightful spectacle; and of all African scenes beheld before or since, no one is more deeply engraven on my mind. The only disappointment was that I was not gazing upon the "Great River of the Makololo" spoken of at Maila, but upon the Zouga or Botletle.

After a few minutes' absence, Tiane announced that a boat had just arrived at the neighbouring halting-place, which was called More oa Maotu, and that the Batowana who were in it were on their way to see me. Accordingly some five or six men advanced from the river, and sitting down after the usual salutations, gave me their news. They were spies, and had been southward to observe the movements of the Bamangwato, it being feared that in the war between Macheng and Sekhome something might transpire which it would be of importance for Lechulatebe, the chief at Lake Ngami, to know. They had now fulfilled their mission, and were on their way home, having still a journey of four or five days before them. They said the place where I had touched the river was at its great bend southwards, and was its nearest point from Maila. I now gave them my news—a plain, straightforward statement of the past events in my journey, and my destination.

"Have you not heard," said the head-man, "that the party of teachers who went in last year to the Makololo are all dead except one man and two little children?"

I replied that I had heard some idle story of that kind at Maila, but that I did not believe it.

"But we left the surviving teacher at Lechulatebe's town," exclaimed the man. "His oxen were all bitten by the tsetse, and he could go no farther. We saw him with our own eyes, and we are sure that you also will be killed by the Makololo if you go there. You had better cross the river, and visit Lechulatebe, who will be glad to see you, and you will see that what we now tell you about your friends is true."

A new suspicion now crossed my mind. Taking it for granted that this story was not true, I thought I could perceive an object for telling it, namely, to get me to visit Lechulatebe. My four waggons were supposed to contain immense wealth; Sekeletu, the enemy of Lechulatebe, had already received two missionaries; it was therefore desired by the Batowana that a share of this distinction should be conferred upon Lechulatebe, and that he also should have his resident white man or missionary. I therefore conceived that these men were skilfully acting a part, and that all they told me was mentioned for the purpose of frightening me from going on to the Makololo, and of inducing me to visit their own chief. I therefore firmly expressed my intention of going on to Linyanti, and that now I had reached the river system, I hoped speedily to complete the journey.

"What message, then, shall we take to our chief?" said the men, at the conclusion of our second interview, in which they had in vain sought to persuade me to cross the river, and give up the journey to the Makololo.

"Greet your chief very much," I replied, "and say that I am now going to Linyanti, but that I hope soon to visit him as a missionary. White men are accustomed to boats in their own country, and I hope soon to be able to visit your master in one after I have seen my friends, and handed over to them their food and their clothing."

They seemed at a loss to understand my determined and sincere unbelief in their story, and left me, declaring I was pre-eminently "tlogo e e thata," hard-headed or difficult to convince.

"But mark our words," said they, as they left for their

boat; "as soon as we get home, and tell your friend that you are here, the teacher is sure to come to you or to write to you, and then you will see that we have spoken truth."

"You will require to make haste," was my answer, "for in a few days I shall have left the Zouga and gone northwards along the Tamalakan."

I noticed two points of difference between the account of these Batowana and that of the Bushmen at Maila. The Bushmen said the wife of the surviving teacher was with him, and he anticipated no detention from tsetse. The Batowana said Mrs. Price had died on the way after leaving the Makololo, and that the missionary's cattle had been bitten by the deadly fly. This looked like truth, supposing the Bushman to have visited the missionary party before the occurrence of these later disasters, which were mentioned by the Batowana. This account, with its apparent discrepancy, caused me some uneasiness; but the prominence given by all to poisoning by charms, and the well-known desire of Lechulatebe to deter Europeans from visiting his enemies, outweighed all such impressions, and I still felt fully convinced that the whole tale was without foundation.

My waggons arrived at the river in the order I had laid down for them; and I had the happiness, before the week was done, of seeing my party again united. Mebalwe explained that after I left they had scarcely enough water, but when the other two waggons followed me he had then plenty for the remainder of the troop. I resolved to give the cattle a few days' rest here, while I endeavoured to obtain information about the country before me, and especially with reference to the whereabouts of the tsetse. I was out one day with the Bushmen hunting, when they pointed to a wooded height at some distance from the river as its nearest habitat. They said that with good guides I could go along the Tamalakan without getting my oxen bitten. While shooting guinea-fowl one day along the banks of the river, one of the barrels of my fowling-piece burst, and damaged the first joint of one of my fingers. The piece of barrel flew into the air with a loud "whirr." I went mechanically to the place where I had seen the guinea-fowl, feeling that something was wrong, but not knowing what it was. Of course, the charge went the wrong way to kill the bird when it went through the side of the barrel. The pain in my finger soon brought me to my senses; and the ugly hole in the breech of the gun left me in no doubt. I had been trying hard to assist in supplying my own wants and those of the party by killing game, and feeling that this was not the kind of thing to establish confidence and respect, either in me or my guns, I laid the damaged gun out of sight, in the waggon, and did not mention to my men the cause of my bound-up hand. Such people believe in "lucky" and "unlucky" masters, and I did not wish them to think that they were in the employment of one who was sure to meet with disasters.

The Batowana residing at Nghabi or Ngami exercise supremacy over the Makobas, who live on the banks of the rivers, as well as over the Bushmen and certain other tribes in the desert. I found that the district of More oa Maotu belonged to a grandee called Lerebola, who played me a trick which is often practised on travellers in Africa. At my request he provided me with guides. When I came to pay beforehand, always an unsafe proceeding, he offered to send them with me as far as Maiketo's, where he affirmed I should find the track of waggons which had gone to the Makololo. But for this he demanded a whole list of articles, —gunpowder, lead, flints, caps, beads, a knife, and a handkerchief. Believing his plausible story, I satisfied him as to the pay, and we proceeded on our journey. At Mpash's village, however, I was assured that the men who had come with me were not Lerebola's at all, but belonged to Mpash, and I must pay again if I wanted guides. Now this seems great extortion to the European. He is indignant at being deceived by a savage. According to some travellers, there never were such unreasonable mortals as the African chiefs through whose country they have passed. But that is only one view of the question. We may think that the chiefs ought to have a fixed charge, or no charge at all; and that our progress should be facilitated by every means in the power of those for whose ultimate benefit we think we are travelling. But the opinions of the chief are entirely different. He does not indeed know the words, so often used in England, about "making hay while the sun shines," but the idea is very vividly present to his mind. It is not every year the locusts come, so when they appear everybody makes the most of them. And so the coming of an Englishman into his country, with several waggons heavily loaded, is an event to be taken advantage of by a chief to the fullest extent. In remote districts, the whole countryside is roused by such an appearance on its horizon, from the man of distinction, who hob-nobs with the Englishman over a cup of coffee, to the Bushman, who hopes to come in for a piece of meat, or a few bones, or a bit of raw hide (which he will roast and eat), or even a pinch of snuff, as his share in the great event of your passing through the country. While the chief or head-man takes you in hand, and gets what he can as a "present," or for guides, his men are busy with your servants, doing the same thing on a smaller scale. You may labour to explain that your journey is for the future benefit of both chief and people. He does not contradict you, but seems to make up his mind that whatever be the contingencies of the future, your present journey shall be made subservient to his immediate advantage. This is only in a rude form what is so often met with in civilized countries, and among all classes of society, —to get as much as you can, for as long a time as you can, and for as little as you can, without much regard to truth or honesty. This is only what the African chief does, and while you are at first disgusted at the imposition, in the end you pay and pass on.

After resting more than a week at More oa Maotu, we left on Thursday the 6th September, proceeding up the river towards its junction with the Tamalakan. On Friday we passed Mpash's village, where we had to hire fresh guides. We observed that in telling us the story of the calamities at Linyanti, a tone of remonstrance and warning was now used by the Batowana. Great prominence was always given to the necessity of our visiting Lechulatebe. Sometimes a clumsy narrator, under a little cross-questioning, contradicted himself, which confirmed us in the belief that the story was concocted, and told by some with greater ability than by others. After a man's statement had been pulled to pieces, and his warnings had fallen unheeded, he would lose all patience, and exclaim, "If you can't believe what is told you, go on to Linyanti and see for yourself."

On Saturday, while we were moving slowly along the bank of the Zouga, and approaching Letsebogo ya Khame, I noticed a party of men advancing from the river, which was here, owing to a bend, at some distance from the course of our waggons. The strangers, without parleying with any one, went up to the leader of the first waggon and told him to halt. Now, I thought, the plot thickens, and the Batowana are making a desperate effort to accomplish their purpose. By calmness and firmness to-day all further trouble may perhaps be averted. I went forward and demanded why he had stopped my waggons in such an unceremonious manner?

"I come from Lechulatebe, the chief," replied the leader of the party, a tall handsome man, drawing himself up to his full height. "He greets you, and sends you boats, by means of which you are to cross the river."

"But who tells your master that I am to cross the river at all?" I inquired, now fully satisfied in my own mind that our surmises of fraud were about to be confirmed. "I am going to the Makololo at present, and may not turn aside. Give my greetings to your chief, and thanks for his invitation. As we are to be neighbours, I hope soon to see him and his people."

The countenance of the man assumed a bewildered expression, and turning to his companions I heard him inquire, "What can we make of this man? What shall I say to make him believe?"

"Tell him about the white man in the boat," suggested one of his men.

"You refuse to believe what everybody tells you. In that boat," pointing to the river, "there sits a white man who says you are his dear friend—the son of his father."

"And why did you not bring him with you that I might see him, if it is true that he is in your boat?"

"Because he is sick and tired, and wished to remain."

Still incredulous, and determined to stick to my course, I brought the conversation to a close by saying, "I shall go on, as I intended, to the Letsebogo (ford), where we shall sleep, and where we shall rest to-morrow (Sunday). If you have got a white man in your boat, bring him to me there, and I shall believe what you say."

Not knowing what turn events might take next, and conceiving that I had been perhaps somewhat abrupt with the men as the messengers of their chief, I now gave them a handsome present, to show that my heart was white towards them, although I was still going on to the Makololo. Highly pleased, they returned to the river; and we pursued our course to the place where I had resolved to spend the Sunday. Left to ourselves, we all felt that the crisis had now come. The stories told so persistently for the last three weeks would be tested this evening, and it would be decided whether we were being deceived, as we had imagined, or whether we were to be called upon to mourn over disaster and death. The interval was spent in canvassing the whole subject afresh—the idea now for the first time being present that it might possibly be true. Towards evening I seated myself in the front waggon to obtain the earliest solution of this mystery. The guides said we were now approaching the river again, and that the halting-place was close at hand. I shall not attempt to describe my anxiety as I gazed forward through the forest, seeking in vain for the solution of my doubts in its solemn stillness. I was roused by the exclamation of the driver, who sat beside me on the waggon, "Ki ena,"—"It is he." I sprang from the waggon, and went forward to meet some one who, I could see through the trees, was a European. At length I saw that it was my dear friend and brother-missionary, Mr. Price.

"But can all this that I hear be true?" I hurriedly asked, before I had grasped his hand.

Alas! I saw what the answer would be before I heard it: "All is true."

I had then to go back and break the news to Mrs. Mackenzie, that her beloved friends Mrs. Helmore and Mrs. Price were no more; and that in short the story which we had so often heard and disbelieved was mournfully true. This was indeed a trying hour. Hopes which had cheered us during our long journey were now dashed to the ground. As the brilliance of the setting sun was now giving place around us to the darkness of night, so the bright pictures which had often filled our minds with pleasure now also gave place to one gloomy scene of desolation and of death. We sat down and wept for those who were not. Our men betokened their sympathy by the solemnity of their countenances; and the simple Makoba stood at some distance, silent witnesses of the scene.

We shrank for some time from inquiring into the details of the disasters through which our friend had passed. We observed with pain that not only was Mr. Price reduced to be the shadow of what he was when in health, but his memory was also for the time somewhat affected; and he repeated the same things several times, without being aware of it. We sought first an explanation of the means by which he had heard of our arrival. Mr. Price said that the messengers of Lechulatebe who had seen us at More oa Maotu on their way up the river from the Bamangwato country, arrived at the courtyard one day while he was present. He heard without interest the recital of their procedure as spies, and an account of the political condition of the Bamangwato. But by and by his attention was riveted when he heard the men state that they had arrived at More oa Maotu at the same time as "a teacher" from Kuruman, who was on his way to the Makololo. He was a red man, and had a span of red oxen. He had a wife and child, and one waggon, but others filled with things were coming after him. Mr. Price, starting up, interrupted the man, and explained to Lechulatebe that this teacher was his friend; and that he must find some way of visiting him. Lechulatebe very kindly placed his own canoe at the service of Mr. Price, who, hearing from the men that we did not credit the story of the disasters at Linyanti, but were intending, as soon as we could, to pass on to the Makololo, embarked as soon as the canoe was ready. He had the idea that he was beginning his voyage on Sunday; but in the long illnesses which he had endured, and surrounded so long by men who themselves had all been an indefinite number of days stricken down by fever, he had lost reckoning of the days of the week, so that what he regarded as Sunday was in reality Wednesday. Mr. Helmore's two surviving little children were so pleased that assistance was near to them that they joyfully consented to remain during Mr. Price's absence in charge of the servants, and under the special care of Lechulatebe's head-wife, who was very kind to them.

Viewed in the light of our recently acquired knowledge of the true condition of our fellow-members of the Makololo mission, our past journey now assumed a consecutiveness and a oneness of purpose beyond anything which we had intended. We started from Kuruman to join the Makololo mission, of which we were members, carrying with us necessary supplies for our friends. Now, it is a fact that when I did join the only surviving member of the mission, and when I supplied him with the assistance which was indispensable to his leaving the lake, not a day had been lost between Kuruman and Lake Ngami. When the boatmen announced to Mr. Price our arrival on the Zouga, it was in reality, as such things go in Africa, an "express" to him from Kuruman. But this was not my intention, because I did not believe that Mr. Price was there at all. I thought of him and of Mr. Helmore as in the Makololo country; and when I left Maila I was under the impression that I was travelling on a new and direct route to that country.

Then the Bushmen of Mokantse at Maila undoubtedly misled me, both as to the route and as to the number of waters which we should find. Had they acknowledged that the "great river" of which they spoke was the Zouga, and not the Sonta or the Mababe, I certainly should not have taken the route proposed by them at all. They deceived me, but for what purpose? The only way I can account for their conduct is, that they determined, in what they regarded as mercy to me, to take me into the country where they knew I must infallibly either hear of my friends as having already passed south, or meet with them on their way out from Linyanti. They therefore schemed to induce me to take that route. I refused to believe the story of disaster which they told; they seem to have determined to avert from me the evil consequences of my unbelief. I told them that I had food and clothing for my friends in the waggons; the Bushmen seem to have resolved that these articles should go into the region where their owners really were. It would be easy to take the teacher to the Zambese near the Victoria Falls, and once there he could find his way to Linyanti. But what did he want there when one-half of his friends were dead, and the rest were on the western and not the eastern road? And so those wild children of the desert took the wayward and unmanageable white man into their charge, and in point of fact led him against his will to the assistance of his friend. Kindly feelings must therefore have prompted these men as they spoke so long together at Maila before they came to a decision. We could not understand their language, but, interpreted by their after conduct, it was that of good-will and sympathy. They no doubt described in their speeches my seeking my friends in the north, and perhaps suffering as they had done, while the survivors sought me in the south, and lamented that they had missed me on the road. All this they most kindly resolved to prevent, and they were successful. I have the utmost pleasure in mentioning this striking instance of genuine benevolence and thoughtful kindness in the Bushmen of the African desert.

But if on the morning of my departure from Maila, Mokantse and his Bushmen arrived just in time to prevent my going to the east under the guidance of the Makalaka, and thus missing Mr. Price, the Batowana voyaging homewards on the Zouga, reached More oa Maotu also in time to meet us there, and without delay to take to Mr. Price the news that help was near him. All of us, missionary, Bushmen, and Batowana, conspired, willingly or unwillingly, to assist Mr. Price at the earliest possible time. These circumstances produced a deep impression on every one in the party. "Sir," said one of my men, who had not professed to be a Christian, "God has been leading us to help Mr. Price." Reverently and thankfully did we acknowledge His merciful guidance. He had led us by a way which we knew not. He raised for us friends even among the wandering Bushmen, who kindly resolved to save us from our own mistaken views, and to bring about a meeting between us and our friends.

I learned afterwards that at the time I was at Maila debating what course to pursue, Dr. Livingstone had arrived in the country of the Makololo, after performing a march on foot of more than 600 miles. Had I accepted the guidance of the Makalaka as I at one time intended, and taken the road to Victoria Falls, it is probable that I should have been in time to meet the Doctor before he returned to the east coast. If any of the Makololo, yielding to the personal influence and advice of Dr. Livingstone, would have removed to Tabacheu, in all probability the mission would have been commenced. But in the exercise of my best judgment, I gave up the eastern for what I considered a better route to the Makololo; and instead of meeting Dr. Livingstone I met Mr. Price.

CHAPTER X.

LINYANTI.

In the quiet of the Sunday following our meeting with Mr. Price, we obtained from him most of the harrowing details of the history of the mission at Linyanti. Messrs. Helmore and Price arrived at that town on Tuesday the 14th of February 1860, after a journey of more than seven months from Kuruman. They were aware that this was perhaps the most unhealthy season of the year to enter that deadly region; but all such considerations were overcome by their anxiety lest Dr. Livingstone should have reached the country before them, and lest by their delay they should miss the opportunity of being introduced by him to the Makololo. They found, however, on their arrival at Linyanti, that they were in advance of the Doctor, who was unexpectedly detained on the lower parts of the Zambese until May 1860. They therefore introduced themselves as the friends of Livingstone, who had come, like Ngake (the Doctor) to teach the people. Their arrival was welcomed by the Makololo in the usual way. Large parties went out to meet them, some two or three days' journey from the town. On the day after their arrival an ox was sent for slaughter, and when next day Sekeletu himself appeared to welcome them, large quantities of beer were brought for the refreshment of the strangers. Everybody seemed pleased: the chief that his name and greatness had brought him white men to reside in his town; the missionaries that a new and populous district of country was about to be opened up to the benign influences of Christianity. Mr. Helmore had preached to the crowds who went out to meet the mission party on the Sunday before their arrival in the town; and every Sunday, as long as he was able, he addressed the Makololo in Sekeletu's court-yard in Linyanti. Some of the head-men who had begun to learn to read under Dr. Livingstone's tuition, now resumed their efforts under Mr. Helmore and Mr. Price. But the missionaries soon saw that whatever influence Dr. Livingstone on his arrival might be able to exert upon Sekeletu and the Makololo, in his absence no one spoke of removing to the highlands north of the Zambese. They said repeatedly that if they removed at all it would be to Lake Ngami, after they had conquered Lechulatebe, and dispossessed him of his country. The missionaries, who were not ignorant of their danger from the insalubrious climate, lost no time in requesting Sekeletu's permission to remove to Sesheke, which Mr. Helmore thought would be a healthier locality than Linyanti, and near enough for them to hear of Dr. Livingstone's arrival as soon as it should take place. The chief, however, would not accede to this. He seemed jealous of the frequent references to Dr. Livingstone, and said that nobody must affect their arrangements with him as chief of the town. He must not be separated from those who had come to teach him and his people; they must live with him at Linyanti. Not wishing to offend Sekeletu, and hoping that Dr. Livingstone would soon arrive, and assist them in coming to some settlement of the question, the missionaries acquiesced in this decision, and Mr. Price built a temporary hut.

In less than a fortnight after their arrival at Linyanti, the whole party, with the exception of Mr. and Mrs. Price and a servant, were stricken down with sickness. Although many of the symptoms of poisoning as practised by natives were present, all these were also characteristic of African fever. It needed no poison in the ox to cause liberal rations of beef, without much exercise, to bring about that bilious state which in the summer months, and in such a region, would be sure to beget fever. It needed no poison in the beer as drunk by Mr. Helmore and Mr. Price, after preaching on the Sunday, to produce the pains in the head and loins and neck of which they complained on their return to their camp. The fatigue of preaching in the open air, the unhealthy atmosphere of the town, with rank vegetation all around, and a hot sun overhead, were abundantly sufficient to produce African fever.

The scene at the camp was now heart-rending. Four sick children, guarded by a sick and enfeebled mother, lay in one place, their sick father at a little distance. "The Bechuana men were lying about," as one of them afterwards said in describing the scene to me, "like logs of wood"—one here and another there, rolled in their blanket or kaross, utterly prostrated by fever, unable to help themselves, and some of them in a deep stupor. The only ray of hope in the picture was that Mr. and Mrs. Price, although suffering severely, were never both ill at once. Either the one or the other was able to wait upon the sick and the helpless. Mr. Price for some time cooked food for the whole party, servants included. On the 2d of March, just seventeen days after their arrival, the first death took place. It was not a European who was first carried away by the deadly influences by which all were surrounded, not even one of the tender children, but Malatsi, the tallest and perhaps the strongest of the Bechuana servants, and who had been driver of Mr. Price's waggon. Five days after this, as Mr. Price was going his

Scott & Ferguson, Edinr.

FEVER-STRICKEN AT LINYANTI.

rounds among his helpless and often unconscious companions, he found, on touching a little face among the four children, beside whom Mrs. Helmore lay, that the cold hand of death had been there before him. It was the face of little Henry Helmore—the first of the children who died. Mr. Price removed the dead from among the living, and placed the little body in the adjoining tent. His father was conscious, and on learning what had taken place, requested that Henry's mother might be spared the knowledge of this bereavement until the morning. But this thoughtfulness was not necessary, for the mother herself was then quite unconscious of all that was passing around her. Henry Helmore was buried by Mr. Price on the day after his death, the 8th of March; his own infant daughter, Eliza, died on the 9th in the arms of its mother, while Mr. Price lay in a wet sheet, endeavouring to get rid of an attack of fever. On the 11th, Selina Helmore followed her brother; and next day the guardian mother, wasted by disease and privation, unable any longer to smooth the pillow or cool the parched lips of her children, was released from her long watching; and heaven, sweet to all who enter it, was surely heaven twice told to Anne Helmore. She had striven long and hard; she could strive no more. In her last conscious moments she said to her husband, "she had no wish to live: she desired to go home to Jesus." In the wanderings of her fevered brain, she had again seen the parched wilderness, and heard her little ones calling to her for water; and once more she fancied she was denying herself everything for the sake of those she loved. In her dreams she recalled the crossing of broad rivers, and the standing of strangers on the distant bank. Her mother's heart could not forget distant loved ones in those half-conscious days and nights. She dreamt of her home as it had been in Africa—of the new home she had hoped to see established on the Zambese; and in the midst of such dreamings and troubled feverish musings, her trustful and enduring spirit passed into the light and joy of the true home of heaven. We can surely say of Mrs. Helmore, as of the little ones whom she followed, and for whose sake she endured so much, "They shall hunger no more, neither thirst any more; neither shall the sun light on them, nor any heat. For the Lamb, which is in the midst of the throne, shall feed them, and shall lead them unto living fountains of waters; and God shall wipe away all tears from their eyes."

Death now seemed to stay its hand. Mr. Helmore and the two surviving children improved in health, and were able again to move about, and the men were now also convalescent. Mr. and Mrs. Price, however, had both severe attacks of fever about this time, from which they happily recovered, although with reduced strength. The condition of the mission was now anxiously discussed by the two missionaries. Was it intended that they should thus build huts and settle at Linyanti? Had not Dr. Livingstone himself said that the place was destroying even the Makololo? But what could be done? Sekeletu refused to remove to the highlands of Tabacheu, and objected to the missionaries going to reside at Sesheke, insisting that as they had come to teach him they should live where he lived. Mr. Price now proposed that they should leave their property in Sekeletu's keeping, as Dr. Livingstone had done—a pledge to the Makololo that they would return, and that they themselves should recross the Chobe, and seek again the free air of the desert, until their health should be somewhat established, and the winter months enable them to return. If, in the meantime, Dr. Livingstone should arrive, messengers could be despatched to give them intimation. This project was considered seriously by Mr. Helmore, and earnestly advocated by both Mr. and Mrs. Price. But to go back any distance seemed to Mr. Helmore like deserting his post. Something might miscarry. The Makololo might misunderstand their movements. When he arrived, Dr. Livingstone might not have time to wait for the going and coming of messengers. At Linyanti he was to meet Livingstone, upon whom he considered the success of the mission depended; at Linyanti therefore he would remain. The result of these consultations must have reached the Makololo, for they told Livingstone at Linyanti in August that Helmore had said that "whoever did, he would never turn back from his work." Now no one thought of "turning back from the work;" this idea was not present to the missionaries, their discussion being about the best method of doing the work.

But the interval of convalescence was not of long duration. After a journey to the town about the middle of April, Mr. Helmore had a relapse of fever, which now entirely prostrated him, and claimed him for its own. Although his friends were now filled with anxiety and alarm about his condition, he himself continued to speak confidently of getting better, and of establishing a mission among the benighted Makololo. The disease, however, was evidently making rapid advances, and while his friend still retained the power of speech, Mr. Price requested to know his wishes concerning his two surviving children. Soon his mind began to wander. He is with his flock at Likatlong; he is now in London assuming the responsibility of leader of the Makololo mission; anon all evil powers seem united to hinder his progress. He wanders in the desert in search of water, and finds none; his waggons lie in the wilderness without oxen to pull them; he stumbles over the fresh graves of those near and dear to him; but still he perseveres. The scene changes in his troubled vision, and he stands, the preacher to the heathen, delivering to them the word of life. But his preaching is interrupted; he waits for some one to assist him. Livingstone has at length arrived! He fancies he hears the greeting of his former friend and fellow-labourer. Difficulties now vanish; churches and schools arise; the imagined voice of praise, in which infants and old men join, fills the soul of the dying missionary with joy. Slowly meanwhile the sands of life run down; dreaming gives place to torpor, and on the 21st of April torpor yields to death. But what is death to this humble and faithful servant of Christ? It is death which opens to his spirit's vision a scene fairer than he had ever dreamt of, and which itself is no dream, but a reality. He awakes from the feverish visions and torpor and death of the tent at Linyanti to the lovely and everlasting life of heaven. He awakes to hear a voice of greeting, more cheering and thrilling than of earthly friend, the voice of Him who has been the witness of his self-sacrificing steadfastness and sincerity, his love to man and to God. It is his Saviour who welcomes him: "Well done, good and faithful servant, thou hast been faithful over a few things: I will make thee ruler over many things; enter thou into the joy of thy Lord. Inasmuch as thou hast done it unto one of the least of these my brethren, thou hast done it unto me."

"What were my feelings," writes Mr. Price to the Directors of the Missionary Society, "on the morning of the 22d of April, as I followed the remains of my dear brother to the silent tomb, can better be imagined than expressed. All then fell on me, and I was so reduced that I was hardly able to move, and my poor wife had entirely lost the use of her limbs."

Tabe, a deacon of the church at Likatlong, died on the 11th of March, and on the 19th Setloke, a Christian native also from Likatlong. Tabe had early been converted from heathenism, and being a person of some ability, as well as of influence in the town, his earnestness and zeal led others to follow his example. He was a teacher of the school and exhorter of the people at Likatlong before the arrival of Mr. Helmore at that station, and while the people were still connected as an out-station with Griqua Town. From the first he was one of Mr. Helmore's right-hand assistants; and it was thought a very happy arrangement when one possessed of so many years' experience consented to join his missionary in what every native in South Bechuanaland from the first regarded as a hazardous enterprise. Had a mission been established, the service of such a man would have been very great. Mr. Price remarked that in Tabe's case, as well as in that of Setloke, there was very great physical pain, along with the same symptoms which were exhibited by the others. Tabe would sometimes come screaming to the front of his waggon in the height of fever and in a paroxysm of pain.

It was the impression of Mr. Price, as well as of the Bechuanas who accompanied the mission party, that the deaths at Linyanti were occasioned by poison administered by the Makololo, and not from fever. But if African fever supplies us with an adequate cause for these deaths, it is unnecessary that we should seek a further reason in the occult administration of native poisons in an ox and in beer. And unfortunately ten years' experience in a district annually visited by this disease, has brought to my knowledge more than one instance of similar disaster among trading and hunting parties, equally deadly, although not equally extensive. Then it must be borne in mind that the missionaries reached Linyanti at one of the most unhealthy seasons in the year, and that they were completely exhausted by the privation and fatigue of their journey. Instead of a life of hardship and daily bodily exertion, they and their men had regular supplies of food without much exercise. In short, all the circumstances were in the highest degree calculated to produce fever.

The suspicion of foul play on the part of Sekeletu would never have been entertained but for his after rapacity and cruelty towards those who were at least his guests, if not his friends. Here his conduct is entirely without justification. But while we remember that "two blacks do not make one white," it is only right to mention that in the matter of plundering the mission property the guilt of Sekeletu was at least equalled by that of another, who tempted him to adopt the unworthy course which he pursued. And, strange to say, this enemy at once to Sekeletu and to the missionary party belonged himself to the latter.

If the native teacher Tabe was a source of strength to a mission among a new tribe, he brought with him a wild and desperate young man called Mahuse, whose influence was calculated to counteract all the good that his master effected. This person's character was well known in the Kuruman district. Mr. Moffat recommended that he should be expelled from the mission party. But he had ingratiated himself with Tabe: and Mr. Helmore, animated by the charity which hopeth all things, and believing that close contact with such a company for months might beneficially affect the young man's character and future life, did not insist on his separation from the expedition. Soon after their arrival at Linyanti, Mahuse found the atmosphere of Sekeletu's court-yard more congenial than the encampment of the missionaries. Of course he figured among the Makololo as a distinguished personage, and was consulted by Sekeletu on all matters affecting the south, or the manners and customs of the white men. Having roamed over a considerable extent of country, Mahuse was able to speak largely of his travels, and his fluency was not at all interrupted when his information came to an end. It is most provoking to observe the credence which such clever unprincipled fellows obtain all over the country. I have known several instances of imposition equally glaring with that of Mahuse, though not attended with such lamentable consequences. When Mr. Helmore died, Mahuse informed Sekeletu, that if this event had taken place in the south, all the property of the deceased would have fallen to the chief in whose country he died. He quoted supposed cases illustrative of his position, in which Moshesh and Sechele and Mahure, and other chieftains, had helped themselves. "Of course," said the tempter, "being ignorant, and afraid of these white people, you, Sekeletu, are likely to let Mr. Price return with all the property intact. The great chiefs whom I have named would not do so." Now Sekeletu must have known perfectly that all this was false; but being as weak and vacillating in his character as Sebetuane his predecessor had been energetic and determined, he yielded to the advice of Mahuse the tempter, who was backed by a party of hare-brained youths acting the part of councillors to this African Rehoboam.

And so while Mr. Price was slowly packing up the property of his deceased friends, and making ready to return to the south, his movements were closely watched by the agents of Sekeletu. A little effort soon prostrated a frame which, however wiry and powerful, was now much impaired by disease, so that it was not till the end of May that Mr. Price had finished his preparations. The presence of sickness and death in the camp had for some time made the Makololo strangers in it; but after Mr. Helmore was buried they crowded the place by day, stealing openly, and almost unchallenged, for Mr. Price was often unable to rise from the pallet where he lay. At night they prowled about the waggons, even lifting the sail-covering, and dragging away the wearing apparel of the sleeping missionary. There was no redress to be obtained from the chief or from the head-men. Sekeletu completely forgot the outward dignity of a chief in his own town, and openly derided the missionary when he made complaints.

When Mr. Price announced that he was now ready to depart, Sekeletu made his appearance at the head of a numerous company of attendants. Pulling aside Mr. Helmore's new waggon, in which Mr. Price had stowed many of his own things, as well as what had belonged to Mr. Helmore, Sekeletu declared it to be his property, and all that it contained. Acting evidently under Mahuse's instructions, he next demanded two front and two hind oxen, in order to train a team for himself; and he postponed the departure of Mr. Price until his men had assisted in the work of training these oxen. When at length, on the 19th of June, Mr. Price took his departure from a place where he had endured so much, he was accompanied by Sekeletu, who rode in his newly acquired waggon! He levied a fine on Mr. Price at every river, delaying the ferrying until his demands were met. "All my guns and ammunition," writes Mr. Price to the Directors, "both tents, and a great many other things, were taken while I was still in town." The meanness of Sekeletu, however, reached its height at the Chobe, which, being the last river, was also the last occasion for levying a fine. "After a good deal of pleading," says Mr. Price, "I was allowed a few things for the journey, such as a couple of shirts, a vest or two, two or three pairs of trousers, an old coat that I had worn in England, an old pair of shoes which I had on, etc. Already they had taken all my bed-clothing, with the exception of what was just sufficient for one bed, for the other we had a kaross. But before my oxen could cross the Chobe, I must needs deliver up our blanket. Every grain of corn which I had for food for the men they had taken; and for all these things I did not get even a goat for slaughter on the road. These were my prospects for a journey of upwards of 1000 miles to Kuruman."

Mr. Price was of opinion that the Mambari, or half-caste Portuguese, who were in the habit of trading with the Makololo for ivory and for slaves, had also used their utmost endeavour to poison the minds of the Makololo against the new missionaries, and against Dr. Livingstone. It was to the advantage of the Mambari that no missionary settlement should take place in that region; and Mr. Price was convinced that they had actively exerted themselves, along with Mahuse, to mislead Sekeletu as to the course which he ought to pursue towards them.

It is thus abundantly evident that it cannot be said on behalf of Sekeletu and the Makololo what I boldly advanced in my ignorance at Maila, "Sekeletu is the friend of missionaries; he would neither kill them nor rob them." So far as character is concerned, that of the Makololo chief and people would not sink much lower in the estimation of natives, even could it be clearly proved that they were guilty of poisoning. Hospitality is a sacred obligation among the tribes of Southern Africa. A chief may refuse admission to his country, but having invited the stranger to enter, his good name demands that no harm should befall him as long as he remains his guest. It was this feeling which protected isolated traders and travellers in Kaffirland during the Kaffir wars. These men had entered the country in time of peace, and were under the protection of the chief. The "leina" (name) of the chief would suffer were anything to happen to them. Now Sekeletu degraded himself in the eyes of all natives, if not in killing his guests with poison, by robbing them when sick and helpless and completely in his power. I have never heard a native speak of this conduct but as an enormous offence—almost the greatest that could be committed. Their argument, indeed, seems to have been: he who could rob the little children of a guest, and send them away hungry and almost naked from his town, had a heart black enough for anything. And seeing that their parents died so suddenly, there is no doubt he murdered them. If he did not murder them, the native goes on to argue, why did he not himself assist Mr. Price to collect all the property, and send a party of his men to narrate to Mr. Helmore's friends the circumstances attending the sudden death of so many in his town? There is no doubt that the majority of South African chiefs would have followed this course in similar circumstances; and there is little question that Sekeletu—impulsive and easily persuaded—would himself have done so had Mahuse been as energetic and eloquent in recommending it as he was in the advocacy of heartless spoliation.

This is fully borne out by what took place about six weeks after Mr. Price left the Makololo. Joseph Arend, a native hunter from Kuruman, then visited the Victoria Falls, and was the first stranger from the south who arrived in the country after the departure of Mr. Price. The Makololo were at first suspicious as to the object of his visit, and came to his camp in their war-dress. Finding however that Arend had not met Mr. Price, and knew nothing of the recent disasters at Linyanti, they proceeded to give their version of the story. Sekeletu sent two messengers to Arend to inform him that the missionary party had died of fever; and that he (Sekeletu) had urged Mr. Price to leave, "lest he also should die, and in order that he might inform his friends what had happened." Mr. Price, they added, had left a waggon behind, which was in

Sekeletu's charge. This wretched weakling had now repented him of the evil counsel of Mahuse, or he dreaded its consequences. Some one with equal eloquence and more sense than this firebrand had come to the assistance of the unworthy successor of Sebetuane. This councillor had no doubt plainly pointed out that if they admitted that they took the waggon by force, every one would believe they had also poisoned the owners. Therefore it must be denied that it was taken by force, and be strongly affirmed by everybody that Mr. Price had left it in their charge. Soon after this Dr. Livingstone arrived at Linyanti; and in addition to this story the Makololo endeavoured to prejudice him against Mr. Price. They had good reason to fear Mr. Price's testimony; and their only chance was to endeavour to damage such an awkward witness. In answer to Dr. Livingstone's inquiries, Sekeletu said Mr. Price had given him Mr. Helmore's waggon. But the suspicions of the Doctor were roused when he saw Mr. Helmore's property lying about, although he seemed at a loss upon whose shoulders to lay the blame.

Sekeletu however soon after made a confession to Sebehwe, another hunter, and son of the native teacher at the Bangwaketse, which may be received as very near the truth. He repudiated the charge of poisoning; and said that if he had intended to kill the white people, how was it that he allowed any to escape? The fact that people weak and helpless had been permitted by him to leave his country, would show that he had not the guilt of killing those who died. But he confessed that he had taken the property of the deceased at the suggestion of two of the mission party—one belonging to Likatlong and the other to Kuruman. He said he was now ready to make restitution; and asked Sebehwe in the meantime to take out the waggon to Mr. Moffat to show that he repented of what he had done. He also expressed his willingness to pay whatever Mr. Moffat might ask for the goods which had been destroyed.

On the 26th June, Mr. Price started from the Chobe river, and left the country of the inhospitable Makololo behind him. Although all very much reduced by sickness, they were now proceeding into a healthier country; the bracing winter had also set in; so there was cause for them to hope and to take courage. The first account which I received of Mr. Price's party was from a Bushman who had seen them at this stage in their journey. Alas! that when I myself met with him two months later, he had to lament another bereavement, which was the bitter dregs of a cup of which my friend had so freely partaken, and a stroke which was all the more severe because entirely unexpected at the time. In describing the lamented death of Mrs. Price, whose lovely character had endeared her to all who knew her, and whose gifts and accomplishments would have enabled her to further the objects of the mission, while she cheered and adorned the home of the missionary,—I shall quote the touching words of her husband:—

"On the plain of the Mababe, on the evening of the 4th of July, Mr. Helmore's two children, my own dear wife, and I met together for our evening meal, when we entered into conversation about what we had seen and suffered; and feeling that we were beginning to breathe again the fresh air of the desert, we admonished one another to forget the past and think of our mercies; for we felt that we had still what might, through the mercy of God, bring us within reach of help. My dear wife had been for a long time utterly helpless, but we all thought she was getting better. She went to sleep that night, alas! to wake no more! In the morning early I found her breathing very hard. I spoke to her, and tried to wake her, but it was too late. I watched her all the morning. She became worse and worse, and a little after mid-day her spirit took its flight to God who gave it. I buried her the same evening under a tree—the only tree on the whole of the immense plain of the Mababe. This was to me a heavy stroke, but 'God was my refuge and strength, a very present help in trouble.' Such things are hard to bear; but God knoweth our frame, and as our day is, so is our strength. With a heavy heart I left that place on the following day, and crossed the Mababe."

It is peculiarly hard for some natures to die in a foreign land; they long for another loving look at the old familiar scene; to hear once more the old familiar voices. But it is surely a more dreary thing to leave behind at death all the home which the spirit knows. It is no doubt sad to think of a young lady, beloved by parents and brothers and sisters in England, being buried by her lonely husband beneath the solitary tree in an African wilderness. But after all the lonesome thought has reference only to the body. The Christian is not alone, even in the valley of the shadow of death. "Lo, I am with you alway; I will come again, and receive you unto myself. Where I am, there shall also my servant be." In the companionship of Jesus there was no loneliness for the gentle spirit which was disembodied on the plain of the Mababe. Many a lonelier soul takes its unbefriended flight from downiest pillow, and from sumptuous sick-chamber crowded with weeping mourners. We need not then weep for her, but for ourselves and our children.

On the southern side of the Mababe Mr. Price met with Bushmen, and the agreement with the Makololo guides who still accompanied the missionary was that their task should be at an end when they could leave him in the hands of the Bushmen. It would seem that the cruelty of the Makololo was not yet complete. Mr. Price afterwards learned that they gave instructions to the Bushmen to lead the waggons into the habitat of the tsetse. Whether the Makololo were guilty of this final act of malice or not, it is certain that the Bushmen led them right into the fly, and then ran away. Now, they had nothing to gain from such treachery, but everything to lose. They lost their pay, and the pleasant life of travelling with a white man's waggon, which a Bushman always enjoys. It is difficult to suppose that this act was not intentional; and it is equally difficult to acquit the Makololo of the chief share in its guilt, inasmuch as Bushmen would be afraid to refuse obedience to their command. Once in the fly, and without guides, Mr. Price despaired of being able to save the forty-four oxen which now constituted his troop. He therefore made straight for the Tamalakan river, which he followed southward to the Zouga. Mr. Helmore's old waggon had broken down, and been left behind on the north of the Mababe; and one of the front wheels of Mr. Price's own waggon broke in the neighbourhood of Lechulatebe's town. With fever still clinging to him, it was with great difficulty Mr. Price made new spokes of such wood as he could find; but although performed in such circumstances, his repairs afterwards sufficed to take the waggon to Kuruman. Lechulatebe had shown great kindness to Mr. Price and the two orphan children of Mr. Helmore. When the waggon broke down, he sent assistance to remove it to the town; and during the month of their stay at the Lake, neither Mr. Price nor the children wanted anything which it was in the power of Lechulatebe to provide. Mr. Price had still a little tea and coffee and sugar left. The chief, who was very partial to these things, gave in exchange abundance of such food as his town supplied. Every day the tribute in meat (the breast of every animal killed) arrived from some outlying district. It might be the flesh of rhinoceros or buffalo, gnu or zebra, giraffe or eland; but whatever it was, Mr. Price was welcome to a share. The missionary was now a fixture at the Lake; for although the waggon was capable of repair, nothing could save the tsetse-bitten oxen from death. With nothing to purchase a fresh team, or even food for himself and his men, it was welcome news to Mr. Price to hear from the boatmen of Lechulatebe that "a missionary on his way to the Makololo, had touched the Zouga at More oa Maotu." Meeting with us on the Zouga after such dark and sorrowful experiences, was, in Mr. Price's own words, "like a resurrection from the dead."

Summing up his personal connection with these calamities, Mr. Price wrote to the Directors of the Society:—"If suffering in mission work is doing anything, then I have done something; if not, then I have done but little. My prayer now is, that God will direct me to some suitable sphere, where I may spend my life in the service of Christ among the heathen." This prayer has been graciously answered. In the active duties of a mission-station, Mr. Price has now spent years of earnest and willing service to Christ. In this work he has companions and fellow-labourers; but in the higher service of suffering, in the dark experiences at the fever-bed and the grave's mouth at inhospitable Linyanti, he is alone among his brethren.

CHAPTER XI.

RETURN JOURNEY FROM LAKE NGAMI.

On Monday the 10th September, we crossed over to the west bank of the Zouga at Letsebogo ya Khame, or Khame's Ford. The Makoba first directed us to a very deep part of the river, where they had collected several boats for the purpose of ferrying over our waggons in pieces, and also our goods. Mr. Price recollected that on the Saturday he had passed a very shallow part of the river, where he thought waggons could cross without being unloaded. The Makoba at first denied that there was a ford, but on being assured that I should give them a much higher reward for the discovery of a ford than for the use of their boats, they guided us to the place. After carefully examining it, we found that waggons could cross without difficulty. We were thus saved some three days' hard work in unloading the waggons and ferrying them across. The same night I was able to make arrangements for leaving three waggons and oxen here, while we accompanied Mr. Price to the lake, where our arrival was eagerly expected by the little children, as well as by the Bechuana servants. In order to expedite our movements, I emptied out the goods from my own waggon, taking only an assortment of articles likely to be of use in buying oxen from Lechulatebe. With a light waggon and two spans of oxen, we proceeded as fast as the dense thorn-trees would allow us.

On our way we passed the remnant of the oxen of Messrs. Helmore and Price. They were grazing in charge of some men at a little village called Matupenyane, and miserable objects they were. Only twelve were now left out of forty-four, and of these only three reached Kuruman. It was Mr. Price's opinion that these three had not been bitten, as they never were ill like the rest. There stood the poor creatures, doomed to die; their hair on end, their eyes sunken, their bones almost piercing the skin, and most of them with a large swelling outside the throat. A native of this district, after speaking about the tsetse and its deadly effects, put to me the following question: "You white people are very wise; you say you have the word of God in your possession, and it is no doubt true, for you can make waggons and guns, and can ride on horses. Explain therefore this difficulty, which baffles all black people. The buffalo and the common ox are so much alike that even Bushmen sometimes mistake the track of the one when it crosses or mixes with that of the other. The tsetse kills the ox, but it cannot kill the buffalo. In the same way, the zebra and the horse, although resembling each other, do not meet with the same fate when bitten by tsetse: the horse dies speedily, the zebra is none the worse. Since you white people have come among us with your wisdom, we blacks say to one another, 'Now we shall be told the mystery of the tsetse-bite.'" To such inquiries, in which there was always suppressed sarcasm, I had to return for answer that I was more ignorant about the tsetse than they themselves. I may also say here that there is some reason to doubt the entire correctness of the statement that donkeys are not killed by the bite of this insect. An English gentleman, who for several years in succession hunted in the tsetse districts on the Limpopo, informed me that he lost several of his donkeys in circumstances which led him strongly to suspect that long exposure to the bite of the fly would prove fatal to this animal. The elephant has sagacity enough to perceive that among the tsetse he is safe from his mounted pursuers. Accordingly, a troop of elephants, in a district often visited by hunters, will, at the approach of danger, make off at once for the habitat of the fly, and there browse in safety. Occasionally, if the troop is numerous, and there are some very large tusks to tempt the hunter, he will return to the waggon, and, tearing up an old waggon sail, make a covering for the whole body of his horse, and fitting closely to it. Next day he selects the oldest or most worthless in his stud, and, enveloping it in the sail covering, enters the tsetse district, and surprises the elephants in their fancied security. The horses sometimes escape through the aid of the covering, and the care that the hunter takes never to loiter until he emerges again from the infested region. Hunting elephants on foot is also occasionally practised in the tsetse districts. Although the tsetse was within two days' journey on foot from the station where I afterwards resided for years, no accident ever happened, except on one occasion, when a troop of cattle, having strayed from their post, entered the fatal district before their loitering herds came up to them, and of course all died.

Boating on the Zouga was a very pleasant mode of locomotion when compared with the jolting ox-waggon. The river was deep, and as placid as a lake. One could hardly tell in what direction the water was flowing. The crocodile sank heavily into the water before our approaching boat. The Makoba seemed to know their way through the tall reeds as the Bushmen knew to thread the sandy wastes. When passing one evening in a canoe the place where the Tamalakan flows into the Zouga, I could not help thinking how easily the evangelist could move from place to place in such a conveyance, and how far he could go in nearly all directions along the vast river system of the interior.

We passed several villages of the Makoba, the blackest people I had yet seen, with large eyes, abundance of woolly hair, and bodies strongly built and well-proportioned. The men had usually beard and whiskers, which, however, they kept closely cropped. Their language belongs to the Bantu family. The Makoba are vassals, like the Bakalahari and Bushmen. Like them also they submit to whomsoever is actual ruler of the country at the time. The Makololo on the Zambese, and the Bechuanas on the Ngami and Zouga, exercised a severe sway over these subject people. While Mr. Price was at Linyanti, he was aware of more than one instance in which a vassal, having given offence, was summarily speared by his master, no one taking any notice of the "dog" whose life had been thus thoughtlessly ended. While Lechulatebe's people were perhaps a little more merciful as to taking away life, his laws were very stringent. The banks of the river are covered with game-pits, which every night secure numbers of game. But only the inside of the animals may be eaten by the vassals; the breast is for the chief; the rest of the meat for the "head-man" who is master of the serfs. Every man of consideration at the Lake has Makoba vassals, and some have both Bushmen and Makoba. The former hunt in the distant wilderness; the latter busy themselves with game-pits by the river bank; the produce of the labour of both being for their liege lords. The master amuses himself as he pleases; sometimes hunting with his Bushmen, on other occasions living with the Makoba in their village, which is his, and embarking in their canoe, which is also his. The following anecdote will show whether or not the Makoba are quite content with this state of vassalage. I had been in the water, and while sitting on the river bank afterwards, one of the Makoba, my only companion, first carefully examined my foot, remarking its whiteness as compared with my face. He then took up my socks, put his hands into them, and examined the knitting. The boots were next inspected. Where was the sewing? He then placed my shoe alongside his very large foot and clumsy sandal, and then, first looking round on all sides to see if we were alone, to my amazement broke out, "Khosi (chief)! you white people ought to come in here and fight with these Bechuanas, and overcome them; they give us no rest, we are never done serving them." Glancing again at the wonderful socks and boots, he went on, "Now, you white people have wisdom; you have something to give those who are your vassals. Your servants are dressed with 'likhai' (cloths), and you have no end of beautiful things in your waggons. Come in and conquer the Bechuanas, and the Makobas will be glad to be *your* servants!" Even this fisherman on the Zouga wished to dispose of his fish in the best market! *He* would not fight with the present owners of the country, but he considered it would be greatly to his advantage if the white people fought with them and took the country and all its belongings into their own possession.

On another occasion I observed a number of Makoba running alongside the waggon, and apparently explaining the action of the wheels to one of their number. They informed me that the man in question had come from a distance, and that this was the first time he had seen a waggon. As I noticed the interest with which he kept up with the waggon for a considerable distance, I was reminded of the Scotchman who, when he first saw a four-wheeled carriage, after protracted observation, applauded the front wheel as the winner of a race, exclaiming, "Weel dune, little wheelie; aye first yet!"

Besides the "perquisites" of the game-pits and the unfailing supplies of fish from the river, the Makoba obtain large quantities of food from the gardens which they cultivate along its banks. But although they are better supplied with food than any other tribe in the country, I cannot report favourably as to their honesty. In fact, more determined pilferers are not to be met with anywhere. We had nowhere to watch our cups, spoons, etc., with such care as among the Makoba. One day a little bag of rice was placed on the ground by the servant, while she went with a cupful to be cooked. When she came back the bag was gone!

Without any hesitation, the Makoba, in answer to my inquiry, expressed their belief in a state of being after death. They seemed to have the notion that all disembodied spirits, at least of the Makoba, proceeded westward. But I could not find that they had any clear ideas about future rewards or punishments in connection with the present life. It is not improbable that their idea about going "towards the setting sun" after death has reference to joining their ancestors. The same people told me that they had formerly lived to the north-west.

On the 18th of September we reached the town of Lechulatebe, chief of the Batowana, a division of the Bamangwato tribe. It was then on the south bank of the Zouga, and not far from Lake Ngami, or Nghabi, as the Batowana call it. We drew up beside Mr. Price's waggon, and found little Lizzie Helmore in good health, but Willie was very sickly. It was touching to see the joy with which the two orphan children welcomed Mr. Price's return, and their gladness when brought to Mrs. Mackenzie. For the next five months we lived together as one family, and it was the daily effort of my wife and myself to cheer and sustain the drooping spirits of our bereaved companions. Lechulatebe received and deserved our special thanks for his kindness to the children as well as to Mr. Price. Having now the means of doing so, Mr. Price made the chief a suitable present, expressing at the same time the sentiment that he was not paying for kindness, or even for hospitality, —he would gladly accept of these as gifts. But now, God having sent him assistance, he did not wish that his friend should be left without some remembrancer of the missionary whom he had so kindly succoured. We now endeavoured to purchase fresh oxen for Mr. Price's waggon. We were willing to sell anything we possessed, but of course offered those things which we could best spare. Knowing the taste of his host, Mr. Price had directed me to bring tea, coffee, sugar, and flour belonging to himself and Mr. Helmore as articles of barter; and when we arrived the chief declared he would purchase nothing but "white man's food." He had been able to keep up a supply of these articles from English traders, who then occasionally visited him from Walvisch Bay on the west coast. Had we wished to buy ivory, instead of cattle, we could have transacted a large business; but we found the Batowana unwilling to sell their oxen. In the course of the week we succeeded in purchasing ten young oxen, which, with the spare ones in my troop, we hoped would be sufficient.

On Sunday the 23d, we had a public service in Lechulatebe's kotla, which was well attended; and our audience included Lechulatebe and all his head men. I delivered an address during the public service; and afterwards we had a very interesting discussion with the chief and his head men.

"What was it which pleased you missionaries in Sekeletu and the Makololo," asked Lechulatebe, "that you should all pass me by, leaving my town in ruins, while you went to build up that of Sekeletu? I desire instruction for myself and my people; I should persecute no one for believing; at any rate, I have shown that I would not eat the missionaries up in my own town, as Sekeletu has done."

"Who has preached the gospel here before?" we asked.

"The Griquas preached a little; Ngake (Dr. Livingstone) taught us during his visits; and several Batlaping have also preached in our town. We retained their instructions for a little time only; they soon faded from our memory. We should not so soon forget were a teacher living amongst us."

The teeming population on the rivers, their accessibility by boats, the attentiveness of the people, and the openly expressed welcome of the chief, made a great impression on my mind. Some time after, in writing to the Directors of the Society, I drew their attention to this wide field for evangelistic effort. The only desideratum for the residence of a European missionary would be a fountain in a high locality at some distance from the river. This will be one of the largest and most inviting fields for native teachers as soon as they are available for such service.

Mr. Price and I returned to the waggons, canvassing the best way of introducing Christianity into this region, when we found that during our absence my little child had been prostrated by fever. Having all necessary medicines with me, and prescriptions for the cure of fever by Dr. Livingstone and Dr. Palgrave, who had passed through the country the year before, I proceeded without delay to administer the proper remedies. We were deeply thankful to see the desired results follow. But this event hastened our departure from the Lake. We had projected a visit round part of its shore; but instead of that I only saw it from a distance.

I had one horse still remaining, and as I knew Lechulatebe was anxious to obtain a number of horses for hunting, I offered him mine in exchange for oxen. But I did a very foolish thing, which quite prevented me from accomplishing my object. I was aware that as many as ten and even twelve oxen were sometimes given by Lechulatebe for a horse; but in order, as I thought, to secure a speedy sale, and remove all necessity for haggling about the bargain, I offered my horse to the chief for four good oxen. Lechulatebe at once took it for granted that my horse was worth nothing at all, when I asked so little for it; so he declined to buy it. He sent his men to find out from my servants the faults of the horse; but being told it had none, refused to believe them. Had I asked ten oxen, and then, after a long talk, yielded a little, and come down to accept eight, I should certainly have obtained them for the same horse for which I could not get four! Happily some Englishmen who now arrived at the Lake from the west coast, wanted a horse, and were quite willing to give four oxen for mine. One day I rode over to their encampment, which was beside a number of baobab trees on the west of the town, and called for the chief on my way. He thought I had come to exhibit the paces of my horse, and began to examine the animal with the air of an accomplished jockey. I remarked that the horse was no longer for sale; I was just going to deliver it to its owners, the newly-arrived Englishmen.

"What did they give you for it?"

"Four oxen."

"Why were you in such a hurry? Don't you know that I sometimes give ten oxen for a horse if it pleases me?"

I replied that I took it for granted that my horse did not please him; for he never offered me four. I left the chief puzzling over two knotty points, arising out of this transaction,—that a man should at once ask what he wanted for an article, and not leave margin for "coming down;" and that I should demand as much from men of my own nation as from a stranger.

On another occasion, when purchasing an ox on the Zouga, I found that the owner would only take gunpowder in exchange. Pointing to a flint musket, he said it was of no more use than a walking-stick without powder. I produced some powder in one-pound paper packages. He viewed them with undisguised suspicion, and after calling his companions to see them, informed me that he would not buy powder in a paper package. He said he knew the powder which was contained in bags, not in packages. As it was of consequence to secure the ox, I got my wife hastily to stitch a bag inside the waggon of the size brought into the interior by traders. Pouring the powder which had been refused in packages into the bag, I found that the man's difficulties at once were removed. This was not only powder, but powder in a bag; so the bartering proceeded, and I purchased the ox.

Lechulatebe showed me a waggon which had been left in his care by Dr. Holden, who had been our fellow-passenger to the Cape from England, and who had also travelled for some time in company with Messrs. Helmore and Price. He had gone from the Lake westward into Ovampoland, and his researches would doubtless have materially increased our knowledge of a district still comparatively unexplored. I learned afterwards that, having pierced into an unhealthy and swampy region, this enterprising traveller fell a victim to fever. Thus science has her martyrs as well as Christianity.

We left the Lake on Wednesday the 26th of September, and after a week's journey reached Khame's Ford, where I had left the three waggons under the charge of Mebalwe. Two oxen had fallen into game-pits in the neighbourhood, owing to the carelessness of the herdsman, and both had died before they were got out. A similar accident afterwards happened, but by promptness the animal was dug out before it was injured. When there is a stake at the bottom of the pit, there is of course no hope of saving the animal; but even when there are no stakes, death, if not so speedy, is nevertheless sure. I have seen in the morning zebras and gnus quite dead in a pit into which they had fallen during the night. They had not been impaled by a stake in the bottom of the pit, but killed by the wedge-shape of the pit itself, into which their own weight and struggling drove them deeper and deeper. The Makoba cut them up in the pit, but afterwards carefully remove all traces of their work, and the least speck of the "moshwang," or contents of the stomach, or other matter which would appeal to the scent of the game, and rouse their suspicions. There is considerable skill shown in placing these pits, and in "laying out" the path in the neighbourhood. Without raising any obstruction so as to excite suspicion, a branch is placed to oppose progress in one direction—the decaying trunk of a tree is used for the same purpose elsewhere: so that the game, having choice of several paths, will find it easier and pleasanter to take the one on which the pit is placed. If these branches were put down suspiciously close, so as to take away the power of choice from the game, and to hedge them in, they would at once turn round and seek another path.

My men informed me with some pride that they had shot six buffaloes during my absence. Before leaving I had supplied them with some native corn, and also coffee;

but for meat I left them guns and powder and lead. I was pleased to find that they had turned these things to good account. To kill an elephant, a rhinoceros, or a buffalo, is the greatest honour to which a Bechuana man can aspire in the chase. He who has accomplished this thinks he need not be silent in any company. There is no end to the tales of wounded animals which a young and inexperienced native huntsman brings home in the evening. According to his own statement he breaks the leg of one animal, wounds another in the ribs, and a third in the flank; but the shot is always a little too high or too low. But when at length he is successful, he cuts off the brush of the animal as the "cupo" or trophy. He walks unconcernedly up to the camp, the tail waving conspicuously from the the stock of his gun if he is walking, or from his saddle if mounted. The sharp eyes of his friends soon discover the cause of his affected indifference, and some older man will say, "Comrades, to-day he has killed; he has shown himself a man; we are no longer asked to believe lies about wounded animals; the 'mogatla' (tail) never deceives." The rest of the party now ask for an account of the exploit, when the silence of the hero comes to an end, and he gives an animated and heightened description of what has taken place.

I had now fulfilled one object of my journey, although under circumstances widely different from what I had anticipated. I had assisted the only surviving member of the Makololo mission with those supplies which I had brought from the south. But what of the mission itself? And what of my own future course? I found that Mr. Price and Dr. Livingstone held opposite views as to the willingness of the Makololo to remove to the north of the Zambese. We had left England on the recommendation of Dr. Livingstone, and on the supposition that they would leave Linyanti; but Mr. Price had no hesitation in affirming, not only that they were unwilling to remove, but that, so far as he could gather, they never intended to do so. While I did not believe that Sekeletu had poisoned those who died, no one could gainsay the fact that he had treated Mr. Price in the most cruel and inhospitable manner, robbing him and the little children of almost everything they possessed. Was I then to go forward to Linyanti after what had taken place? It seemed absurd to do so, until at least the Directors of the Society under whose auspices we had come to the country had had an opportunity of considering the whole matter. But it was not without reluctance that I came to this decision. One does not feel satisfied in turning back without seeing and judging for one's-self. I had a long conversation with old Mebalwe before making up my mind. He assured me there was not a man in the party who would accompany me to the Makololo after the accounts they had received from Mr. Helmore and Mr. Price's men. It was thus plainly enough my duty to return with Mr. Price to Kuruman, and there wait fresh instructions from the Directors in London.

Leaving Khame's Ford about the middle of October, we proceeded slowly southward along the west bank of the Zouga.

The whole course of this river on both banks is infested with lions. Where the water was approached by a gently sloping bank, and therefore frequented as a drinking-place by the game, I have seen so many tracks of lions that I do not believe one could have taken a step in any direction without lighting on or passing over a lion "spoor." But in such districts they seldom interfere with the passing traveller. We spent a night close to a drinking-place such as I have described, and our encampment was undisturbed. I need hardly say that we did not select such a spot as the most suitable for a night's bivouac; we were compelled to halt here on account of an accident which happened to one of the waggons. Its driver had forgot to replace the linch-pin of one of the wheels after greasing the axle-tree; and the wheel keeping its place for miles, rolled off at this spot, when the waggon fell down and the axle-tree was broken. A piece of wood partially dressed, and kept by me in reserve for such an accident, was soon prepared and inserted, and next day we resumed our journey.

One of my men caught fever on the Zouga. He had come into my employment lean and hungry-looking, but in spite of the hardships of the journey had gradually swelled out; and after my return from the Lake I noticed that he was exceedingly stout, and very slow in his movements when doing his work. He had now a severe attack of African fever, and for some time seemed to be proof against the strongest medicines. I am sure that he must have had five or six ordinary doses before the slightest effect was produced. He lay in a dull lethargic state, the disease seeming to find in his gross system its most appropriate food. An impression once made, however, by the medicine, the fever was effectually checked, and after the lapse of some days the man was again at his place at the fire-side, distinguishing himself as formerly by his attention to the flesh-pot. This was the only case of fever among the men. The disease hung about our little child during the whole time we were on the Zouga. But as soon as we emerged from the dense foliage of the Lake river, and proceeded into the open plains of the Bushman country, a complete change took place in his health and spirits. The face which had become pale when not flushed with fever, regained its own healthy appearance; the eye which had been dull and listless became clear and bright; and the child who along the river sat wearily beside its mother, devoid of energy and spirit, was now once more full of vivacity. What the utmost solicitude and attention could not accomplish in the humid atmosphere of the Zouga, was effected without the aid of medicine by the pure air of the desert.

A marked improvement also took place in the health of Mr. Price and the children of Mr. Helmore as we journeyed southward.

I found it difficult to manage the men who had formed part of the expedition to Linyanti, a task which I readily undertook at Mr. Price's request. They were thoroughly soured and disappointed. They had expected pleasant times among the Makololo, and perhaps dreamt of enriching themselves, instead of which they had barely escaped with their lives. One man who was suspected of joining in Mahuse's evil counsels at Linyanti received the appointment of goat-herd under my dispensation. He was accustomed to walk about with the air of a man who had a grievance, and as a matter of course left his goats and sheep to look after themselves. He would answer a command from ten to twenty minutes after it was given, and seldom obeyed without growling and swearing at all and sundry. Then my own men were disappointed also. They had looked forward to an opportunity for trading with the Makololo, and hunting elephants on their way home. Grumbling being an infectious complaint, the presence of such a fellow as our sweet-tempered goat-herd was enough to poison the best party of men. As each person became less diligent more fell upon him who had the charge of all; and I found it a very different thing to journey south with men in this temper from what it was to travel north, every mind animated with hope. Furu no longer herded the cattle at night as before, and neither he nor his master

Galiboi seemed to care when I said that if he did not perform the extra work he could not get the extra pay which I had promised. I had therefore to tell off a man to do this work, and to see that it was done. One night, when half-way between Lotlakane and Nkowane on our way south, the oxen strayed in the night, and were found next day at noon far on their way back to the water. It was late in the day before they were brought again to the waggons, and the poor creatures were exhausted with their bootless journey. We had fortunately plenty of water for our own use. While waiting for the cattle to come back, and feeling all the chagrin and disappointment which my circumstances were calculated to produce, I overheard a conversation between Mr. Helmore's two children which affected me deeply.

Little Willie remarked to his sister that he was very thirsty. Was the water all done? His sister, who was older than he, answered that "he must be a good boy, and not ask for water. The oxen had gone astray. Did he not remember how they had been thirsty long ago, when mamma was still living? They must not ask for water." The poor little fellow had nothing more to say, but lay still, not very thirsty, but very unhappy. In a little I called him to me, and, without appearing to have heard their conversation, poured out a large cup of water, and gave him to drink. I assured him that there was abundance of water, and that as soon as he felt even a little thirsty he must come again, and I should give him a large drink. I observed that he drank only a little, and the idea of danger or uncertainty once driven from his youthful mind, he played in the shade of the waggons as usual, and I heard no more of thirst. Of course this was easy where there were not many children. But I cannot fancy a more trying position than to have charge of a number of little children in the desert where the supply of water is short.

We reached Shoshong on the 1st of December, where we remained for two months, experiencing much kindness and hospitality from Mr. Schulenborg of the Hermannsburg Society, who was at that time labouring as a missionary among the Bamangwato. A week after leaving Shoshong we were agreeably surprised to meet our veteran friend Mr. Moffat, who was, as he explained to us, on his way to search for us, and to bring us relief. The news of the calamity at Linyanti had reached Kuruman, through Joseph Arend, the native hunter, who had visited the Victoria Falls. Mr. Moffat informed us that having communicated the sad intelligence to friends in Cape Town, a public subscription had been there set on foot to send relief to the surviving members of a mission, all the members of which had but a short time before left that town in good health and spirits. Mr. Moffat, whose Kuruman home since 1855 was, in his own words, "more like the lodge of a wayfaring man than a permanent abode," had cheerfully volunteered to act as agent for those kind Christian friends at the Cape; and thus the pleasure of meeting him was enhanced by the consideration that he was on this occasion, in a peculiar sense, the "messenger of the churches." We were much gratified to learn that the expedition which now met us represented the Christian sympathy of all the churches at the Cape,—thus teaching us that whatever apparent schisms or divisions there might be in the Church of Christ, "all had been baptized by one Spirit into one body," and thus "whether one member suffer, all the members suffer with it." I may add, that with that clannish feeling which is characteristic of my country, I was particularly pleased to find among the contributors the name of Bishop Mackenzie of the English Universities Zambese Mission. Alas that in the death of this admirable Christian bishop the churches should have been called upon so soon after to mourn a calamity similar to that at Linyanti! Deeply grateful for the assistance which Mr. Moffat now proffered, I was still more thankful to be able to say that I stood in need of nothing, and to allay the solicitude of our dear friend by assuring him that no one travelling in our company had ever endured a day's hunger or thirst.

We again reached Kuruman on the 14th of February, exactly one year after the entry of Messrs. Helmore and Price into Linyanti. My own journey had extended over nine months, and I was glad when I had paid off the men, returned the hired waggons, with whose "weak places" I was now painfully familiar, and once more entered a Christian home under the hospitable roof of Mr. Ashton.

Some weeks after our return to Kuruman, my wife, who had enjoyed very good health while in the interior, was prostrated by a severe attack of fever. It was of a type unusual in the neighbourhood of Kuruman; and similar to what I was afterwards familiar with in the district of Shoshong. After reducing her very much, it assumed an intermittent form; and nothing which Mr. Moffat or Mr. Ashton could assist me in prescribing was effective in dislodging it from the system. Quinine, which is of great service in warding off recurrent attacks, became so distasteful that it instantly acted as an emetic. Given in the form of pills, covered or disguised in any way, the result was the same. I had not then met with a most useful preparation of quinine for South African fever, and one which the system does not reject—the citrate of iron and quinine. It will be remembered that Mrs. Livingstone, before her death from fever at Shupanga on the Zambese, was affected by quinine in the same way as Mrs. Mackenzie.

This fever, in its most malignant form, is closely allied to that on the west coast of Africa. The bodies of Dutchmen who died of it in the hunting-grounds near to the Zambese changed to a darkish yellow colour before death. In such severe cases the stupor comes on very soon, and death follows in a few days. Probably change of air would always be necessary to the complete cure of this type of the disease.

One year an elephant hunting-party ventured too early into a low-lying and swampy district in Mashona-land. The country abounded with elephants, and they were loath to give up the hunt and to remove for the sake of their health. They thought the winter, which was at hand, would itself restore their vigour; so they loitered in the deadly region, hunting one day, and confined to their waggons the next. When at length it became apparent, even to their unwilling minds, that they must remove to a more elevated region, it was too late. The disease had gained the mastery. They reached a healthier region only to die. Five grown-up people and one child were thus swept off within twenty-four hours of one another.

I have also observed several instances in which the sufferer from fever has had acute muscular pain, like Tabe the native teacher; the other symptoms being those of an ordinary attack. The fever which usually prevails in Bechuana-land comes on with headache, disinclination to exertion, even to change your position. The pulse quickens, the face flushes; the eyes are heavy and incapable of bearing light; the lips and mouth are very parched, and the whole body is dry and hot. If the fever is allowed to run its course without the interference of medicine, delirium to a greater or less extent supervenes. The mind wanders, recalling past scenes with remarkable distinctness. The preacher delivers part of a sermon, or sings some favourite hymn;

the trader talks of beads and ivory and ostrich-feathers; the hunter is in difficulties among elephants, which he is shooting in his dreams. At this stage the invalid experiences almost a duality of being. With an effort he listens to the question which is put to him by friend or attendant, and answers it; but all the while a phantasmagoria surrounds him, which is seen only by himself. In some cases, from constitutional and at times accidental causes, while the patient has the same rapid pulse, and the same dry skin and parched mouth and throat,—instead of complaining of heat and unconsciously pulling off all covering from his body to get relief, he lies shivering and his teeth chattering under the warmest blankets. In both cases this hurry and excitement of the system ends in a state of profuse perspiration and great exhaustion. The head, however, is now again clear, and the patient declares he is well again. But in three or four days the same symptoms may again appear—leaving the man weaker after every attack, until at length he sinks into a state of insensibility, which gives place to death.

Fever is unknown in winter in Bechuana-land. In the middle of summer, after the rains have fallen, it is not common. It is in spring, before the rains come, and in autumn, when the moisture is drying up, and vegetation is ripening and decaying, that we find the greatest number of fever cases, and, indeed, the greatest amount of sickness generally. What would be a bilious attack in a healthy season of the year, often resolves itself into fever in spring or autumn. The huntsman or traveller is tempted to remain without any additional covering, in the chill evening air, the little clothing he has on being damp with perspiration. In winter this might not produce any appreciable evil consequences, or at most what is called a common cold; but in the unhealthy seasons such exposure often leads to fever. If then a man avoids what would give him a cold or a bilious attack, he is taking the best means of averting the fever of Bechuanaland. Quinine is a most efficacious curative; it would seem sometimes to fail as a preventive. Where it has been much used to ward off the disease, it is of course necessary to give larger doses as a curative. The first prescription which I tried began with a purgative; then a sudorific; and lastly tonics. But I soon gave it up for Dr. Livingstone's plan, which dispenses with the second dose entirely, and combines the third with the first. Although it would only increase fever to administer quinine alone at the outset, Dr. Livingstone found that it might be safely given along with the purgative. Its presence with the other medicines affects the system in a way which the simple purgative does not accomplish. Profuse perspiration usually accompanies the action of this medicine upon the bowels, and thus the sudorific is unnecessary. There is indeed no doubt that Livingstone's prescription is a specific for African fever as it is found between the Orange and Zambese rivers. As a missionary, I have had every year several cases under my care, and with God's blessing, in every instance a cure was effected by means of this remedy. The cure is indeed a somewhat rough one. I believe Bishop Mackenzie remarked that it was "worse than the disease." But it is not so. The system is in such a state that Livingstone's prescription produces no injurious result. I have met with several people who thought a more tender treatment would suffice. In every instance they have been glad in the end to take the "big dose." I have tried to substitute an emetic for Livingstone's prescription, and thus to prepare the system for quinine. It never produced the desired result. But as the European population increases in the country, and numbers of qualified medical men settle in it, a more elegant cure for this dangerous disease will no doubt be found out. I have heard ardent believers in homœopathy declare that they could cure African fever very speedily with their pleasant little doses. I can only invite them to try; and I sincerely hope they may succeed.

Fairly baffled in our attempts to cure Mrs. Mackenzie, and remembering the beneficial effect of change of air on our little child, we resolved to try its effect upon his mother. And in order, at the same time, to secure the advice of medical men, we resolved to journey towards the Cape Colony. But before we had been gone a week a marked change for the better was observable in Mrs. Mackenzie's health, and my joy in her convalescence was shared by Miss Moffat, who had very kindly accompanied us, and by Mr. Price, who was then on his way to the Colony with Mr. Helmore's little children. After our departure from Kuruman, instead of recurring with the regularity of tertian ague, the fever returned only twice, at long intervals, and then left her entirely. It being unnecessary to go into the Colony, we renewed our friendships in Philippolis and Fauresmith, and returned to Kuruman, with my dear wife's health fully restored. At Fauresmith I was gratified with the assurance which I received from friends that during our absence in the interior the prayers of Christian people there had been ascending on our behalf; and I was informed that some of the inhabitants of Fauresmith were about to equip an expedition from their little town to search for us in the interior, when they learned that the matter had been taken up in Cape Town. It was pleasant to think that when isolated from Christian friends such true sympathy and prayers followed us.

CHAPTER XII.

THE LAST OF THE MAKOLOLO.

In giving the Directors of the Society an account of my journey into the interior, I expressed the opinion that if they intended to persevere in introducing Christianity into the Zambese country, operations could be best carried on from the east coast; and offered to proceed thither with that object in view. If, however, the Society intended to work the Zambese district from the south, and in connection with missions already established, it was evident that there must be a chain of intervening stations. To go from Kuruman to the Zambese country at one bound was to separate the advance guard too far from the main body, and was sure to lead to disaster. This view of the case had also been pressed upon their attention by the other missionaries when on their way into the interior. At this time liberty had been given to resume the work of evangelizing Madagascar; and in case there should be any lack of men to take advantage of the opening, I mentioned to the Directors my willingness to undertake work in that island, and, in short, placed myself entirely in their hands.

While waiting their decision, I itinerated in the towns and villages of South Bechuana-land, and also made two additions to the Sechuana literature, in the compilation of a little book on geography, and in the translation of the well-known work by the Rev. Newman Hall, *Come to Jesus.* I suggested to native teachers that along with their own discourses (which were not always to the point) they should occasionally read to their people one of the short addresses given in that volume.

The Directors of the Society would seem to have been somewhat at a loss to know how to dispose of Mr. Price and myself. I was kept more than a year in suspense. At length, in May 1862, I received an appointment to Shoshong, the town of the Bamangwato. Dr. Livingstone was the first missionary who preached to the Bamangwato. His first visit to them was in 1842, that of Mr. Moffat in 1855. The importance of the place as a station was pointed out by the latter missionary; and a native teacher from Kuruman conducted a school for some time at Shoshong. But in arranging for their interior missions in 1858 this important station was unfortunately passed over by the Directors of the Society. Its population of thirty thousand souls ought alone to have led to a different decision; and its importance, with reference to the country beyond, was hardly less striking. Had a mission been first planted here, at a point four hundred miles farther north than Kuruman, it would have been easy afterwards to communicate with the Makololo concerning the residence of missionaries among them. Shoshong indeed was the true point from which to have commenced both the Matebele and Makololo missions.

In 1859 a missionary of the Hermannsburg Society commenced operations among the Bamangwato. Owing, however, to some misunderstanding between the managers of the Society and its agents in Bechuana-land, the latter were for a time denied pecuniary assistance from Europe, and were compelled to resort to trading with the natives for support. It was reported that in these circumstances the station of Shoshong was abandoned by the missionary, who had returned to Natal; and the Directors of the London Society requested me to occupy the town as one of their stations. The above report, however, was not strictly correct; so I felt it to be my duty to inform the Directors that I did not regard a Bechuana town to be vacant while another European missionary resided in it; although, in this case, the desultory and often interrupted efforts of one man, unconnected with any Society, were not to be taken into account by a Society carrying on an extensive work in the country. At Shoshong I should at least be able to communicate with the interior tribes, and especially with the Makololo.

Travelling with two waggons, I left Kuruman immediately after receiving the letter of instructions from the Directors. Besides some spare oxen, I had bought a few cows for the general benefit of my establishment in the interior, and with the view of replacing old and enfeebled oxen in my team. The Missionary Society supplies its South African agent with the first team of oxen which he needs on entering the country, but he is afterwards supposed to be able to supply oxen for himself. I had also purchased about twenty sheep, which the men were driving in front of the waggons with the spare oxen and cows. I now performed a journey of some four hundred miles at the rate of twenty-four miles a day. This is considered very good travelling in that country.

On my way north I paid another pleasant visit to the Barolong at Montsiwe's town. I was again deeply interested in the condition of the little church here, under the care of Moleme and Jan. Considerable progress had been made since my last visit. The leaven of Christianity was steadily operating on the community. The young people especially were losing confidence in the old customs, and giving increased attention to the doctrines taught from the Word of God. But, as I was informed by Moleme on this latter occasion, the "kingdom of darkness" did not allow this change to go on without violent opposition. In particular, Montsiwe, the chief, assumed an attitude of open hostility to his Christian subjects. Matters were brought to a crisis by the unusually large number of young people who, under religious impression, ceased to take an interest in those subjects which engage the attention of the young in a heathen town. When these inquirers were about to be enrolled in classes, and thus take up a position as "bathu ba lehuku" (people of the Word), the chief resolved to prevent their doing so. His decision was that they must first observe the usual customs of their forefathers, and especially that they must join in the reed-dance, and that afterwards they might, if they chose, "join the Word of God." Moleme and the disciples were opposed to this course, as one which virtually obliged them to serve two masters—a thing which, they said, God's Word told them no one could do. One can imagine what would be the result of resistance to the will of the chief in such a town as Montsiwe's: the consequent pitshos, accusations, defences, and general loud talk in public; the asseverations, the upbraidings, the family strifes in private. All this Moleme informed me was enacted among the Barolong when the young people resisted the will of their king, and broke off from the custom of their forefathers.

The next cause of offence was the refusal of the Christian young men and inquirers to go to a certain hunt (letshulo) enjoined by the rain-doctors. This was followed by their declining to join in digging the "garden of rain" (tsimo ea pula). This is a heathen ceremony, and those who take part in it are of course abettors of rain-making. Moleme and Jan, with the other believers and the inquirers, refusing to join in digging this "garden of rain," requested that, if the king wished a test of their loyalty, he should appoint them another field, which they would be quite willing to dig at his command. "Do not accuse us of disobedience," said they to the chief; "you are still our father, and in all things belonging to your kingdom we continue your most willing subjects; only concerning our old customs and the Word of God, we have believed the latter, have entered into the Word, and therefore may not join in the dark deeds of our forefathers, who had not the knowledge which we possess."

Baffled in these endeavours, Montsiwe had recourse to another plan. In the absence of the two chief men among the believers, he gave out the order that on the following Sabbath there should be no meeting in the little chapel, and all were to join in the customary singing and dancing by moonlight. In spite of the chief, the believers met as usual, led on and encouraged by two women, whose names I forget, but who certainly acted in a manner worthy of their Christianity.

Finding that his command was unheeded, the chief resolved personally to scatter the little company and terrify the females, who, he knew, animated the rest. Accordingly, while one of the male members of the church was engaged in prayer, Montsiwe appeared at the chapel door, a naked sword in hand; the services were interrupted, and doubtless many were terrified. Montsiwe ordered the worshippers immediately to disperse; but he was answered by one of the two women that they were doing nothing but what was required of them as "people of God's Word," and that they should just go on with the service. Then followed what must have frightened many, and what was meant to terrify all. The chief in a great rage, indignant at being opposed to the face by women, threatened the most dreadful things if they did not at once leave the place. I believe he ultimately succeeded in clearing the little church, but he was utterly foiled, nevertheless, in his endeavour to put a stop to the regular meetings for worship, which were taking place up to the time of my visit.

But perhaps the most interesting part of this account remains to be told. Montsiwe had a daughter, not more than twenty years of age, who was married to a serious-thinking young man, and who herself was a believer. After it had occurred to the chief to crush Christianity among his people, he felt of course that he must "begin at home." Accordingly he forbade his daughter to attend the public worship. He was obeyed in this; but the heads of the church endeavoured to make up to her what loss she might sustain by her obedience to this cruel command, by regularly sending one of their number to read to her the portions of Scripture which had been read in the meeting, and to mention something of what had been said. Montsiwe finding this out, and learning that she continued to sing and to pray in private, separated her from her husband, and removed her to his own house. She was forbidden to read or pray, or, in short, *to be a Christian.* The young disciple evaded part of this injunction by carrying about with her her Sechuana hymn-book, which she read in her secret devotions. This being discovered, she was ordered to doff her European clothing, and to return to heathen attire, which it was supposed would afford her less means of secreting books about her person. However, she was not to be baffled, but with the assistance of the old women contrived a plan by which she continued to carry about with her the Sechuana hymn-book. She also paid stolen visits to old Moleme, who encouraged her to hold fast her confidence, and who, in giving me this account of her, said, "I fear not for her; the Spirit of God is strong within her." Being forbidden the company of Christians, she could only remain with me a few minutes. I am not sure that she was allowed to attend the preaching, which was in the court-yard and not in the chapel.

My visits to the Barolong cheered my heart as a missionary, and especially encouraged me to hope and believe that the Bechuanas, known to the world chiefly in connection with strongly-drawn pictures of their degradation, may yet in many cases force themselves into favourable notice on account of their steadfast faith in the gospel. Especially gratifying will it be to Wesleyans to hear, as it is to me to publish, that their labours among the Barolong are yet bearing precious fruit, although the field is at present without the oversight of a resident European missionary.

I found that the district between Sechele's Town and Shoshong was very dry, there being only two available waters on the road which I took, in a distance of about 140 miles. It was therefore necessary to travel a good deal by night. In such circumstances, it was my custom to unyoke about an hour before sunset, that all might prepare for the work of the night. After having supper, my wife made all necessary arrangements for retiring to rest in the waggon with the little ones. The sail-covering having been tightly fastened down at both ends, the precious freight composed themselves to rest, rocked to sleep by the jolting of the rude waggon, and awoke only if it halted for any length of time on the way. My place was on the front of the waggon, beside the driver. It was this latter arrangement that gave confidence to my inside passengers: they fully believed that I would lead them into no danger. The men, who had just had a good supper, were in capital spirits, and the oxen, which had improved the opportunity to the best of their ability in their attentions to the grass of the prairie, stepped out with the waggons, during the cool hours of the delicious moonlight, at a much brisker pace than during the day. Having learned, soon after entering the country, to use the long whip of the waggon-driver, I now and then relieved one of my men, who meanwhile lit his pipe, and told me some story of the olden time.

After toiling for hours one night in the sand we were all heartily glad when we ascended the bank of the old river course of Bonnononyane, and found ourselves rumbling along at a fine pace over the hard road approaching Boatlanama. We were going so fast that the drivers of the spare oxen in front could hardly keep their charge out of the way of the teams. As this was our second night without rest, the poor fellows who were driving them were very tired, and I found, on going forward to assist them, that one man especially, who had had a severe illness at Kuruman, was actually asleep while walking. He was nodding his head, and walking as if he had St. Vitus's dance; when he occasionally ejaculated to the oxen his voice died away before he could finish the word. The cattle which he professed to be driving were—some before him, others on each side, and a few had got behind him, and were driven by the leader of the first waggon! I suggested that he should take a good pinch of snuff, but although not at all loath to do so, he said it had lost its power: the "sleep had conquered the tobacco." But something soon occurred which roused him most effectually, as well as every other member of the party, except the happy sleepers inside the waggon. I had been walking some time in front of the waggons, whistling to the cattle which we were driving, and keeping up the spirits of the men, when, not more than a hundred yards in front of us on the road, the unwelcome roar of a lion suddenly brought every ox to a stand-still. They raised their ears, and stretched forward their heads, sniffing for the animal whose voice had alarmed them. What was to be done? Even if I halted and tied up the oxen which were in the yoke, the loose cattle would certainly be scattered by the lion. The place was just suited for his skulking movements, being dotted over with thorn-bushes. In order to inspire my companions with confidence, I ran to the waggon, and, seizing my gun, returned to drive the loose cattle on. I asked the men if their assegais were ready, and they said they were, but I did not anticipate much help in that direction. I hoped that as it was a bright moonlight night our right of way would be conceded by the loud-voiced foot-pad in front. The oxen were very unwilling to go on, especially some old ones which had been in the interior before. The younger and inexperienced animals led the way. I now looked out for a spring to be made upon them as they passed. The drivers behind stood on the waggon-chests, and made the welkin ring with their large whips. At length, urging on the most timid of the oxen, we passed the place where we judged the lion to be. After this the oxen went on more willingly. The waggons passed also unscathed. In a little my companions began to congratulate themselves on what they had done. "It (the lion) knows how to distinguish people; it knows that we are valiant men (literally bull-calves of men). Monare (Sir), are we not men to-night?" When I thought that one of them had been so exhausted a little before as to be unable to drive his oxen, that they were now only armed with one assegai each, I could not withhold the praise they sought. "Yes," I said; "you have done well; you are really men to-night." A little afterwards one of them said, perhaps in consideration of this compliment, "Monare had now better go and rest on the front of the waggon; we are fairly awake now, and the oxen don't need much driving." I was not at all satisfied, however, that we were out of danger, although I found on returning to the waggon that the drivers thought so. "That lion has only the heart of a wolf," said one man, who himself was not the bravest of our party. I made up my mind that as we had got safely past the lion, our best plan would be to travel right on without unyoking till daybreak. I had heard that lions in certain districts got acquainted with the waggon-roads, and often lay in wait in their neighbourhood; and that they would proceed for miles upon the fresh track of travellers. After proceeding some time, the night became intensely cold, and my men beginning to feel their weariness return, asked leave to unyoke. We were now, they said, within an easy distance of the water. I refused for some time, although I felt sorry for the poor fellows, who had been toiling in the heat of the sun, but whose teeth were now chattering with cold as they sat in front of the waggons. Having gone on for fully two hours after we passed the lion, I at length unwisely yielded, against my own judgment, to the importunity of the men, and gave them permission to unyoke. I appointed two of the freshest and best men to watch the oxen till daylight, which was thought now to be near at hand. Pulling the waggon sail over me, I lay down on the front box of the waggon, and, overcome with the fatigues of our long march, fell fast asleep. When I awoke the eastern horizon could just be distinguished by the grey brightness of the advancing light of day. On looking out I missed the oxen from the place where they had gone to rest sometime before I fell asleep. Springing from the waggon, I found the men all sitting round the fire in silence. I knew there was something wrong now; otherwise they would have been sound asleep. The men appointed to watch said that some time after I went to the waggon, the lion had passed the encampment, until he got on the windward side of the oxen, when he made a noise which not only awoke the wearied cattle, but with the scent of the dreaded animal carried to them by the wind, caused them to start in terror and rush past the fire at the top of their speed. The two men tried to stop them, but of course could not succeed. I verified these statements next day.

As soon as it was daylight the men started on the track of the oxen. Fearing that the cattle might separate in their flight, I retained only two young lads at the waggon. After drinking a cup of coffee, I thought I should like to know at least in what direction the cattle had run. Like the Bushmen, I felt that if the lion had killed anything, I ought to come in for a share of it, having also, in this instance, I thought, a good right to what was my own. One of the boys accompanied me, and after proceeding some time on the track of men, lion, and cattle, I found as we entered a thicket that the men had here turned aside; and there remained only the track of cattle with that of a large lion on it. Looking through the trees, which were here pretty close, and perceiving the men some distance on before, I asked the boy how they had got there, seeing they had left the track?

"We thought we heard a sound last night in this thicket," the boy replied, as he followed after me, "as of something dying; and perhaps they have given the lion a wide berth, and taken up the track again on in front."

This was a reason for leaving the track which I had not thought of. While we were speaking I heard a movement among the bushes a little before me, and to the left. Looking in that direction, I found we were close to the carcase of one of my oxen, which the lion had just left. He had eaten the greater part of the entrails of the ox; but our approach had interfered with his doing justice to the more solid part of the repast. The carcase lay at the edge of the copse. Beyond there stretched an immense field of prairie-grass fully four feet high, into which the lion had reluctantly retired as we appeared. I now sent the boy to the waggons for his companion and for knives, that we might get the Bushman's portion of our own ox. I found that the animal which had fallen victim was a young ox which a few days before had become slightly crippled through over-exertion in pulling the waggon. As he was content with such an ordinary quarry, I felt convinced that our acquaintance of the previous night must be an old lion, glad to pounce upon the animal which he could first overtake. Although such old lions are regarded as the most daring and pertinacious, this one had now twice "given place to his betters." For some time he proceeded in silence through the long grass; but in a little, while the boys were skinning the ox and dividing the meat so as to carry it to the waggons, we heard him, perhaps a mile away, utter an occasional low growl, which died away as he proceeded in the direction of the water.

It apparently did not occur to the lion that we would remove any part of the meat; for being ourselves delayed the whole day waiting for our oxen, we found as soon as the sun went down that the old fellow had invited his whole family to partake of the beef which he had so suddenly deserted in the morning. When they came to the place, and found little or nothing there, they set up a chorus of disappointment, to which it was not at all pleasant to listen. We had made a strong fence for the sheep; and I gave a gun to each of the boys, more to encourage them than from any expectation of our requiring to use them. One of the lads, however, thought he might as well use the powder and lead which had come so easily into his possession, so he commenced an "opposition demonstration," firing into the darkness in the direction of our visitors. Whether a bullet found its way in the dark inconveniently near to one of the lions, or whether it had only struck against a tree in their neighbourhood, the boy himself did not profess to say, but all at once the roaring ceased, and was not again resumed. Contrary to our expectation, we were able to sleep soundly, and arose refreshed. Soon after daybreak the men appeared with the oxen. The affrighted animals, forgetting their weariness and thirst, had struck out into the open country to the east of the waggon-road, and must have run more than a dozen miles. Fortunately they kept together in one troop. It was after mid-day when the men found them.

Although they returned as speedily as possible, the men saw that they would not be able to get to the waggons till after sunset: and knowing that the lion would be sure to return to finish his meal, they remained during the night in the open country, at a small Bakalahari town, from which they started before dawn. The men were now ready to admit that the loss of the ox was owing to their haste in unyoking before daylight. "Cold is stronger than a lion," said these wiseacres; "we held out and passed the lion, but we were overcome by the cold."

The deep pool of Selinye, which we reached after this adventure, is supplied entirely by rain, but so retentive of water is its slightly brackish bed, that I have never known it to be dried up except on one occasion. We here met a waggon belonging to native hunters who were on their way south. They announced the arrival of Mebalwe from Moselekatse's country, whither he had gone in the service of Mr. John Moffat. They narrated the Matebele news, and the history of their journey to Shoshong in the company of Mebalwe. At length some one asked—"Has he a white man with him?" "Yes," was the answer, "he has got Yonie" (Mr. John Moffat). The whole expedition had been mentioned as if belonging to Mebalwe, who was then in Mr. Moffat's employment, as he had been in mine. The Bechuanas are naturally most interested in their own people, and I have since often heard them describe the arrival of one of their friends, and find it only mentioned, as a minor incident, that he was in the employment of a traveller or trader.

On arriving at Shoshong in June, I found that Mr. Price, who had been appointed to reinforce the Matebele mission, had remained here, having taken the precaution of sending forward letters to the Matebele missionaries from himself and from Mr. Moffat, in order that his approach to the country might be announced to Moselekatse, and the feelings of the chief ascertained before he proceeded further. Moselekatse had no hesitation in returning an answer. Neither he nor his people desired more missionaries. Mr. John Moffat was the bearer of this message. Mr. Price was busily engaged when I arrived teaching the Bamangwato, in the temporary absence of the German missionary. I found that Mr. John Moffat entertained a strong desire to assist in the establishment of a mission to the north of the Zambese, having corresponded on the subject with his brother-in-law, Dr. Livingstone, who had given him many valuable hints as to the country and the best manner of procedure. This desire was strengthened when he found that I seriously contemplated a journey to that country next travelling season. Mr. Price also joined in this fresh attempt to open up the region of the Zambese to the gospel. Sebehwe, the native trader, who had already brought out a message from Sekeletu to Mr. Moffat, was now at Shoshong on his way back to the Makololo country. We therefore resolved to write a joint-letter to Sekeletu, informing him that with his consent we would next year cross the Zambese, and proceed to Tabacheu, and endeavour to select a suitable site for a mission station. We expressed our desire to teach any of his people who might come to reside in that healthy locality, reminding him of his cruel conduct at Linyanti, but saying that God desired us to wish well even to those who injured us. We were now sanguine of success. Sekeletu had no doubt become thoroughly ashamed of his heartless conduct to the former missionary party. Once settled in a healthy region, we hoped gradually to open up communication with the east coast through the intervening stations of the English Universities Missions under Bishop Mackenzie. Soon after writing to Sekeletu Mr. John Moffat left for Kuruman. In August Mr. Price and I engaged an artisan who had been connected with the Hermannsburg mission, to cross the Zambese with us, and assist in the introductory work of the new station. I also purchased two horses for the projected journey, and sent out my waggon for the necessary supplies to Kuruman, whither Mr. Price also went for the same purpose about the end of the year.

Sechele, who is not the most modest or self-abasing of men, had taken upon himself the office of representative or champion of the missionary party whose goods had been plundered by Sekeletu, and early this year sent in a waggon to "demand the things of the white people." This party arrived at Shoshong in October on its way home. The Bakwena of Sechele were accompanied by four Makololo, sent as ambassadors to that chief. We were told by the Bakwena that Sechele had not succeeded in his application for restitution of the white men's things. But the presence of the Makololo did not altogether favour the idea that this self-imposed effort had been entirely unsuccessful. We trusted, however, to receive definite information from Sebehwe, our own messenger to Sekeletu. Modiane and Tlaripane, and the rest of the Makololo, when confronted with Mr. Price, endeavoured to put the best face on past events at Linyanti. It was evident, however, that our questions were answered with extreme reluctance, and that they wished if possible to avoid the whole subject. We were kind to them, and fully explained to them our message to their chief, and our intention to cross the river next year. In December Sebehwe returned from the Makololo country, bearing a message from Sekeletu, which he had committed to writing, lest he should forget it on the way. The answer to our letter was much more favourable than I had anticipated. Sekeletu himself promised to remove to Tabacheu as soon as he should hear of our arrival at the Victoria Falls. His readiness was perhaps partly to be accounted for by the fact that he was very ill, and had been given to understand that we should be able to help him with medicine. Other hunters bore testimony to the correctness of Sebehwe's statement. One thing was very evident to us, that whether our mission were established or not, the office of messenger from the missionaries to Sekeletu had been a very profitable one to Sebehwe. He brought out a large quantity of ivory; and according to his own account had received public honours as our representative, from which we ourselves would have shrunk. Afraid lest we should start without him next year, Sebehwe laid special stress upon the importance of our going in his company, in order that he might "place us" before the chief, when he said his work would be at an end.

The solicitude of this shrewd native, who no doubt had an eye to another load of the ivory of the Makololo, was shared by our own friends at a distance, as soon as they learned that we were again to attempt the establishment of the mission in connection with which we left England. But the projected journey from Shoshong to the Victoria Falls was through a comparatively healthy country. There was already a waggon road much better supplied with water than our previous route; and if Dr. Livingstone was not mistaken in his estimate of the healthiness of the region of Tabacheu, we had now the reasonable prospect of beginning operations as missionaries under favourable auspices. Some of our friends, however, in their kind letters to us, were most vigorously shutting the door after the horse had been stolen. Now that negotiations had taken place, and there was, so to speak, a straight path from Shoshong to Tabacheu, some hastened to tender us the advice as to caution, necessity of previous negotiation, the leaving wives and children behind, etc., which had been in vain tendered at Kuruman under widely different circumstances.

This whole project, however, was destined to fall to the ground, from a combination of causes entirely beyond our control. Most singularly, every detail seemed to miscarry, so that at the time we had proposed to start, it was obviously impossible for any of us to do so. Mr. Price had a serious attack of illness while absent for supplies, which induced him reluctantly to give up the idea of again entering the Zambese country. Instead of being able speedily to return to the interior, and there make arrangements to join in our expedition, Mr. John Moffat was delayed by sadder duties, through the lamented and sudden decease of his only brother a few hours after he had left his father's house on a journey to Natal. Even the supplies which I had ordered were not forthcoming, although ample time had been allowed. And to crown all, the whole idea upon which the two missions had been founded in England was itself entirely dissolved by the attack of the Matebele upon the Bamangwato. It was thought that missionaries would be able so to sway the councils of the Matebele, as that their old enemies, the Makololo, might with safety live in the open country of Tabacheu, provided they also had missionaries with them. But, as will be seen in the next chapter, Moselekatse attacked the Bamangwato without any provocation; although he had been told that missionaries were residing with Sekhome, and indeed that one of them (Mr. Price) had married the daughter of his friend Mr. Moffat. It was therefore certain that the same chief would not be deterred from attacking the Makololo if they removed within his reach, even although missionaries were residing with them.

In June 1863 I had an opportunity of communicating with Sekeletu by a party of English gentlemen, who were visiting the Victoria Falls. I announced to him that we should not be able to cross the Zambese as we had intended, and that he must also take notice that the presence of missionaries in his town had not prevented Sekhome from being attacked by Moselekatse. I still held out to him the hope that in the course of time missionaries might be able to reside with his tribe, but that we could not be a shield to him from his enemies. This was the last communication which we had with Sekeletu. He died soon after, a victim to leprosy, with which he had been afflicted for some time.

And now began the last brief chapter in the history of the Makololo tribe. Dr. Livingstone narrates how Sekeletu himself had to combat opposition after the death of Sebetuane, and how one of his opponents was put to death while the young chief was travelling with the Doctor. On Sekeletu's death, there was again bloodshed; and as the reign of Impololo, his successor, was of short duration, the intrigues and assassinations were hardly at an end when they were resumed in the interest of another claimant for the chieftainship. During these disturbances, the people of a small town of Makololo escaped, and were hospitably received by Lechulatebe at Lake Ngami. Others sought among their enemies the Matebele an asylum, which was granted. The Barotse, the Batoka, the Bashubea, and other tribes which had been conquered by Sebetuane, were not uninterested spectators of the feuds which were thus decimating their proud masters. The fights as to the succession to the chieftainship took place when the Makololo were assembled at the capital, and it was observed by the keen-eyed vassals, that after the tumult was over for the time, and the lords were dispersed among their villages, their numbers kept steadily decreasing. At length the Makololo were so few that even the timid and unwarlike tribes which had borne their yoke so long, resolved by one united effort to regain their freedom by the destruction of their oppressors. A plot was accordingly concocted, which seems to have been closely concealed and well carried out by those who had the execution of it. The subject tribes rose in one night on their masters, and put them to death. Some Makololo, however, whose character had endeared them to their slaves, or whose vassals were perfidious to their own countrymen, were able to collect their families and their property and to escape across the Mababe into the Bushman country, which we have already described. A few also again escaped to Moselekatse. But the Makololo as a tribe were destroyed in this insurrection of their vassals. The Makololo women and little children were spared; and Lotanku, the Barotse chief, gained considerable prestige, even among his own people, by taking to wife Mamochisane, the daughter of Sebetuane. The Barotse now regarded themselves as revenged for the years of oppression which they had endured; and from a native point of view, in the possession of the wives, cattle, and "other possessions" of their former lords, their triumph was complete.

An evil destiny hung over the party of fugitives who had escaped across the Mababe. Although some of their countrymen had been favourably received by Lechulatebe at the Lake, this party decided not to trust to one who had so long been their enemy, but rather to seek protection from Sekhome the chief of the Bamangwato at Shoshong. But Lechulatebe was unwilling that his enemies should thus escape out of his hand. There was living in his town one of the Makololo who was under great obligation to Lechulatebe for protection afforded him many years before, when he had fled to him as a refugee. He was now willing to further the interests of his benefactor to the best of his ability. And so it was treacherously planned by Lechulatebe and this refugee that the latter should waylay his passing countrymen and endeavour to decoy them towards the Lake. He accordingly crossed the river and made his appearance among the Makololo as they were pursuing the route towards Sekhome.

"Who has told you about Sekhome?" asked the traitor, "that you should go to him? Does he ever slaughter? Does he ever make beer like a king? Are not his people thin and ill-favoured? Who then encourages you to go to him?" Pointing towards the Lake, he went on: "At the Lake there dwells a true chief, a man who really has a heart. Look at me. You know I fled from the wrath of Sebetuane. I arrived at the Lake in poverty and in terror, for it was the town of our enemies. But Lechulatebe has been a father to me. He did not make me a dog, but constituted me a great man; and people are silent when I speak in the council of the Batowana. As to meat, only Sebetuane excelled Lechulatebe in providing for his people; his men also drink pots of beer every day in the court-yard. I am a Lekololo; I am your brother; and I have come to assure you that if you want a father and a defender, you will find these in Lechulatebe." By such speeches, which he artfully adapted to suit the character of those whom he addressed, this envoy succeeded in his mission, and after some delay and negotiation, the Makololo gave up the idea of going south, and turned aside in the direction of the Lake. After they reached the Zouga, Lechulatebe's messenger, who of course acted as guide to the party, so managed matters as to succeed in separating the fighting men from the women and children and camp-followers carrying the baggage and driving the cattle. These were left on the eastern bank of the river; those were ferried over to the western side, where they were told Lechulatebe was advancing to meet them and to welcome them to his town. The guide, who was all the while secretly communicating with his master, took every step according to instructions which he received from him. When the tragedy was ripe for its final act, the guide one morning announced to his fellow-countrymen that a short march would now bring them to the presence of their future king. Lechulatebe, to show his attention to them, and his wish to receive them into his town, not as slaves, but as freemen, had come out to meet them, and he expected that in a little they would reach the royal party. A short time after this intimation, the guide stopped the Makololo, and, pointing to a thicket on the bank of the river, informed them that the great chief of the Lake country was there sitting in the shade, and waiting to receive them. "It will be necessary for you now," he added, "to lay aside your arms during the ceremony of being presented to the chief. It is not his custom to speak with men in arms." The Makololo at first demurred at this proposal, afraid of some plot. But when they came to consider their position, it seemed to them that they had now gone too far to return. Where were their women and children, their servants and cattle? They knew not. They had no boats by which again to reach them. If they resisted Lechulatebe now, they knew that they must lose all that was dear to them. And had they any true cause for alarm? Did not their guide smile at their hesitation, and assure them that they were only going to greet the chief, and receive refreshments from him? At length, half ashamed of their own hesitation, the now devoted Makololo went forward unarmed into the grove where Lechulatebe sat apparently surrounded by only a few attendants. And now the greeting commenced: the Makololo shouting out the praises of "the chief who befriends the strangers," the chief answering with hollow words of welcome. At a given signal from Lechulatebe, each surrounding bush poured forth its armed men, who completely overpowered the betrayed and helpless Makololo, and stabbed them to death with their assegais. Not one escaped, and only one youth was spared, whose sister, a member of Lechulatebe's harem, had pleaded for his life. The Makololo women, separated by forests and by the river from the scene of this tragedy, were conducted towards the town, entirely ignorant of the fate of their husbands. The servants followed, carrying on their heads the property of their murdered masters. The cattle were at once seized, and driven to Lechulatebe's posts. The Makololo refugees, who for a long period had resided with Lechulatebe, and who up to this time had enjoyed his protection and favour, were now one by one put to death on the nominal charge of witchcraft, until at length the insatiable assegai desisted, not because it was appeased, but because there no longer remained a Lekololo of birth or distinction to put to death!

Thus perished the Makololo from among the number of South African tribes. No one can put his finger on the map of Africa and say, Here dwell the Makololo. And yet this is the mighty people who more than forty years ago spread dismay in the neighbourhood of Kuruman—who in their northward journey conquered the Bangwakatse, the Bakwena, and other tribes in that region—who drove the Bamangwato before them like antelopes before the lion—whose track can be marked by the usual signs of savage conquest: the wasted towns, the devastated country, the silent grief of the widowed and orphaned captives. By the measure which they had meted out to others, was it now measured to them again. They had taken the sword and lived by it; by the sword they now perished. As long as the genius and resources of Sebetuane presided over their councils, prosperity attended their footsteps. This chief knew how to secure the affections of his vassals in peace, as well as to overcome his enemies in war. But Sebetuane had no successor. Sekeletu was a weakling; and pride, presumption, and effeminacy, characterized the children of Sebetuane's warriors.

I do not venture to affirm the presence of Divine retribution in this tragic end of the Makololo. Our Saviour discourages us from forwardness in interpreting the motives which influence the Divine mind. To those who would assert that the Makololo were sinners above all the tribes in their neighbourhood, and that therefore they suffered such things, our Saviour's sharp warning would seem to apply: "Except ye repent, ye shall all likewise perish." But in Bechuana-land, and especially among the heathen community in the northern part, the feeling is very general that the destruction of the Makololo, so soon after their inhospitable and perfidious conduct towards the missionaries, is to be traced to the vengeance of God. Nor is this mere theory in the native mind; for in some of our difficulties at Shoshong, which are hereafter to be mentioned, when sinister councils had well-nigh prevailed, some Gamaliel was sure to stand up and advise, "Let the missionary alone: the Makololo injured the missionaries, and where are the Makololo?"

Wooden Pillow—Zambese tribes.

CHAPTER XIII.

FIRST YEAR AT SHOSHONG.

ALTHOUGH I did not regard Shoshong as my permanent station in 1862, I proceeded, soon after my arrival, to build a temporary hut. I availed myself of the custom of the natives, and asked the chief to point out where I might build, which he was very willing to do. I bought nothing in connection with the building except the labour of the people who assisted me. The structure itself, whose outward appearance was more picturesque than symmetrical, was made of poles, plastered on both sides, and thatched with reeds. The house was divided into three rooms, to which a fourth was afterwards added. The kitchen was outside. Our "windows" were covered with white calico; they were therefore not very bright "eyes" to the house, but allowed of the free passage of "wind," so that our lowly abode was deliciously cool. When the hut was built we expected to occupy it only for a few months: it was however our only dwelling for three years.

Soon after my arrival, the Hanoverian missionary returned from the Transvaal country. I explained to him that I had been sent to Shoshong by the London Missionary Society, but that I hoped to be able to pierce farther into the interior next season. Mr. Price and I explained also that as we were to reside for some months in the midst of a large heathen population, we should of course engage in instructing the people. We expressed our willingness to co-operate with our Lutheran friend if he desired it, during the time we were together, and suggested that our teaching should not extend to the points upon which we differed. The other alternative was that we should ourselves conduct public worship and day-school in another part of the town. Mr. Schulenborg chose that we should co-operate with him, sharing the public services of the Sunday, and teaching certain classes in the school. Perhaps we had the best part of this bargain, for the points upon which we were to be silent did not bulk so largely in our creed as in that of our friend. It was no effort to us to keep sacraments and ceremonies in the background; but it was a different matter with our colleague. The arrangement, however, was carried on very harmoniously; and we all found scope and verge enough for our teaching in the cardinal truths of our religion, upon which we were truly agreed, and which it was of the first importance that the heathen should know. The London Society never censured us for taking this step; but I afterwards learned with regret that our friend's conduct had been disapproved of by his superiors. I even heard it hinted by others of his Society that our colleague was half suspected of having been inoculated during our co-operation with some of our dangerous "English views," and I could see that such a catastrophe as the slightest falling away from inherited Lutheranism would be deeply deplored.

In spite of all the charms and spells of the priests and doctors of Shoshong, small-pox made its appearance in the town at this time, the infection having been brought by some travellers from a village in the south, in which it was then raging. The early Dutch colonial records speak of an "infectious disease" as appearing among the Hottentots in 1663 and in 1666. Again in 1674 an "infectious disease" broke out among the people of a certain tribe. Perhaps these were fevers of an epidemic character, such as a few years ago visited the colony. In 1713 small-pox was introduced into the country from a vessel which had several cases on board. The disease seems to have committed fearful ravages at the Cape, probably such as I myself witnessed in Bechuana-land. The Rev. Mr. Valentyn, who was an eye-witness, describes it as a "sweeping pestilence." When it was at its height hundreds of natives were lying dead along the roads. In 1755 small-pox again visited the colony, and in Cape Town alone carried off 2000 people. In 1767 it returned, and numbered 1000 victims in Cape Town. In 1812 the wave again passed over the country; in 1831-2 it reappeared; and its last visit was that of 1858.

When we landed in Cape Town in 1858, this loathsome disease had just broken out, and was gradually spreading among the population of the town. The epidemic soon found its way into the country districts. Our own waggons were often looked upon with suspicion as we travelled northwards. On one occasion, one of the missionaries happened to unyoke his waggon for the night a little in front of the rest. We had difficulty in contradicting the story which was consequently spread by some Dutchmen who hastily rode past us, and who affirmed that the English missionaries had certainly the "pokjes" in their party, for one waggon had been drawn aside from the rest! But if this disease did not travel north so fast as we did, it nevertheless steadily followed us. It took four years to travel a thousand miles, turning aside to visit every glen and lingering at every farm-steading. A railway train can carry infection speedily, as it does everything else. But even diseases "take time to bait" in their progress through Africa. When the deadly wave, however, has rolled slowly over a district, it does not return for years. Hence the timidity of the country people in the colony, whose farms are widely separated. They placed in quarantine all strangers who approached their farm. They firmly believed that if they strictly isolated themselves until the tide of infection had passed their district, they would then be able without danger to mingle in general society. And they all trusted to this isolation, much more than to vaccination, which was unpopular among them.

On this occasion small-pox was accompanied by measles —where the one went the other was sure to follow. The two diseases were known in Bechuana-land by the same names, Sekoripane and Sekhonkhwane, the distinction being conveyed by the adjective "great" applied to small-pox, and "little" applied to measles. The names in Sechuana, like the word "measles," have reference to the "dotted" appearance of the skin of those suffering from these diseases.

I found that the Bamangwato were in the habit of inoculating for small-pox—sometimes in the forehead, but more frequently on the front of the leg, a little above the knee. It was no doubt unwise to inoculate in the forehead; but among those whose knees and arms were equally bare, the other Bamangwato custom was natural enough. As in other communities, however, a large number of people refused to bestir themselves in the matter. Sekoripane, they said, would kill those it intended to kill; and so they just let it alone. On several occasions I had received vaccine virus from the Colony, but had not succeeded with it. In order therefore to stay the ravages of the dreadful disease, we strongly recommended inoculation to Sekhome and his people, and offered to inoculate as many as came. We selected children with a mild form of the disease, some of whom indeed we found playing in the streets, and propagated that type by inoculation. We remembered that our own forefathers had done this for many a year before Dr. Jenner satisfactorily proved the value of vaccination. Sekhome, and most of the grown-up people, had had the small-pox on the occasion of its last visit to the country. "It killed me before," was the usual remark of such persons, pointing at the same time to the marks in their face. I inoculated several of Sekhome's sons, and also a good many people. Only one person, of those to whom I thus gave the disease, was compelled to take to bed, and he only for two days. But in such a large town the number of deaths was very great. The careless and the heedless who had not been inoculated, the poor people and the vassals, died every day. At length the people seemed to weary of burying the dead; especially in the case of friendless dependants. A long thong was tied to the body of such, which was dragged by this means behind some rock or bush, or into the dry bed of a ravine, and there left. The hyenas and tigers battened by night, the dogs and vultures and crows held carnival by day, on these exposed and putrefying corpses. Several times I stumbled over these hideous objects, and scattered the dogs from their revolting feast. I remonstrated with the chief, but little attention was paid. "The hearts of the people are dead within them," was the answer, and it really seemed to be so with many. After the disease had passed away, I met with several people in Shoshong and elsewhere who had become blind by the eruption appearing in the eye.

The wolf or spotted hyena (phiri) of Bechuana-land is a large and powerful animal. Its fore-quarters are especially strong; so that it can run with considerable speed with its prey in its mouth. Its jaw is also powerful, but the teeth are blunted by the bones which it is often compelled to break for food. It is very cowardly, is seldom seen in daylight, and at night is extremely cautious in its mode of attacks. A gentleman who had joined a party of elephant-hunters, for some reason or other used to make his bed away from the fire and his companions. When the hunters arrived at Shoshong this gentleman as usual slept apart. His friends were awoke in the middle of the night by the vehement shouts of Captain ——, round whose solitary bed (as the tracks testified next morning) a wolf had paced for some time, until at last it mustered courage to lay hold of the dressed skin which served as a mattress, and to drag off its sleeping prize as fast as it could! The shouts of the alarmed captive, and the noise of the half-wakened sleepers at the fire, induced the wolf to relinquish its hold. When the captain next made his bed, it was nearer the fire and his companions.

A boy who was for some time my own goatherd, had some years before been seized by a wolf, which had crept through the frail fence round his mother's dwelling. Holding the boy by the head, the wolf made for the mountain as fast as it could. The boy's screams awoke the neighbours, who followed in pursuit. The little fellow seems to have had all his wits about him, for he seized a sharp-edged stone against which his hand was dragged in the wolf's flight, and applying it to his captor's face and eye, induced it to let him go, when he was recovered by his mother and the neighbours. He lost an ear on this occasion, and received wounds on his head and face which would have killed many children. Another little child was taken by the wolf soon after we reached Shoshong, and was never seen again. The mother was annoyed in her house by "tampans," insects whose bite is more distressing than that of mosquitoes. Getting up in the night, she plied her brush on the floor of her hut, and having now well-nigh collected her tormentors, she asked her child to stand for a little outside the door while she swept them out. It so happened that a wolf was just passing the woman's hut at the time; it seized the child and made off with it to the hill. After feeding on human bodies for a considerable period during the prevalence of small-pox, it seemed as if these creatures grew bolder when the supply ceased. A grown-up woman was dragged away one night, and so severely bitten that she died in the course of next day. Sekhome actually came to me and proposed that the woman's body should be exposed next night, and that I should put some strychnine into the flesh! I encouraged the chief rather to give rewards for every wolf's skin that his people brought to him; and when he demurred, I myself offered four pounds of lead for every skin—the skin to remain in the natives' possession. At this time we were every night disturbed by the cackling and howling and hideous laughing of these hyenas. One Sunday evening our rest was disturbed by a specially loquacious fellow, who discoursed from the other side of the native town in front of our house, until I could stand it no longer, but had to go out half-dressed to chase it away. Round our own dwelling no hyena dared come. I had at this time a very fine dog, of no particular breed, but perhaps nearer to a mastiff than anything else. He had been trained to guard sheep in the Colony; and seemed to have a profound contempt for his nightly combatants. If one ventured to approach my calf-pen, Nero drove it back at once, following it for some distance, and finishing up with a note of triumph which I soon learned to recognise. In the middle of the night I have heard their first encounter—the retreat of the hyena—the note of triumph; and next minute I would hear faithful Nero sniffing about the door or the calico window, as if to indicate to me that he was at his post.

One evening Sekhome informed me that he was going to appoint two men to waylay the hyena beside the carcase of a horse which had that day died of "horse-sickness." It was therefore necessary for me to tie up my dog, otherwise no wolf could have passed. It was amusing to hear the whinings and pleadings of Nero, as he scented the approaching hyena, and was unable to go out to meet it. By and bye I heard the report of a gun, and going down to the place where the men had been stationed, found them groping about in the dark. They said they were sure they had wounded the wolf, and were expecting every moment to stumble over its body! I went and loosened Nero, and brought him to the place. He was not long in finding the wounded animal, and commenced barking about one hundred yards up the hill. The men did not seem inclined to go up, so I led the way.

As we approached the spot where Nero stood baiting the wolf, the man whose gun was still loaded came up to me and said, "You know how to fire better than I do; take the gun." The previous bullet had injured one of the wolf's legs, but it was still able to make progress up the hill. Nero however now laid hold of him, and a bullet from the flint musket settled the question. The Bamangwato actually ate this horrid creature, although it was believed by all to be the one which had carried away the little child. Latterly its food must have been rather of an indigestible description; the greater part of a lady's boot being one of the articles found in its stomach by those who skinned it! The skin of both this animal and of the baboon are sacred to the use of the doctors or priests. No common person dare wear them.

The rains were delayed till November this year; and as a dry spring is here always an unhealthy one, the ravages of small-pox were succeeded by fever and dysentery. Mr.

Price and I therefore sought a few days' change of air and scene for ourselves and our families in the open country of Mashue. As we had both purchased horses for our projected journey to the Zambese, we thought this a good opportunity for exercising both them and ourselves. One day Mr. Price left the waggons after breakfast to look for a giraffe or an eland, to supply the wants of our party. Some hours afterwards a Bushman made his appearance to say that elands were grazing close in our neighbourhood. My horse's back was in wretched condition when I bought it, and was not yet whole; but the message that the game was so near to the waggons made me improvise additional padding for the saddle, so as to protect the wound, and guided by the Bushmen and two of my own men, I started on the eland spoor. I found, however, that the track was not so fresh as I had been led to believe; and when some miles from the camp I saw from the tracks that Mr. Price had already lighted on it. While thinking of at once returning to the waggons, I was surprised to notice that the track of Mr. Price's horse led through places where a horse alone could go, but not with a rider upon it. On examining the tracks more carefully, we could see Mr. Price's own footmark on the ground. What had happened? If horse and rider had been thus separated, we must evidently hasten on and render assistance. So on we went for a considerable distance without reaching any solution of the cause of our anxiety. The Bushman now drew my attention to the setting sun and to a large thunder-cloud which seemed to advance in our direction. We reluctantly made our way for the camp, feeling that we could do no more to explain the mystery of the riderless steed.

Our own difficulties were soon to begin. We had gone much farther than I had thought. Darkness set in while we were still far from the waggons. In a short time no object whatever was visible. I could not see the Bushman in front of the horse, nor the horse's head, nor my own hand —for I held it out to try. By and bye the Bushman said he could no longer see the path, and was afraid he would wander. I encouraged him to proceed; and while we went on, rain began to fall in torrents. The Bushman now doggedly sat down with his back against the stem of a tree, and would go no farther. In order to avoid disputes, I suppose, he refused to answer me in Sechuana, speaking only Bushman, which I did not understand. I now dismounted, already thoroughly drenched with rain. The only thing that was dry was my gun, which was now our only protection in a country infested with lions. The rain fell steadily for about three hours. I held the horse's bridle myself, afraid lest, if affrighted, he should suddenly disengage himself from the hands of one of the men. When the rain abated we began to bethink ourselves of a fire. I had some very good matches. We now groped in likely places for dry grass or wood; but everything seemed to be thoroughly soaked. My matches were exhausted before we got the fire to burn. One of my men had a tinder-box; we set to work again, and again failed. The Bushman now began to move his limbs a little, and at length condescended to give us a piece of his mind. "The white man's fire is quick and bright, but it soon burns out. It is not made for the rain. The Bechuana's tinder-box needs a great deal of puffing and blowing, and ends in smoke and darkness. Make way for the Bushman." He now produced his hunting-bag, still nearly dry; how he had kept it so was to me a mystery. Its contents were perfectly dry. He sought the flat piece of wood in which the fire is produced, and placed it above some dry shavings of another and very inflammable tree, which he carried for the purpose. The slender rod which is used in producing the friction and the fire was next brought out; and to work the Bushman went, chanting meantime something which was possibly some spell or charm. Little bits of fire soon fell upon the shavings from the hole in which the friction-rod was revolving. When the operator thought there was enough of this fire produced, he commenced cautiously to blow, still keeping the flat piece of wood on the top. After failing once or twice, the Bushman succeeded in getting a fire. The next thing was to dry ourselves and our clothes, which was soon accomplished; and then we forgot our adventure in sleep, my saddle being a pillow and the soft moist sand a bed. Such a night in certain latitudes would give a person "his death of cold;" in Africa travellers often endure it, and are seldom the worse for it.

Next morning we hastened to the waggons to obtain an explanation concerning Mr. Price, and indeed to find if he had arrived at the camp. I found that my well-meant exertions had been entirely gratuitous, and that Mr. Price had reached the waggons at an early hour the previous afternoon! He had not met with any game, and after some hours' search, had saddled off his horse to let it graze for a few minutes before returning to the waggons. Now Bluebuck had an unfortunate trick of resisting all efforts to catch him when knee-haltered, until he found himself fairly surrounded. As on this occasion he had only his master to attempt to catch him, he could easily keep at a convenient distance, nibbling away at the grass in a provoking manner, and apparently enjoying the sport. At last Mr. Price was fain to carry the saddle himself, and drive his wilful horse before him, and in this fashion reached the waggons. This was the explanation of the mysterious tracks which had filled us with anxiety, and caused us to spend a dreary night in the rain and darkness. He whom we sought was comfortably ensconced in his waggon, whilst we, who flattered ourselves that we were to deliver him from some calamity, were benighted, and in our turn supposed to be lost!

But although Bluebuck had little ways of his own, which were not altogether pleasant, he was a fine strong horse, with wind which never failed. On this excursion, and mounted on Bluebuck, Mr. Price killed two giraffes, and I an oryx or gemsbuck, which is said to be the fleetest of the antelopes. I gave chase under the impression that the half-dozen creatures before me were elands, but as I approached I could see that they were gemsbucks or kukamas. I separated one from the rest, and Bluebuck seemed to enjoy his work, although at the last he needed considerable urging. We had a fine open country; the holes of the wild hog, and the trunks of fallen trees, being thus avoidable as we went along. All at once the gemsbuck turned sharp round, and stood on the defensive, its tongue visible in its open mouth, its nostrils dilated, its whole appearance betokening terror, anger, and exhaustion. In such circumstances, this animal is more combative than eland or giraffe. A bullet speedily ended its sufferings. In the gemsbuck I had secured a nobler prize than the eland, although the flesh of the latter would have gone further in supplying the wants of our party. Following the custom of the country, I tied the brush of the tail to Bluebuck's saddle. There are many fleet horses in Bechuanaland that cannot run down a gemsbuck.

As soon as the young grass began to appear, the horses which Mr. Price and I had purchased, as well as those bought by Sekhome for the purpose of hunting, fell sick, one after the other, of what is, by way of pre-eminence, called in Southern Africa "the horse-sickness." The horse is seen grazing in its usual health; an hour after it stands in the utmost distress, its eyes sunken, with a swelling above the upper eyelid; the breathing is rapid, laboured, and stertorous; froth fills the mouth and nostrils, and perspiration drops from the animal, which, however wild or skittish before, is tame enough now. This acute inflammation frequently runs its course in an hour or two. After death, a large quantity of a frothy, greenish-coloured liquid is discharged from mouth and nostrils. It is considered a good sign, if, when seized with this deadly disease, the horse coughs frequently, and brings up quantities of this froth. This cough often lingers weeks after the recovery is otherwise complete; but there is no discharge after the acute symptoms pass away. There is no cure for this disease; indeed, the seat of the disease itself does not seem to be very well understood. Examination of the horse after death throws little light upon the subject. The Dutch call it "gall-ziekte;" the English, inflammation. A medical friend gave me a prescription, which he said he had found successful in another part of the country. But at Shoshong it entirely failed. I sat up many a night with sick horses endeavouring to cure them. In one or two instances the disease was checked for the time, but in every case it returned afterwards with fatal result. Out of some seventeen which were passing their first summer at Shoshong, only one survived, which belonged to myself. A horse which has recovered from this sickness never gets it again, and, according to the colonial phrase, he is now a "salted horse." This term is used in certificates and other documents, and is taken to mean a horse which has recovered from the distemper. It is observed that when breeding is carried on in a district subject to the annual return of this disease, its ravages are more severe in the case of horses introduced from a distance than those reared on the spot. At Shoshong, several of the chief's horses are from a mare which he some years ago bought from a Dutchman. In the course of years acclimatization thus takes place, and the disease does not return every year. For instance, some of the districts which are now famous for rearing horses were unsuited for them in the time of Barrow's visit to the Cape, some seventy years ago. He mentions that in the Hautam the horse-disease committed great ravages, and that horses were safe only on the tops of mountains. Horses are now safe far to the north of this district; there is no annual return of the disease, although in a wet season it is still well known in the colony. The "salting" of the districts where the disease has thus become mitigated, does not stand good in the interior. I have known horses which have had the colonial form of the disease die in the interior of horse-sickness. There are some districts of the Transvaal where horses now live without being attacked by this disease, and in the course of years there is little doubt that this noble and useful animal will live in Bechuana-land and on the Zambese as it now exists in districts where formerly its death was certain. Horses were lately kept one summer on the top of one of the Bamangwato hills, where there was an ample plateau of grass, and the mountain was so surrounded with rocks and precipices that it was possible to confine them as in a cattle-pen. They were every day driven down to the water, and again hastily enclosed in their elevated sanatarium. That year not a horse was lost, but then not one of the animals was "salted." Next year they might all take the disease and die. The elephant-hunter likes a horse with which he can go anywhere, and at any season; therefore he will hazard a few horses in a deadly district in the hope that at least one will survive. In the colony you can buy a good horse for £10 or £15; the same animal, if salted, at Shoshong would fetch from £30 to £75.

One day Mogomotsi, a head man among the Bamangwato, and a constant attendant at church and school, came to my house with a miserable-looking Makalaka woman, who was unable to stand erect, but crept on her hands and knees. Mogomotsi explained that as he was coming down the kloof or gorge, he found a number of boys stoning the poor woman, shouting out Legoru! (thief) at the top of their voices. It seemed the woman, in the extremity of hunger, had stolen some sour milk from a "lekuka," or leathern bottle, which was hanging in the sun, and, being perfectly friendless and helpless, the cruel heathen children were stoning her in the river. Turning to the poor wounded creature, I found two bright eyes fixed upon me, half in terror, half in supplication. She had no relatives. Her friends or owners had cast her off. They said she might as well die, seeing she could no longer work for them. I noticed that in giving an account of herself she hesitated and stammered in her speech, and I learned that she had for some time been afflicted with St. Vitus's dance. Mogomotsi said,—now that the word of God had come to the town, it ought to prevent such cruel deeds, and therefore he had brought her to me. A short time after, Sekhome made his appearance to pay me a visit, followed by perhaps twenty of his head men. I showed him the woman, and told him how she had come to me. "It is well," said the chief carelessly; "if you care to feed such a creature as that you may do so." "But what I want to know is this," I said, profiting by previous knowledge; "if this woman should get well under my care, and her friends or owners, who have now cruelly cast her out, come and demand her back again, against her own will, what side will you, as chief of the town, take? I call you to witness that she has been stoned with stones, having been driven away by her own people. If she does not wish to return to them after her recovery, will you sanction their compelling her to do so?" Sekhome answered at once, "The woman is as good as dead; if you raise her up again she is yours. Her Makalaka masters cannot claim her again." Turning to his followers, he called them to witness that the woman was now the missionary's if she lived. There was a broad grin on every face as the attendants responded to Sekhome, and all seemed to think that too many words had been wasted on such a subject. Mabu (as she called herself) ensconced herself at once in the kitchen, and testified her gratitude by endeavouring to perform such little acts of service as she could render without walking, which was quite beyond her power. The regular supply of food, and some medicines given with the view of restoring and establishing her general health, produced a favourable change, and by and bye she was able to move a few paces. For a long time, however, her gait was decidedly zigzag; and it required some courage to pass her as she steered her uncertain course to the kitchen with a pot or other vessel in her hand. If Mabu, however, came to grief (which was not often), there was no louder or heartier laugh than her own. She strove to show her gratitude especially by her devotion to the wishes of Ma-Willie; and we were sincerely thankful that we were able to rescue a fellow-creature from a most cruel death, and introduce her to some of the enjoyments and privileges of a Christian household.

When we first resided in Shoshong we had little hope of being able to distinguish the Bamangwato by their features as one does in a crowd at home. They seemed to us to be all very much alike. But gradually as our eyes got accustomed to the colour of the people and to their dress, we began readily enough to distinguish between the features of one person and those of another. Indeed, we have since been often struck with the resemblance between certain Bamangwato and friends and acquaintances in our native country. I have sometimes called my wife, and without telling her my own opinion, asked her who a certain person was like who was then standing at the door? The resemblance has often been so striking, that it also occurred to my wife, who at once mentioned the name of the friend or acquaintance of whom I had been thinking. Of course we were never guilty of the indiscretion of informing our friends in England that we had found their African counterpart! I was amused to find that the Bechuanas are equally bewildered at first among a number of white men. "How can I know him?" I have heard a native frequently say; "these white people are all so like one another." After having resided for years in the town, I frequently heard discussions in passing which showed that I was not readily recognised by the people.

Our Hanoverian colleague left again for the south after a short residence on the station; and in the beginning of 1863 Mr. Price started for supplies for our projected journey into the interior. I was thus left in charge of the station, and had some months of quiet and steady work—teaching during the week and preaching on the Sunday. I began to find that my knowledge of medicine greatly increased my influence with the people, and would be of real service to me as a missionary. The successful treatment of a case of fever in a near relative of Sekhome became widely known; and I found that the native doctors themselves came to me for advice. This young woman's fever had been improperly treated; and when I was called I found that she was considerably reduced and in high delirium. Afraid that I had come to kill her, she darted past me like an arrow, and endeavoured to make off. She refused to take the medicine I prescribed until her attendants told her it was not mine but Sekhome's. As soon as she came to herself and found out who had been her benefactor, she was as lavish of her expressions of gratitude as she had formerly been of her curses.

Another case illustrates the character of the people, and the manner in which our influence was extended. An old man with weak eyes, hearing of the cures of ophthalmia which had been effected by simple lotions, requested Sekhome to introduce him to me. "Be your own introducer," said the chief; "your sore eyes will speak for you; the teacher will be sure to give you 'eye-water.'" The old man made his appearance at the door of our hut, and begged for medicine for his eyes. I gave him a lotion which did not colour the water in the cup, and told him how it was to be used. "But, Monare," said the man, "this is nothing but water." I told him to try it when he got home, and he would find it was an eye-lotion. He laid down the cup in displeasure, remarking that he was an old man, and did not like to be a laughing-stock for a boy—meaning myself. So away he went to report in the court-yard how he had been slighted by the missionary, who would give him nothing to use for his eyes but pure water in a cup. The chief and several other head men at once saw the mistake which he had made, and sent him back again. "I am ordered to take away your water," said the man to me, meaning that he still adhered to his own opinion, but had been commanded to use the lotion by the chief. Wishing to enjoy his surprise, I now poured some into his eyes; and as he had been very opinionative, and expected only pure water, the smartness of the lotion was increased by the suddenness of his surprise. The value of an eye-lotion, in the estimation of Bechuanas, is in proportion to the pain it gives in the eye. This old man went off to the court-yard with the cup in his hand, to show everybody how the white man had "charmed" pure water, and made it very "bogale" or powerful. His idea was, that if there was anything mixed in the water, it would be visible.

CHAPTER XIV.

THE MATEBELE RAID.

When the traders and hunters passed Shoshong from Moselekatse's country at the end of the hunting season of 1862, they brought the report that the Matebele meditated an attack upon the Bamangwato as soon as the rains should fall. Native wars are seldom or never carried on in winter. The waters are then too scarce on the road; the weather is too cold; and there are few edible roots procurable on the way, and no fruits standing in their enemies' gardens to supply the army with food. Dutchmen on the other hand, as we saw in the war with the Batlaping, never attack till winter comes, in order that they may be able with safety to use their horses. Since the first unsuccessful march of Dutchmen on foot against Hottentots near to Cape Town, soon after the arrival of the former in the country, horses have been regarded as indispensable to the success of a commando or war party. The Dutch carry their own supplies of food in their waggons, which always accompany them on such occasions; and the cold, which is not much felt by the Dutchmen, almost paralyses their enemies in the winter mornings.

The past history of the Bamangwato gave them no reason to presume on the friendship of the Matebele. They had dared to be independent—had rescued their cattle when in the hands of machaha, and instead of submitting to pay tribute had put the Matebele tax-gatherers to death. Still, twenty years had intervened since these events had taken place. Missionaries were now residing with Moselekatse; and peaceful trading waggons passed every year to Matebele-land. Although Sekhome had opposed the entrance of Mr. Moffat into Moselekatse's country, both he and his people had lent a certain amount of credence to the messages which Mr. Moffat had brought back from their old enemy. Moselekatse informed Sekhome once and again that he had laid his spear in the water (which is the same as to beat it into a pruning-hook); that the Bamangwato might sleep; and that their cattle-posts might without fear be extended towards the confines of his territory. The Bamangwato showed their confidence in these protestations, by advancing as far as the river Motloutse with their cattle, which left about two days' journey between them and the Batalowta at Mahuku's town, who were vassals of Moselekatse, and at the same time relatives and friends of some of the Bamangwato.

Between the Matebele country and the Bamangwato there stretched an irregular line of Makalaka towns, the inhabitants of which spent a most wretched existence, having the difficult task to perform of serving two masters. They were in the power of the Matebele, who entered their towns when they chose, depriving them of their children as soon as they grew up to be of use. On the other hand, it was their interest to keep up friendly intercourse with their old masters, the Bamangwato, because if Moselekatse's rule became intolerable, they hoped to be received into the town of the Bamangwato. Sometimes in the same Makalaka town there would arrive scouts from the two opposing tribes, the Matebele and the Bamangwato, to "hear the news." In such circumstances the Bamangwato messengers, who were often themselves Makalaka by birth, were passed off as inhabitants of a neighbouring Makalaka town, or if they were Bamangwato, and unable to speak the Sekalaka language, they were hidden in a hut or amongst the rocks, until the Matebele soldiers left. The intolerable severity of the Matebele has broken up this line now, the people having fled to the Bamangwato for protection; but in 1862 there was a considerable Makalaka population stretching along the southern and south-western boundary of Moselekatse's country. When the Bamangwato herdsmen advanced northwards with their cattle, they trusted to the assistance of these Batalouta and Makalaka to give them secret warning of the Matebele plans. A little uneasiness had been excited among the Bamangwato by the flight from Shoshong of an under-chief called Kirekilwe, who was related to the Batalowta at Mahuku's, and who was not long at the latter place when he passed on to Moselekatse's residence. Sekhome at once said, when he heard the reports of war brought out by the traders, "If war takes place, it will be through the treachery of Kirekilwe."

On Thursday the 5th March definite intelligence reached Shoshong that a Matebele army was on its way to attack the Bamangwato. Already the farthest advanced cattle-posts of the latter tribe had fallen into their hands, and some of the herds had been put to death while defending their charge. A village of the inoffensive and industrious Machwapong had also been destroyed, only two of its inhabitants escaping to tell the tale. Such was the story told Sekhome by the dust-covered messenger, who himself had nearly fallen into the hands of the Matebele. Not knowing what was going on, I arrived in the public courtyard while the man was speaking, having finished my work in the school for that day. Sekhome recapitulated the items of the unwelcome intelligence to me, and to his sons, who had come with me from school.

By order of the chief a man at once ascended some

rocks at the outskirts of the town, and sounded loud and shrill the war-cry of the Bamangwato. Disturbed in their mid-day repose, in their skin-dressing and kaross-making, the men of the town obeyed the unwonted summons, and streamed into the kotla or court-yard, some armed with guns, and others with assegais and ox-hide shields. The news was laid before the people, and steps were at once taken to collect the cattle from the various posts, with the sheep and goats. All were to be driven toward the Bamangwato mountains, there being at this season of the year both grass and water on its lofty plateaus and within its hidden ravines. While some were despatched to the posts, others were sent as sentinels to guard the paths radiating from the town, and a few picked men were sent forward as spies, to find out the present position of the enemy. Having made all such arrangements, the chief now turned his attention to the force available for the defence of the town. Some parties were still in the country at their cattle-post or their hunting station; and while their friends were afraid that they would be cut off, the chief lamented their absence from their various regiments. Marching out of the town at the head of his men, Sekhome held what might be called a review, although it was certainly a different spectacle from what is indicated by that expression in civilized countries. There was no marching, no defiling, no sham fighting; but the chief, squatted on the ground, dealt out ammunition, etc., to those who required such supplies, inspected the faulty lock of one gun, and the frail stock of another,—all the while inquiring after the absent, conversing with those around him, and listening to the account of the herdsmen who continued to arrive, and who had fled for their life after leaving their charge in the hands of the Matebele.

In passing my house after holding this "review," Sekhome jocularly asked me if I were going to help him against the Matebele? I replied in the negative, and reminded him that I was a promulgator of peace and goodwill amongst men; that I had no quarrel with the Matebele, and that I was persuaded they also would regard me as a neutral party. His reply was to the effect that Matebele warriors did not make nice distinctions, and that the colour of a man's skin was not easily discovered in the darkness of night. He then informed me that they expected to be attacked during the night or very early in the morning. "In olden time," added the chief, "whilst our herdsmen were still informing us of the loss of our cattle, the Matebele themselves fell upon us before we could make any preparation for self-defence; but to-night they will find us ready; and should they choose to enter the town from the plain they will find it empty."

Sekhome having given orders that all the women and children should take refuge on the mountains, and that all property should be removed thither also, a strange and melancholy spectacle presented itself to the eye. The several narrow paths leading to the top of the steep rugged mountains were for some time densely crowded with those fleeing from the bloodthirsty Matebele. Many mothers carrying large bundles on their heads had also a child on their back, while the rest of the family struggled up the ascent before them. For some time the old men and women and servants and children followed each other up the hill as closely as people do in Cheapside. It will be remembered that my fellow-missionaries, with their families, were then absent from the station. That night therefore Mrs. Mackenzie was the only female in the town of the Bamangwato, and our children the only little ones who had not been removed to the mountain fastnesses.

People passed to and fro the whole night under arms; every one was on the alert, and we slept as little as the Bamangwato. About ten o'clock the young chiefs paid us a visit, with several of those who attended church and school—surrounded by whom I offered up prayer before our door in the bright moonlight. I besought a blessing on those who fought for home and family and property; and prayed that God would frustrate the counsels of the nation delighting in war. Fully expecting that an engagement would take place before we met again, I said to Khame in parting that I hoped it would be seen that those who feared God would be found to be the bravest in defence of all that was dear to them. During the night we collected our letters, portraits, accounts, etc., in a little box so as to be easily removed. My wife also selected some provisions, which, with the children's clothes, were placed in readiness in case of sudden alarm. Although we could not sleep like our children, we could commend them and ourselves to the merciful protection of God, our heavenly Father, and enjoy the peace of those whose minds are stayed on Him.

Friday.—At length the morning dawned without any attack having taken place. The cattle, sheep, and goats from the outposts came pouring in, and were hastily driven up the mountains. The "kloof" for a time resounded with the lowing of cattle, the bleating of sheep and goats, and the shouts of their drivers. This morning, in stating his plan of defence, the chief informed me that, should the enemy make the attempt from the plain, they were to be allowed to enter the town, and to set it on fire if they chose; that a number of cattle were to be kept in sight (as a bait for the Matebele) on the side of the mountain behind Mr. Price's house, and opposite my own; and that the fight would therefore take place, as it were, on our premises. Sekhome said he was sure to beat them on this ground; and that should they approach from the plain, he would not risk an engagement elsewhere. He added that he was sorry our houses were in the way, but that he could not help it. In the event of the Matebele endeavouring to reach the town from the north side, which was nearest the scene of their depredations, the Bamangwato were to meet them on a "haugh" in the heart of the mountains, and, if beaten, were to fall back on the vantage-ground before referred to.

After seriously considering our position in connection with the statement of Sekhome, and taking into account the merciless character of the Matebele, I came to the conclusion that it would be best for my family to retire to the mountains until the danger became less imminent. When I heard one cattle-herd after another narrate the cowardly and bloody deeds which had been enacted at the cattle-posts, my resolution was confirmed. Whilst they remained in the house I could not but feel uneasy as to the result of a midnight rush of such savages, every one of whose spears had repeatedly drunk the blood of the aged and the decrepit, the defenceless female and the tender infant. "Let Ma-Willie go on the mountain beside my mother," said the sincere and affectionate Khame, the eldest son of Sekhome, "and the Matebele will then reach her only when we are all dead." I consented to this, and my young friend kindly furnished me with a few men, who conveyed to the top of the mountain the articles which we had resolved to remove from the house. Accompanied by these people and by our servants, Mrs. Mackenzie with the newly-wakened and wondering children took her departure at early dawn. I afterwards followed with the cattle, and found my little family seated on the grass beneath a tree, their nearest neighbour being the chief wife of Sekhome. It was Wednesday evening of the following week before they left their refuge on the mountain top; and the native women remained for two or three days longer.

I cannot describe this life on the mountain as having been at all pleasant; for the place itself was well known to be a haunt for wolves and tigers; in fact, but a few days before, a sheep had been killed in daylight not many hundred yards from where Mrs. Mackenzie and the little ones slept in the open air. But we heard nothing of such unwelcome visitors, and cannot but think that the overwhelming rush of people into their haunts must have driven both wolves and tigers to seek a lair elsewhere.

It was my intention to remain in the house during the night, that, in the event of an attack, I might be able to inform the assailants that the premises belonged to a missionary; but such was my wife's description of her first night on the mountain, alone with her little ones, that I considered it necessary afterwards to form one of the party. Our house was thus left without an occupant during the night; but Mabu, the woman whose life we had saved a few months before, slept on the premises. Although able to have gone with her mistress, she was still weak, and preferred to remain among our pots; and we allowed her to do what she pleased. I have to record, to the credit of the Bamangwato, that although Mr. Price's premises were now entirely deserted, and my own left in the charge of a single woman, no attempt at theft was made.

While we were scaling the mountains on Friday morning, the Bamangwato had assembled in the haugh already referred to. It seems there was a good deal of talking among the head men, and Sekhome, who besides being chief is also "ngaka" (doctor or sorcerer), engaged earnestly in reading his dice, and repeating his incantations. He was interrupted by Khame, who very abruptly informed his father that he was taking up too much time with these things; and that as for himself, he (Khame) wished to fight and have done with it. The

Scott & Ferguson Edin.

REFUGE ON THE MOUNTAIN.

chief, who felt proud of his son, "pocketed" the insult which in his priestly character he had sustained, and immediately ordered out the two youngest "mepato" or regiments, viz., that of Khame and of his brother Khamane. The people were pleased with the conduct of their young chief, and several old men, who of course did not belong to his regiment, tried to join it as it moved off, but were seen by Sekhome, and ordered back. The two chiefs next in rank to Sekhome however attached themselves to Khame's party, followed by their men.

So far as I can judge, the whole force under Khame did not exceed two hundred. Of these, the majority had guns, and about eight were mounted on horseback. Before he rode off, Khame was addressed by Sekhome, to the effect that he must not imagine he was going on an elephant hunt; that he was marching against men, and not merely men, but Matebele.

It was late in the afternoon before the Bamangwato came in sight of the Matebele, who, contrary to their usual custom, had been advancing slowly, apparently in no hurry to attack the town. They were marching in three companies, two of which were together, and these the Bamangwato attacked.

At first the machaga (Matebele soldiers), who were armed with spears and shields, made light of the guns, imitating their report; but they soon changed their mind. Moving in compact bodies, they found that every ball told on some of them; so that, when charged by those on horseback they gave way, some of them throwing down their arms and fleeing. These, however, were rallied by the others shouting to them that they were disobeying the great law of Moselekatse, which forbids any of his warriors to run from the enemy. But while the day was thus with the Bamangwato, the third company of Matebele, which had been following up a cattle-track at some distance, hearing the report of fire-arms, hastened to the scene of action, and seeing how matters were going, crept along under cover of the tall grass, until they got close behind the Bamangwato. They advanced until they were discovered, when they sprang to their feet, and, raising their wild war-cry, rushed as one man on the forces of Khame. The retreating Matebele, finding that their comrades had come to their assistance, turned round on their pursuers; so that now the Bamangwato found themselves surrounded by the enemy. Khame shouted to his men to keep together and fight their way out; but his authority was soon at an end. Many of the older Bamangwato men had shown symptoms of fear from the beginning, and fought only after they saw that Khame and his young comrades were gaining the day. Now, when they beheld machaga on every side, the old fear of the Matebele seemed to return to them, and they fled in all directions, the horsemen doing their best to cover their retreat. The Matebele did not pursue them far; and the Bamangwato returned during the night, leaving about twenty dead on the field. According to trustworthy reports afterwards received, the loss on the other side was much greater.

Late on Friday night, Patopato, a Matebele refugee, who had long resided under Sekhome's protection, and who had been sent as a spy to observe the movements of the advancing Matebele, returned with the message that a detachment of the enemy was on its way round the mountain; and that therefore the attack on the town might be expected from the plain on the south of the town.

Keeping watch over my premises, I heard about midnight the shrill war-cry rise from the rocks near the kotla. It resounded through the deserted town, was re-echoed by the mountains, and caught up and repeated by the sentinels on the heights. Every one took it for granted that an engagement was at hand. My wife told me that she had been surrounded by native women a minute before the cry was heard; in a few minutes more she found herself alone with her three children on the mountain top. She could see nothing in the moonlight but the rocks, into whose dark caverns her companions had suddenly rushed.

Out of many incidents which occurred in the fight, I shall narrate one or two. Pelutona, one of the chief men who went with Khame, being very fat, and on foot, soon fell behind in the retreat, and would have been killed but for the gallant conduct of one of his men. This devoted servant put himself between his master and his pursuers, saying to the former, "Now, take a good breathing, they have to kill me first, and before they do so you will be well rested, and able to escape." Instead of firing at once at the Matebele (who by this time had a very wholesome dread of the guns), this man kept them at a distance by now and then pointing his musket at them, until at length, thinking they were now too far from the main body, and seeing that the Bamangwato were no longer afraid of them, the Matebele gave up the chase.

In the course of the retreat of the Bamangwato, one of them found himself at some distance from the others, and closely pursued by a Letebele. His gun was loaded, and cocked too, but he had not courage enough to enable him to stand and fire; so he ran as fast as he could, carrying his gun on his shoulder. To the surprise of both pursuer and pursued, something having caught the trigger, bang went the gun, its terrified bearer still running at the top of his speed. Whether the ball had passed somewhat near to the Letebele behind is not known, but at any rate he at once gave up the pursuit, evidently of opinion that he was altogether too dangerous a fellow who could thus fire over his shoulder without slackening his pace.

Another man was brought to me five days after the battle with nine spear wounds, all deep, and one completely maiming one of his legs. He said he had shot three Matebele, but was surrounded while re-loading, his gun taken from him, and he himself repeatedly stabbed, and left for dead. Coming to himself during the night, he crawled out of the way to a place of safety, but it took him five days to get home, as he could not walk. I dressed his wounds, which, being all clean cuts, soon healed, and in a few weeks the man was quite well.

Saturday.—Among other things which I had conveyed to the mountain was my medicine-chest, for which I felt sure I should find some use. A man called Ralitau made his appearance at our retreat to-day, carrying a Letebele spear as a trophy. Pointing to his arm, I saw that it had been pierced above the elbow, and the man explained that it was done by the spear which he carried in his hand. He was one of four men in charge of a flock of sheep and goats, which they had driven to the top of a hill in the neighbourhood of the Machwapong. On the approach of the Matebele, two of his companions fled, and the third was killed. While endeavouring to make his escape, Ralitau was confronted by a Letebele. Both discharged their missiles at once. The bullet from Ralitau's gun missed the Lechaga himself, but it drove his shield out of his hand. The spear of the Letebele pierced Ralitau's arm, and stuck in it. Hastily pulling it out, the herdsman challenged the Letebele to combat with his own spear, exclaiming, "We have now a spear each, and neither of us has a shield : come on!" The Letebele declined the combat ; and Ralitau was proud of both spear and wound.

It was confidently expected by the Bamangwato that

to-day they would be attacked, and their expectations were confirmed by the report of the scouts that the Matebele were advancing. It was taken for granted that after enemies whom they formerly despised as unworthy of their steel, had met them in the open plain, the Matebele warriors would consider themselves in honour bound to vindicate their character by destroying the town and gardens of those who had been guilty of such temerity. But the day and night passed, and Sabbath dawned, and still the Matebele came not.

Sunday.—I conducted divine service in my house, the congregation under arms, and momentarily expecting the news that the attack had begun. Strange to say, I had that morning come, in the course of regular expositions of the Sermon on the Mount, to the 43d and 44th verses of the fifth chapter of Matthew: "Ye have heard that it hath been said, Thou shalt love thy neighbour and hate thine enemy. But I say unto you, Love your enemies; bless them that curse you, do good to them that hate you, and pray for them which despitefully use you, and persecute you." This was the "lesson of the day" for my congregation as they stood round me in arms. I endeavoured to explain to them that the covetousness and selfishness, which were at the bottom of all aggressive wars, would yet be overcome by the power of Christianity in the world, teaching men to love their neighbours as themselves. But in the meantime, while tribes existed which still revelled in bloodshed, and lived after the manner of beasts of prey, their neighbours must stand on the defensive. It was as reasonable for a man to defend his person and his home from the assegai of midnight assassins as from the assault of lion or snake. God had given the man a stronger body than the woman, that he might work for her and defend her. A man's mother, or wife, or sister, ought to be reached by enemies only over his lifeless body. But the spirit of the covetous man engaged in an aggressive war, and that of the Christian man defending his family and his home, were widely different. The one was a dark and murderous spirit, finding satisfaction in pillage, in outrage, and in bloodshed. The other was a noble and worthy feeling, stern to the assailant, and yet regretful because it was necessary to defend human life at such a cost. Aggressors fought for what was before them, and not their own, the possessions and the homes of their neighbours. The defenders fought, not for anything before them, or in the possession of others, but in defence of what was their own, and dear to their hearts, in their homes behind them. Gloomy malice filled the heart and blackened the visage of the one combatant; mildness and calm determination animated the other. The one desired only the ruin and destruction of his adversaries; the other went forth to fight that he might preserve and build up, and cherished no hatred in his breast towards his misguided fellow-men. "Thus," I concluded, "while you defend yourselves and your relatives from the Matebele, do not give way to the spirit of revenge. Wish well to the Matebele. Wish that they may give up war, and visit you only on peaceful errands. Wish that the teaching and spirit of Jesus Christ may find its way into their hearts, and prevent them from coming to desolate the homes of their neighbours any more." We concluded by an earnest prayer for the Matebele, in which I feel assured I was heartily joined by some of my audience. The lesson of that morning was communicated to many who were not assembled for worship. "The teacher had said that God would bless and help those whose minds were not filled with covetousness, but who were only defending their own homes and families." Sekhome himself came and expressed his pleasure at the "word" which had been spoken, and said that "I must pray very much that God would help them, and give them the victory." The Bamangwato head men came also to speak of the bravery and cheerfulness of the young chiefs and others who were members of the congregation. "We were told," said they, "that when a man became a Christian he was bound not to fight in any cause, and that his relatives would have to defend the believer as well as his wife and family. We therefore expected that all the 'men of the word of God' would have ascended the mountain with the women and children. But to-day those who pray to God are our leaders."

"In forbidding covetousness," said an old man, "the word of God stops all war, for all Bechuana wars are begun through covetousness."

In my own retirement I craved that wherever the lessons which I ventured to teach in the name of Christ fell short of what He himself would have given at Shoshong, he would mercifully forgive, and lead His servant into full obedience to His will.

As one means of putting an end to this state of suspense, the idea occurred to me this morning to visit the Matebele camp, with the undefined hope that earnest expostulation might avert further bloodshed. I communicated my desire to Khame and some other Bamangwato, but they unanimously urged me not to go; that my counsels would be unheeded, and my own life placed in danger. They said that when the Bamangwato horsemen first made their appearance on the battle-field, the Matebele called out, "These are 'Makhoa'" (white men), and that some might still labour under this impression. Out of curiosity I called two Matebele refugees, and laid the matter before them. I asked them, if they were still in the Matebele army, and while on duty as sentinels saw me approaching their camp, what would they do? would they waylay me in the long grass, or meet me openly and demand my business? The men seemed puzzled; hesitated some time; looked at my face and then at one another; and at last replied, that they thought that they would show themselves to me and demand my business. On some one asking them if they had taken into account the facts of the late engagement, especially in connection with the terror inspired by the horsemen, the countenances of the two Matebele assumed a rather embarrassed aspect, and they at length answered, "Your reception would depend very much on the individual character of the advanced sentinels." "Does the teacher know," continued one of them, "that it is reckoned an honour among my former comrades to kill a white man? It is only old Matebele that can boast of having done so. Then in the event of any investigation by the chief, it would be easy to say that they thought you were a Boer, or even a native spy." Their manner as much as the words of their answer, induced me to relinquish the idea, for I was convinced that the risk incurred in taking this step was not counterbalanced by any well-grounded hope that my advice would be taken. I remembered that the army of the Matebele had left their country in opposition to the expressed, or at any rate well understood, wishes of Messrs. Thomas and Sykes, and I had no grounds for supposing that a stranger would have more influence with them than their own missionaries, or that they themselves would be more open to reason after the irritation of a fight in which one half of their army had been forced to retreat before enemies whom they despised, than they were before they left their own country.

It rained heavily during the night of Sunday; it was as dark as pitch, and in every way suitable for deeds of blood. My poor wife had to draw herself and the children into small compass below the bush, for the kaross above did not afford much shelter. I spent the weary hours of the night over our fire, which consisted of one huge log, the burning end of which the rain failed to extinguish. Now was the time for the Matebele to attack; for the fire-arms of the Bamangwato got more or less out of order through exposure to the rain, especially the old-fashioned flint muskets, whose owners had frequently nothing but a tattered handkerchief with which to cover the lock. To the astonishment of all, the night, which had been one of discomfort and anxiety, passed over in peace. Early in the morning, however, Sekhome's advanced sentinels brought the intelligence that the Matebele had advanced to the foot of the mountains, within a few minutes' walk of the place where the Bamangwato lay in waiting for them. Every one was in readiness for immediate action. The chief gave orders that no cattle should descend from the hill to drink. We could distinctly hear the report of the guns fired by the Matebele, being those which had fallen into their hands in the fight.

After an hour or two spent in this way, it became evident that the enemy did not intend to advance on the town. They were reported as eating water-melons, and destroying what they could not eat in the outlying Bamangwato gardens. It was evident that they were ready again to fight in the open plain; and it was equally plain that they were afraid to venture into the narrow passes leading into the town of the Bamangwato. In a short time the report came that the enemy was moving off, and afterwards it was ascertained that they were retracing their own steps, and not, as it was imagined, moving round the mountain to the more accessible side of the town. The news had a wonderful effect in brightening up the countenances of the Bamangwato, although they were not without suspicion that the retreat was a feint; and that, as in olden time, the Matebele would return when they thought their enemies would be off their guard. Men were therefore selected for the purpose of following the enemy and watching their movements. They were to sleep where they slept, and in the event of their returning to the attack, were to hasten before them and inform the chief. On Tuesday morning a second party was sent off; and in the afternoon the first returned, bringing the intelligence that the Matebele were still retreating. On Wednesday, it was ascertained that the oxen, sheep, and goats which they had secured, and which had remained at a distance under strong guards, were being collected by their captors, who were now in full retreat homewards. Feeling convinced that all danger was now over, we that evening re-entered our house, thankfully cherishing the hope that the disturbance and anxiety were now at an end.

On Thursday the message was brought to Sekhome, that a Letebele, found without spear or shield, had been taken prisoner, and that they awaited his orders as to his fate. The order was that he should be put to death. I learned this from Khame, who said the men who were to kill him had already left the town. I immediately sought the chief, but was kept waiting some time. At length he appeared, and I expostulated with him both as to the cruelty and bad policy of such conduct. He at once despatched a messenger to countermand his order, professing that he had given me the man's life. But what was my regret while I was still in the courtyard to see the men first despatched advance into the kotla, and announce that the chief's command had been obeyed. The poor defenceless wretch had been put to a cruel death, although, as I afterwards learned, he pleaded with pitiable earnestness that his life should be spared. I was gratified to find that all who attended church were opposed to such revengeful bloodshed. Indeed, it was with the idea that

I might be able to save the man's life that the young chief had informed me of the circumstance. This was certainly acting in the spirit of our last Sunday's discourse.

In this incursion the warriors of Moselekatse more than sustained their character for bloodthirstiness. They butchered old men, women, and little children, at the Bamangwato cattle-posts. Young women and boys they spared, driving them as captives; the former to cultivate their gardens and the latter to be trained as "machaga," or warriors.

About a fortnight after the departure of the Matebele, Sekhome organized and secretly despatched a party of his best men to "lift" the cattle from posts lying to the south-east of the Matebele country. Of course it was a dangerous expedition, it being very easy for the Matebele to have intercepted them on their return. But the Bamangwato relied on being out of reach before the army, which they knew had been sent for a time to the north-west of Moselekatse's country, could be led against them. And in this hope they were not disappointed. After more than a month's absence they arrived with the oxen of two large Matebele posts, and a drove of sheep and goats. The chief kept this business a secret from me, as also from Khame; it being given out that the men had gone to collect the Bushmen who had been scattered by the Matebele. On the arrival of the party, Sekhome, who professed to be ashamed to come himself, sent Khame with the message that he knew I should blame him; but that he wished to obtain something in place of the cattle which the Matebele had stolen from him. On this occasion Khame refused what must have been to him a most tempting present, in the shape of a handsome number of the stolen cattle. He told his father that he disapproved of the expedition, and would not share its spoils.

CHAPTER XV.

JOURNEY TO MATEBELE LAND.

On the arrival of my friends Messrs. Price and J. S. Moffat at Shoshong, in the end of June 1863, our consultations were not, as we had at one time hoped they would be, concerning the mission to the north of the Zambese, but with reference to the continuance of the mission already established among the Matebele. It was nearly a year since we had heard from Messrs. Sykes and Thomas, the missionaries at Inyate, and their last letters had contained the mournful intelligence of the death of Mrs. Thomas from fever. Mr. and Mrs. J. Moffat were extremely anxious to proceed to the assistance of their friends; but the disturbed state of the country presented an obstacle to their proceeding alone. After protracted deliberation, "it was thought necessary," as I wrote to the Directors at the time, "temporarily to reinforce the Matebele mission at this unsettled juncture, on account of the indifferent health of some members of the mission, and the contemplated absence of others from the scene of their labours. The Directors, I thought, would agree that it would be very unadvisable for any one family to be left alone in such a country as the Matebele; and it was in order to prevent this possibility that I undertook the present journey. My own health was very good; and it was some time since Mrs. Mackenzie had had an attack of fever. We were therefore happy in making the present attempt; hoping that, having assisted the Matebele mission to weather a storm, our own path for the future would be made plain to us." In fact, I was not without hope that I might afterwards meet with such encouragement as would induce me to remain in the Matebele country, or to visit some of the tribes beyond it. Although it was abundantly evident that the traditional war policy of the Matebele was not to be given up all at once by the chief and people, I also hoped to be able to represent to Moselekatse some of the evil consequences of war with the Bamangwato, in stopping communication between the Matebele and the south, from which quarter they were annually visited by European traders. Sekhome gave me a half-defiant message to Moselekatse, in which he compared himself to a certain insignificant but pertinacious insect, well known to both Matebele and Bamangwato; but I consulted my own feelings and Sekhome's interests by not delivering it.

We left Shoshong about the middle of July. We had not gone two days from the station when we met a second war-party of Bamangwato, who were driving before them sheep and goats which they had captured at the Matebele outposts. We were afraid that this pertinacity on the part of Sekhome to secure something in place of his stolen cattle, might bring down the signal vengeance of the haughty Zulu chief, who was not accustomed to such reprisals from a Bechuana adversary. At Palatshwe, about three days from Shoshong, we came to the large enclosures which the Matebele had built for the reception of the stolen cattle of the Bamangwato. Here Mangwane, the son of Moselekatse, had his headquarters, while the Matebele forces were scouring the country. During the rest of our journey, not a day passed that we did not see in these fresh cattle-pens along the road, the evidence of the recent presence in the country of the warlike people to whom we were journeying.

The country lying to the north-east of Shoshong is intersected by a number of rivers which are all tributaries of the Ouri or Limpopo. The Mahalapye flows close to the Bamangwato mountains, and was the first of these rivers which we crossed. The Mitle and the Teuane were only a few miles beyond; and the Lotsane, with its bed of slate rock, was the next river on our route. To our east the tsetse is found over a wide expanse of country, leaving, however, many unoccupied tracts within the radius of its habitat. At a place called Tshakane the fly approaches close to the waggon road; indeed the Bamangwato asserted it was on the road itself. But we saw nothing of it, and it had probably shifted its quarters with the game, which of course every year became less numerous on frequented highways. Near to Serule we passed the ruins of a village whose inhabitants had been killed or scattered by the Matebele. Not a soul was visible in the country—not a fresh human foot-mark on the sand. The broad trail of the Matebele soldiers had swept all life before it.

Before reaching Seribe river, which joins the Motloutse a short distance below the road, a troop of buffaloes passed our mid-day resting-place. Some of the men seized their guns and fired, but without result. The dogs gave chase and caught a calf, whose bellowing we soon heard in the forest. It was of considerable size, which I suppose explains why its mother did not return to defend it or to seek it. When we came up to it, Mr. Moffat's dogs and my own were holding fast the indignant animal in spite of its violent efforts to get away. A bullet carefully placed put an end to the struggle, and supplied the party with some veal. This is a kind of meat which natives do not much relish. They seem to regard it pretty much as they do unripe fruits, which are good enough in a season of scarcity, but much improved if allowed to arrive at maturity. In hunting buffaloes the object is to secure a cow in good condition, the bull buffalo being very dry and tough eating. A troop of buffaloes pursued by mounted huntsmen keep together for a short distance, but gradually the old bulls drop to one side under the shelter of the thick bushes. These grim-looking animals remain here in ambush, and spring out upon the unwary hunter, should he unfortunately pass that way. But experienced men keep their eye on such awkward customers, and give them a wide berth by not following exactly upon the track of the buffaloes.

I once rode seventy miles to attend a Dutch hunter, who, strange to say, had been not only way-laid but shot by one of these old buffalo bulls. It rushed from behind a bush upon the Dutchman, throwing both horse and rider to the ground with the fury of its first attack. It gored the horse to death before it could recover its feet, and next attacked the rider. The Dutchman says he lay as flat as he could on the ground, in order to prevent the curved horns of the buffalo from getting below him to toss him. Whilst irresolute what to do next, the buffalo unfortunately trod upon the Dutchman's gun as it lay on the ground, and some twigs having got about the hair-trigger, the gun went off, and the contents of the barrel went through the Dutchman's bent arm, entering above the elbow, and passing out below it. The buffalo was frightened by its own exploit, and left the wounded hunter, with his gun and saddle and wounded arm, to make his way on foot to his waggon. Several splinters of bone came away, and the man again recovered the use of his arm. I learned that when the pain became very great with the motion of the waggon, the Dutchman had been in the habit of slaughtering a goat, of which he had a flock with him, extracting its still warm stomach, and inserting the wounded arm into it. The "trekking" or drawing was described by the man as very severe as soon as the arm was introduced into this strange poultice of herbs. I was informed that the stomach of a sheep had not the same virtue; and in explanation was reminded that the goats fed upon bushes, many of which had medical properties, while the sheep contented itself with grass. That this application removed acute pain I had the fullest evidence in the case of this hunter. I found also that his companions were applying, as an ordinary dressing to the wound, a poultice composed of certain proportions of ostrich-egg and flour, which seemed to answer very well. On the whole, I have a much higher idea of the Dutch appliances to external wounds than their prescriptions for internal maladies.

I was detained a little behind Mr. J. S. Moffat while disposing of the young buffalo behind my spare waggon, so that it was nearly sunset before we came to the Seribe. Here we were fated to spend the night. In pulling the waggon up the steep bank of the river, the gear of the oxen gave way repeatedly, and the waggon rolled back into the deep sand of the dry river bed. Whilst patiently repairing these accidents, both men and oxen were startled by the loud roar of the lion in our vicinity. Bringing the front of the team round to the waggon, I made the two leaders fast to the wheel, so that the team could neither pull the waggon nor break away. Whilst we were doing this, a young ox, which had been standing loose, made off through the bushes. As there was no response among the men to my request for volunteers to bring it back, I had myself a good chase in the moonlight after "Bleisman" before he would consent to return to the waggon. The wolves (hyenas) abounded in the river, so we lighted a large fire near the end of the little waggon, which was still on the other side of the river, lest we should be robbed of our veal. We lighted also another fire close to the front of my own waggon, the entrance to which was, owing to the depth of the river bank, on a level with the ground. Seated at this fire we had our usual evening worship, and the whole night was spent in watchfulness. I taught my men some new psalm-tunes, by way of passing the tedious hours, till daylight brought complete safety. The lion no doubt found his supper in our neighbourhood; but in the morning none of us was sufficiently curious to seek to discover what had formed his meal.

The Motloutse river, which we next crossed, had on its bank the ruins of the most advanced cattle-post of the Bamangwato, and the first which had fallen into the hands of the Matebele in the late raid. Crossing the Shashe and the Tatie, we were now in the heart of what was until recently one of the most famous resorts of the elephant. Immense troops still visit this district every year; and hunters here loiter to fill up their waggons at the end of their hunt, or to draw fresh blood at the commencement of a new season, and while they are on their way to more distant fields. Near to the confluence of the Impakwe and Ramokwebane, there are some acacia thickets into which no hunter can follow the elephant, and towards which the sagacious creatures, when alarmed, at once direct their course. Not long ago a hunter shot six elephants in one day in this district. He was on horseback, and carried a gun with an immense bore, shooting four bullets to the pound of lead. On this occasion he was accompanied by a young Scotchman, then taking his first lessons in elephant-hunting. Following a wounded elephant into a dense thicket, this young hunter was unhorsed by another of the troop, and narrowly escaped being killed. The enraged animal stood for some time over the wounded horse and the rider, lying low in the dust, and then, apparently satisfied, took its departure.

Another party, headed by Mr. Hartley, a well-known hunter, whose locks have grown grey on the elephant "spoor," also got into circumstances of extreme danger in this locality. It was at the beginning of the season, and the usual caution was not observed in the general anxiety to secure some of the troop. This temerity led some of the hunters into the dense thorn bushes, through which sometimes there was only the single path which the bulky elephants made as they fled before them. In such a thicket, and only a few yards in front of them, an elephant cow raised its shrill shriek of rage, and with uplifted trunk rushed towards them. One huntsman glided from the saddle, and crept away under the bushes, leaving his horse to take its chance. Others who were not so far in advance hastily retreated. The elephant made at once for the foremost huntsman. One glance assured this gentleman that his only hope was in retreat, there being no outlet whatever in front of him. Wheeling round in an instant, he dug his spurs into his horse and made a rush for life. For a moment it appeared he was too late. The trunk of the elephant was over him; but, sure of her victim, instead of seizing him at once, she preferred to strike him with her tusk. She fortunately missed her first blow; but was about to repeat the stroke, when, the bushes being now a little less dense, Mr. Hartley observed the imminent peril of his friend, and bravely hastened to his assistance. Riding close up to the elephant, and discharging the contents of his gun in her side, he galloped off in another direction. The well-executed ruse was successful; the attention of the elephant being withdrawn from the hunter who was within her power, and directed to her new assailant, who having thus saved his friend's life, made good his own escape also.

In the beginning of August we crossed the Inkwezi river, and halted near Mahuku's town. Instead, however, of presenting the usual indications of a large and industrious population, the whole country looked forlorn and desolate. The long grass was waving over the untrodden paths which led to the gardens from the town. The corn, pumpkins, and melons, and other fruits, were standing unharvested in the fields. I visited the town itself, which had been a few months before the scene of life and activity, and found only charred ruins, with here and there the skeletons of some of its former inhabitants. Soon after our arrival, a handful of Batalowta descended to our waggons from the fastnesses of the mountain, which had now become their abode since their escape from the general ruin of their people. From them we heard the confirmation of reports which we had previously received, concerning the massacre of this tribe by their masters, the Matebele.

When Moselekatse first approached their country from the south, the division of the Batalowta under Makobe submitted to him as his vassals. On his death, Makobe was succeeded by Mahuku, who continued his obedience to Moselekatse. At the same time he kept up constant communication with his friends and relatives at Shoshong, and his brother Kirekilwe deserted Moselekatse, and fled to Sekhome. Kirekilwe lived under this chief for several years; and was a person of consideration in the town. He seems however to have been animated by an insatiable love of change or adventure; for soon after I took up my residence at Shoshong, Kirekilwe fled back again to his brother Mahuku. It was said that he suggested to Moselekatse the facilities for making a raid upon the

Bamangwato cattle-posts. "Did not the chief hear the cattle of Sekhome in the still evenings?" it was asked. "Their cattle had advanced so close to his country that if the chief listened he would hear them." The bait was too strong for Moselekatse. He had made promises to live at peace, but had never kept them; to attack Sekhome would only be throwing off the mask. Had not Sekhome long ago killed forty of his warriors, and was the vengeance of Moselekatse, although long deferred, not to fall? So the war against Sekhome was agreed upon by Moselekatse, but kept secret from the missionaries. They saw the preparations for war; they knew when the army left; but there was not a soul who dared to inform them of its destination, because Moselekatse had said they must be kept ignorant until after the war-party had started.

One division of the army was ordered to pass the town of the Batalowta, and to obtain guides from among the people of Mahuku, who would show the cattle-posts of the Bamangwato, and the best paths into their country. But the Batalowta remembered they were Bechuanas, although vassals of Moselekatse. Mahuku and his people excused themselves from such traitorous service. They said they were faithful to Moselekatse as vassals and as herdsmen. But they declined to guide his soldiers to attack their own countrymen. Even the restless and meddling Kirekilwe refused to accompany the army against the town whose hospitality he had so recently enjoyed. What was to be done? The whole army halted while messengers hastened back to inform Moselekatse of the unexpected conduct of the Batalowta. The chief's reply to the leaders of the war-party was simply that the army must go on and bring Sekhome's cattle. At the same time, however, he ordered another body of men to go to Mahuku's, and there wait for the return of the army from Shoshong. They were to live in open friendship with the Batalowta; but as soon as the army returned they were to be ready to execute orders which they should then receive. The instructions of the chief were faithfully obeyed. While the rest of the Matebele army were toiling through an unknown country, enduring hunger and thirst, their comrades at Mahuku's were living in continual revelry. Every night they assembled for beer-drinking and for dancing. The surrounding mountains, so silent when I gazed upon them, re-echoed the deep voices of the soldiers and the shrill notes of the Batalowta women, as they joined in the song and in the dance.

After weeks spent in this manner, their comrades returned from the raid upon Shoshong. They sent forward a message to Moselekatse to say that they had brought some Bamangwato cattle; but their sufferings had been great for want of guides, and the Bamangwato were assisted by white men, from whose shooting they had suffered loss. Confirmed in his belief that he had been betrayed by the Batalowta, Moselekatse took steps to wreak on them his heaviest vengeance. He told the commanders of the war-party that they were not to see his face until they had destroyed Mahuku and Kirekilwe, and every one belonging to them. This order was carried out in the spirit in which it was given. The commanders of the army sent for the two brothers, professedly to receive the cattle, sheep, and goats which Moselekatse was to intrust to their care. At the same time the Matebele in the town were secretly informed that they must be ready to take their part in the tragedy which was about to be enacted. The Batalowta were completely deceived. Only Kirekilwe seems to have suspected foul play, and therefore secreted a battle-axe below his mantle. Several young men followed Mahuku without invitation, hoping to be "treated" by their "balekane" or comrades among the Matebele soldiers. They advanced unsuspectingly into the heart of the camp, greeting the soldiers, and being greeted in return. But in an instant the guests became the victims. In vain they craved for mercy; they were overpowered by their betrayers, and put to death with every indignity and cruelty of which savages could conceive. But before he died, Kirekiḷwe had killed one and wounded another of the soldiers.

The Batalowta women, working in their gardens, heard that day a dreadful noise in the camp of the Matebele; sounds were borne to their ears so like the cries of the dying, and the shouts of their murderers, that they fled from the gardens and hastened home to give the alarm. They learned that their chief and some of their head men had gone to the camp; but what of that? There sat their Matebele guests as merry as ever, in friendly conversation with the men who had remained at home. The women whispered their fears and misgivings to some of their friends; but no heed was given to what was regarded as an idle tale. They were told that they had heard nothing but the sounds of rejoicing in the camp, mingled with the lowing of the Bamangwato cattle, and the bleating of their sheep and goats. But by and bye the merry mood of their Matebele guests seemed to abate; in spite of themselves they looked uneasy, and directed eager glances towards the outside of the town; meanwhile striving to dissemble and to carry on the playful talk. In an instant they started to their feet; the friends now changed into furies, the laughing guests into betrayers and murderers. They stabbed each man his host, each soldier the man whose comrade or particular friend he had been. Their eager glances had been in expectation of a signal outside the town, to notify that it had been surrounded with

Matebele soldiers. Now the Batalowta old men, roused from their mid-day repose by the din of murder, and seeking to escape to the neighbouring hill, were received upon the spears of the Matebele who encircled the town. The aged women who unbared their breasts to bespeak men's mercy, instead of mercy received a spear. Even the harmless infants were put to death; "for," as a Matebele soldier explained to me, "when their mothers are killed, did we not also kill the infants, they would only be eaten by the wolves." Only young women, and boys and girls, were spared. Some of these wretched captives told me that at first they knew not the fate of some of their relatives, but that hope died within them when they beheld an armlet or a necklace of beads, or other well-known ornament, now decking the body of a Matebele soldier. A large slit, made with the assegai in the ear of every captive, announced to them that they were now the property of Moselekatse. The last heathenish act was to strip the dead, to cut up the clothing of the murdered parents into the cinctures worn by the Matebele, and then compel the terrified children to wear them.

Strange to say, in the midst of this slaughter, the Matebele spared all the Batalowta who had been employed as servants by the missionaries at Inyate. Having no idea of the connection between master and servant as obtaining in England, they seemed to regard these men as the property of the missionaries, and therefore not to be put to death with the rest of their townsmen.

Three of these Batalowta were despatched on the Monday after our arrival at Mahuku's to inform Moselekatse of our approach. No stranger is admitted into the Matebele country without the permission of the chief first asked and obtained. And after he enters the country, if he is a trader or hunter, he is under constant surveillance until he is again beyond the boundary of the Matebele country. I found that great stress was laid by the Batalowta on the fact that I had been at Sekhome's during the late war; in fact, that I was to be announced to the king as "Sekhome's missionary." While not caring to hide my connection with the Bamangwato, I endeavoured to impress on their minds that I had been only one year at Sekhome's; that I had come from England at the same time as the Matebele missionaries, and that I was one with them in entire neutrality in all political matters. I learned afterwards that all my explanations had been given in vain—all that reached Moselekatse's ear being that "Yonie (Mr. J. Moffat) was coming, accompanied by Sekhome's missionary."

Taking it for granted that Moselekatse would admit us, we did not wait at Mahuku's for an answer, as is sometimes done, but slowly followed in the rear of our messengers. In this way we passed through what is called the Makalaka country, which is the ridge or backbone from which on one side the rivers flow first to the north-west and then northward to the Zambese, and on the other side flowed to the south-east and joined the Limpopo. This elevated region appeared to be healthy, as well as beautiful and fruitful. Although this was the dry season, we found the country abounding with water. We found here the sugar-bush, and for days were free from the acacia jungles of the lower-lying country which we had left behind us. After leaving Monyama's town we entered the Matebele country proper, and began the descent from the high lands in which we had spent the last few days. We had now an escort in old Monyama himself, who was responsible for letting us pass his village before our messengers had returned with the permission of the chief.

On the evening of Tuesday the 19th August, our attention was directed to the fierce barking of our dogs at something among the neighbouring trees, and some of the men, having taken their guns, proceeded to the spot. Hearing shots fired, Mr. Moffat and I followed. My wife handed me what we both took for granted was my rifle, and I hastened to the scene of action. As I approached I was met by my two drivers, who were running at full speed. I inquired what was chasing them, but they had no time to tell me. Proceeding a little farther, I saw a black rhinoceros cow with its calf, the latter of which was baited by the dogs. I came up just in time to see one of my dogs tossed into the air by the enraged mother. Sadly shaken, but with no bones broken, "Celt" crept away among the bushes, and did not show face again until the danger was past. The rhinoceros had already received several shots from Mr. Moffat and from the men: I now discharged the contents of both barrels into its body, being perhaps fifty yards from the animal. When I fired the second time the rhinoceros staggered. The calf was now shot, and another bullet or two were placed in the body of the mother, when the men said it was dead, and began to advance towards it. I had just been observing its little eye, and saw there was life in it still, when a sudden movement of its body sent back at the top of their speed those who were advancing. But it was only a spasmodic jerk. The creature was unable to rise again to its feet. It was however too stubborn to roll over in the helplessness of some wounded animals, and died resting on its knees.

"Hallo! who has been firing at a rhinoceros with small shot?" asked some one as soon as we went up to the body. Every one now looked at his gun. To my chagrin I found that I was the hero of the small shot. I had been riding in Mr. Moffat's waggon that afternoon, and in my absence my driver had begged my rifle from my wife. When I afterwards hastily asked it, she mechanically handed to me my fowling-piece, which was also loaded and capped! It was amusing now to remember the applause with which the men had greeted my second shot, and the staggering of the rhinoceros! The noise of the report may have disconcerted the animal, but certainly the hail of small shot did it no harm whatever, only mottling its hide so as to resemble what a rhinoceros with small-pox might be! As the sun was nearly set, we drew our waggons up to the two carcasses, and there spent the night. Before the waggons were unyoked, the children had climbed on the back of the rhinoceros, and were examining its horns and fierce little eye. The meat from the ribs of the rhinoceros is considered best; and it is said the flesh of the mohohu or white rhinoceros is very good. I cannot recommend that of the borile or black rhinoceros, although with the appetite of camp life in Africa it was palatable enough.

Two messengers from Moselekatse met us here next morning before we had commenced our day's journey. They had brought the "mouth" of the king to us. Of course Mr. J. Moffat was going home; the chief was glad to hear of his return. Turning his attention to me, the men began to put a great many questions, to which I returned plain and straightforward answers. "The chief wished to know what I wanted in his country?" I replied that I wished to see the chief himself, and my friends at Inyate. After patiently answering a great many questions—explanations being also given by Mr. Moffat on any point where it was necessary,—to my surprise and disappointment the messenger began, not without some confusion, after our unreserved conversation, to deliver to me the decision of his master. Moselekatse ordered me to return; Yonie was to come on; but the chief did not wish to see one of the Bamangwato. I learned, however, that this decision was not final; one of the men was to return with such explanations as I might have to give. Mr. Moffat and I again went over our position and our objects with the different tribes where we resided as missionaries, and that my visit to the Matebele had no political meaning whatever. Having already ascertained that our friends at Inyate were in good health, I might have returned at once; but I confess I felt a strong disinclination to do so. I did not like the indignity of being sent about my business in so summary a manner; but above that, I felt it would enhance our reputation as missionaries among the natives were we able to pass over from one contending tribe to another during the time of war, and be recognised as the friends of all and the enemies of none. "Say to your chief," I added, when the man was about to depart, "that my heart is sore at having to turn back here, although not because I shall lose the opportunity to take something out of the Matebele country, or to enrich myself at the king's expense. I can also bear to return without seeing either the chief or my friends who have lived so long under his protection; but my heart is sore because in turning me back the chief says I am one of the Bamangwato. Now my chief is not Sekhome, although I taught his people for some time the Word of God. The chief to whom I owe allegiance is the Sovereign of all the white people you see, and lives beyond the ocean. I go back because Moselekatse commands me; and the only sore place in my heart is that he treats me not as a missionary from England, but as a subject of Sekhome." Mr. J. Moffat also assured the soldiers that he would be responsible for my good conduct at Inyate, and would be willing to take upon his shoulders the blame of admitting me into the Matebele country.

Being without water at our present encampment, the soldiers with some reluctance agreed that we should go forward to where we could obtain some for ourselves and our oxen. There being none at Boherehere river, we advanced to Kumalo, there to await the final decision of the chief. We learned in our conversations with the messengers that the announcement that "Sekhome's missionary" was coming with Yonie had given rise to a good deal of pleasantry and joking at the court of Moselekatse. "Make haste and milk some of Sekhome's cows for Sekhome's missionary," said the chief to those near him, "for he must be hungry after so long a journey." This was received with roars of laughter. "Why, if I admit this man," he added, "he will see everything in the country, and then return and inform Sekhome." One of the chief's wives, greatly puzzled at my coming, exclaimed, "What crimes do these white men commit which cause them to flee from their own country in this way?"

On Thursday the 21st August, the messenger returned from the chief—his feet and legs covered with dust, but with a smiling countenance. Instead of delivering his message to us as we expected, he passed us with a word of greeting, and sitting down before his fellow-soldier, who was, I suppose, his superior, narrated to him the reply which the chief had sent. After he had fully mastered the report, the head man of the two now addressed us, and announced that "I was to come on; but where was my present to the chief, and that of Mr. J. Moffat? He had not seen them."

The next Sunday we spent at a river called Tlapa Baloi (Wizard's Stone), where Mr. Moffat preached in Setebele to the people of the neighbouring village. A considerable number of soldiers were present when the service began, but before it was over they had all left except one or two old men, who at the conclusion demanded "tusho," a reward for their good conduct! I noticed that almost every grown-up man had his body marked somewhere with the cuts of the spear or battle-axe. I had afterwards frequent opportunities of noticing the same thing. The vast majority of the men I saw in the country bore the marks of these hand-to-hand encounters with their enemies. I have heard it said that an African's head is the last place at which an adversary ought to aim with sword or spear; but the Africans do not think so themselves, for the majority of the wounds which I saw among the Matebele were in the head, or near to it. With their scars I noticed an orderliness among the soldiers, and a politeness on the part of their officers, which I had not seen among the Bechuanas.

We reached the camp of Moselekatse on Monday afternoon, but did not see the chief till next morning. He was not living in a town, but at the foot of a mountain not far from a village called Sesentene. His four waggons were drawn up near to each other; behind these were the temporary huts of his harem and servants, closed in by a hedge of thorn branches, and in front a large pen for cattle and another for sheep and goats. Such were the "quarters" in which we found the chief of the Matebele. As in other things, his changes of residence seem to be guided by caprice. After living for some time at a place, suddenly the order is issued to pack the waggons and yoke the oxen, and before all the attendants know whither they are going, the waggons are moving, and the temporary huts left in a blaze. Perhaps the old chief's craving for new encampments, and fresh green boughs for his fences, had to do with the common belief in charms and spells. His enemies were supposed to be constantly at work to bewitch him and compass his death. The removal of his camp to new quarters would be supposed to break all these enchantments, and render them nugatory. In the same way, if one of his people becomes ill, he is removed from the village in which he is residing, and placed in a booth or temporary hut, away from all human residence, and the sufferer in this lonely retreat is watched by the doctor and by one attendant until recovery takes place, or death puts an end to his sufferings.

And now for my reception by this African despot, whose

name was a terror far and near. After passing the little booths and the waggons, we were shown into the sheep-pen, at the door of which sat a number of soldiers. A fire had been placed in the middle of the pen, and near to it, seated in an old-fashioned arm-chair, the gift of Mr. Moffat, sat Moselekatse. As we advanced, we got each a warm and rather lengthy shake of the hand, the attendants shouting lustily, "Great king! man-eater!" etc. We took our places on the ground, opposite the arm-chair, and had a full view of its occupant, who was the object of this abject praise. We saw an old frail man, so frail that he could not stand by himself or walk a single step. His legs were paralysed; his arms moved with difficulty, and in a spasmodic manner; his head was grey, and his face bore the wrinkles of old age. The only clothing of the chief at the time of our introduction to him consisted of an English blanket brought loosely round his loins, and a naval officer's cap on his head. An old greatcoat, the original colour of which was to me matter of speculation, served as a footstool, and was removed with the chair when the chief desired to change his position. I sought in the countenance of Moselekatse some explanation of his bloody and successful career, but I cannot say that I found it in the face of the old man before me. He had a good head and large eyes, almost the largest I have seen in an African face. And if we were in the presence of one who could listen unmoved to the voice of justice and mercy, we had little to remind us of the fact. A bright-eyed child sat near the chief, and waited upon him. He was a captive, and his parents had no doubt been ruthlessly murdered. He sat beside the arm-chair of Moselekatse like a favourite lap-dog, the chief occasionally taking notice of him, and smiling at his apparently happy looks.[1]

[1] Strange to say, this little favoured captive boy did not like his position as spaniel or plaything to Moselekatse. Although I never spoke

Some of Moselekatse's "wives," of whom I was told there were hundreds in the country, sat near to their lord, ready to obey his slightest wish. We were presented with boyalwa or native beer in a drinking vessel neatly woven of grass. The women held in their hands elegant spoons, also made of grass, for skimming away flies or other objects from the beer. No notice was taken of the two great-coats which we had sent on the previous day as presents; but immediate application was made for additional "help," as the Matebele express it. However, our reception on the whole was gracious enough, as things go there. Moselekatse seemed to lose sight of my connection with Sekhome, and recognised me as a missionary from England or Kuruman—the difference or distance between those two places not being understood by the Matebele.[1] The chief had

to him, except perhaps by a kindly glance of the eye, I found after leaving the chief's camp, on my departure from the country, that this little fellow had forsaken the smiles and the dainties of Moselekatse and secretly ensconced himself in one of my waggons. Poor boy! I could not let him stay. But it was with a heavy heart that I led him out, and delivered him to two soldiers to take back to his heathen master.

[1] I have been amused to observe the hazy notions as to places and persons which prevail in the interior. Till the day of his death Moselekatse thought of his friend Mr. Moffat as chief of the traders and hunters who annually visited his country. An Englishman who never saw Mr. Moffat, and certainly never visited Kuruman, delivered every year at his first interview with Moselekatse an improvised message to the chief, with which he said he had been intrusted by Mr. Moffat. Again, on leaving the country at the end of the season, this person went regularly to the chief to receive a message for his chief at Kuruman, his journey all the while leading him hundreds of miles away from that place. Then the people of Kuruman invariably gave themselves out in the interior as subjects of Moffat. "Mahure," they said, "was chief at Taung—Moffat was chief at Kuruman." This insured for them more consideration than they would otherwise have received. At Lake Ngami an English trader most gravely assured the chief that he could not again show face at Kuruman and answer to Moffat for the goods in his waggon, unless Lechulatebe gave him more ivory for them than he was then offering! And after all there was great reason for the current report that Mr. Moffat was the chief of Kuruman. As the land belonged to the missionary society, the kingly

been noted for the hospitable custom of detaining visitors long after the time when they desired to depart. But lung-sickness had considerably diminished the quantity of beef at his disposal, and visitors were no longer entertained as guests at the chief's expense. In our own case, after a stay of two days, the chief's politely expressed reluctance at our departure was fully met by the promise of an early visit after we had seen our friends at Inyate.

Leaving the sylvan abode of Moselekatse, near Sesentene, we reached Inyate on Saturday, the 29th of August, having been more than a month, including all delays, in performing a journey of about 330 miles. We had now the pleasure of again meeting our dear friends, Mr. Thomas and Mr. and Mrs. Sykes. This pleasure, however, had its sad alloy in the absence of Mrs. Thomas. All we could see of her, except in the features of her two little boys, was her grave. The influence which this lady had obtained over the Matebele was attested by all. The rude and boisterous soldiers were mild and civil to her. They could be rough to others, they were always gentle as lambs to Ma-Mogelė. She spoke the simple words of gospel to the little children who came to serve her, to the women who sometimes visited her, and even to the men as they crowded round her door. Her death from fever in June 1862 was a heavy loss, not only to her husband and children, but to the mission at Inyate; and the Matebele mourned for her with a sorrow as deep as their admiration had been high.

office of apportioning the gardens rested for fifty years with him. Then the residents on the station belonged to different and sometimes distant tribes, and it was their custom to bring their quarrels to Mr. Moffat for settlement. And no chief in the country entertained strangers with more regularity and cheerfulness than this venerable missionary, the maize and the corn which the guests received for food being reaped in the gardens laid out and irrigated by his skill and industry.

CHAPTER XVI.

MOSELEKATSE.

Moselekatse, the son of a Zulu chief called Matshobane, spent his youth in and around what is now the colony of Natal. The names of some of the rivers in that distant country were well known to the chief, and to other old men whom I met in Matebele-land. Some fifty years ago Moselekatse's tribe was conquered by the dreaded Tshaka, the greatest chief of the Zulus, at the time when he was "eating up" all the inhabitants of that region. Moselekatse became a captain in the army of this fierce despot, and performed in that capacity some daring exploits. Having thus secured the affection of his men, instead of returning from a certain raid on a distant tribe, with the captives and the cattle which he had taken, Moselekatse hastened northwards, placing the Drakensberg mountains between him and his master. He then entered what is now the Transvaal Republic, finding it in the possession of the Bakhatla and other unwarlike Bechuana tribes. After a time his headquarters were established in what is now the district of Marikwe in the Transvaal country, where on almost every mountain side are to be seen the ruins of his towns and cattle-pens. The inhabitants fled before him, leaving their country and their property an easy prey. His kingdom was established on the ruins of the peaceful towns of the more industrious Bechuanas, who were workers in iron, copper, and in wood. Both English Episcopal and American missionaries attempted unsuccessfully to establish a mission among the Matebele while they resided in this district.

Moselekatse was here twice visited by Mr. Moffat; and some head men were sent to visit Kuruman, while about 1836 two went as far as Cape Town, with Dr. (now Sir) Andrew Smith. The impression made upon the mind of Moselekatse by the first Englishmen whom he himself had seen, and by the accounts of his ambassadors to the "white men's country," was never afterwards effaced. The superior skill and power, the higher and self-denying morality, the kindliness of heart of Mr. Moffat, and his mysterious words about God the Father of all and Jesus Christ his Son, excited the highest admiration of this Zulu chief. His son who was to reign after him he named Kuruman; and the name and character of "Moshete" (Moffat) followed the despot, as something peculiarly precious, in all his wanderings. But little or no impression was produced in his outward conduct, his men continuing to ravage and destroy, as if the Divine Word to love one another and to be merciful had not been spoken to them.

Berend Berend, a Griqua chief, remembering how the Batlaping had been saved from the Mantatees by his people, conceived the idea of delivering the Bakone and Bakhatla tribes from the terrible bondage of the Matebele under which they were groaning. Proceeding at the head of a war-party, he attacked the Matebele, and succeeded in collecting a large number of their cattle. On their way home, however, the Griquas were followed by the Matebele, and when off their guard were surrounded in the night, and their victory was turned into complete defeat. The insult which had been offered to Tshaka by Moselekatse was not forgotten by that chief and his successor

Dingaan. Although the march was a long one, they despatched war-parties to destroy the renegade. Last of all, another and more formidable enemy to Moselekatse appeared in the emigrant Dutch colonists, who were now in detached camps or parties, each "fighting for his own hand." In 1836 a party of these men under Gerrit Maritz defeated the Matebele; and soon after, Moselekatse, thinking that his enemies had become too many for him, left the Transvaal country, and pursued his way northward, intending to cross the Zambese.

He was detained on the southern bank of that river by tsetse and by the rebellion of one of his sons. This young man remained behind his father on the march, thinking to imitate Moselekatse's early example, and, at the head of his own men, to become an independent chief. He paid the penalty of his audacity with his life and the lives of his followers. The chief then settled in the country of the industrious Makshona and Makalaka, whom he destroyed as he had done the Bechuanas before. Finding, after a time, that his soldiers were paying too much attention to the Makalaka young women, the relentless tyrant commanded his men to put to death those whose charms beguiled them from sterner work. The command was of course obeyed, and there was lamentation and dismay among the Makalaka at the ruthless butchery of their sisters and their daughters by those "hounds of war" who had formerly professed to be their admirers.

The Dutchmen, under Hendrike Potgieter, ventured to pursue Moselekatse into his distant retreat. They succeeded in capturing some cattle, and were on their way home with their booty, when the regiment of Matebele called Sokindaba recaptured the cattle, and killed some of the Dutchmen. This was the last engagement between them and Moselekatse. Those who had performed this distinguished service were much honoured among the Matebele; and I have more than once heard men of Sokindaba describe their share in the glories of the rescue of Moselekatse's cattle. One man showed me wounds which he had received on the occasion; another wiry little fellow imitated the way in which he had rushed upon a Dutchman who was loading his gun, wrestled with him, and put him to death. It is quite an accomplishment among these people to be able to mimic successfully the various cries of distress which are heard upon the field of battle. Young men especially were disagreeably demonstrative in this way; older soldiers were in general quieter, allowing the hacks and cuts about their head and body to testify to their prowess.

In 1855 Moselekatse was visited in his new territory by his old friend Mr. Moffat, and thus a waggon track was made to his country. It is the opinion of all natives that if a country is to remain unknown to Englishmen a waggon must not be allowed to traverse it. They say, "Where one waggon goes another is sure to follow." The road to the Matebele was soon an illustration of this. In 1857 Mr. Moffat paid Moselekatse a second visit, and obtained his consent to the establishment of a mission among his people; and in 1859 he returned with his son Mr. John Moffat, and with Messrs. Sykes and Thomas. The track of the missionary soon became a frequented road, upon which, at all seasons, are now to be found the waggons of traders and hunters.

As to the personal character of this South African despot, from all that I could gather from my friends at Inyate, or from the Matebele themselves, Moselekatse seemed to be possessed of tender feelings, and keenly alive to the sufferings of others. Such apparent contradictions are not unfrequent; a man is sometimes better, and sometimes worse than public report makes him to be. Although Moselekatse was able by the help of his admiring soldiers to achieve his independence, he would not have been able, even had he desired, at once to cease from plunder and from bloodshed. His soldiers had been trained and enrolled for this very purpose. As in other military despotisms, war was a necessary part of the Matebele scheme of society. In order to secure the continued allegiance of his men, Moselekatse had to devise work for them, in which they would meet with the gratification of their savage passions. The clamour to be led forth to pillage, outrage, and bloodshed never ceased to issue from men forced to live under the restraints of Matebele barracks. This dreadful organization, created by the chief, and guided by his wisdom, came by and bye to act with great precision. Every year a war-party marched against some neighbouring tribe; every year multiplied the number of murdered innocents, whose blood cried to Heaven for vengeance. But as a matter of fact the master spirit animating and regulating all these movements was personally averse to pain and suffering. Even his oxen Moselekatse did not permit to be lashed severely by the long whip of the waggon-driver; his men were allowed to beat them only with green wands cut from the bushes in the forest. When, some weeks after my arrival, Mr. Thomas, on his way to the colony, brought his little children to take leave of the chief, Moselekatse cried out in the most feeling manner, "Take the poor motherless dear ones to the waggon, for I cannot bear the sight!" And yet how many motherless children arrived in his own dominions every year, made orphans by the insatiable spears of his soldiers!

Moselekatse's admiration for Englishmen was very great, and could not possibly have long survived the advent of the "mixed" society which has recently found its way into his country. I have heard him say to his congregated officers and men, pointing to the Englishmen present, "These are the masters of the world. Don't you take notice how they sleep in the open country alone and unprotected, and are not afraid? They are in my country one day; they pass on to the towns of other chiefs; they go fearlessly, for they bear no malice, but are the friends of all. And when the great men in the white man's country send their traders for my ivory, do you think they give me beautiful things in exchange because they could not take the ivory by force? They could come and take it by force, and all my cattle also. And yet look at them! They are humble and quiet and easily pleased. The Englishmen are the friends of Moselekatse; and they are the masters of the world."

The missionaries destined to preach the gospel among the Matebele arrived at the head-quarters of Moselekatse on the 28th October 1859. As pneumonia, a deadly and infectious disease, had broken out among their cattle, as soon as they reached the borders of Moselekatse's country they sent forward a messenger to beg the use of the chief's draught oxen, in order that they might be able to keep their own outside the country, until the disease should disappear from among them. They dreaded the consequence of associating their arrival in the country with the coming of a disease which had produced such ravages wherever it had hitherto appeared. At first the chief invited them to come on, with the assurance that no one would blame them even if the disease did break out; but afterwards, on a second messenger being despatched to him, he took the warning, and expressing his thanks to the missionaries for their interest in his prosperity, promised to send them assistance. Instead of oxen, however, to pull the waggons, he sent men, who took to their task cheerfully, but after all were not able to compensate for the absence of the steady and patient oxen. The party certainly presented a novel appearance, with Matebele soldiers in the place of oxen, and the sides of the waggons covered with shields and spears. Having also the nightly noise of the men at their camp-fires close to the waggons, and witnessing daily the slaughtering and eating of the cattle with which the chief kept his soldiers supplied, the young missionaries and their wives became somewhat accustomed to the Matebele before they reached their destination. At length the chief was pleased to accede to the request of the missionaries, and sent his draught oxen to relieve the soldiers and bring forward the waggons to his encampment.

During the first two months after the arrival of the mission party in the Matebele country, their position was a very unpleasant and trying one. After the first civilities were over, the manner of both chief and people completely changed. Confidence and regard gave place to distrust and unconcealed aversion. One morning, about three weeks after their arrival, the missionaries observed an unusual stir about the chief's quarters. He was leaving for another locality; the waggons were already moving; and yet the guests had received no intimation or explanation from Moselekatse. Having no oxen in the country, they were of course fixtures where they stood. Mr. Moffat resolved to ascertain the meaning of this movement, and followed the receding party for some distance for that purpose. But as soon as he approached the chief's waggon, he was turned back by the attendants of Moselekatse. The old attachment between the chief and his friend was for a time entirely inoperative. As to the young missionaries, their first impressions of Moselekatse were very unfavourable. They were disappointed at the manner of their reception. Instead of generosity, or even friendliness, they met with excessive selfishness, meanness, and duplicity. Instead of their imaginary "noble savage," they found a greedy, unreasonable, and cunning old man. But they had to content themselves with the exercise of patience, a virtue which is needed everywhere, but nowhere more than in the establishment of a new mission in Southern Africa. Insulting messages were now sent to them from the chief. They were told that they were spies, and had come to find out the resources of the Matebele country. They must pay the chief for his assistance in pulling their waggons during the latter part of their journey. One waggon-load of goods must be given to him at once, etc. For about two months the mission party were virtually prisoners. They were forbidden to leave the waggons or to kill game; and the Matebele were commanded not to sell them food, or even milk for their coffee. They asked permission to purchase cows, the chief replied he had ivory but no cows for sale; and he wished in return guns and ammunition. Determined not to compromise their character at the very outset, the missionaries refused to purchase a single pound of ivory. They explained that other men would come to trade with him; they had come to teach him and his people.

The chief reasons for this disaffection towards those whom he had promised to receive as his own children are easily given. When he promised to receive missionaries, Moselekatse took the precaution to send messengers to Mahure, the chief of the Batlaping, in whose country Kuruman is situated, for the purpose of inquiring into the whole bearing and scope of the missionary's work. He had heard the missionary state his case, he would now hear the chief in whose country Mr. Moffat had been so long carrying on his work. The report of these messengers was unfavourable to the missionary. They found the Batlaping in 1857 in complications with their Dutch neighbours, and in danger of being dispossessed of their country. In their report to Moselekatse, the messengers blamed the missionaries for these disasters. They had come first; the Dutchmen had followed.[1] Then the Matebele themselves remembered that the only missionaries (Americans) who had resided with them at Mosiga in the Transvaal country, had been only a short time among them, when the town where they were stationed was attacked by the emigrant farmers, and the missionaries, instead of fleeing with the Matebele, or even remaining after the flight, went away with their enemies, as if they had been privy to the attack, which, of course, was not the case. The Matebele therefore were fully of opinion, that if they allowed the missionaries to build in the country, other white men would come, and in the end the land would be taken from them. Moselekatse himself did not seem to hold this opinion; but then he had his own grievances in the matter. He had agreed in his own mind, that if a visit from Mr. Moffat had been to him such a profitable as well as pleasant thing, what must be the residence of his son in his country?

[1] This was only a repetition of what had taken place in a distant country some forty years before, in somewhat similar circumstances. It is said that a certain Kaffir who had led a wandering life in the Cape Colony, and who had been imprisoned on Robben Island for cattle-stealing, found his way, after his release, to Zulu-land, and was employed by Tshaka as interpreter or agent between him and the Englishmen who had then just begun to settle near to Port Natal. Besides the knowledge of the world to which he laid claim, this person also assumed the prophetic character, and predicted to Tshaka that in the course of time a white man called an "umfundisi" (missionary) would make his appearance, and ask permission from Tshaka to build a house in his country, that he might teach them the "Great Word." Afterward another and another would come until the country would be filled with white men. Then they would fight with the chief's people, and dispossess them of their land. Some years afterwards, when Captain Allen Gardiner applied for permission to open up a mission in Zulu-land, it was held by the Zulus that part of the Kaffir interpreter's prophecy had been fulfilled, and Captain Gardiner was told that if the chief permitted him to build, the rest of the prophecy would be fulfilled also, and the white people would multiply and destroy the Zulus!

Now services may be rendered and favours conferred by one who is on a visit to a native chief which a resident missionary would find it impossible to fulfil as every-day engagements.[1] Moselekatse seemed determined to employ the new missionaries in his service in this way. Despite all explanations to the contrary, he insisted for some time that one of the missionaries should commence a trade in ivory, and offered to load up the "missionary trader's" waggon at once, that he might return to the colony and bring back such articles as the chief desired. It was this battle that was fought during the two months of suspense at the commencement of the Matebele mission. The more powerful and dictatorial the chief, the more necessary was it that those who were to reside with him should, at the outset, avoid all occasion of future complication or misunderstanding. Moselekatse's views concerning a missionary must fall to the ground, and they must be received on the simple footing of "teachers of the Word of God." Once established in this position, it would be for them to render such daily services and favours as their feelings might dictate, and as their opportunity and skill enabled them to perform.

At length, on the 15th December, the missionaries received instructions to meet the chief at the town to which he had removed. On the 23d, they were shown the foun-

[1] I once saw a certain native chief in whose own family and household there were several women who had learned to sew, when a button happened to come off his vest, at once despatch vest and button to the wife of his missionary, with the request, which was uttered as a command, that she would sew on the button at once, and the man was ordered to wait for the vest and bring it back again! I had not the pleasure of being acquainted with the good lady in question, but have little doubt that she had in kindness and inexperience begun such services, and they had multiplied day after day. It is the duty of the missionary to conciliate and to help those among whom he labours; but when he or his wife habitually renders unnecessary menial services, they will gradually cease to have influence in the town, and come to be regarded as mere adjuncts to the possessions and glory of the chief.

tain and valley of Inyate, and Monyebe, the chief's officer, told them that if the situation pleased them, Moselekatse granted them both the fountain and the land, to occupy and to cultivate according to their own ideas. This was a happy deliverance from their difficulties. The missionaries gave thanks to God, who had so far changed the minds of the Matebele, and given them acceptance in their eyes as teachers of the Word of God. Mr. Moffat, upon whom, as leader of the expedition, a two-fold responsibility and anxiety had devolved, now felt that a heavy load was taken from his mind. The mission was to be established. His son was here to live over again his father's life at Kuruman. That life was spent near the Orange river: this was near the Zambese. So slowly, but surely, was the blessed light of the gospel travelling northwards.

The missionaries next requested that interpreters might be provided who understood Sechuana and Setebele, from whom they could learn the latter language, and through whose aid they might begin to preach to the people. Moselekatse did not show any anxiety for the commencement of such labours, but put off giving interpreters month after month, although he still promised to furnish them. At length, in the end of April, the interpreters were produced, and the missionaries were able to commence preaching to the Matebele. The first services were held in the large cattle-pen of the town, and were attended by great numbers of the soldiers. Moselekatse was always present, and showed at once his knowledge of Sechuana and the doctrines of the Word of God, as previously taught him by Mr. Moffat, by occasionally interrupting the interpreter, and helping him with the right word. As every utterance of Moselekatse is applauded, these corrections were received with the usual demonstrations, every soldier present shouting out "Great King!" etc., in the middle of the sermon. The chief also considered himself bound once or twice to express his dissent from the doctrines which were proclaimed. For instance, when one of the missionaries, some time after their arrival in the country, was preaching concerning the accessibility of God, he said that all might repair to Him in prayer, the poor people as well as the greatest kings, and that God would hear the one as soon as the other. "That's a lie!" interjected Moselekatse, who did not like to be thus publicly ranked with the poor and abject. The missionary was immediately interrupted by the shouts of applause which greeted the emendation of their chief. As he found, however, that his disapprobation did not alter the preaching, and that in every discourse there was a good deal which was unpleasant for him to hear, the Matebele chief did what people in somewhat similar circumstances do in England and elsewhere,—he gave up attending the public worship. His outward friendliness to the missionaries, however, suffered no abatement.

In less than a year after their arrival in the country, the missionaries obtained permission to preach at other towns and villages as well as at Inyate, and they began to visit regularly the three which were nearest them. Mr. Thomas, who obtained this liberty for himself and his fellow-labourers, was now able to speak to the people in their own language. Being a very good shot, it was easy for him, at almost every preaching visit, to kill a gnu or a zebra in the open country between Inyate and the scene of his evangelistic labours. The whole or the greater part of the meat he usually gave to the people. Mr. Thomas's fellow-labourers, although not so successful Nimrods, were still able to supply the people occasionally with meat, which cost them nothing but a bullet and perhaps an hour's additional walking. It is not at all to be wondered at if the Matebele sometimes followed the missionaries, not on account of their preaching, but because they ate of the game which they killed for them. A Greater than the missionaries had been followed for similar reasons. The Matebele were all the more inclined to give heed to the preaching after they had seen the prowess of the preachers in the field, as well as their kindliness of heart.

I one day requested a Matebele head man to give me an account of all that he knew concerning the past history of the Word of God in the tribe. Listening to his recital, I was able to form an estimate of the position of Christianity in the minds of the people. But as he went on with his story, my informant mentioned an episode of which I had not before heard. Having described some of the events which we have already narrated, the head man introduced among his list of evangelists the name of Sechele, the chief of the Bakwena, who visited the Matebele shortly before the arrival of the missionary party in 1859.

"Sechele preached regularly in the chief's court-yard and before Moselekatse," said my informant; "and all the people in the town where the chief was residing attended the service. When Sechele departed, Moselekatse resolved to keep up the service."

"And did Moselekatse himself pray and preach and sing?" I asked, with some curiosity.

"No; the chief said that Monyebe was to take the 'pina ea sekhoa'" (the white man's dance or religious service).

"Upon what grounds was Monyebe chosen to pray after the white man's fashion?" I inquired.

"Because the chief thought Monyebe knew more about white people and their ways than any one else!"

It must have been a singular spectacle to see Moselekatse and his people assembled to worship "after the white man's fashion," under the presidency of one of themselves, whose recommendation was that as prime minister he had come into most frequent contact with white men, and had had the best chance of learning their ways! This strange and sad service, which must have been a burlesque, was not kept up long, having been discontinued before the appearance of the missionaries in the country.

When the missionaries began to reside with the Matebele, it was suggested that they should approach the chief with the form of salutation used by the common soldiers, which is to crouch down to the ground and advance, shouting all the while the praises of the chief. The missionaries objected to this, and were permitted to greet by bowing and shaking hands. This point settled, the next question was, Were they to be allowed to sit on chairs or camp-stools at the public worship in presence of the chief? No head man among the Matebele would sit on a stool under any circumstances. If asked to do so, he at once declined, saying that "Moselekatse alone sat on a stool." But the missionaries carried this point also. They said they had always been accustomed to sit on stools or chairs in their own country, and if they did so still, it was not because they wished to dishonour Moselekatse! But the Matebele positively refused to allow old Mebalwe, the native teacher, and other Bechuanas in the missionaries' party, to take their chairs into the presence of Moselekatse. I have seen some of these people going half-way with their chairs on Sunday morning, forgetting where they were, till some soldier passing by indignantly demanded "if dogs like them were venturing before the chief with a stool?"

After a little time it was arranged that missionaries and white men generally were to rank in the country as the "sons of Moselekatse." This was a high honour, and had many direct privileges. The people throughout the country were bound to honour those whom the chief had thus virtually adopted. A boisterous soldier, haggling over a bargain, would, after a little reflection, address the white man in a more submissive tone,—" Child of the king, just a few more beads, and I will go away ! " White men were allowed to approach the person of the chief, and usually sat down beside him. His officers in attendance sat next; his own children at a still further distance, but within a few yards. At the door of the enclosure if the place was small, or at some thirty yards' distance if in a large yard, sat the common soldiers in a semicircle. Each person, on entering the enclosure, loudly and repeatedly greeted the chief, and then took his place among those of his own rank. The only women admitted into the chief's presence were two or three of his wives. Their place was behind Moselekatse's chair.

About four o'clock in the afternoon was what may very appropriately be called " feeding time " at Moselekatse's quarters. The cattle had been killed in the morning, and the beef had been stewing all the day in a pot, the lid of which was kept closely sealed with cow-dung. The meat was very tender, and having been stewed rather than boiled retained its richness. The cook having announced to the chief that dinner was ready, received from him minute orders how to dispose of it. First of all, a certain portion was brought to Moselekatse himself, in a dish which had been just before handed to the cook by one of the wives. This wooden vessel, in which the chief always ate his meat, was never washed, and never removed from his immediate neighbourhood. These precautions were taken on account of the prevailing fear of witchcraft. The congealed fat at the bottom of the dish was at least an inch in thickness. On its sides the " deposit " was not so thick, and the colour and contour were more variegated from having been frequently disturbed by the presence of fresh pieces of beef. White men who visited Moselekatse at this auspicious hour were always invited to dine; and it would have been altogether unaccountable had any one refused. A portion was ordered for his visitors in a separate dish, and what they did not eat they were expected to send to their waggons. Nothing was to be returned. If the chief wished specially to honour a visitor, he would ask him to eat out of the royal dish. Occasionally I have seen a missionary advanced to a position even more dignified, and asked to cut down the meat for Moselekatse. When he felt inclined to present any of his visitors with the remains of the piece of which he had been partaking, it was carefully removed from the "unwashed" to another dish, and in that carried to the waggon.

While the visitors were eating, the cook and his assistants handed round the immense dishes of beef to the various companies of soldiers present, according to the orders of the chief. Each company shouted out their thanks when the dish was placed before them. Not only was the chair sacred to Moselekatse, but so was the knife in eating. No one may use a knife at meals except the chief, the white men, and the chief's family. But the Matebele are at no loss without knives; although, I confess, their appearance when thus engaged in eating beef is singularly repulsive, and suggestive of great degradation. The soldier who is next to the dish seizes one of the large pieces of beef into which the oxen have been cut. I believe Moselekatse's beef was always cut up in one way, and every piece had its name. Laying hold of the beef with both his hands, the soldier seizes it with his teeth, and pulls off as much as he can from the piece. What comes off is his. Passing the large piece to the man next him, he sets to work to masticate and swallow the bit which he has secured. By the time he is quite ready for another bite, the piece of beef has travelled from man to man, becoming, of course, less in bulk on its journey; and is again presented to him who first attacked it. And so it goes round until it is demolished. But if it is very large, and the party are not numerous, they may be seen seated in a circle, supporting the meat by their hands in the centre, while they all simultaneously tear and pull away at it with their teeth in vigorous style. Not a word is spoken; each one conducts himself as if he had no time to lose. And certainly what one man does not seize is soon swallowed by the man next him. In no circumstances are good teeth of such evident and immense advantage; the old and toothless man can have no chance at such a dinner-party. After the beef has been disposed of, large calabashes of beer are brought in, and placed where the dishes of meat had stood. Each man in his turn raises the vessel to his mouth, and takes a long draught. The old have now the advantage, being long-winded, experienced beer-drinkers, and make up for any deficiency in their share of the beef.

CHAPTER XVII.

A MILITARY TRIBE AND CHRISTIANITY.

DURING the five months which I spent among the Matebele, I gave some attention to their customs, and to the peculiarities of their social life as a warlike people —every able-bodied man of whom is a soldier, and every year a year of war. No more complete military despotism ever existed. Stripped of all its attractiveness to European eyes, war is seen in its unmitigated horrors when carried on by Zulus and Matebele every year, and as a matter of course. Such a society needs a head—one guiding mind. No council or oligarchy suits the purely military organization; without one man able to wield it, such a tribe falls to pieces; with a man who can conceive and execute, encourage and compel, the weapon in his hands is a terrible one—stripping a country of its population as the reaper cuts down the corn in the harvest-field.

Matebele society may be said to exist for the chief. His claims are supreme and unquestioned. To him belongs every person and everything in the country. The droves of cattle which you meet in every part of the country belong to the chief; and if one dies he is informed of it. The herd-boy who follows the cattle, and his master who lives in the adjoining town, belong alike to the chief. The troops of girls who rush out from every Matebele town to see the passing waggons, belong all of them to the chief;

the immensely fat women who slowly follow are introduced to the traveller as the wives of Moselekatse. The chief's officers or head men may indeed possess private property; but the chief has only to raise his finger, and their goods are confiscated and they themselves put to death.

The head men lead perhaps the most wretched lives under this wretched government. The private soldier has little in possession or enjoyment, but he has also little care. The officer, on the other hand, knows that jealous eyes are upon him. His equals in rank and station covet his possessions, and regard the favours which he receives from the chief as so much personal loss to themselves. Therefore the head men are continually plotting and counter-plotting against one another. "We never know," whispered one of them to me, having first looked carefully round to see if we were quite alone, "we never know when we enter our house at night if we shall again look upon the light of the sun." As a matter of fact such men seldom fall asleep sober, they every night call in the aid of boyalwa (beer) to deepen their slumbers. One day a small wiry man was introduced to me at Inyate by one of the missionaries. He was asked where he had been the night before, and with a smile mentioned the name of a certain village. This person had sharp restless eyes, the thinnest lips I had seen among natives; his mouth was wide, and his teeth large and white. I was told after he left that this was one of the chief's executioners; and from the frequency of his domiciliary visits, he was called by the Matebele "the chief's knife." I thought his face befitted his office. Waiting in the neighbourhood till his victim has drunk the last cup of beer, he gives him time to fall into that stupor of sleep and drunkenness out of which he is never to awake. The chief's knife has his assistants, who are in readiness to "mak' siccar" any bloody work; for Moselekatse could not carry on his paternal administration with only one "knife." According to the testimony of one of the missionaries, it is nothing for him to send in one night four or five different parties of vengeance, to hurry the inhabitants of four or five different villages into eternity.

The death of Monyebe, who was the favourite officer of Moselekatse when the missionaries arrived, illustrates the social life of the Matebele, and especially the position of the head men. Monyebe was a wise councillor, as he had been a brave soldier. Moselekatse kept him always near his person. But the man who is thus in attendance on a Zulu chief receives many valuable presents. Horses, saddles, clothes, guns, beads, were given by Moselekatse to the officer in whom he had such pleasure. The other officers became violently jealous of Monyebe's prosperity. They laid their heads together and plotted his destruction. Jealous of one another, they were united against him who was preferred before them all. Innuendos were first thrown out in the hearing of the chief; vague surmises and fears were expressed; and at length a definite charge was made against Monyebe for witchcraft and intended murder—murder not of a subject but of the king himself. For some time the king turned a deaf ear to these charges, but the head men were indefatigable. They gave Moselekatse no rest. His life was at stake, they declared, and love to their chief was their sole motive. At length, sorrowfully and reluctantly, the chief gave the officers permission to kill Monyebe. The next morning nothing remained of the favoured prime minister, or his wives or his relatives or his servants, or his property, or his village, but a blackened and smoking ruin. The sharp assegai had done its work, and fire was left to complete the destruction. Jealousy was for the time appeased.

"The chief has made a narrow escape," said the deceivers and murderers, as they hastened to acquaint Moselekatse of Monyebe's death. "We found your enemy's house filled with medicines and charms of the most deadly description; the wizard we have killed; his medicines we have burned in the houses where we found them."

The law of Moselekatse, like that of Tshaka, from whom he broke away, forbade his soldiers to marry, so that the increase of the Matebele depended on their success in taking children in war. I found therefore that this strange people (they can hardly with propriety be termed a tribe) consisted of a few Zulus, who had been the life-long companions of Moselekatse, and who, under him, exercised authority over some ten or twelve thousand soldiers, who were a heterogeneous assemblage of members of every tribe through which Moselekatse had forced his way north. These Zulus were all advanced in years. The middle-aged and full-grown men were Bechuanas, being the captives taken when the Matebele resided in the Transvaal. Lastly, the young men were Makalaka and Mashona, the captives whom they had seized since they came into the country which they now inhabit. The captives grow up in the service of their captors, or of those to whom they sell them within the tribe. They herd cattle in time of peace; they carry the impedimenta of the soldier when he goes to war. At home they practise fighting and running with boys of their own age; in the field they are familiarized with deeds of blood. Their physical frame thus becomes more fully developed than if they had grown up in their own unwarlike and ill-fed tribes. I have seen children of Bushmen among the Matebele whose personal appearance formed a perfect contrast to their ill-favoured relatives in the desert. As the captive boys grow older, they become impatient of the restraints of their position, and laying their heads together, all living in a certain town march off in a body to the chief's quarters and present their petition to Moselekatse: "We are men, O King; we are no longer boys; give us cattle to herd and to defend." If the chief approves of their petition, he drives out a few cows as their

Zulu Herd-boy with Musical Instrument. Herd-boy—Fanciful Head-dress.

herd, and gives these boys in charge of an experienced soldier, with some assistants, who, in the new town or barracks which they erect, proceed to train them as Matebele soldiers. This is called to "bota." It is in this way that the Matebele army is supplied with men.

The new military town or regiment is called by the

same name as the one in which they lived as captive boys. When they go to war now, it is as a company of that regiment. But they are no longer baggage-carriers ; they bear their own weapons now like their former masters. Should they succeed in killing and in taking captive, they at once occupy the position of their former owners, and on a second war have their boy to carry their food and water. Should they not succeed in killing man, woman, or little child, their position is still one of dishonour. They are not men. If at the camp fire they sit in the presence of comrades whose spears have drunk blood, the latter will sometimes show contempt for them by rubbing their portion of meat in the sand, and then throwing it to them as to a dog. There is therefore every possible inducement to animate the youth to shed blood speedily. On their return journey from a successful raid, the captives are during the night tied to their captors, or to trees, to prevent their escape. Should a captive fail on the march after his master is tired urging him forward, he stabs him and leaves his body on the path. The Matebele soldier-town has nothing domestic about it; it is not a town, but barracks. The voice of the infant, the song of the mother, are almost unknown there. Only after some signal service does the chief bestow, as a great reward to the soldier, a captive girl to be his wife, who has no choice in the matter, but is delivered over to her new owner as an ox is given to another man, whose deeds have been less meritorious.

Theoretically all distinctions as to birth are unknown among soldiers whose ears have all been slit open with the spear, and who are equally the property of Moselekatse. But this was not carried out in practice. I noticed that soldiers of Zulu extraction, in quarrelling with perhaps finer-looking men than themselves—but who had been originally captive boys—when better arguments failed, did not forget to demand what right Mashona or Makalaka dogs had to open their mouths to dispute with their superiors. In this I saw an element of weakness and danger to the Matebele as a tribe. Soldiers who are reminded that they are captive dogs will cease to regard with interest or affection the cause of their captors. They

Matebele Soldiers.

need only a certain amount of intelligence and resolution to assert their independence.

These soldiers have little chance of obtaining any training in native religion or superstition. Captured in early youth, they do not learn the mekhua (*mores*) of their own forefathers; and not being Zulus, they are initiated by the Matebele into little else than the service of Moselekatse. The Zulus are careful to keep up their own customs among themselves; but I did not learn that they inculcated them among their Makalaka and Mashona vassals. Like other conquerors, Moselekatse himself paid a certain deference to the religions of the countries which he conquered. For instance, he sent to "inquire" on certain occasions at the "Morimo" (god) of the Makalaka. When I was in the country, about a dozen Malokwana priests or doctors from the south-east of the Matebele country, were busily engaged in making rain at the chief's camp. They were in the employment of Moselekatse, and would be handsomely paid for their services. But then these religious acts were public and official, and supposed to be proper to Moselekatse as chief. All such questions were far removed from the common soldier's thoughts, which were debased in the extreme. My own impression of the Matebele soldiers was, that the mental and spiritual parts of their nature had become very much dwarfed by disuse; and that they were very seldom indeed occupied with thoughts about the Unseen in their every-day life. Their whole training as youths; their incentives in the prime of life; their aims and their objects at home and in the field, were very brutal and degraded. If the missionaries approached the youths with the words of Jesus Christ, they found them the most impracticable and unruly class in the country, having their minds eagerly set on the attainment of their full manhood through the shedding of human blood. If they spoke to the men who had gained this distinction, and were glorying in their strength, every word which as evangelists they uttered, tended, according to Matebele ideas, to unman them,—to neutralize the deeds of which they were vaunting. The men wear a necklace of wood, every link of which represents an enemy slain in battle. In the war-dance they step out and give one proud thrust with the assegai for every enemy they have killed. Christianity would rob them of their necklace, and deprive them of their public boasting. If the missionaries approached the old men, who, alas! were not numerous in such a land, they found in every case that the man's nature, blunted by the deeds of his manhood, was now still further debased by habitual drunkenness and excess. And if such were the men, what, in the light of the religion of Jesus Christ, were the women of the Matebele, who were not the equals but the creatures of such men? We leave their condition undescribed.

The people of Moselekatse are truly far from God. If there is such a state as preparedness of mind for the gospel, then the Matebele were unprepared. No people could need it more; none could be less prepared or inclined to receive it. To preach the gospel, in point of fact, was to condemn their whole social system from its very roots. To call upon them to "join the word of God" was, in the estimation of the people, to tell them to desert or defy Moselekatse. "The chief must speak first, and then we shall give attention to the word of God." This was the language of several soldiers to me, when conversing with them on this subject. You may go on to say that "Morimo" (God) is greater than Moselekatse, and ought to be first served; that the service of the one is the bondage of fear, that of the other a labour of love. If the man is alone, some impression may be produced in his mind; at any rate he will wonder as to what the meaning of this new idea may be. But in the presence of several Matebele, a remark such as the above would only lead to opposition,—every word throwing the slightest slur on the chief being, as a matter of course in such circumstances, received with loud tokens of dissent.

In other countries the opposition of rulers and governments has not been able to prevent the spread of Christianity among the people. It will no doubt be so in the case of the Matebele. "When a strong man armed keepeth his palace, his goods are in peace; but when a stronger than he shall come upon him, and overcome him, he taketh from him all his armour wherein he trusted, and divideth his spoils." But the strong man is not often vanquished in one day. He is not stripped of all his armour at once. The Christian missionary in such a country as the Matebele, is glad as a beginning to observe that the pride in the heathenish armour decreases, the pleasure in its use diminishes; and he hopes that at length each part will be thrown aside.

Now, there are some supporters of missionary societies in whom patience is not a conspicuous virtue. Forgetting the past history of Christianity in their own and other lands, they seem to expect to see the yellow harvest-field as soon as the husbandman appears on the wild furze-covered moorland. There is to be no laborious or preparatory process: the end is to be attained at once. "Is not the Spirit of God all-powerful?" it is asked. Now, the Holy Spirit is indeed all-powerful, and His operations are not to be limited, nor His coming or going to be explained, any more than that of the wind to which He is likened. The power and the presence of this Divine Helper constitute the grounds of the confidence of the evangelist in Pagan lands. The minds and hearts of the heathen, however, upon which the Spirit acts, are not everywhere in the same condition. Occasionally there has been a special preparedness for the work of the evangelist. For instance, the Karens had a tradition that religious teaching was to come to them from the west. When, therefore, the missionaries appeared, they were received with open arms, being hailed as the expected benefactors. Here was "good soil" specially prepared for the husbandman, and the seed sprang up at once. But when missionaries found their way into the country of the Matebele, their position was very different. The natives of that land expected not good but evil from the white man. They were not simple, unsophisticated savages, but habitual murderers and assassins—perpetrators of outrages and enormities that may not be named. The difficulties connected with a mission in such a country must, on a moment's reflection, be apparent to every one. The fact that men preaching such doctrines as the missionaries advocated were not speedily expelled from the country, would seem to show that the doctrines themselves touched chords which were not entirely destroyed even in the hearts of the Matebele, although constantly ignored in their every-day life. And if the missionaries who were received with suspicion and distrust at the outset, and who constantly advocated doctrines unpopular, unpatriotic, and illegal to the Matebele, nevertheless grew personally in the favour of both chief and people, we cannot but accord to them individually high commendation in connection with such a result. Nothing but the rectitude and the kindliness of the Christian character could have procured and preserved for them the friendship of such a people. Above all must thanks be given to God whose Spirit accompanied His servants, commending their words and their lives to the hearts and consciences of the Matebele, giving them favour and respect in their sight.

It seems to me that no illustration can be taken from the New Testament of the experiences of Christianity in such a land. Nor does the history of the earlier Jewish Church of the Old Testament supply us with a parallel. In the Matebele we have an organized band of savages, far more ignorant and degraded than the Hebrew slaves who left the bondage of Egypt for the promised land of Canaan.

And in the case of the South African tribe, we have the attempt made to benefit them spiritually, not in a solitary wilderness, where they would be completely open to Divine influences, and under the immediate control of their Divine teacher, but while the people remain under a more galling and debasing yoke than that of the Pharaohs.

It is true that men have all gone astray like lost sheep; but some would seem to have wandered farther than others—have indeed gone so far that the shepherd must call repeatedly before his voice is recognised, and must himself assist their return by clearing away many miles of entangling thicket before they reach the fold and the rest of the flock. When such a lost soul hears the Divine voice, and responding, although with faint, uncertain accent, "I will arise," sets out on the journey—"turning round" with dissatisfaction from old courses—few would allow that the still degraded man is "converted." He was very far away, and is long in returning. He sometimes fails, and forgets again to rise and resume his journey. He sees, as in a distant land, the life which he dimly admires, and wonders if he can ever attain unto it. In many instances the man dies without having reached the intelligence, stability, consistency of a "convert."

Thus in the Matebele country I found that after four years' teaching by my friends the missionaries, many of the men with whom they had come into contact would admit that their views were right, and that the Word of God was "truly a good Word." But such admissions would be made only if the person were alone with yourself; the presence of another, in that land of mutual distrust, would put a stop to all such remarks. "How am I ever to learn," said a soldier to me, "seeing that after I have made a beginning, I am sure to be called away on the business of the chief, and the war party starts before I have made any progress. And when we come back from the war we are tired, perhaps wounded, and need to rest before we can begin again." Poor Matebele soldier! His was a wretched lot; yet in it there was to me one cheering thought—he himself began to be displeased with it.

In tribes which do not possess the knowledge of letters, it takes some time before people, who do not give personal and minute attention to the subject, are able to comprehend the true use of books or of writing. Sekhome, the chief of the Bamangwato, once asked me if Mr. Price was on his way back to the station, and upon my saying that I did not know, his reply was, "Well, then, ask your 'likwalo' (books); will they not tell you?" In the Matebele country "the books" were regarded at the time of my visit, and by almost all with whom I came into contact, as the "sacred things" or the "divining things" of the white man's religion. To "learn the books" was therefore regarded as a formal entrance upon the practice of the white man's mode of worship. It occupied an initial position in their minds similar to that which baptism really occupies. They had no idea that a man might learn to read, and still choose to remain a heathen.

During one of my visits to Moselekatse, I had a conversation with the chief upon this subject, which will show his skill in avoiding what was unpleasant, as well as his deep aversion to the work of the missionary. I began by expressing my great pleasure and thankfulness to see that my friends at Inyate had enjoyed his protection and his hospitality. "But there is one thing which very much surprises me," I added. The chief was now all attention to hear the complaint, and so were his head men sitting near. "I am surprised that no one has learned to read the Word of God during these years. My friends are quite capable of teaching it: it is indeed what they have specially learned to do.

When I see that your people are more handsome than all their neighbours, I cannot believe that they are unable to learn. You know you yourself invited the teachers, and they came; but no one is taught, although they have been here for years. I thought I should ask yourself for an explanation of this strange thing."

After a pause, during which every one seemed to wonder what the reply would be, the chief said, "We Matebele like many wives."

"But," I rejoined, "a man with many wives may learn the Word of God, and after he understands it, accept of it or otherwise; and as for the children, they might surely all learn."

Again a pause, and again the same reply: "We Matebele like many wives." Each time the answer was given, it was loudly cheered by the head men who sat near. Moselekatse was too politic to enter into a discussion on such a subject. He seized the most unpopular tenet of the "Word of God" from the Matebele point of view, and held it up to scorn. I learned from one of his men that the chief, after we left his presence, proceeded, amid the merriment of his attendants, to draw a ludicrous picture of the state of Matebele society were the Christian views adopted. It was thus apparent that whatever obstacles might arise in other quarters, the greatest of all was the determined opposition of the chief.

The following anecdote will illustrate the amount of knowledge possessed by some of Moselekatse's sons, and two or three head men of the Matebele, at the date of my visit. It is to be noted that none of them resided in the district regularly visited by the missionaries, but they must nevertheless have come into frequent contact with them, both at Inyate and at the head-quarters of the chief. Mr. Sykes and I were on a visit to Moselekatse, and the former, who is a diligent and most successful student of the Zulu language, of which Setebele is a corruption, was availing himself of the opportunity of meeting with the chief's sons and other Zulus, to compare the language as spoken by them with that given in a Zulu lexicon which he held in his hand. The young men were amazed when Mr. Sykes read off to them the Zulu form of certain words which had become changed in the Setebele dialect. They recognised some of the expressions as still used by the old men. "To-day I see your books are not 'dice' or 'divining things,'" said one of Moselekatse's sons, "but contain real words." Some of the company, however, thought this praise was too hastily given, and expressed their dissent. Mr. Sykes bethought him of a plan by which he hoped to enlighten and convince all as to the use and power of letters. Calling upon the man who had expressed his doubts to follow him, they left the tent together. When they were alone outside, Mr. Sykes requested him to suggest a word—any one he liked—which he would write down; assuring him that I, although now out of hearing, would be able to tell the word to every one in the tent as soon as I saw the paper. This was a challenge which the man at once accepted, and whispered a word to Mr. Sykes which was duly written down. The two then re-entered the tent, and the man explained to his friends what had been done. The paper was now handed to me, amid the breathless attention of all. When I at once pronounced the word written, the surprise was universal and genuine. But some of a "sceptical" turn of mind, or perhaps with greater curiosity than others, requested Mr. Sykes to go out with them also. As every experiment produced the same result, the paper always telling me what the man had whispered into Mr. Sykes's ear, conviction was at length produced; and their language was ransacked for encomiums with which to characterize the wisdom of the white men. Even then, however, they could have only a very imperfect idea of the manner in which the letters were formed into words.

I found on inquiry that as the result of the advice of Mr. Moffat and of the resident missionaries, the enforced celibacy of the common soldiers had been considerably relaxed by Moselekatse. The soldiers admitted this to me, and owned that a change had been produced in the administration of the chief in this respect as a result of the advice of missionaries. But as far as barracks are changed into homes, so far is a deadly blow struck at the brutal war-parties of the Matebele. When they have wives and children at home, one great inducement to go on such parties will be removed. At the time of my visit the counsels of the missionaries had not prevailed in putting a stop to these war-parties. But latterly the chief seemed to be more anxious for them than the people. Uneasiness and disinclination to go to war were not always hidden from the missionaries by the people, although they dreaded to impugn the conduct of their chief. Up to the time of his death Moselekatse continued every year to assemble his forces and let them loose on the Mashona or some other neighbouring tribe. To have caused these war-parties to cease would have been to accomplish a complete revolution in the supreme policy of the tribe. It could only have been effected by the action of the chief himself, and a large majority of the head men and common soldiers.

But the bloodthirstiness of the Matebele has certainly decreased since their contact with missionaries. The latter have repeatedly told the soldiers of Moselekatse that it is a disgrace to kill old people and women and children in war, and that English soldiers fight only with those who are armed. I never saw greater "shame and confusion of face" in a black man than in the case of a party of soldiers at Inyate, before whom I was imitating the retreating form of a decrepit old man hobbling away into the bushes, and the aged woman appealing to their mercy, while they followed and speared all indiscriminately. Had they been white men the blush on their faces would have been deep. In black men this expression is chiefly to be detected about the eyes and mouth. On one occasion, while we were on a visit to his quarters, Moselekatse called Mr. Sykes to his waggon to converse with him. He wished the missionary to give up residing at Inyate, and to come and live with him. "I am always glad when you missionaries are near to me," said the aged chief. "My heart is white when I see you. When I have you at my encampment I say to myself, God is with me." Distrusting his own men, the chief knew he could always trust the missionary. "We always take notice," the officers of the chief remarked on another occasion, "that the chief does not kill so many people when you white men are at his camp. He loves the white men, and he knows they don't like bloodshed."

When some people are told that converts to Christianity are not likely—so far as man can judge—to appear speedily in such countries as the Matebele, they rush to the conclusion that Christianity cannot produce the desired change at all. Like the ignorant practitioner who having tried one remedy without result, hastens to administer another, these people exclaim, "You must civilize before you Christianize the savage tribes." Others again hold the very opposite opinion, and assert that Christianity may be calculated to improve rude and savage men, but is effete in the ethereal regions of modern culture. According to another view Christianity and civilisation lead only to the deterioration of barbarous nations. Le Vaillant, one of the earliest writers on South Africa, propounds this notion. He says: "In a state of nature man is essentially good; why should the Hottentot be an exception to the rule?"[1] Why, indeed! Le Vaillant was very much pleased with the "fair Narina" in her African attire; and if others might object to the buchu-scent and the smearing of the body, these were objections only to externals; the girl herself was, like her countrymen, and everybody else, "in a state of nature, essentially good."

But the theorists in question would not be agreed as to the "chief end" of man's existence, or the standard toward which the nations are to be raised. Indeed Le Vaillant would affirm that we must all return to a "state of nature"—whatever that might mean. I for one would object to this. I have had some years' experience of man in the state to which the Frenchman probably referred, and even in this chapter have given abundant proof that he is not therein "essentially good." The moral standard of others is not perhaps much higher than that of Le Vaillant, although they are more fastidious as to outward appearances. But what is civilisation without the sanctions and restraints of religion? Mere refinement, however arrayed in elegance and beauty and affluence, may be after all only the selfishness of the heathen in gaudier attire. Or, if we affirm that it is "French polish," our meaning will probably not be misunderstood. Now this article is very thin, and easily rubbed off, as we have often seen, and the ugliness which is then revealed is all the more glaring on account of the fair and prepossessing exterior.

But let us take it for granted that our object is to induce men everywhere to love God and to love one another. How is this to be accomplished? It will be admitted that

[1] Le Vaillant's *Travels*, vol. ii. p. 149.

this end would not of necessity be attained, although the savage had become the artisan, or the man who now beats out his assegai on a stone had learned to fashion a breech-loading rifle or a mitrailleuse. For my own part I come from the mission-field with the earnest belief that the teaching and the living of Christianity in a heathen land is the only practicable method of leading men to love God and to love one another. I believe in the gospel of Jesus Christ for "every creature." But then, religion does not despise civilisation and the useful arts, as if she had no need of them. Foolish men may flaunt an empty name before us, and affirm that civilisation[1] without religion is enough to bless mankind; and others may have been led into the region of theory, in speaking of what religion could do without civilisation. But as a practical question, in connection with the elevation of the heathen nations, it seems to me a gratuitous thing to separate in theory those things which are never separated in practice. As a matter of fact, religion and civilisation always have gone hand in hand in African missions. The missionary endeavours to introduce and to exhibit both, in his teaching and in his life. Religion is the mistress; civilisation her attendant and servant. The one appeals to the deepest and strongest feelings of man; the other enables him to carry into practice his new thoughts. Industry and civilisation at a mission station are religion in practice. Its divinest fragrance ascends like precious incense to Heaven, but its fruits are visible to men. Christianity may be long in

[1] We all know who spoke of "a certain rich man," who lived in all the elegance of Eastern refinement, and of the poor beggar who was left at his door to be fed with crumbs, and whose only medical attendants were the dogs who licked his sores. Religion raised the faithful beggar to heaven. Civilisation and refinement engrossed the attention of the rich man in a life of elegant selfishness. He lived neither for God nor for his fellow-men. "In hell he lifted up his eyes, being in torment."

swaying the heathen; nothing else would move him so soon. There may be an interval between the first introduction of Christianity and its reception by the people. Such intervals are the rule rather than the exception in modern missions. Whatever name we choose to apply to this sometimes protracted stage in the history of a mission, it is of importance to remember that Christianity is the leading agent which is silently working the change. When Christian churches return to a primitive model, and make the spreading of Christianity in the world the great end of their organization, one of the questions which will no doubt occupy their attention will be—how practical and industrial Christianity may be best exhibited in barbarous countries in connection with our missions, on a more extensive scale than at present.

In Southern Africa, in those districts of which I am treating, Providence would seem to have linked together the introduction of Christianity with the destruction of all possibility of the old way of living. The spread of Europeans in the country, and the gradual introduction of guns and horses into the interior, lead to the wholesale destruction of game, upon which formerly the natives largely subsisted. An extensive and deadly epidemic among the cattle still further curtailed their means of living the old lazy heathen life. As a matter of fact those events render industry absolutely necessary on the part of the natives. They must work, if they would eat.

In the Matebele country as soon as missionaries made their appearance, traders followed them. Ivory, which Moselekatse had kept in store for years, was then disposed of on terms which were satisfactory to both the chief and the traders. As an adjunct to the work of the missionary, this trading was of great consequence. It directed the minds of the people into other channels besides rapine and blood. The ivory in store was soon exhausted, and then the Matebele, with their recently purchased guns, began to kill elephants and ostriches, for the sake of trade. The produce of the chase, like everything else, belonged to the chief, but he was pleased to waive his claim to the feathers of the ostrich. Thus it was possible for a common soldier to obtain the things of the white men; and property could now be held by those who a short time before had little else than their spears and their shields. One drawback to their engaging in such a career with pleasure was that the Bechuanas already excelled in hunting, and were usually dressed in European clothes when they entered the Matebele country in the service of white men. To hunt, therefore, or to be dressed in the clothes which the traders brought, was to descend to the position of the Bechuanas, who were despised by the Matebele, as less powerful than themselves in war. And it did not comfort them to think that the white men also wore such clothing, because when the Matebele donned the European dress they found they were not so much like Englishmen as they were like Bechuanas! Thinking that an athletic people might appreciate the supposed freedom of the "Garb of old Gaul," Mr. Moffat presented Moselekatse with a Highland kilt and appurtenances. But it was never worn. The Matebele preferred their own cincture of wild-cats' tails to the cincture of the Scotch mountaineers. If they doffed their own dress at all, it was only to don the clothing which they saw in use among the white men around them.

As long as I was in the country I continued to be known as "Sekhome's missionary." During one of my visits to the chief's quarters, a regiment of soldiers was assembled, which had formed part of the war-party against Sekhome. While walking near my waggons in company with Mbego, the head man of Sokindaba, I observed these men looking and pointing to me. I asked my companion what they meant. "They say they recognise you; and that you fought against them at Sekhome's." I went up to the men, and asked them why they were pointing at me.

They smiled, and said, "Because it was you who shot us at Sekhome's."

"But do you really mean to assert that you saw me there?" I inquired. "Take a good look now—not at the clothes, but at the face."

"Well, we are not quite sure, but we think so; and the Bamangwato prisoners told us that the white men were helping Sekhome."

Seeing that they were all young men, I replied, "Some of you say I was fighting against you, some of you say you are not sure. It is evident you have never seen white men fight. Should you ever meet them in battle, depend on it there will not be two opinions among you as to who your opponents are. You will at once perceive that they are neither Bamangwato nor Mashona." I went on to assure them that not a single white man had fired a shot in behalf of Sekhome. Those whom they mistook for white men were Sekhome's sons and their servants, who were dressed in white men's clothing. I occupied at Sekhome's the position which their own missionaries did there, and they all knew they were the enemies of war. The head man enjoyed my reply, and was glad to amplify my remarks, declaring that the soldiers had seen nothing at Sekhome's in comparison to what he and his equals had experienced in the "old wars," etc. I often saw my horse pointed out by the Matebele soldiers, as they passed Inyate, with the remark, "That is the horse of Sekhome's missionary, who shot so many of us in the fight." Now, my horse was a roan, and there was not a single one of that colour in the possession of those who fought under Khame. But the

Matebele are not much accustomed to horses; and when I heard these remarks, made with such confidence, I was thankful that I had not carried out my intention of visiting the camp of the Matebele while they were close to Shoshong, as I at one time proposed to do. The Matebele were still very reluctant to believe that Bamangwato could manage guns and horses with such effect; and they had been deceived by the Bamangwato prisoners, who magnified the strength of the town as much as they could, and roundly asserted that a party of white men were fighting for their chief.

During my stay in his country, Moselekatse agreed to allow me to form a new station on the same terms that my friends enjoyed at Inyate. But when I considered the facilities for instruction afforded by the milder government of the Bechuana chiefs, as contrasted with the unyielding sway of Moselekatse, I resolved in the meantime to return to Shoshong, and submit the offer of Moselekatse and the circumstances of the Matebele mission to the consideration of the Directors in London. That mission was now happily through the crisis on account of which I had joined it; and I did not conceive it to be right for me to relinquish the direct and active work of instruction elsewhere for such a position as my friends occupied among the Matebele. When I had made up my mind, I rode over to Moselekatse's quarters to thank him for the offer of a site for a station which he had given; but said that I should first return to Shoshong, where my "bagolu" (fathers, directors) had placed me; and if they agreed to my returning I should come back. This elicited the commendations of the chief: "This is how the white men prevail, by the obedience which they render to superiors." Turning to me, he asked, "Will you come back in the winter?" I replied that I did not think so; indeed, it was uncertain whether I should come back at all. This answer also met with approval: "Makense is no deceiver; other white men speak pleasantly, and tell me they will be back soon, but never return."

Every year the Matebele celebrate the "pina ea Morimo" (the dance or religious service of God) before the departure of the war-parties which are organized by the chief. This annual assembly was about to take place when I left the country. The soldiers had begun to arrive in full dress, with their large war-shields, and their heads and arms decorated with the black feathers of the ostrich, which are so arranged as almost to hide the contour of the human form, and enable the soldier to represent a fury or war-demon more than a man. One of the last ceremonies performed by the soldiers before their departure, is to catch a bull devoted to this purpose, holding it fast without the aid of rope or halter, while a large piece of meat is cut out of one of its hind-legs. When this operation is complete, the bull is let free; but of course it cannot go far. The meat which has been taken from the leg of the living animal is now thrown upon the embers of a fire lighted for the purpose, and after being turned once or twice on the coals, and long before it is roasted, it is taken off the fire, and every soldier in turn partakes of it. This ceremony is supposed to qualify them for the part they shall have to play in the coming campaign.

When I last saw Moselekatse, he was very ill, unable to lift the cup to his own lips. He begged hard for medicine. But it would have been a hazardous thing for "Sekhome's missionary" to have dosed Moselekatse just before leaving the country. Any temporary discomfort produced by the medicine would have roused the suspicions of those who never cease speaking of witchcraft and poisoning. Besides, the old man's disease was practically incurable; and my answer to him was that "I had no medicine which would make him better."

"Would you tell that to your own father, if he were in my position to-day?" pleaded the aged chief.

I was heartily sorry for him; and was glad to be able to say that his own missionaries would be ready to assist him in this way, as they had done before. To show the respect entertained by the chief for missionaries, and something akin to the dignity attaching to his own character, I may mention that, as we entered the yard previous to my final interview, we were informed by an attendant that "we must not be offended, the chief's heart was white toward us; but there would be no shaking of hands in greeting that day." We soon saw the reason: the chief had not power to move his arms from where they lay.

When I was leaving the country, my waggons stuck fast in a deep rut opposite one of the towns. Some scores of soldiers came out to witness the efforts of the oxen to pull the waggon out.

"Go back to Inyate and live there," said the men; "don't you see that the waggon refuses to go again to Sekhome?"

I had now an opportunity of witnessing the united strength of these men in pulling a waggon. I begged their assistance from their officer, who was present; but the men consented to pull the waggon out only on condition that I would unyoke my oxen, and leave it entirely in their hands. As soon as I had done this, they raised a chorus; and during the singing of the first line or two they were all making preparations, and securing good hold of the waggon. When they reached a certain word in the song, every energy was put forth by common consent, and the waggon was at once in motion. "Tusa! tusa!" (help) was now the cry. Not being able to pay nearly a hundred men, I persuaded the officer to take the payment, and give it to his soldiers. I first gave some bullets; these were scattered in the crowd of men, who growled and roared as they pressed on one another in the scramble. The officer now said that I must give a bit of calico also.

"But," I said, "I have not enough to go over them all."

"Never mind; hand what you wish to give to me."

I gave the man two or three yards of thin print, which, gathering into a lump in his hand, he threw among the men. There was now another scramble, and in a few minutes I beheld one man with a shred of cloth encircling his brow, another had enough to tie round his neck, a third stuck his portion as an ornament into his ear! Every one was now pleased; so I again yoked my oxen and proceeded on my way.

Our friends Mr. and Mrs. Sykes accompanied us as far as the borders of Moselekatse's country. In that distant mission-field such a journey in the waggon is appreciated as a "change" in the life of the missionary. Families usually return to their station with recruited health and vigour after a week or fortnight's tour, during which missionary work has been done in villages and by the wayside.

Late one Saturday we reached the Shashane river, in the Makalaka country. We were benighted before the last waggon was pulled through the sandy bed of the river, both men and oxen being exhausted after a long day's ride. To complete our discomfort, it commenced to rain while we were still working in the drift, arranging twenty or thirty weary oxen before one waggon. Instead of a cheerful camp with a bright fire, our waggons were standing under some spreading acacias in complete darkness—a small fire struggling with the rain being completely surrounded by some Matebele soldiers who were then with us. Instead of a comfortable pen for our cattle near to the waggons, there was no pen at all, and the cattle were lying about on all sides. There was, however, a cheerful light inside my waggon, and a bright face too, and a warm cup of coffee ready to refresh me after my day's work. But there is many a slip between the cup and the lip. Before I had tasted it I heard first the howl of the hyena, and then the low growl of the lion. There was no mistaking either, so I had at once to see to the safety of the camp. We were certainly in a nice predicament—without a cattle-pen—without a fire—without even firewood! Between the darkness of the night and the shadow of the trees I could see nothing whatever outside. Having a good glass lantern, I succeeded in inducing some of the men to accompany me to collect firewood, and to light new fires, so as to encircle our camp. Mr. Sykes did the same at another side with the aid of his men. What was the lion doing all the while? He never had a better chance of getting beef, but his courage failed him. My dog Nero, which had been in a decidedly pugnacious humour that evening, having had a long and severe fight with another dog, as soon as he heard the lion and hyena, went out to meet them, and barked loudly between them and the cattle. When our fires were ready, we collected the cattle, and brought them inside our enclosure. I may explain that the lion had approached on the leeward side; therefore, while the oxen were uneasy at the sound of his first and only low growl, they were not so terrified and unmanageable as they might have become had our enemy approached us from the windward, so as to enable them to get his scent. Aware of this, the lion endeavoured once or twice to get past the dog, and round the circle of fires to the other side. He succeeded twice, but was on both occasions followed in the darkness by our noble defender. But do I mean to affirm that a dog ventured to attack a lion? The dog of course could not have gone near to the lion, for a single stroke of his paw would have killed it at once. At one time it must have ventured too close, for it suddenly gave a scream of terror, and then its bark was silent. I thought it was all over with my faithful dog. But after a rush through the bushes, which I could distinctly hear, his loud deep bark was heard in a different quarter. The lion must have made a spring at the dog, and just missing him, run for the other side of the oxen; when, nothing daunted by his narrow escape, the dog stuck to his place between the lion and his master's property. But why did not the lion rush past him at once, entirely ignoring his existence and his barking? The dog no doubt would have given way. Now, I don't know why the lion was not bolder than he showed himself to be. All I know is, Nero never let him get past him toward the cattle. I conjecture that the lion was prevented from making a spring, not on account of the dog's presence, but on account of his barking. If all thieves had bells tied to them which they could not keep from ringing, or even if loud-barking dogs always accompanied them, and baited them, they might not fear the dogs much, and the bells not at all, but they would consider it very awkward to ply their stealthy work in such unfavourable circumstances. And so the lion cared nothing for the dog as an opponent; but how was he to know how many invisible enemies were roused by so much noise? Go where he liked, the barking went with him. When this had gone on for some hours, I felt at a loss to know what to think of it, and hazarded the opinion that it was only a wolf or hyena, and no lion at all. On my saying this to old Mebalwe, he demanded if I had ever heard a wolf make such a noise as that growl? "That did not come from a wolf's throat," said this old native traveller. "But did you ever hear of a lion kept at bay by a dog, while men are gathering wood and making fires, and collecting their cattle?" I replied. Mebalwe admitted that this was something new to him, but stuck to his firm belief that it was a lion. The conduct of the oxen did not throw much light on the question, for when the dog and his invisible opponent rushed to the windward, although they raised their ears and looked excited, they were quieted by the whistling of the men and the sight of the fires all round them. About an hour or two before dawn, the barking ceased, the oxen lay down, and our danger was evidently at an end. As soon as Mebalwe could see a spoor, he examined those round the encampment, and especially in the sand of the river near my waggon, where they were plainly visible. There was no longer any doubt: it was a large lion which had been kept at bay by one dog in a pitch-dark night. We had now the choice of spending the Sunday in building a cattle-pen, and preparing ourselves for another night's attack, or of proceeding on our journey to the village of Monyame, which was within a short distance of our camp. We chose the latter course, as involving less labour, with the certainty of repose for ourselves and our cattle, and for Nero our faithful defender. A few days after Nero fell sick, and could not cross a deep rapid river through which the waggons had gone. I went back for him myself, carried him over in my arms, and prepared a place for him in the second waggon. In a few days, however, he died, much to my own and my children's regret. We dug a grave for him by the roadside, and raised a heap of stones over it. I am sure any boy who reads about Nero's exploits will agree that he deserved this honour, for he was no common dog.

We reached Shoshong in the end of February. Khame and Khamane, and other attendants at church and school, rode out to meet us, and expressed their joy at our return.

A year after his discovery of gold at the Tatie river, Mr.

Mauch also ascertained that the same precious metal was to be found over an extensive tract of country some four days' journey to the north-east of Inyate, in a country now in the possession of Moselekatse, its former owners, the Mashona having been killed by him, or obliged to flee. This gold was some years ago collected by half-caste Portuguese traders from the east coast. These men visited Moselekatse once, but as their views did not seem to accord with those of the Zulu chief, the visit was not repeated. As soon as the discovery of gold was announced in the south, an ambassador from the Transvaal government visited Moselekatse to obtain authority over the gold field in behalf of the Transvaal government. But the old chief would not yield. "Your people may come in and take away this stone (quartz) as they take away ivory in their waggons. They may load up as much as they please of it, but on no account are they to bring with them a Dutch woman, a cow, a ewe, or a she-goat, because the permission is to carry away stones, not to build houses and towns in my country." This gold-yielding region is still unexplored.

Since the period of my visit in 1864, the missionaries have been pursuing their quiet labours among the Matebele—their influence increasing, but without any open adherents to their doctrines. The death of Moselekatse, which took place in 1868, was felt to be a crisis in the history of the tribe and the mission; but in all the discussions and difficulties with reference to his successor, the influence and presence of the missionaries have been recognised with thankfulness by all parties. According to Zulu custom, Moselekatse sent away in a secret manner his son, called Kuruman, whom he declared to one or two confidential head men to be his successor. The young heir was sent to a neighbouring chief, who was to have the care of bringing him up, and the responsibility of seeing that he "got his own" on the death of his father. But Moselekatse lived twenty years after this private arrangement. At his death, Umbate, the only surviving councillor, started a party of men to bring home the young chief. But Kuruman could not be found. It was at one time rumoured that he had made his appearance in the Matebele country, and Mangwane and other sons of Moselekatse fled for fear of him. They had good reason to flee; for one of the first acts of a young Zulu chief is to put to death all possible claimants to the chieftainship, and all councillors of his predecessor, who might continually annoy him by saying that his wisdom and prowess did not equal those of his father. But Kuruman has never been found. There is indeed a romantic story told of a Zulu called Kanda, at present living in Natal, who claims to be, if not Kuruman, at least a son of Moselekatse. This person has been for some time in the employment of Mr. Shepstone, the respected Agent for Native Affairs in Natal. The story goes that, unlike the other servants, Kanda declined to receive the usual wages from his master, with the explanation that he was a great man in his own country, and did not wish to receive pay. It was not beneath his dignity, however, to beg, so when he wanted a blanket or other article of clothing, he went to his master and begged them. In this way he no doubt took care to keep his account balanced on the right side. When the news of Moselekatse's death reached Natal, Kanda declared himself to be the person the Matebele were looking for. But Umbate did not share this opinion. The old councillor gave his verdict that this was another son, and that Kuruman was dead. Lobingole, the next in rank, was accordingly appointed by Umbate and a number of the head men as successor to Moselekatse. The large town of Sokindaba, however, and others, professed to believe that Kanda was no pretender, but the true heir to the chieftainship. A battle was recently fought, in which, after considerable bloodshed, Lobingole was victor, so that his claims are no longer likely to be questioned. The wounded of both sides on this occasion hastened to the missionaries at Inyate for protection and for medical assistance. The missionaries also visited the field of battle, to assist those who were left there. At Inyate the wounded did not all know which side had gained the victory; they saw they were sitting down with adversaries; but so far, "old things had passed away." They were content thus to mingle together at the mission station; and the chief cheerfully granted the petition of the missionaries that none of his wounded enemies should be put to death.

It will be a blessing to themselves and the whole country when the military organization of the Matebele is at an end. But it is to be hoped that this breaking up of the old system will be accomplished without the dispersion of the heterogeneous elements of the tribe, and without the march of some of its component parts to the northward to carry devastation beyond the Zambese.

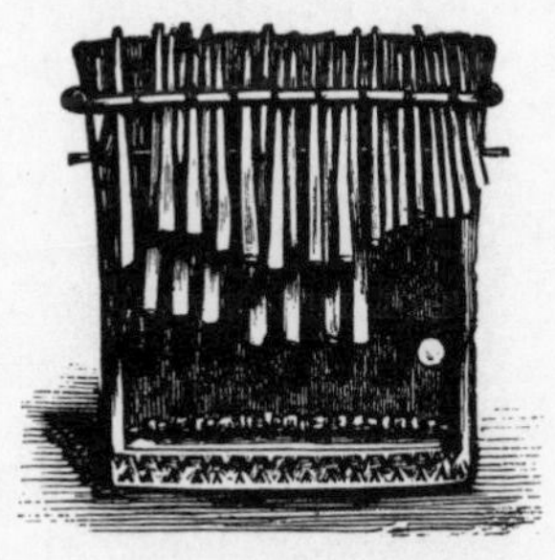

Musical Instrument—Mashona-land.

CHAPTER XVIII.

A CHAPTER OF BAMANGWATO HISTORY.

AFTER my return from Matebele-land in February 1864, I resumed my labours as a missionary at Shoshong. During our absence our dear friends Mr. and Mrs. Price had been earnestly and assiduously carrying on the work of instruction. It was amicably arranged that, in accordance with the expressed wishes of the chief and people, the station should be occupied by the London Missionary Society. The German missionaries carried on their work in districts within the Transvaal Republic, and on its border.

Without the knowledge of letters, the Bamangwato are not able to recall much of the past history of their ancestors. They have preserved the names of seven chiefs, but beyond that they cannot go. The precedence as to rank among the tribes in North Bechuana-land is taken by the Bahurutse. The first-fruits of a new harvest must be first partaken of by Moilwe, the present chief of that tribe. For another chief to "loma," without waiting to hear that his superior had done so, would be a public insult and a cause of war. But in recent times such transgressions have been numerous, for the Bahurutse are not now a powerful tribe. The Bangwaketse, the Bakwena, and the Bamangwato were originally one people. Tradition retains a glimmering of the circumstances of their separation. The Bakwena included the Bamangwato when they separated from the Bangwaketse; but afterwards a subdivision took place, the Bamangwato being the younger or minor party. We have already seen that afterwards the Bamangwato again divided, the minor party being now the Batowana, at present residing at Lake Ngami.

The division of the Bamangwato took place in the time of Matipi, the great-grandfather of the present chief. Matipi loved Towane, the younger son, and disliked Khame, the elder. Before the death of their father the sons quarrelled, and Towane, aided by the influence of his father, over whom he began to exercise control, secured the suffrages of nearly half the tribe, and the property belonging by right to the chief. Accompanied by his father and their adherents, Towane separated from his brother, and proceeding into the region of the Botletle river, eventually settled at Lake Ngami. Ungrateful for the kindness lavished upon him by his father, Towane was soon impatient of his presence in the town; and having now secured to himself the support of all the people, heaped indignities upon the parent through whose partiality he had risen to power. Turning with a bitter heart from the home of this unnatural child, the aged chief was fain to try the affection of Khame, whom he had wronged and robbed of part of his birthright. He approached the town of the Bamangwato, then standing at a different place in the same range of mountains, and sent messengers to beseech the forgiveness of his son.

The answer was a stern one: "Say to Matipi that he has no son called Khame; his only son is Towane. It would not be meet that Matipi should reside in the town of Khame, the despised vassal. But if the chief Matipi chooses to reside in his own country, let him select a fountain and build."

The grey-headed sire was now filled with grief and

remorse. He had destroyed the "lehae," the home of the Bamangwato—few of whom remained with himself now. The son whom he had injured was more merciful than the one he had favoured, but neither the one nor the other now regarded him with filial affection. Without children—without people—without a lehae or home—the heart of the old man failed him, and he hanged himself to a tree in one of the deep ravines among the Bamangwato mountains. He was buried with the honours of a chief, and his grave is visited by the Bamangwato for the purpose of sacrifice and prayer to this day.

Khari is the chief whose name is most cherished among the Bamangwato. Brave in the field, wise in the council, kind to his vassals, Khari was all that Bechuanas desire their chief to be. Under his sway the Bamangwato acquired great influence. The Makalaka sent presents or tribute of hoes from distant villages; even some outlying towns of the Mashona, whose country the Matebele now inhabit, were glad partially to own the sway of this chief. But the lust of conquest brings ever its own punishment, although sometimes it may come speedily, and at others be long deferred. Not content with his ample possessions, Khari had gone against an unsubdued town of the Mashona with the strength and flower of his tribe. The Mashona had noticed in previous engagements the tactics of the Bamangwato, and now resolved to counteract them. They pressed forward their young regiments to meet the soldiers of the Bamangwato, sending round their best men by a concealed route, so as to attack the Bamangwato reserve, which was headed by Khari in person. The main body of the Mashona, as on other occasions, fled before the Bamangwato, who, thrown completely off their guard, chased their retreating enemies to some distance. The noise and tumult of war in their rear was the first indication to them of the danger into which they had fallen. Those whom they were pursuing all at once turned round and fell on their pursuers. Khari was surprised by the covert attack on his reserve by the second division of the Mashona army. The chief and his head men fell together. Few indeed of the army returned; and the Bamangwato never again attacked the Mashona. Indeed, the tribe may be said at this time to have been nearly destroyed.

While the Bamangwato were in this disorganized state, their country was traversed by Sebetuane at the head of the Makololo, and by Moselekatse at the head of the Matebele. Sekhome, the eldest son of Khari, was for a short time a prisoner of the Makololo, in the district of the Mababe. But gradually the scattered people re-assembled. The energy and wisdom of Khari seemed to animate the conduct of Sekhome, who managed to escape from his captors. A fatal obstacle, however, to his sway was that his mother was not the first wife of Khari as to rank. One brother was put to death by the Bamangwato head men, with Sekhome's connivance, and Macheng, the only remaining rival, and who was then a child, was saved by the flight of his mother to the Bakwena.

A tribe from Basuto-land endeavoured at this time to follow the Makololo into the interior; but the Bamangwato fell upon them in a pass which has been pointed out to me, and completely destroyed them. The name of the tribe is now almost forgotten.

For some years after his settlement in the present Matebele country, Moselekatse sent his warriors to bring in the cattle which he had left among the tribes he had conquered in Bechuana-land. Every year these hordes passed through the Bamangwato country, lifting cattle, destroying the gardens and driving the men and women to seek a refuge in the numerous caves on the top of the mountains. But at length the courage of despair was given to them. A young man, whose name I have forgotten, stood up and addressed his countrymen, as from the mouths of their caves they beheld the Matebele driving away their cattle on the plain below, "Bamangwato! let us die to-day. Have we not been dying the death of women for years? To-day let us die as men. Have we not seen our mothers killed before our eyes; our wives and sisters and daughters led away by our enemies? Have we not seen our own infants thrown into the air, and caught on the point of a Matebele spear? Have we not seen the same spear which had transfixed the old man, thrust also at once through the infant and the mother on whose breast it hung? This is worse than death! Therefore let us go and fight with these destroyers of our people and die like men."

The Bamangwato listened to this heroic counsel, placed themselves under the speaker as a leader, and engaged the Matebele on the plain. After a severe struggle they retook their cattle, and inflicted severe punishment on their enemies. The worsted Matebele retired, and waited for the arrival of the other divisions of their army, which had gone to the Bangwaketse and Bakwena countries. But even after they were united, they did not again attack the Bamangwato, but passed their stronghold in two companies, one going through the pass of Monakalongwe, the other taking what is now the waggon-road to the Matebele, which passes Bonnapitse.

Some time after this, a party of forty men was sent by Moselekatse to the town of the Bamangwato to "khetisa" or raise tribute for their master. The "tribute" of Sekhome was a heathenish as well as a daring one. He put the forty men to death. His people as well as himself were thus pledged to one another and to independence or death. From this time till 1863, when the raid took place which has been already described, there was no intercourse between the Matebele and the Bamangwato; the former neither seeking more tribute nor revenge for the death of the former tax-gatherers. Other smaller tribes now sought the protection of Sekhome. The Mapaleng, the Batalowta, the Maownatlala, the Bakhurutse, the Makalaka, and others, sought refuge from the Matebele with Sekhome in the hills of the Bamangwato.

The history of Macheng will further illustrate the social customs of the Bamangwato. After his mother fled to the Bakwena, Macheng was taken prisoner by the Matebele. He was then liberated by his friends; but falling into their hands a second time, he was carried away captive into the present Matebele country, and trained as a lechaga or common soldier. As the guardian from whom he had been taken captive, Sechele, the chief of the Bakwena, had some natural regret at the loss of his relative. The desire to free him was increased also by another kind of motive. The Bakwena taking the precedence of the Bamangwato as to rank, it has been the life-long endeavour of Sechele to obtain such influence in the town of the Bamangwato as would enable him to secure some of the treasures of ivory and ostrich-feathers and furs which are brought from its extensive hunting-grounds, extending northward to the Zambese. Sechele, however, found Sekhome a most unmanageable person. Having achieved the independence of his people, Sekhome refused to own the supremacy of Sechele in any tangible way. Strifes were fomented in the Bamangwato town, but Sekhome was too vigilant, his power too great. So Sechele, with great grief for the little boy that had been stolen from his town twenty years before, and with greater desire to liberate one who, according to Bechuana customs, was the rightful chief of the Bamangwato, once and again requested Mr. Moffat to plead with Moselekatse for the liberation of Macheng. At length Mr. Moffat's influence prevailed with the Matebele despot. Macheng was set free, and accompanied Mr. Moffat into Bechuana-land. He was received with suspicion by Sekhome, but with an ovation by Sechele, who called the neighbouring chiefs to a grand assembly, where Macheng was publicly introduced to those who were to be his neighbours in Bechuana-land. In his speech on the occasion, Sechele likened the appearance of Macheng among them to the resurrection from the dead. But although the assembled chiefs took Sechele's speeches for what they were worth, all were agreed that the missionary had performed a disinterested and worthy action. They said it was becoming that such men should go among the tribes, for they did not go to betray but to deliver and to bless.

Tshukuru, the next in rank in the Bamangwato town to Sekhome, had been secretly in league with Sechele in this intrigue against Sekhome. He now appeared at the head of a party of Bamangwato, to welcome and receive their chief from the hand of Sechele. Macheng was established as chief of the Bamangwato, and Sechele received a very handsome present in ivory and other valuables. Sekhome was now afraid that Macheng, in self-preservation, would put him to death; for the latter could not but feel that he was a stranger in his own town, whereas Sekhome knew every man in it. Sekhome fled, therefore, to Sechele, who was delighted to afford him an asylum in his town. His presence there gave Sechele so much additional power and influence in all Bamangwato affairs. The training which Macheng had received as a lechaga did not very well qualify him to fill the office of a Bechuana chief. It is true he had received valuable instruction from Mr. Moffat, and some capital advice from Moselekatse before his departure. But Moselekatse had been teaching him after a very different fashion all his life as a soldier, and the lesson of years had more effect than a few kindly words spoken at parting. So Macheng began to introduce some of the Matebele customs into the Bechuana town. He ignored the head men. He struck a blow at all buying or selling, except through him and with his consent. He slaughtered oxen which were not his own property according to Bechuana customs; and one of the head men who had begun to complain was found dead in the town one morning. Every one now grieved that Macheng had ever arrived. "They were not Matebele; they were Bamangwato, and they did not like such practices." Tshukuru was now foremost in negotiating the return of Sekhome. Sechele was ready to oblige them again. Khosilintsi, his brother, was sent with an armed force to reinstate Sekhome. On their appearance Macheng fled with a few adherents; Khosilintsi and Sekhome took possession of the town, and the armed force of Bakwena made a raid upon the Bamangwato cattle-posts, taking home to Sechele a rich reward for his services. Chief-making had thus become a favourite pastime with Sechele; so that when Macheng, after having in vain sought assistance from Moselekatse, made overtures to the chief of the Bakwena to be permitted to reside in his town, this accommodating man was as usual very gracious, and Macheng lived for a longer period than Sekhome had done under Sechele's protection. When I first saw Sechele in 1859 his people had just returned from placing Sekhome as chief at Shoshong, and the timidity of the Bakalahari and Bushmen whom we met in the interior was owing to this disturbance. When I passed Sechele in 1862, Macheng, against whom he fought in 1859, was a refugee in his town, and plots were being concocted for the displacing of Sekhome. Both Sechele and Macheng gravely informed me that they were going to fight, and that they would not answer for my safety if I went in. My answer was that if he did not stop me forcibly I should go where I was sent; and I ventured to express the opinion that Sechele might give the Bamangwato a little rest, either with the one chief or the other. Such had been the history of the Bamangwato and of their chiefs when I appeared at Shoshong in 1862.

One thing remains unexplained. Macheng is a much younger man than Sekhome. But according to Bechuana custom this does not affect his title, as his mother was the recognised "head wife." As a matter of fact, Macheng was not born till some years after the death of Khari, his reputed and "legal" father. Neither does this affect his title to be chief. Khari having elevated the mother of Macheng to the dignity of head wife, and having paid her price in cattle, she and her offspring are to be reckoned to Khari, although the children should be born a dozen years after his death. It is not etiquette ever to refer to the man who thus "raises up seed" to another, in connection with such children. They are not his children. They are the children of him who is dead. But when Sekhome was vexed, he sometimes sarcastically declared that his rival was the "child of cattle," meaning that the price paid for Macheng's mother at her marriage with Khari was her son's only title to the chieftainship. There is never any question, however, among the natives as to the validity of this title. Even the most ardent friends of Sekhome admit that according to their customs Macheng is the rightful chief.

The Bamangwato mountains have afforded shelter to restless and roving tribes for many centuries. The earliest tradition points to Makalaka as their occupants. They were dispossessed by the Bakaa, who in turn gave way to the Bamangwato. But the mountains themselves speak of earlier inhabitants. On their summits I have noticed the small stone enclosures of ancient dwellings. Situated at a distance from fountain and garden, and in the most inaccessible heights, these dilapidated fences teach us at least that their builders lived the insecure and distrustful life of all rude and warlike clans. I never heard Bechuanas speak with affection of the open country. Perhaps the reason was that good garden ground, and grazing and hunting stations, could be readily obtained. But I have often heard them speak fondly of the mountains which they inhabit, and which form their refuge in times of war. The Kaffirs also spoke with the same affection of the Amatola mountains, not on account of their beauty, but because when guarded they were almost inaccessible to an enemy. The Scotch, the Swiss, and the Welsh speak and write fondly of the "land of the mountain and the flood" which gave them birth. This strong sentiment which animates all European mountaineers is perhaps an inheritance from their rude forefathers, who, like some Africans in our own time, had reason to be gratefully attached to the wild and inaccessible retreats which aided them to secure and to retain their independence.

Shoshong, the town of the Bamangwato, contains a population of some 30,000. It is situated at the foot of a mountain range of primary rock stretching from east to west for more than a dozen miles. About three miles to the south of this range there is another basaltic mountain called Marutlwe, in the neighbourhood of which both sandstone and limestone are to be found. The ground lying between the hills is occupied by the gardens of the Bamangwato. The main town spreads along the foot of the mountain, and some distance along the gorge in the mountain range, where the stream flows which supplies the town with water. There are also five divisions of the town in a beautifully sheltered position among the mountains. Again, there are small towns along the range to the west to the distance of some six miles, all being under one chief, whose decision in every case is final. The most distant villages are those of Makalaka refugees, who fled recently from the enormities of the Matebele sway. They chose to remain at a distance from the large town for the sake of their gardens, for it takes some of the Bamangwato who reside in the large town more than an hour to reach their cultivated fields.

A little more than a day's journey to the north-east of Shoshong, and along a range of mountains running north and south, which is visible to the traveller on his way to the Matebele country, there resides a subject tribe called the Machwapong. The mountains among which they reside abound with iron, and the Machwapong are famous among the tribes for their skill in smelting ore, and making the iron into hoes, axes, adzes, etc. They had found out that a certain tree yields charcoal, which gives great heat, with hardly any ashes. They therefore supply all their furnaces with this charcoal. Again, they observed that the lumps of smelted iron which remained longest mixed up with the charcoal were the hardest, and made the best axes. They thus may be said to have had the knowledge of making steel. They render a certain tribute to the Bamangwato, but are permitted to enjoy, after a somewhat precarious fashion, their own flocks and herds, and other personal property. They are also of service to the Bamangwato in announcing when a troop of elephants leaves the habitat of the tsetse, and passes into the open country. A party of men is at once despatched by the chief. Sleeping halfway, they reach the elephants the next day.

About three days' journey to the east of Shoshong, and

near the Limpopo river, here called the Ouri, there resides a small tribe of Bechuanas called Basilika. These people were once incorporated with the Bamangwato, but are now independent. They reside in a very romantic locality, well wooded and well watered. Their town is built on the crest of a high rock, and within the habitat of the tsetse. They have chosen this position for defence against their enemies. Their cattle they hide in belts of country known to them to be free from the destructive fly. Their enemies, however, even if they found the cattle, could not hope to drive them out without entering some place infested by the fly, in which case their prize would be worth nothing, as they would all die. When traders visit the Basilika, they have to halt a day's journey from the town, and either remove the goods to the town by bearers, or wait till the Basilika come to the waggons to trade. The latter is decidedly the safer procedure, as in the other case, the unfortunate stranger with only a man or two of his own, is not able to remove his own property back again to the waggons, and has therefore to sell his stock for prices which are much more profitable to those sharp-witted and unscrupulous denizens of the precipitous rock, than to the trader, who has a long bill to pay at the store at which he has filled his waggon. The district between Shoshong and Silika is well watered, and suitable for agriculture; but the greater part of it is at present infested with tsetse. It is believed that when the game is shot down and driven away, the tsetse will also disappear. The natives will then find in this district a place suitable for irrigation, upon which in a few years they will all be depending for subsistence.

In laying out a Bechuana town, the first thing is to ascertain where the chief's court-yard with the public cattle-pen is to be placed. As soon as this is settled the remainder is simple. As, after the tabernacle was placed in the wilderness, each one of the twelve tribes knew on which side he had to take up his position, so in the case of a Bechuana town; as soon as the chief's position is ascertained, one says, "My place is always next the chief on this side;" another adds, "And mine is always next on that side," and so on till the whole town is laid out. The chief is umpire in all such matters, and settles all disputes about ground, etc. When duly laid out, a Bechuana town is called "motse" (*urbs*) or town, and "lehae" or home. It is the mark of a freeman to have a residence in the town, while the vassals are doomed always to live in the open country (*pagus*). Bushmen indeed are not allowed to enter the precincts of the town during the day. They must wait outside till the sun has set before they appear in the "home" of their masters.

In general, those head men whose towns are on the east of the chief have their cattle-posts and their hunting-stations towards the east of the country; those on the west branch out towards the west, and so on. Thus within three or four days' journey from Shoshong, every fountain or available grazing station has some head man who does not exactly claim the ground as his property, but would regard the appearance there of another man's flocks and herds as an intrusion. The chief is not subjected to such stringent usages; for while his vassals have their allotted places, the chief's cattle in time of drought, or for other reason, may be shifted to any part of the grazing country. Then between one cattle-post and another there is always an understood boundary, except in cases where they are so wide apart that the cattle do not meet in grazing. Sometimes the herdsmen of two or more cattle-posts water their flocks and herds at the same fountain or well. In this case all have equal rights; those who are earliest at the fountain have the privilege of first watering their charge. As the Bechuanas do not water their cattle every day in winter, an arrangement is made, if the water is scarce, by which two cattle-posts do not visit the water on the same day. There are frequent quarrels among the herdsmen, which are often settled by blows.

Between one tribe and another there are no proper boundary lines. From the town as a centre, there are footpaths to most of the hunting stations. A certain fountain is known as the furthest hunting station on each road. These fountains are not equidistant from the town. If we drew a line from one of these frontier hunting-stations to the other, we should include within this zigzag boundary all the country of the tribe. To trace such a line, however, is an idea which never occurs to the natives.

Living respectively at their furthest hunting-station, the members of neighbouring tribes meet in time of peace, when they treat one another to snuff, and tell the news. In time of war, the vassals who live at those outlying villages are expected to be on the alert to convey to their chief the earliest information of any movement of an enemy. Therefore if an army intends to surprise a certain town, and attack it while it is quite unprepared, a necessary preliminary is to secure the vassals at every hunting-station on a certain path. Sometimes the enemy endeavours to pierce through the open country between the radiating paths; but it is not often that a Bechuana town can be thus surprised. In case of a protracted feud between two tribes, both call in their vassals; there is no longer any hunting; no longer any friendly intercourse. "The wayfaring man ceaseth" in such circumstances, and the intervening country becomes a desert, traversed only by the armed scouts of the adverse tribes.

The idea of buying land was unknown to the Bechuanas. Neither the house in town, nor the garden, nor the cattle-post, nor the hunting-station was ever bought. When a tribe, driven by its enemies, or moved by its own enterprise, advanced into a new country, the whole scheme of their social life was gradually re-developed there; and domestic, agricultural, pastoral, and hunting pursuits were there carried on as before. Every question as to the occupation of the territory was finally decided by the chief; the new settlement being, indeed, as much as possible a counterpart of the old; the divisions in the town keeping up their old inter-tribal names, which of course apply also to the possessions in the country. Thus one part of the town of Shoshong (or rather a division of its people living together) is called Maloshu. A certain belt of garden ground also goes by that name, as well as a cattle-post and hunting station.

Gourd Snuff-box.

CHAPTER XIX.

RELIGION AND POLITY OF THE BAMANGWATO.

THE "bogosi" or chieftainship is hereditary among the Bechuanas. A chief generally unites in his own person the offices of king, supreme judge, commander-in-chief, and high-priest or sorcerer. Sekhome exercised the functions belonging to all these offices, and was held by his admirers to excel in them all. Although a strong-minded man will always rule weaker men under any sort of government, a Bechuana chief has often a good deal of canvassing, "treating," etc., to perform before he can carry his point. Every important matter is supposed to be decided before the pitsho or public assembly of the free-men of the town. But in reality all "business" is transacted by the chief and the head men in secret. The chief knows how far he can go in a certain course before the pitsho takes place, and so do his opponents. In the public assembly there is a great deal of talking; but the matter in hand is carried or lost, not by what takes place there, so much as on account of the previous secret wire-pulling. The people are called to a public assembly by a recognised functionary of the chief, who leaves the twig of a certain tree in the public court-yard of each division of the town. In time of war the public assembly is generally held outside the town, when it is called a letshulo. The same name is given to an assembly for hunting certain animals employed in rain-making, or for hunting elephants, ostriches, or lions at the command and under the leadership of the chief.

Lions have twice attacked live stock at the town of Shoshong during my residence there; and once my own cattle-post was attacked by two lions, and four oxen were killed. A letshulo is ordered out on such occasions; the lion is surrounded and put to death. All the Englishmen on the place, as well as a letshulo of Bamangwato, kindly turned out to follow the lions which attacked my post. Only one of them was found. There being such a large party, there was some rivalry as to who should hit the lion first; for it is the man who first hits the animal who is said to have killed it, although it should need a good many shots afterwards. On this occasion an Englishman and a native fired nearly at the same time, and both bullets entered the lion's body.

In a letshulo after elephants many narrow escapes have come to my own knowledge. Mogomotsi, the brother-in-law of Sekhome, was pulled off his horse by an elephant, and thrown into the air. He luckily fell to leeward of the elephant, into a dense thicket of thorns. He was injured by the fall, and bleeding from the thorns, but had sense enough left to lie still. The elephant sought him to windward, going farther and farther away, until at last the man mustered courage to creep out and seek the rest of his party. At another letshulo an elephant charged a man who had only the native mantle on. When the elephant was fast gaining on him he unfortunately fell, and fortunately lost his mantle in the fall. The man instinctively rolled to one side on falling, and the elephant coming up, tramped the mantle into the earth, squealing and shrieking with satisfaction at having secured its enemy. But the letshulo or public hunting of ostriches is dangerous for other reasons. The Bamangwato do not take into account that the gun and the assegai are very different weapons, but continue to surround the ostriches, until they have them in a comparatively small circle, when, without any order or any hesitation, each man fires his rifle or his musket at the ostrich next him. Wherever he stands in the circle he is of course sure to have a fellow-townsman opposite to him. I have known several accidents take place on these public hunts. I believe there is generally less danger in a Bechuana war-party than in a letshulo which surrounds ostriches or antelopes.

In assembling at one of these public gatherings, the men march under their own head men; and in cases of dispute the head men range themselves under the chiefs they prefer, and thus march to the council. The relative strength of parties is thus discovered, and such things as *coups d'état* are not unknown in the history of the Bamangwato.

The head men have power over their own towns and over their own vassals and property. No Bechuana chief, when he wants to slaughter an ox, may summarily send for it to the cattle-post of one of his head men, or otherwise invade his right of property. In this matter the chief himself is distinguished from other head men only by having a larger number of vassals and more live-stock. In cases of dispute, the head man of the locality where one or both litigants reside endeavours to settle the matter; but his decision may be carried before the chief, whose verdict is final. The chief's court is conducted with decorum and order. His assessors are the head men of the various subdivisions of the town, and all men of distinction in it. A stranger of consideration sitting in the court-yard during a trial would be asked by the chief to assist with his opinion. All Bechuanas are more or less "accustomed to speak in public;" but there are generally in each town a few men whose shrewdness and power of speech, as well as social position, render them powerful advocates before such a court. The evidences of clear-headedness and close reasoning in speeches to which I have often listened are really remarkable, in people whose only training has been to listen to previous cases before their chief. But justice frequently miscarries when the culprit is a person of influence. For instance, a man speared his wife in Shoshong in a fit of rage. As he was one of Sekhome's adherents, and party spirit ran high in the town at the time, no notice was taken of the crime. When a theft takes place it is announced to the chief, who sends the town-crier round to give public notice that a certain article has been stolen, and is "wanted" by the chief, and must be forthcoming. It is usually restored in the darkness of night, and the culprit is thus allowed to escape detection. One of my men once lost a pair of trousers, and having given notice to Sekhome, the crier went round with a strong proclamation from the chief, and next morning the trousers were found suspended at the entrance to my cattle-pen!

There is nothing which irritates Europeans travelling or trading in such a country more than the bungling and uncertain manner in which justice is frequently administered. Shutting their eyes to the past history of their own country, these people seem to expect policemen with their batons, detectives, and a bridewell in every Bechuana town. And when, with considerable trouble, they have proved the guilt of some man of influence, their impatience and disgust are unbounded when the criminal escapes without the infliction of any punishment. In rude countries punishment must be either by fine, corporal punishment, the maiming of the body, or death. Imprisonment is not possible; besides, it would not be a severe punishment. In Potchefstroom the government of the Transvaal Republic has a prison; but able-bodied men usually found little difficulty in escaping from it, until the authorities had recourse to the ancient custom of making the feet of prisoners fast in the stocks at night. Among the Bamangwato a fine is the usual punishment for all offences. For murder the theory of the law demands the death of the murderer; its practice is usually satisfied with a fine.[1] For theft the theory is to restore fourfold; but the practice is to be content if you can get back your own property. When a person becomes "by habit and repute" a thief in Bechuana-land, after fining and beating have been tried, maiming the body is next resorted to. The fingers of the culprit are forced into a pot of boiling fat, and if the offence is repeated the whole hand is thrust in. I have seen persons with their hands maimed in this manner. I believe death would be inflicted if theft were persisted in after this mutilation had been resorted to.

As commander of the able-bodied men of the tribe, the Bechuana chief finds an organization ready to his hand, which he has only to exercise and direct. The rite of circumcision is administered throughout Bechuana-land to boys between perhaps eight and fourteen years of age. It is not performed every year, but whensoever there is a sufficient number of youths waiting for its observance. No single ceremony has a wider significance; it may be said to introduce the youth to heathen manhood, with all its duties and responsibilities. No honourable marriage

[1] Certain words in the Scottish language, such as *cro* or *croy* (compensation, satisfaction), and *kelchyn* (a fine), lead us back to a time when similarly rude arrangements possessed the sanction of law in the northern part of our island. It would seem that the compensation or satisfaction made for the slaughter of a man was formally arranged according to his rank. "The cro of ane Erle of Scotland is seven tymes twentie kye, or for ilk kow thrie pieces of Gold Ora; of an Erles sonne, or of ane Thane, is ane hundreth kye; or of the sonne of an Thane thrie score sax kye; or of ane husbandman saxtene kye." A *kelchyn* or fine was also paid in Scotland by one guilty of manslaughter, generally to the kindred of the person killed.—Jamieson's *Scottish Dictionary:* "Cro," "Kelchyn."

could take place with a man who had not gone through the "boguera" or initial ceremony. It is also the season when the youths are instructed in the wisdom of the ancestors of the tribe. But above all, it is the introduction of the youths into social life, under a regimental name which they receive during the progress of the ceremony, and which will be their collective designation as long as they live. The chief endeavours to keep back or to hasten forward the circumcision of his own sons so as that one shall be in each succeeding regiment; but failing that, one of the children of a near relative of the chief is appointed captain of the newly-collected force. The first and great lesson which the Bechuana youth is taught is to endure pain. The elders in his own family collect moretlwa rods (corresponding to the "birch" rods of our own country), and, headed by the priests, march in procession to the encampment of the novices. They join in a sacred dance; and afterwards the initiated select their own relatives from among the boys. The men now testify the depth of their affection for their sons and younger brothers, and the genuineness of their interest in their future welfare, by the severity of the flogging which they inflict upon them. I never saw a Bechuana man throw aside his mantle without exposing on his back the deep, broad marks of the chastisement which he had received while being introduced to Bechuana manhood.

"How deeply you are marked!" I said to one of my men.

"Monare" (Sir), was the sapient reply, "you must, no doubt, have also observed my superior wisdom. You see my father did not beat me so severely in vain!"[1]

[1] It was formerly almost as severe an ordeal to the flesh to become a Scottish burgess as it is at present to become a Bechuana citizen. We are told that in "riding the marches" of a town in Scotland, it was customary to take those who had been made burgesses during the year, and to strike

There is a second ceremony usually performed in the succeeding year, and which, although of subordinate character and importance, is still necessary to the completion of the training of the young man. After the first year's ceremony the regiment of boys is sent out under the command of their own captain to hunt antelopes. Every one must prove that he has at least killed one before they return. On the completion of the second year's ceremony, the youths are again ordered to the field, now to kill a rhinoceros, a buffalo, or an elephant. Having accomplished this, the Bechuana youths have won for themselves the position of men in the tribe. They live in different parts of the town; and as civilians own allegiance to different head men, but they are nevertheless one compact body for warlike or other purposes. The chief has only to announce to their captain that they must assemble at a certain time, to have his order obeyed. The only way a Bechuana man has of telling you his age is to mention the name of his regiment, and the names of one or two men in it whom you know. The idea of counting years or days was unknown to Bechuanas. Sometimes for practical purposes, if a regiment has been cut up in war, it may be united with another next it in age; but the name is not changed. It is sad to see a whole company of Bechuana old men marching together, nearly every one showing some indication of failing powers. Few of these men have learned to shoot with the gun, a weapon which is eagerly sought after by

their buttocks on a stone. This was called "burgessing." "This harsh custom, besides the diversion afforded to the unpolished agents, might be supposed to have the same influence in assisting the local memory of the patients, as that said to exist among the native and more wild Irish, who during the night go the round of the estates to which they still lay claim, as having belonged to their ancestors; and for the purpose of more deeply impressing on the memories of their children the boundaries of the several properties, at certain resting-places give them a sound flogging."—Jamieson's *Scot. Dict.*: "Burgess."

younger men, but more for the purpose of hunting than as a weapon of war.

The early missionaries opposed circumcision as a religious rite; therefore in the course of years it came to be the token of a young man's sincerity and of his parents' Christian principle that he should refrain from this heathen ceremony. The missionaries said, in effect, to the people, "There are two ways and two rites: the way of God's Word and the way of heathenism; the rite of baptism and the rite of circumcision. Let all give up the one and adopt the other." If all had done so, some other method of social and military organization would no doubt have been adopted by the various tribes. But the chiefs who stuck to the old customs blamed the converts in their towns, not only for changing their religion but for refusing to enrol themselves as subjects, and to enlist as militia-men or soldiers. I once pleaded with Sekhome that he would institute some new token of obedience and of social and military organization at Shoshong, mentioning the wearing of a certain head-dress or the carrying of certain colours; and to dispense with the present ceremony for all who did not wish to attend it. I admitted that I wished the people to leave him as priest, but declared that I desired his people to be subject to him as commander of the army of the tribe. I wished all to be Christians, and yet all to remain Bamangwato. But, as was to be expected, no new thing was so inviting to Sekhome as the customs which had the sanctions of immemorial usage.

Bechuana women do not occupy a very dignified position in the country; still they have a corporate existence in regiments as well as the men. During the administration of "boyali," the rite initiatory to womanhood, the girls are assembled every day in the town, under the leadership of two or more old women, who instruct them in all the duties of their future life. They draw water and bring home firewood, and perform other female duties, the clothing of the poor creatures being, in the meantime, nothing but coils of rough reeds, cut into pieces and strung like beads. Their faces and limbs are smeared over with white earth. Wherever they go they sing in chorus; but they presented a very sorry spectacle in the cold winter mornings when they passed my house shivering, with their water-pots on their heads. They are kept night after

Water-pot, with Gourd for drawing water.

night from sleeping, being caused to sit on the "motse" or mortar in which the corn is pounded. Should they sleep, they themselves speedily give notice of the fact by falling over. In all this blindness and misery there is again the noble idea of bearing up under hardship and pain. And they learn the lesson well. I once extracted a bullet from a man's face, which, entering at one cheek, had destroyed his nose and rested beneath the cheek-bone on the other side. The man never winced, and certainly he was not spared pain by the skill of the operator. He is now almost as handsome as he was before! the nose, however, being less prominent. I have been perfectly astonished at the power of endurance exhibited by the

Bechuana women. Sekhome one day brought one of his female relatives to have a tooth extracted. It was partly decayed, and unfortunately broke while being pulled out. The woman did not show the slightest impatience, but waited with outward impassiveness till I had extracted the last piece; then clearing her mouth, she gathered her mantle about her and walked away.

"That is a true woman," said the chief to his attendants, who had been witnesses of the operation.

"Yes," they replied; "she has a large heart."

To endure is the lot of man on earth. In Bechuanaland, as elsewhere, human life is a struggle. But it is surely a nobler and higher attitude of the mind to endure suffering and trial in the spirit of the Christian, as the will of a Father rather than doggedly to sit down and bear what is held to be inevitable fate. The missionary does not wish to change the feelings of the Bechuanas as to the worthiness of him who can endure; but rather to heighten and purify this feeling by the examples of suffering in God's Word, and especially in the life and death of Him "who bore our griefs and carried our sorrows," "yet opened not his mouth." And Christianity adds yet other ideas, of which the enduring dark-minded heathen sufferer did not dream. Human suffering is moral discipline, not only ennobling the present life, but fitting for a future state of existence,—the chastening and training of a Father for the benefit of His child. The Christian Bechuanas are therefore taught to endure pain and suffering with even greater composure than their heathen neighbours. There is an object in their sufferings—their own highest well-being; and the pain is inflicted, not by the callous hand of an earthly priest, but is meted out by a Father's love, and shared by the Great High Priest of the Christian: "For we have not an high priest who cannot be touched with the feeling of our infirmities; but was in all points tempted like as we are, yet without sin."

As ngaka or priest, the chief is supported by a class of men (lingaka) who not only practise the art of healing but are professors of witchcraft, and have taken degrees in rain-making. In Shoshong there are a good many of this influential class. Admission to the profession is to be obtained on the payment of a fee, and going through a course of learning under one or more of the initiated. An ox is the usual fee on entrance. The instruction is called "teaching to dig," because most medicines and charms are obtained from plants which are dug up in the fields. So the Bechuana lecturer takes his pupil or pupils with him to the open country one day, and to the mountains the next, and shows him where the healing plants are to be found. In the course of time he communicates to his pupil all his own knowledge. The disciple now begins to practise in the town, and is permitted to wear the baboon-skin mantle or head-dress, and to sit on a hyena-skin mat, which are both sacred to this profession.

Prayers and incantations are used by the doctors when they are preparing and administering their medicine, and frequently the divining-dice are thrown, and the doctor will then assure his patient that he will soon be better.

"Why don't you throw the dice, Monare?" said the wife of a man whom I was attending, and who had been given up by the native doctors; "your medicines are no doubt good, but you ought also to throw the divining-dice."

She hardly confided in one who did not come with the fuss and noise of the man of many ceremonies, who had attended her husband as long as he got any fees, but afterwards gave up the case.

The belief in divination by throwing dice is exemplified

in a remarkable way by the Bechuana doctors in cases of severe illness. A consultation of medical men is the last resort in such extreme cases in England; but in Bechuanaland there is still another appeal. When a case has baffled all medical skill the Bamangwato doctors produce their divining-dice. Certain herbs are represented by certain positions of the dice; and the medicine which is thus prescribed for their patient is unhesitatingly administered by the doctors, whatever the result should be. They had before exercised their own highest judgment; they now follow the supposed unseen guidance which they invoke.

When a Bechuana doctor is attending a stingy patient, he has ways and means of extracting a fee which seem to be peculiar to that part of the world. He tells the patient that in order to be cured he must lie upon a skin of a certain colour, and that his blanket must be of a kind which he specifies. The doctor's keen eyes have observed both the articles which he describes hanging in the sick man's house. In the course of his attendance the practititioner causes his patient to perspire violently, and next morning rubs all his body very carefully with his bare hand. The dirt which falls from the body on the skin, and which adheres to the blanket, is declared by the medical attendant to be the seeds of the disease of which the man has been complaining. Therefore these articles are unclean and dangerous, and henceforth of use only to the doctor, who has powerful charms to counteract the disease which is upon them. So the Bechuana doctor carefully sweeps all the dirt into the skins, proceeds to the open country, digs a hole, and buries, not the skins, but the dirt, and the imaginary disease, and having vigorously charmed the skins sells them, or wears them himself.

The only surgical operation which is performed by Bechuanas for the cure of disease is that of cupping, which is not so often done by the regular doctors as by certain "skilled women," who charge a fee for their services.

But while the lingaka have thus their own private practice, there are also certain public duties devolving upon them in virtue of their profession. The Bamangwato have no town-idol like the piece of wood which is erected by the Makalaka in their town, and to which they make offerings from time to time. But there are the "lipeku" or town-charms, which are renewed every year, and which are supposed to protect and bless the town. The varied ingredients are concocted by the united wisdom of the chief doctor and all his assistants. It is held to be the highest and most sacred and mysterious service performed in the town. One of the observances is to select an ox, which is caught, and its eyelids sewed together, when it is again allowed to rejoin the troop. It is called the "ox of the lipeku or charms." It is eventually slaughtered as a religious rite by the priests. When the concoction of the charms is completed, part of the contents of the sacred vessels in which they have been prepared is emptied into small calabashes or gourds, more than a dozen of which hang from the person of the head sorcerer on public occasions, especially in time of war. During the attack by the Matebele Sekhome was always arrayed with these calabashes round his shoulders and waist, which gave him a most fantastic appearance. By means of them he was supposed to be able to protect his own people, and to bring evil upon his enemies. Another portion of the "lipeku" is conveyed outside the town by the priests, and placed on all the paths which lead into it. Nothing is visible above the ground but a pair of horns, it may be of a koodoo or some other antelope. A native would not touch these horns for the world. I was once in my ignorance about to pull them up, when one of my servants ran to interrupt me with the gravest face, and informed me that "these were not mere horns: it was lipeku, and had been placed there by the town priests." Sometimes a native pot is used for these charms, and is then always turned upside down. To uncover it would be regarded as a profane and insulting action. A few years ago a white man, ignorant of these things, was trading at a Bechuana town, and trying one of his guns before a number of people. Noticing a small object on the adjoining hill, he took aim and hit it. To his surprise he found that he had committed a grave offence, having broken a pot containing charms which had been placed in that conspicuous position by the priests!

The "making of rain" is attended to by this class of men. But it is a great mistake to call them rain-makers, as if that were their only task. It is only one of the numerous duties which they undertake to perform. The most popular rain-makers must come from a well-watered country. This is always mentioned in commendation of any "doctor" or priest who has come to make rain for the gardens, and who appears laden with medical roots and barks and leaves, which he sells to the people for beads and for other articles. During one or two years Sekhome contented himself with his own efforts and those of his fellow priests at Shoshong; but on other occasions Malokwana from the east made their appearance, and undertook to water the gardens for the season. They come from what is now the northern part of the Transvaal country. I rather puzzled one of them by asking him if the rain still fell in his country after the Dutchmen had taken possession of it?

"O yes, it rains a great deal every year." "That's strange," I replied. "Who makes it now? The Dutch don't make rain; they have taken the country from you, the rain-makers, and yet it continues to rain there! Does not that prove that while the country was in your possession your medicines had not so very much to do with the rain which then fell?"

When digging the gardens is to commence, their owners proceed to the lingaka, and purchase from them a small quantity of seed-corn which they have blessed or charmed, and which is to be planted in the corners of the garden. Having done this, the people may not work more that day. On the morrow they may proceed with the digging of the garden. As soon as the digging commences, it is held to be improper to cut down the branches of green trees or the trees themselves during the day. Such work can only be done early in the morning or in the evening. But although every green tree is forbidden, the hack-thorn (*acacia detinens*) is especially sacred; it would be a great offence to cut down a bough from this tree and to carry it into the town at mid-day in the rainy season. As the sacred mistletoe was cut with formality by the Druid priest, so when the corn is ripe in the ear, the Bechuana chief holds a public assembly, when the people proceed with axes to the field, and each man brings home on his shoulder a branch of the sacred hack-thorn, with which they repair the cattle enclosure belonging to the town. It is also forbidden during this season to carry about uncovered any of the fruits of the earth. Ivory must also be covered if carried from one place to another. If rain falls during the night, and continues in the morning, public notice is given that no one must go to their gardens that day. It would stop the rain to turn up the ground while it is still falling! At this season the lingaka are frequently to be seen on the heights of the mountains near to the town, lighting their fires, blowing their horns, whistling, and shouting. They have also numerous processions, and a multitude of observances, which indeed take up all their time. If the rain is delayed, it is thought to be occasioned by some remissness in administering the affairs of the town. For instance, it is a custom that all widows and widowers are ceremonially unclean [1] until they shall have separated themselves from their families, and lived for some time outside the town in booths erected for the purpose. Their heads are shaved after a peculiar fashion, and they are purified by the priests before they are allowed again to join their family. This custom is sometimes relaxed; but should the rain be long in coming, a row of booths may be seen outside the town, the lingaka having resolved that they could not expect rain unless they attended to the old customs. Again, each fireplace is supplied with three stones, upon which the pot rests when being cooked. It is held that these may become unclean or impure, and need to be changed, not by the owner of the house, but by the lingaka or doctors. The old stones are collected in a heap outside the town. This is also attended to if the rain fails. The fires themselves become impure, and the lingaka order them all to be put out. The priests then go round with lighted sticks, which have been previously charmed. Having seen that the hearth has been thoroughly cleared out, they relight the fire from the pure source which they carry with them for the purpose.[2] One day a priest made his appearance at my house, carrying in his hand a lighted stick, which had the appearance of having been smeared over with "medicines." It

[1] See Numbers v. 2, 3.

[2] In Pagan times in Scotland it was the custom every autumn, on what was afterwards called Hallow-eve, to extinguish all the fires in the country. Next morning the people were supplied with holy fire, which was kindled and consecrated by the Druids. In Ireland, the Druids lighted two solemn fires every year on the summits of the highest hills. On these occasions the inhabitants of the country quenched their fires, and relighted them from those sacred fires. In the Western Islands of Scotland the Druids extinguished the people's fires in case of wrong-doing, and

was the first time I had heard of this ceremony, which would seem to be the African version of the fire which was represented to come down annually from Jupiter in Southern Europe, and almost the same as the sacred fire which was dealt out to our own forefathers in ancient Britain by their priests. I civilly declined the assistance of this priest, telling him that my fireplace was regularly swept, and that as to all other impurity, I trusted to the mercy of God in Christ Jesus. But Khamane, the second son of Sekhome, who was standing with me at the time, could not pass the matter over so lightly.

"Do you mean to say that you are capable of teaching or of doctoring the missionary?" asked Khamane. "What can you show for yourself—what can your countrymen, the Malokwana, show, who are now the vassals of the Boers? You may deceive us, who are ignorant Bamangwato; but it seems to me to be arrant presumption in you, a feeble vassal clothed in rags, to proffer your priestly aid to a man like Makense, or to any of his nation."

The priests also direct that all defilement should be removed from the country. Exposed human bones are accordingly buried, and other objects removed, by direction of the chief doctor. Should the rain still delay, a procession headed by the priests proceeds to the grave of some distinguished ancestor, and there a sacrifice is offered of a sheep or a goat, to appease the spirit of the deceased, and a prayer is presented to him, in which he is invoked to look upon the distress of his children, and to help

also on account of the non-payment of their dues as priests.—Jamieson's *Scottish Dictionary*: "Shannach;" Martin's *Western Islands*, p. 105. In our own time, in the Highlands, the first day of May is called Beltane-day, *i.e.*, the day of Baal's fire. When a boy, I myself rolled on the green-sward round cakes of a peculiar kind on Beltane-day. Fires were also lighted at night on prominent places. These were called Baal-fires. We did not know, as children, that we were taking part in the lingering Pagan worship of our rude forefathers.

them. This ceremony is always spoken of with solemnity, and is regarded as most efficacious.

The wildest remarks are made by the lingaka when their charms and incantations are of no avail. I heard it suggested by one of them that "there were too many white waggons in the town for rain to fall." Sekhome, however, did not agree in this opinion. I often heard that the traders and hunters were ordered "to cease firing guns when the clouds were so near,—the report of the guns would frighten them away!"

At Shoshong, however, it was usually an easy matter to "make rain." It might be late, but it always came. Some years both "the former and the latter rains" fell in abundance, and there was always either the one or the other. After copious rains had fallen, an offering of joy and thanksgiving is placed in the most crowded street of the town, consisting of two or three large dishes filled with the rain-water, and with certain herbs and charms. In the evenings, the town, which had been hushed under the calamity of drought, now resounds with the boisterous dance, which is carried on in almost every little kotla or court-yard. The little children gather on the street, and shout and sing and clap their hands for joy. The lingaka, and the old men generally, show their gladness in a quieter if not more sober fashion, informing their wives that they must not be stingy any more with the corn for the beer. "The rain has fallen," is the joyous cry of every one.

There is a certain amount of suspicion connected with the word "ngaka" (doctor, sorcerer); but when the superhuman power is supposed to be brought into requisition for an evil purpose, the name is changed and the man is called a "moloi" (wizard). But the wizard is always a doctor, and his crime is that he turns his knowledge to evil purposes. This is the most hateful term you can apply to a Bechuana man, combining the ideas of murderer and sneak. It is to be explained that in doctoring the simplest case, the lingaka inculcate the belief that although they choose to give medicines, they, and not the medicines, effect the cure. They "charm" the sickness by power in them, and do not "cure" it by the mere action of the medicine. And so when members of this profession lend themselves to advance the interests of a chief or a party, they "charm" or cast spells over houses, over persons when asleep, and over footpaths or other places resorted to by the objects of their enmity. A moloi is represented as often gliding about through the streets of the town at night. He makes no noise. The dogs do not bark at him. He can go where he likes. One says he saw a wizard mounted on the back of a hyena flying through the streets at night; another declares one glided past him quite close, and seemed to be all spirit or shadow without any body. "The baloi" (the wizards) is an expression often used to frighten naughty children by the Bamangwato mothers. For my own part, while I have often met the hyenas prowling about the streets when coming home late at night, I never saw one mounted by a wizard!

The Bechuana sorcerers believe that if they can make rain, they can also drive it away. One of the readiest and most powerful spells by which to accomplish this end, is to thrust the green branches of a certain bush into the fire, the proper charms being repeated at the same time. I have frequently seen this done, and sometimes in earnest, by heathen men, who did not wish when travelling to have themselves and their possessions soaked with the tropical thunder-shower. It will be evident that malice and superstition would find ample scope in this direction. For instance, Sekhome sent with Mr. Price one summer a party of men who were secretly charged by the old moloi or wizard to "loa" or "bewitch" the corn-fields of Sechele.

Mr. Price was entirely ignorant of their object, some lawful and plausible story having been told him by Sekhome as to their errand. Sechele caught these men, with all their charms, almost in the very act of bewitching his cornfields. Notwithstanding the deception which had been practised on himself, Mr. Price interceded with the Bakwena for the wizards' lives, and having obtained a promise that they would not be put to death, left them to their punishment, and went on his journey. The Bakwena conveyed the men, with their charms still in their possession, as far as the borders of Sekhome's territory, when they mixed all the medicines together, and stripping the wizards, smeared their bodies with their own preparations, and set them free. The discomfited "baloi" were ashamed to go into the town, but turned aside to some cattle-post or village till they had removed all marks of such a deep disgrace. I afterwards questioned Sechele as to whether he believed in the potency of these charms to injure his crops. He replied in the affirmative.

It may be mentioned that the wizards are supposed to use parts of the bodies of men, which they secure after death. A still-born child is said to supply their favourite and most potent spells. A certain white pebble, which I have never myself seen, is also used. It is thrown into the court-yard of a rival, in the belief that it will disorder his ideas, turn and warp his judgment, so that his followers shall forsake him, and he become a prey to his enemies. The deadliest poison is said to be obtained from the body of the crocodile, therefore it was forbidden to kill them in the Matebele country. To illustrate the length to which superstition will lead men in evil and in credulity, it is held to be possible for a sorcerer to "give over" a certain man, who has gone to hunt, to a buffalo, or elephant, or other animal. The wizard is believed to be able to "charge" the animal to put the man to death! If two men quarrel, the one will wait till the other goes to hunt, when he employs and pays for the secret services of some wizard, with the view of compassing his absent enemy's death while engaged in the hunt. And so when it is announced that a certain person has been killed in the hunting-field, some of his friends will remark, "It is the work of enemies; he was 'given' to the wild beast. The wizards will finish all the men in the town with their witchcraft."

If lighting fires on the tops of mountains by the Bechuana priests reminds one of the ancient worship on the heights or "high places of Baal," as practised both in Asia and in Europe, the following ceremony would seem to be allied to the grove-worship, which was as extensively resorted to. It seems that if a Bechuana man, while either hunting or journeying, finds himself in the depths of a forest, when he reaches what seems the darkest or gloomiest part, he will select the largest tree in his neighbourhood, and prostrate himself before it in prayer. "To whom, or to what, does he pray?" I have asked. "Oa rapela hela"—"He just prays." This was all the answer I could obtain on that point. Of course there was no hesitation as to the burden of the prayer itself. It was for all the elements of prosperity from the suppliant's point of view—in his house, his garden, his cattle-post, his hunting trip or journey, as the case might be.

On entering a Bechuana town you see numbers of stones caught between the forked branches of trees on each side of the road. They have been placed there by men entering the town on some important matter, and who have performed this act as the means of procuring for themselves success in the business which they had in hand.

There are very many things which occur in the daily life of a Bechuana man to cause him misfortune according to the old belief. Each tribe has its "sacred animal" to which it is said to "dance." The puti was the sacred animal of the Bamangwato. To look on it was a calamity to the hunter or to the women going to the gardens. The Makalaka, however, kill the same animal, and dress its skins, but they may not wear them in the town. They are therefore often sold to the traders. I had at one time a mat of puti skin at my door, at a time when I did not know so much about these customs. Sekhome called to see me, and not noticing the skin on entering, walked over it. But on his way out, just as he was about to tread on it again, my attention was excited by the antics of the chief, who, in the most undignified manner, was springing first to one side, then to another of the dreaded skin! Although Sekhome made no remark, I of course lifted the mat, and put in its place another, upon which my visitors would not be afraid to tread. If an owl rests on a house it is a great calamity. The ngaka is sent for at once, who scrambles up to the place where the unclean bird sat, and purifies the place with his charms. If a goat climbs upon the roof of a house it is speared at once; it has "transgressed," gone beyond what is proper in a goat, and would bewitch its owner if it were not put to death. If the native owner of cattle visits his pen at night, and hears a dull sound at intervals from among the cattle, he creeps up stealthily to see from which animal the alarming noise proceeds. It is one of his cows or oxen quietly beating the ground with its tail. This is a very serious matter. It is an offence which has got a special designation. The cow is said to "tiba," and this implies that she is no longer a mere cow; she is bewitched, and she only waits her opportunity to bring disease or death upon her owner or his household. A man who is rich in cattle would not hesitate to spear such an animal at once. A poorer man will proceed with the cow next morning to the missionary or to a trader, and offer her for sale. As it is almost a rule with the natives never to sell their breeding cows, it was only through this superstition that we could purchase such animals from them. The neighbouring Matshwapong were not afraid of cattle which had this habit, and the Bamangwato could sometimes exchange cattle with them. Such are a few of the numberless terrors which haunt the minds of the benighted pagan. What a thrilling message to deliver to these bond-slaves of superstition, "Fear no one but God; fear nothing but evil!"

There are many ceremonies in a Bechuana town which remind one of the Levitical code. Some of these are the purifying of weapons of war; the cleansing of those who have been in the fight before they are allowed to re-enter the town; the cleansing of captives and refugees, as also of cattle or goods taken in war; their antipathy to swine; the uncleanness of such as have touched or approached a dead body, and the mode of purification; the seclusion of a woman after childbirth, extending among Bechuana "ladies" to two and three months, and even among poor people to one month; the custom of "raising up seed" to a deceased brother or relative; the practice of "shutting up" a sick person, after it is supposed he is seriously ill, when not even his nearest relatives may enter his enclosure without being defiled; the practice of shaving round the head in purification, and yet not "causing baldness." In making a public covenant or agreement with one another, two chiefs "tshwaragana moshwang;" that is to say, an animal is slaughtered, and some of the contents of its stomach are laid hold of by both covenanting parties, their hands meeting together and laying hold of each other, while covered over with the contents of the sacrificed animal's stomach. This would seem to be the most solemn form of public agreement known in the country. It was performed more than once at Shoshong while I was there, in the case of chiefs who, with their people, placed themselves under Sekhome's protection.

Morimo (God) has not been mentioned in the preceding description of native worship and superstition. When missionaries first met with Bechuanas they addressed them through the Dutch language. They found Bechuanas who could already speak both languages, and who therefore acted as interpreters. At Griqua Town there were (and are still) regular services in both languages. The invariable equivalent for *God* in Dutch, given by all the interpreters, was *Morimo.* It was no suggestion of the missionaries: the Bechuana interpreters, after hearing concerning God in the Dutch language, said that their name for Him was Morimo. But it is a singular fact that, on further inquiry, there was found to be little else known to the people besides this Name. There was no worship or service rendered to Morimo in all Bechuana-land. Like the good deities in India and elsewhere, Morimo had been apparently lost sight of and well-nigh forgotten by the people in their eagerness to propitiate the evil influences by which they believed themselves to be immediately surrounded. It is said that the condition of some men with reference to the knowledge of God may be likened to a state well known to all of us,—when we know a name but cannot recollect it. But the Bechuanas would seem never to have entirely forgotten God. His name was found by the missionaries still floating in their language. Even this name (Morimo) however would seem to have been tampered with in the course of the long ages of increasing darkness. The word has two plurals—one of which means not *gods*, but *spirits of the dead* (*manes*). But how does it appear that this latter meaning is the secondary and not the primary one? Because in the sense of *spirits of the dead* (*barimo*), the word has no singular; whereas, in the sense of *God*, it has both the singular and plural forms. In Sechuana, *ba* is the plural prefix and particle used to denote people; *eo* is its singular form. Now it is correct Sechuana to say, *Ba*rimo *ba ba* arabileng, the spirits of the dead who have answered; but there is no singular form agreeing to this. You cannot say, Morimo *eo* o arabileng—the spirit of the dead who has answered. The only particle (*o*) which can grammatically follow *Morimo* in the singular has no reference to human beings; Morimo *o* o arabileng—the God who has answered. Plural, Merimo e e arabileng—the gods who have answered.

What lesson does Sechuana grammar here teach us in theology and in the moral history of the Bechuanas? Is it that men have been ever rising in knowledge and intelligence, and that thus *ba*rimo is a higher step than *me*rimo, a form which has no reference to human beings? There being no sex-distinctions in Sechuana, the grammar does not prove so much. *Me*rimo is not necessarily lower than *ba*rimo. Or is *ba*rimo—spirits of the dead—the afterthought of men lapsing into greater ignorance of the Divine Being? And was that ignorance caused by the dislike of parents to retain God in their own knowledge, and to teach their children concerning Him; so that less and less was spoken of Him, more and more about priests and spells, during the long weary ages, until just the name for God remains in the language—the sole remembrancer of a knowledge higher than is now possessed? This is the explanation given by the Bechuanas themselves:—"Our forefathers, no doubt, knew more about Morimo than we do; but they did not persevere in speaking of Him to their children." But the grammar leaves this an open question. What it would seem to prove is that *Mo*rimo (God), *Me*rimo (Gods), are older thoughts in the Bechuana mind than *ba*rimo (spirits of the dead). The readiness of the Bechuanas to give Morimo as an equivalent for the God of the Bible certainly accords best with the view that they thought of *Mo*rimo, *Me*rimo, as higher and not lower than human beings.

CHAPTER XX.

THE LEAVEN OF THE GOSPEL.

THE Bechuanas have a misleading custom of feigning extreme ignorance when conversing with some white men. Their motive is perhaps partly to pay a compliment to their instructor; partly, and perhaps chiefly, the desire to "draw him out." On such occasions they have great command of feature; nothing shows the Englishman engaged in arguing with them that their ignorance and stupidity are assumed. Those who adopt least of a hectoring style with the natives are least likely to be deceived in this manner. But if a man rushed to narrate in his first letter to his friends in England the impressions produced by such a conversation, he would be likely to affirm of the natives not only that they were so degraded as not to believe in a future state, but also so ignorant as to be unable to count their own flocks and herds; and so stupid as to be seized with a violent headache whenever they tried to think!

The Rev. John Campbell, who was the first missionary to visit a Bechuana town, and to study their religious and social customs, was impressed with the tenacity with which they clung to the customs of their forefathers; and expressed the opinion that "their 'caste' feeling was perhaps no less strong a barrier against the reception of the gospel than in India." At Shoshong, the opposition to the gospel has always been based upon this feeling. It is not that the people cannot comprehend what is preached to them, but that they prefer the customs in which they have been brought up. Just as there are thousands of professing Christians in England who could give no better reason for their religious belief than that it was the belief of their fathers, so Bechuanas look upon their customs with reverence for the same reason—it was the religion of their ancestors.

"How should I answer to Khari if I changed the customs of the town?" said Sekhome to me on one occasion when we were conversing on this subject.

My argument was, "How are you to know that Khari would not have changed the customs himself, if the Word of God had come in his time? You say you will live and die like your ancestors. As a matter of fact you are not doing it. You have changed your weapons of war; you ride on horses and shoot with guns. Your customs, which you say are inviolable, you have already broken. Indeed it is impossible for you to live and die like your ancestors. You can never be like Khari; for he never refused the Word of God, whereas you do refuse it at present. From all you tell me of Khari, I form the opinion that he would have probably believed the Word of God himself if it had ever been made known to him. You must therefore live your own life, in the circumstances in which God has placed you; and not seek to live the life of an ancestor to whom these circumstances were unknown."

In the course of the year 1864 we were able to begin two district schools, as well as to carry on the more advanced classes which had been for some time under instruction. Mr. Price took the towns lying in the centre of the mountain range, meeting in the courtyard of the Maownatlala. He was assisted by Khamane, the second son of Sekhome, and two or three others. My district was to the west, at the town of the Mapaleng. I was accompanied by Khame, the eldest son of Sekhome, and by Mogomotsi, his uncle. These native assistants were of service in introducing us to the people, and also in the practical work of teaching. The chief of the Mapaleng made a long speech when we requested permission to teach the children in his town, to the effect that "he himself was too old to learn; he was content with the path in which his father had placed him; but as for the young people, they might all be taught. Whoever wished to learn himself, or to have his children instructed, need not be afraid; they were doing no harm; the learning was good." We opened this school with some thirty scholars, and were encouraged by the progress which many of the children made. We found also that the work of instructing others was beneficial to our more advanced pupils.

In conducting school among the Bamangwato, I observed a great difference in the capacities of the various learners. Some were easily taught, being able to understand your meaning at once; others were slow and dull, and it was as if a mist were before their mental vision. These last were chiefly grown-up people. I came to the conclusion that the mental ability of those I was teaching was probably as great as in a village school in a country district in England. Since I came to England I have met with the following remarks from gentlemen better able to judge than myself, having had different races in one school. The Rev. Henry Calderwood, whose labours, both as missionary and as Civil Commissioner on the Kaffir frontier, were of great advantage both to the natives and to his own countrymen, gives the following opinion on the subject:—

"I have often observed with much interest the progress

which children of both sexes have made at school; and in equal circumstances the Kaffir or Fingo boy is quite a match for a respectable youth of European origin in the acquisition of knowledge, whether classical or mechanical, notwithstanding the Saxon superiority in energy of character."[1]

The Rev. Dr. Wilson of Bombay, at present Moderator of the General Assembly of the Free Church of Scotland, kindly furnishes me with the following statement as to the comparative intellectual endowments of Africans and Asiatics:—

"Though I am a missionary to India, I have had much to do with natives of the shores and inner countries of Eastern Africa, from Abyssinia, south to Zengebar; and I must say, that after my experiences in attempts to instruct and educate them in our Bombay mission, I have been led to form a very favourable opinion of their talents and aptitude to learn. In those respects I do not think them inferior to the average specimens of the Hindus. I have seen individuals of them at the top of some of our largest classes. I have not observed in them, when properly attended to, anything of the fickleness, caprice, and idleness often laid to the charge of the negro races; while I have felt myself bound to respect their common sense, straightforwardness, fidelity, and strength of affection. The people of Africa, when christianized and civilized, will be found to occupy a respectable position in the scale of humanity."

Dr. Livingstone also, speaking of the Bakwena, says:— "They might be called stupid in matters which had not come within the sphere of their observation; but in other things they showed more intelligence than is to be met with in our own uneducated peasantry."[2]

[1] *Caffres and Caffre Missions*, page 34.

[2] *Missionary Travels*, p. 19.

In all matters pertaining to the habits of animals, the plants and trees of the country, the political history of the various tribes, the casuistic difficulties as to relationship and property arising out of polygamy—in these and many such questions they are quite at home. Bechuanas have remarkably retentive memories, owing no doubt to the fact, that having no written language, all their knowledge on every subject must be either treasured in the memory or lost. Having broken up into many separate tribes, each one strong enough to stand alone and assert its independence, these South African clans were never without their feuds and raids. And the chief reason for Highland raids was also the moving cause of of South African forays —the possession of cattle; with occasionally a quarrel on the interesting subject of the marriage or the marriage-portion of some young scion of a chieftain's family. But while Bechuanas sometimes fight with their spears, they decidedly prefer to do so with their tongues, and are indeed much better qualified for the latter warfare than for the former. And so diplomacy played a prominent part in the public business of each little court, without letters and without a secret cipher. Each chief had usually three or four confidential officers whom he employed on these public and sometimes delicate errands. It was the custom to send one of these ambassadors with four or five men as an escort. Before starting, the party is assembled to hear the message of their chief. The leader of the expedition then repeats it; and should he hesitate, one of his men helps him with the word or thought. They now start on a journey of six or ten or more days, going over the message once or twice at their evening fire, and especially reviving it in their minds the night before their arrival at their destination. Next morning they proceed into the public courtyard, and salute the chief in the name of their master, reciting some items of news which they deem suitable for the ears of the public. They then retire with the chief into the private court of the latter, ostensibly for the purpose of drinking beer, but in reality to deliver their message. At other times the message will be delivered at once in the public yard. The leader of the messengers is the speaker. He proceeds without any break in his story till he comes to the "gist" of the whole matter, the refusing or granting, as the case may be; he then pauses, and, turning to his attendants, demands, "Am I lying? does not our chief say so?" "You speak the true words of our master," say all the attendants. And thus, without writing, the message is faithfully delivered; without attesting signatures to a document, the testimony of four or five men is presented to the chief, to declare that such is the opinion and determination of his neighbour. Missionaries in Bechuana-land find that many of those who listen to their discourses are able again to repeat what they hear—at any rate to give all the ideas.

According to a principle of English law, the person on trial is not bound to criminate himself. The public prosecutor undertakes to prove his guilt. But this principle is not carried into private life. In an English family the office of prosecutor is not necessary; the culprit usually comes forward and criminates himself at the family tribunal, where love and forgiveness are known as well as punishment. But Bechuanas take the very fullest advantage of the plea of Not Guilty. Their power of personating injured innocence is wonderful. Equally astounding is the coolness with which, when the process of proof is complete, the air of injured innocence is at once thrown off, with the remark, "Ah, now he has beaten me; I have nothing more to say." It is a principle among Bechuanas that a fault is never to be confessed. It seems to these shrewd heathen the height of absurdity for a man to confess, and, giving up all chance of escape, become his own accuser. Therefore in private and social life "Not Guilty" is always the Bechuana's plea; and he will stick to it, unless you can prove his guilt. Once a cook was in the habit of stealing my maize, and carrying it home to the town. I several times nearly detected him; but failed to catch him just in the act. He knew that I was aware of his guilt; but his parents at home pressed him to steal, and he continued to risk all consequences. Afraid that my maize should have all disappeared before I could bring the theft home to such a clever fellow, I called him one day, and, giving him his wages, dismissed him without saying a word about the theft which I could not prove. The first thing a native demands, when you charge him with a fault, is "Who saw me?" or "Who told you?" Related to this phase in their character is their great disinclination to inform on one another. Suspicious and jealous of each other, dreading evil-eye, charms, etc., they are unwilling to make to themselves enemies; and therefore give information which will criminate others with great reluctance. For this reason, a chief, in the conduct of public affairs, has to resort to many a scheme to collect evidence of which he can avail himself in public. But when matters become desperate, when a side in a dispute must be taken, then the people will make a virtue of necessity, and secretly volunteer information to damage those against whom they have arrayed themselves.

The bearing of this trait of character on the work of the missionary is obvious. Church-discipline can only be exercised upon information duly attested. The people as a rule do not entirely overcome their reluctance to give evidence against others, even in the Christian Church; nor are the church-members, as a rule, distinguished for the readiness and fulness of their confessions of wrong-doing, until evidence is duly produced against them.

In summer, the houses of the natives, and the hedges round them, are covered over with climbing gourds or calabash plants. Maize, sugar-cane, and pumpkins also grow in every available corner round the houses. When viewed from the adjoining mountain, the town thus clothed in green is really beautiful. But however charming in the distance, it is not at all pleasant to thread those narrow, winding, and gourd-shaded lanes. When daily returning from school soon after noon, I found the atmosphere of the town to be quite oppressive, and constantly wondered that cases of fever were not even more numerous. Early in 1865, I had an attack of African fever, no doubt induced by constant exposure to this miasma. I had recourse to strong measures, dosing myself at once with Livingstone's prescription, and was only a few days an invalid. I have elsewhere described some of the symptoms of this disease.

About this time a Matebele soldier made his appearance at Sekhome's as a refugee, being accompanied by one of those women who occupy the station of "wives of the chief" in the country of the Matebele. The man was well received by Sekhome, and a place appointed for him in the town. Every day, however, he came to my house, ostensibly because he had known me in his own country. But I soon learned from him the true cause of his coming so often: he was afraid of being put to death by the Bamangwato, but thought he would be safe as long as he was on my premises. I did my best to assure him that he was in no danger. By and bye I missed the tall handsome soldier from his usual place in my yard; and in a few days I learned that he had hanged himself. He laboured under the disadvantage of not understanding Sechuana; and his fears coloured every gesture and look of the Bamangwato. One night he stole away from Shoshong with the woman who might be called his wife, and who had given up a position of distinction and of ease for his sake. They endeavoured to find their way to another town; but their courage seemed to fail them, and for some days they lived secreted in the mountain called Marutlwe, about three miles to the south of Shoshong. At length the man proposed that they should terminate their sufferings by death. "The Bamangwato," he said, "will kill us both; they will torture and insult us: let us rather die by our own hands. We escaped the anger of Moselekatse only to fall into the hands of those who hate us." His plan was to kill the woman first and then take his own life. But the woman was not so despairing as the soldier, whose mind would seem to have been affected by the constant pressure of anxiety, and she evidently had no desire to follow her lover in his present course. She succeeded in calming his mind, and secured also his consent to her returning to the town, for the purpose of ascertaining from Sekhome himself whether or not their lives were in danger. Accordingly the woman made her appearance before Sekhome, who told her to return and bring her husband home at once, assuring her that their fears were entirely groundless. But when the poor woman, now the bearer of joyous intelligence, again reached their place of concealment, she found that the soldier had already taken his fate into his own hands, and had hanged himself with a thong from a tree.

In the end of 1864 our peaceful labours were disturbed by news of an inroad from an unexpected quarter. One of Sekhome's Bakalahari had come across the track of a large number of men accompanied by horsemen, but with no waggons, and avoiding all public paths. The suspicions of the vassal were at once excited, and instead of proceeding on his hunt, he hastened back to give warning to his family, and to the members of the little village. Taking with him a companion, he then returned and followed on the track till sunset, when they stealthily approached the bivouac to inspect more narrowly its leaders and members. They found it was a war-party of Bakwena under Khosilintsi, the brother of Sechele, and Sebele, the eldest son of that chief. So close had the Bakalahari gone that they were able to repeat part of the conversation of the Bakwena at their camp-fire. Some preparations were made by Sekhome, but in a very different spirit from what was shown when he anticipated an invasion of Matebele. Not a woman left the town; they said they had nothing to fear from Bakwena; it was only Matebele who killed women and children. The night after the notice had been given to Sekhome, the Bakwena approached Shoshong, sleeping about three miles from the town, and near to the mountain called Libobe. Before daylight they commenced their march, making for the mountain range so as to be able to command the town. But the Bamangwato were waiting for them, and easily drove them back. Accompanied by Mr. Price and two Englishmen, I climbed this range from the other side, and found we were just in time to see with our glasses Sechele's "braves" retreat in confusion. They had calculated on being able to gain the vantage-ground of the mountain; but certainly the manner in which they retreated seemed to show that the place must be very strong indeed in which they would venture to fight. Sekhome's sons gave orders to their men to advance and cut off the retreat of the Bakwena; but their father countermanded this order, and the Bakwena were allowed to return home unmolested, with a few cattle, which they managed to collect in the district through which they passed. Sechele had made the raid professedly to indemnify himself for losses and insults inflicted on him and his people by Sekhome, especially by the party of "baloi" or wizards whom Sekhome had sent to wither up the corn-fields of the Bakwena. It was evidently not Sekhome's interest to have a quarrel with the Bakwena at this time, while expecting another visit from the soldiers of Moselekatse.

One night a report came to Shoshong that the Matebele were advancing to retake the cattle which Sekhome had lifted from their posts. It turned out to be an unfounded rumour, but while it lasted it caused great uneasiness. The Bamangwato were aware that the cattle which they had taken two years before had been followed for some distance by a party of Matebele, who, when they found that they had taken the way to Sekhome's, placed branches of trees on the track, and went through certain ceremonies, in course of which they pledged themselves to come back and take up the "spoor" at another time, and follow it to Shoshong. The Bamangwato now expected a fulfilment of this vow, so that when Sekhome came to me to announce their rumoured approach, nothing could have been more likely. "I am resolved to die rather than succumb to the Matebele," said the chief; "but if I thought the Boers (Dutchmen of the Transvaal) would assist me for a certain number of cattle, I should be willing to pay the cattle. I have already laid them under obligation, having spared the lives of those hunters whom Sechele urged me to kill, after the Dutch had destroyed the town of the Bakwena. I spared their lives, and sent Tshukuru into their own country with their waggons and property, which they deserted in their fear. But I hear from the Bakone that Dutchmen have no gratitude; and I am afraid that if I called them to assist me, they would afterwards reckon me a mere Mokalahari (vassal), make me pay tribute, and eventually possess themselves of my land. I am in difficulties, Monare, and you must try and help me." Fortunately the danger passed over without Sekhome having become the tributary of Dutchmen or Matebele.

About this time I had frequent visits from Sekhome. On these occasions he had no attendant. Rising from the public yard after dusk, he withdrew first to his mother's premises, and then by a private gateway found his way to my house. During these interviews the subject of Christianity was sometimes brought before his notice; and I found that this man with the sinister face, who was the greatest sorcerer in Bechuana-land, who was hated by many and mistrusted by all his neighbours, had a keen appreciation of the character and the object of the gospel of Jesus Christ. He referred more than once to an Englishman, not a missionary, who had long before taken pains to explain to him the doctrines of God's Word. He had often heard preaching since, but Sekhome's mind continued to be most impressed with the view of our religion which he had first heard as a novelty from his early instructor. I could never find out who this traveller was who explained Christianity to the Bechuana chief. Sekhome never failed to mention that he was not a missionary. There would seem to be the same feeling among the Bechuanas as amongst Englishmen, that preaching is to be expected from a minister, as it is his proper work. Hence the store set on the kindly explanations or good counsel tendered by a passing layman. Sekhome indeed had not forgotten this person's name, but it was not recognisable to me as he pronounced it. But it is likely that his story of the gospel will remain in this chief's mind as long as he lives. Would to God there were many travellers and hunters of this kind!

"It is all very good for you white men to follow the Word of God," Sekhome more than once said. "God made you with straight hearts like this,"—holding out his finger straight; "but it is a very different thing with us black people. God made us with a crooked heart like this,"—holding out his bent finger. "Now, suppose a black man tells a story, he goes round and round, so,"—drawing a number of circles on the floor; "but when you open your mouth your tale proceeds like a straight line, so,"—drawing a vigorous stroke through all the circles he had previously made. "No, do not oppose me; I know I am right. Your heart is white from your birth; the hearts of all black people are black and bad."

"Nay, Sekhome, you are completely wrong. We have all bad hearts. There may be worse thoughts in some than in others; there are bad thoughts in all. Those who turn to God and often think of Him and of His words, get a new heart and better thoughts."

"Not black people," he interrupted; "and yet"—after a pause—"and yet, after all, Khame's heart is perhaps right. Yes,"—after another pause—"Khame's heart is right."

I was glad that he had this opinion of his eldest son. I now reminded him that all white people were not alike—that he himself knew the difference between them was often very great. "There is F— now," I said, mentioning the name of a young lad of English parentage who had grown up among the natives in Bechuana-land, "what kind of heart has he got? is his a white or a black man's heart? You know he prefers the company of black people to that of white men, and he can speak Sechuana a great deal better than English. Of what value to him is the colour of his skin? He was brought up as a Bechuana, and you know the people's nickname for him goes to show that they think of him as one of themselves."

"Yes, F— is one of us," said Sekhome; "I can't deny that."

"Well," I said, "but if he would change to-morrow—give up his associates in the town—open his heart, like Khame, to the teaching of God's Word—learn to read and to write—in a few years no one would think of him as he does now. It would just be as difficult for him to do this as for a black man, but not more so; inasmuch as he has received a black man's bringing up, having gone about in youth a naked herd-boy with Bechuana boys of his own age, and having also acted as the leader of his native master's oxen when travelling with his waggon.—Sekhome, why shouldn't you 'enter the Word of God'?" I added suddenly.

"Monare," said the chief, rising to leave, "you don't know what you say. The Word of God is far from me. When I think of 'entering the Word of God,' I can compare it to nothing except going out to the plain and meeting single-handed all the forces of the Matebele! That is what it would be for me now to 'enter the Word of God.'"

Poor Sekhome! Such was his own estimate of his position, surrounded by the thralls of priestcraft and polygamy; but, above all, misled by his own darkened and wayward heart!

CHAPTER XXI.

THE TRIAL OF FAITH.

POLYGAMY is sanctioned by the traditional customs of the Bechuanas. Practically a plurality of wives falls only to the lot of chiefs and head men. The common freemen of the town have seldom two wives. The head men have usually from three to six, according to their wealth and social standing. Sekhome had twelve wives. Their houses were in a semicircular row fronting the court-yard of the town. The chief did not reside with any of his "partners in life," but in his mother's house, which stood in the middle of the row. His personal property was stored in his mother's premises. It will not be necessary to enter into the domestic arrangements of such a family. But it is necessary to the perspicuity of our narrative to point out that this system not only destroys all family affection, but surrounds the chief with never-ceasing complaints and jealousies. A certain provision in servants and cattle is made for each wife by the chief when he takes her home. In return, she furnishes every year a certain quantity of corn for the chief's use. The division of the town out of which each wife comes is always ready to advocate the cause of its representative in the harem, and that of her offspring. The gifts of the chief in cattle or karosses or beads to one wife are jealously watched by the others, as are also his presents of horses or clothing or guns to any one of his sons. In early childhood nothing divides the children of the chief; but as they grow up they learn to regard one another as rivals for the chief's favour. They learn to espouse the side of their mother, and the views of the division of the town to which she belongs. Those whose birth places them in the first rank are the objects of malicious whisperings and half-expressed accusations to the chief. Those who are of inferior birth are accused of plotting, whether guilty or not. But while all this is going on, great outward propriety and etiquette are observed. The jealous wives daily greet each other with smiles, calling one another "mother" with apparent affection. The children vie with one another in outward demonstrations of respect to their father and to all his wives. A stranger might imagine from a single inspection that he never saw such a "happy family;" but this system is nevertheless the fruitful source of most of the internal strifes, often attended by bloodshed, which characterize the ordinary life of a Bechuana community.

The ceremony of "boguera" (circumcision) was administered at Shoshong in April 1865. Each head man mustered his retainers, and, surrounded by his own sons and near relatives, marched daily to the camp of the neophytes. Proud is the Bechuana father who is surrounded by a number of sons on these occasions. There is an honour connected with this which no distinction of rank can supply. Sekhome's mortification was therefore very great when he found himself marching to the camp alone—not one of his five eldest sons accompanying him. They were all at our school instead, and every Sunday they were in their places at church. They themselves resolved that they would not go to this heathen ceremony. Here began a period of trouble for our mission. Sekhome, in inviting missionaries to his town, had evidently not anticipated opposition of this kind. He had hoped to be able to regulate all matters connected with the Word of God in his town as he exercised control over everything else. To a certain point it might advance, but no further. So when he found himself deserted by his sons on this public occasion, he was deeply offended, and threatened extreme measures if they did not at once yield obedience to him. Failing to overcome them by threats, he next proceeded to work upon their feelings in private. He is said to have shed tears in presence of some of his sons, when expostulating with them on their desertion of him and of the old tribal customs. He was successful in winning over two of his sons. But promises and threats were alike unavailing with the other three. Even when he declared he would disinherit them, they continued faithful. After a time Sekhome publicly announced that it was his intention to give all his property, and in the end the chieftainship, to those sons who had obeyed him. He at once presented them with valuable articles of European manufacture, such as guns, saddles, clothing, etc. He forbade the Bamangwato to follow the disobedient sons; and told them that those who had gone to the "boguera" were alone to be regarded as his children. As to the Word of God, it was bad, seeing it led to disobedience on the part of children to their parents; and whoever attended church or school might henceforth look upon Sekhome as his personal enemy. This opposition had an immediate effect upon the number of those who sought instruction in Christianity; only those came who resolved to brave the wrath of the chief, and occasionally some of their vassals and attendants. On Monday the chief would seek out some one who was perhaps halting between two opinions, and who had been seen attending church on the Sunday. Taking him aside, Sekhome would ply him with threats of vengeance. As he exercised the office of priest as well as chief, he professed to be able and determined completely to blast and ruin the man unless he gave up attending church and school. Knowing also the individual character of most of the people, he was able to attack them at their weak point. One was fond of his flocks and herds: he threatened him with the immediate confiscation of his property. Another was peculiarly open to superstitious fears: him he vowed so to bewitch and encompass with the spells of necromancy, that his property would be destroyed, his name blasted, and the affections of even his nearest relatives alienated from him. For more than twelve months the mission made no progress whatever, except, indeed, in the development of character among those who took, perhaps not joyfully, but resignedly, "the spoiling of their goods" for Christ's sake. Those who after all his efforts still continued to attend our services became marked men; and in their steadfastness the Bamangwato, as well as ourselves, understood by a fresh illustration the power of the gospel of Christ.

It was under such circumstances that I resolved to build a better dwelling-house than the wattle-and-daub hut in which I had hitherto dwelt. I had to begin at the beginning, and make the moulds for the bricks. Brick-making was then proceeded with. I next went to the forest with a party of men, and felled timber, which we conveyed to Shoshong to be dressed there. The stone foundation of the house was laid by myself, and I had begun with the bricks, laying them down according to a scheme which I found in a book on the mechanical arts, when a bricklayer who had recently begun trading in ivory and feathers arrived at the station. I got several lessons from him on the practical detail of bricklaying, which I did not find in the book; and he was also kind enough to raise the wall a considerable height before he left. I was equally fortunate in obtaining assistance in the making of doors and window-sashes from English traders, who were on the station at the time. Before I entered the new house at the end of the year, I made the following entry in my note-book:—"Have to record that for many months I cannot remember having been seated for half an hour during the day with either book or newspaper. Continually at out-door work." Indeed, during all the period of our life at Shoshong reading and correspondence were seldom overtaken during the day, but carried on in the silence of night. Although without European society, we never felt lonely, for our hands were constantly filled with one engagement after another.

Up to this time Sekhome had shown friendship and respect towards the missionaries. But if the teaching was bad the teachers could not be good. If he quarrelled with the scholars and with the doctrines taught, he could not remain on friendly terms with their teachers. He had nothing against either Mr. Price or myself. A charge must therefore be concocted. Accordingly he first quarrelled with Mr. Price, and afterwards with me. When I began house-building I had hired four men from Sekhome, who were to obtain payment of a heifer each for a year's service. When this period had half expired, Sekhome demanded their wages. It was evident that he sought occasion against us, and as I could not hope to have a better case at a future time, I resolved to refuse his glaringly unjust demand. I reminded him of our public engagement, and mentioned the names of head men who were witnesses of the transaction, desiring them to be called to support my statement. I said I was resolved to be his friend, and to fulfil my word in all things. It was for him also to stick to his engagement. But the chief doggedly reiterated his demand, and then left me in a passion, declaring I should know that the anger of Sekhome was not a trifle. In this he was quite right. He succeeded in annoying me very much, especially by removing all our servants, so that we had no one left to assist us belonging to the Bamangwato. They were forbidden to serve us in anything, even to draw water for us from the river. But about this time a young Makalaka lad, who had known me in the Matebele country, came out of his own accord to Shoshong, and placed himself in my hands. Then some Englishmen, who were going to hunt in Moselekatse's country found that they could not take Zulus thither on account of the jealousy still existing between Moselekatse and the tribes from which he separated. Two Zulu men were therefore left with me by these sportsmen, so that after a time I was not dependent upon Sekhome's assistance.

In the course of the strife between Sekhome and the small Christian party in the town, which was headed by his own two eldest sons, every occasion was sought against the believers, but in vain. There was positively nothing of which they could be accused. It was only in this matter pertaining to the service of God in which the chief could find ground of complaint. The bulk of the people were fond of the two young chiefs, and showed their respect and regard in many ways. But the head men in the town were bitterly set against them, although not for the same reason which animated Sekhome. Khame and Khamane had married sisters, the daughters of Tshukuru, the chief who was next in rank to Sekhome. The ground of the complaint of the head men was that this Tshukuru was thus raised to pre-eminent rank in the town, inasmuch as the young chiefs, being Christians, would not "add to" the number of their wives, according to heathen custom, so as to elevate several other families to this intimate connection with that of the chief. Hostility to Tshukuru was therefore gradually introduced into the quarrel by

Sekhome and his coadjutors, and allowed to mingle with and strengthen the opposition which arose from their hostility to the Word of God. At this juncture it was brought to the remembrance of Sekhome that some years before he had negotiated a marriage for Khame, his eldest son, with the daughter of Pelutona, one of the head men, a famous sorcerer, and a great favourite with the chief. The cattle had been paid for this young woman by Sekhome, and the marriage was thus ratified according to Bechuana custom; but Khame had never given his consent to the match at all, and at last prevailed upon his father to break it off. The cattle were never returned, however, to Sekhome, and it was now thought by the heathen party that they had here a suitable cause for quarrel. They said to Sekhome that as the cattle had been paid for Pelutona's daughter she was Khame's wife, and Sekhome must show his zeal for the customs, and his power over his son, by compelling him to take this woman to his house as his head wife, and to place his present one, the daughter of Tshukuru, whom he had married "after the customs of the Word of God," in a subordinate position. Sekhome was willing to take up this ground, because it secured him increased support. Instead therefore of saying to his son as before, "Give up going to church and to school," Sekhome now added the command to take home his proper wife, and to put Mabese, his present wife, into the position of an inferior wife. Khame's answer was a respectful and straightforward refusal: "I refuse on account of the Word of God to take a second wife; but you know that I was always averse to this woman, having declined to receive her from you as my wife before I became a Christian. I thought you had given up the match. I understood you to say, before your mind was poisoned against me, that you were pleased with my present wife. Lay the hardest task upon me with reference to hunting elephants for ivory, or any service you can think of as a token of my obedience, but I cannot take the daughter of Pelutona to wife." This was the answer which the head men had expected, and which they desired, for their grudge was not so much against Khame as against Tshukuru. They said therefore to Sekhome that it was evident that the father-in-law of his sons was poisoning their minds; and that he no doubt intended to kill Sekhome, and then, through his sons-in-law, obtain supreme power in the town. They advised that Tshukuru should first be put to death, otherwise he would kill the chief. Now there is no doubt that Tshukuru was very proud of his sons-in-law, and especially pleased that they were Christians—not because he believed in Jesus Christ, but because through the Word of God his daughters would have no rivals as wives of the young chiefs, and he would have no head men rivals to himself as their fathers-in-law. Tshukuru therefore withstood all the solicitations of the chief and the priests, that his second daughter, the betrothed wife of Khamane, should go through the ceremony of "boyali" before marriage. He said he would leave it to her future husband; if he wished her to go she was to go, but not otherwise. Khamane declared she was not to go, and carried his point. She was the first in Shoshong to be married without introduction to the "boyali," and the women confidently affirmed that she would be barren as a punishment for her departure from the old customs. In this, however, they were mistaken, for in her first-born she had the happiness, so eagerly desired by Bechuana women, of presenting her husband with a son. As the enmity of the head men was increasingly directed against him, Tshukuru, as a heathen, sought to meet his enemies on their own ground, and to raise up a party against them. In this, however, he obtained no countenance from the young chiefs, who abstained entirely from plotting against their father. Tshukuru was however joined by several head men who had secret grounds for fearing or for hating Sekhome; men who had not the slightest attachment to Christianity, or appreciation of the position which the young chiefs had taken up. For months angry words were heard, chiefly uttered by Sekhome—never by his sons. Sekhome now secretly offered a reward to any one who would assassinate Tshukuru. He called several Matebele refugees, who were supposed to be more habituated to such ruthless work, and intimated that he wished them to put Tshukuru to death. But the Matebele knew that Tshukuru was the best shot among the Bamangwato, and a man whose powers with the assegai were known over the country. Besides, they were merely refugees; why should they meddle with the quarrels of the Bamangwato? So without positively refusing to do what they were commanded, they put off time, professing to be seeking a convenient opportunity to transact this bloody deed.

In January 1866, Sekhome considered that he was in a position to carry everything before him, and with one blow to crush all opposition. But when the night came on which he intended to kill or to banish his own sons, and all who adhered to them, he found at the last hour that there was a deep unwillingness on the part of the people to move a hand against the young chiefs. He ordered his men to fire. "Upon whom?" "Upon these huts," said the misguided chief, pointing to the houses of his two sons. Not a man would obey. At length Sekhome hastened himself to load a double-barrelled rifle. One of his own head men came up, and with that amount of compulsion which on certain occasions may be used even toward a chief, laid the rifle aside. Sekhome saw that however much jealousy might be roused against Tshukuru, there was only respect and affection on the part of the body of the people toward his children. The chief was now in great terror. Judging his sons by himself, he took it for granted that as he was now completely in their hands they would order him to be put to death. So he fled from the midst of followers whom he now distrusted, and hid himself in an outhouse behind his mother's dwelling, while every entrance to his place of retreat was guarded by picked retainers in whom he still had confidence. In the olden time, in a Bechuana town, such a failure as that of Sekhome's would have led to immediate and most disastrous results. The man who had secured in this unmistakeable way the suffrages of the people would have asserted his right to reign at once in the town, and his opponent would have been compelled to flee or have been put to death. But Khame and Khamane, the sons of Sekhome, had no such thought. They sent their uncle, the brother-in-law of their father, to assure him that he need fear no harm from them. They would not lift a hand against him. But for the satisfaction of the people, who had been long troubled with those needless quarrels, they wished him publicly to announce what his future policy was to be as to this marriage question; and if there was to be now peace in the town? Mogomotsi had the utmost difficulty in obtaining admission to his brother-in-law. Sekhome could not believe that there was no treachery. At length the messenger of his sons stood before him, and delivered to their guilty and trembling father the statement of their forgiveness for the past and their inquiry with reference to the future. Sekhome eagerly answered every question in the way which he knew would give satisfaction—scarcely believing it possible that those upon whom he had shortly before given the order to fire, were addressing him thus respectfully, although he was completely in their power. It was now given out that the strife was at end; Khame was not to be forced to take Pelutona's daughter to wife, and those who were attending church were not to be molested.

I expressed to the young chiefs my satisfaction on hearing this news, and my hopes that Sekhome would now resume his former manner toward them and toward the mission. I was grieved, however, to find that they had no such hope. They did not believe he was sincere in his public statements. They said his past rule had been characterized by a determination to carry through every project which he began. If he gave up the attempt to put down the Word of God after threatening to do so, it would be the first instance in which he had ever failed in an enterprise to which he had committed himself. Some time after they assured me that their father had returned to his old machinations, and with apparently greater vehemence than ever. They expressed their determination to take no steps whatever to counteract what their father was doing, but to trust in that Providence which had already delivered them.

A short time after the signal failure of Sekhome's plot against his sons, I learned from them that their father had secretly despatched a messenger to his brother Macheng, who was then residing at the town of Sechele. Determined not to relinquish the unnatural strife, Sekhome resolved on the bold policy of inviting Macheng back to Shoshong, and of outwardly investing him with the chieftainship. In the event of his own death he maliciously determined that his Christian sons, at any rate, should not enjoy the chieftainship after him. And Sekhome was bold enough to trust that after he had used his brother as a tool, and through him had accomplished all his wishes, he would be able, when he pleased, to rid himself of Macheng also, and resume the rule over the Bamangwato with no one to dispute his authority, and with no Christianity to hold up its persistent torch-light in his town, and even in his heart, saying of certain actions, "They are wrong, and displeasing to God." In the meantime, however, the town of Shoshong was in daily and nightly ferment. Sekhome and his friends met no longer in open day, but in the darkness of night. But even in these innermost ranks of heathenism there were sure to be some waverers; and Khame and his brother were duly informed of the plans which were being hatched against them.

Khame awoke one night and was alarmed to find his premises lighted up as if on fire. On hastening outside he discovered the "baloi" or wizards at their enchantments opposite the entrance to his house. They were casting plant after plant, charm after charm, into the fire, mumbling and muttering their dark prayers and curses as an accompaniment. Who would wonder if a shudder passed through the mind of the young man, to find the previously dreaded customs of his ancestors thus actively directed against him, the eldest son of the chief? But the weird appearance of the old wizards, whose faces were lighted up by the flames of their fire, failed to strike terror into the heart of Khame. Advancing unobserved to the hedge of his yard, he suddenly raised himself within a short distance of the baloi. Surprised in their wickedness, these evil-doers fled panic-stricken from the scene, leaving their spells and charms hissing and crackling in the flames. Fearless of its powers to harm him, Khame now put out the fire and went again to sleep. But if the young chiefs were not affected by this necromancy, it was far otherwise with many who sympathized with them personally, and desired to see them enjoying their proper position in the town. These heathen came to inquire if Khame could not return in kind the cursing of his father; and by the employment of other baloi, counteract the mischief, which they declared had already come upon him through the perseverance of Sekhome. "Unless you use these things also, the people will be frightened to remain with you. We are not afraid of Sekhome, but who can withstand the power of baloi?" The young chiefs, however, were impracticable: the Word of God forbade them to curse any one, and especially their own father. And as to the spells themselves, they were worthless observances. The missionaries agreed with Bechuanas, that people could be poisoned in their food, but taught that spells had no power over any one; and this was their own opinion and experience also. Had not their father long tried to injure them by such means, and had he not failed? Had they not all health and prosperity in their homes and families? The heathen men answered that the Word of God no doubt threw its protection over them; but what was to become of those who did not believe "the books" when the necromancy was turned against them? They said that the people loved the young chiefs, but there was one power which would cause them to desert, and that was the power of witchcraft. No doubt Tshukuru did his best as a sorcerer to counteract all these influences, but he was so unpopular, through the jealousy of the head men, that little notice was taken of his practice of the "black art." And his efforts were further neutralized by the open and repeated declarations of his sons-in-law, that they had nothing to do with his spells, and had no confidence in them.

CHAPTER XXII.

THE FATHER AGAINST THE SON.

In February 1866, our friends Mr. and Mrs. Price left us to visit their relatives at Kuruman. But what we hoped was only a separation for a month or two, turned out to be our severance as colleagues at the same station. There were at that time so few missionaries in Bechuana-land, that it was thought unadvisable that two should reside at one station, even although it had a population of 30,000. The chief, Sechele, was also so urgent for a missionary, "who would teach him as Livingstone had done," that it was thought best that Mr. Price should at once take charge of that station. This step entailed additional labour and inconvenience upon Mr. Price, who having built a house at Shoshong, found himself again in a hut at Sechele's. We were sorry that this separation was necessary, and especially regretted its cause, in the fewness of missionaries in the country. The loss of our friends' society was much felt by us, and all the more on account of the disturbed circumstances of the mission at the time. At Sechele's, however, they have been able to organize an extensive work of instruction. They found among the Bakwena a general desire to learn to read, and it was with some difficulty that the wants of the people could for some time be met as to spelling-books and Testaments, all of which, with very few exceptions, the learners purchased with such articles of barter as they possessed.

I may state here that Mr. Price has since been able to organize, or perhaps to re-organize, the Church at this old station of Dr. Livingstone. In doing so he required great firmness to deal with Sechele. This chief, as a matter of course, expected to enter the church. Baptized by Ngake (the doctor), welcomed into the communion of the Lutheran Church, Sechele was disappointed to find that some of his own servants were admitted into the church by Mr. Price before their master. He could also point to the fact that he had built a large church in his town entirely at his own and his people's expense. The missionary, however, had weighty reasons for thus treating the application of the chief—reasons which the latter could not gainsay. On the occasion of one of my visits to the station he renewed his application, thinking perhaps that he would secure my support. But I felt, with his own missionary, that many of his doings were inconsistent with the discipleship of the Lord Jesus Christ.

"But," said Sechele, when he found he had little to hope for from my presence, "what if either myself or my wife were to die as we are now, out of the Church? The thought is fearful. Yet life is uncertain, and you refuse to admit us."

And when it was explained that the whole of the saving of the soul is the work of Christ, and none of it the work of man, or of the Church, Sechele's wife very strongly broke in—"Of what use is a missionary then?"

I do not know how far this doctrine of faith in the Church and in its sacraments was taught by the Lutheran missionaries to the Bakwena. But such was the apparent result of their teaching on the minds of these people. I am quite aware, however, that it would be very unfair to attribute every crude notion held by Bechuanas to the missionaries who taught them. However this may be, it is a miserable thing for people to trust in church, or sacrament, or ceremony, instead of directly, personally, and wholly in the ever-living Saviour.

Some of the minor tribes living under Sechele's protection have made even greater progress in knowledge and in civilisation than the Bakwena. The whole circumstances of this mission are at present very encouraging, and there is the prospect of a deep impression being made upon the dense population of the district. The Missionary Society has recently appointed a second missionary to assist Mr. Price in this work.

On the evening of the 8th of March 1866, Khame was hastily accosted by a Matebele refugee, resident in Shoshong, who in a few words warned him that Sekhome's plans were laid for that very night. The old chief thought his enemies were off their guard. A decisive blow was now to be struck to retrieve the defeat and disgrace of the last attempt. Many of the people had been secured by the most dreadful pledges to be faithful to Sekhome. "I myself," said the Matebele soldier, "have been commissioned to attack you in your house, at the head of a party of my countrymen and others appointed by the chief. My heart is very sore; we Matebele respect chiefs, and obey their commands—we have put this off for a long time, and can do so no longer. But my own heart is white toward you—it has no malice; and I therefore sought this opportunity to warn you." Khame was within five minutes' walk of my house when he received this warning; so he came at once and informed me that if I heard the report of guns during the night neither I nor Ma-Willie was to be alarmed. He was convinced that no one would harm us. I expressed the hope that it would blow over again as before; but I could see that Khame was desponding. He said that his father had filled the minds of the people, and almost maddened himself, with his necromancy; and that those who before spoke boldly on their behalf were now afraid to say a word. I could only invoke God's blessing and protection upon those who sought to serve Him, and who were so hemmed in by heathenism in the ranks of their friends as well as among their enemies.

After leaving me, Khame went to inform his brother and his father-in-law of their danger. Although they anticipated an outbreak at some time, Sekhome had completely taken them by surprise. Not suspecting any danger, Khamane and Tshukuru had gone to the gardens on horseback, and had not returned when Khame made his appearance at his father-in-law's town. When Khame reached his own dwelling, he found that armed men were fast gathering around the entrance. They made way for him, however, and allowed him to take out of his house whatever he wanted; and also to remove his relatives in peace. My last advice to him was, not to leave his own house, and not to fire a shot. But finding his premises already in the occupation of Sekhome's adherents, he was obliged reluctantly to retreat from his own dwelling. Crossing the river he took up his quarters outside the town, near to the walls of a building which had been begun by the Hanoverian missionaries, and intended for a church. Neither building nor site was suitable for our operations, and the roofless walls had become a ruin. Driven by their own father from their home, the young chiefs here took up their head-quarters. Hearing what had taken place, their friends hastened to join them. Some who attempted to do so were forcibly prevented by their relations and friends. Others found that their guns had been hidden by the older members of their families who favoured the views of the chief. The argument used by these old men to their sons was to this effect: "Two parties so opposed to each other as Sekhome and his sons cannot live in one town. We preferred the sons, and we gave them their chance. They might have been chiefs of the town to-day but for their being in the Word of God, which makes them so impracticable. Now, the town cannot be thus disturbed. As the sons refused to take any steps against their father, the people for the sake of peace, as well as through fear of Sekhome's medicines, have many of them gone with the chief this time; and only those who are heedless of death will now join Khame. To-night Sekhome will have the majority on his side, and he will assuredly not imitate the example of Khame by doing nothing—he has already given orders concerning the occupation of his son's premises." With such cautions and remonstrances many young men were deterred from joining Khame. During the night each party sent for its cattle to their posts, and drove them to separate places of security on the mountain range,—Khame's cattle climbing the mountain on the east, and Sekhome's on the west of the town.

We spent a very uncomfortable night, revolving what could be done for the sake of peace, which had not been already attempted. At grey dawn the report of musketry announced that actual fighting had begun. We heard first a few shots, and then repeated volleys, which resounded from side to side of the kloof or gorge. "May God help the right!" was our sincere prayer, as we listened to the firing, which began this most unnatural and cruel war. I hastened to the door, and found that one party was stationed opposite the front of my house—another half way up the mountain to the south of the house. I learnt afterwards that hostilities were commenced by Sekhome's party —the first shot, it was said, having been actually fired by a brother of the young chiefs, called Ralitlari. Khame and Khamane now ascended the mountain behind the ruined building already described, which was that day held by a party of their men under Mogomotsi. Sekhome and his men held the town, occupying Khame's premises and those in the neighbourhood. By stooping down, they could pass along the hedges from one place to another in the town, unseen by those outside. On the other hand, those on the mountain were more conspicuous, although they took every advantage of the shelter afforded by the rocks and bushes on its side. Tshukuru and his party occupied a strong position above his own town, and were expending large quantities of ammunition, with little or no result, as we afterwards learned. Kope, the head man of the village on the brow of the mountains, had vacated the houses, and taken up his position among the rocks opposite to my house, and overlooking it. He kept up a pretty constant fire against Tshukuru, who however replied with vigour. After taking a survey from the hill at the back of my house, I was satisfied that my premises were being respected by the combatants. I could see Khame's men firing from the mountain side; and though I could not see those of Sekhome in the town, the smoke from their guns gave frequent evidence of their whereabouts.

As soon as I heard from Khame the previous evening of the imminence of a fresh disturbance, I sent word to some English traders who were then on the station. Two brothers, who were then trading in the town, found themselves involved in the fray before they were well aware of it. Their waggons stood near the church walls, where Khame spent the night. When hostilities commenced, they found themselves mixed up with Khame's men. A bullet passed through one waggon while one of the brothers was asleep in it. The hut in which part of their goods was kept, and in which the other brother and a friend were sitting, was battered with bullets. Sekhome's men argued that if these Englishmen did not sympathize with the young chiefs, they could have removed their waggons in the night. This was no doubt what the traders would have done, if they had known what was to take place. At the same time, every Englishman in the country was sorry for Khame, and convinced of his sincerity and love of peace. His present position was calculated to excite their sympathy. He represented to them that he had been unable to remove all his own ammunition from his premises; his men's guns had been hidden by their relatives; the men had absconded in the night, but were now without arms. He was willing to pay for everything he received. The result of his statement was that the Englishmen helped him to provide suitable equipment for those who had cast in their lot with him. As morning approached Khame gave strict orders to his men to avoid giving the least provocation to their opponents, and that those who loved war must remember that they were entirely unprepared to fight.

It was probably reported to Sekhome in the night by spies that the Englishmen were assisting Khame, and the order had been given to respect neither their lives nor their property. Finding that their hut was untenable, the traders retired for protection behind the walls of the church. It is perhaps not remarkable that young Englishmen, one of them not long from school, should in such circumstances fire upon those who had already damaged their property and seemed to wish to take their lives. They thought indeed that they were unperceived by the other side, and that while having what they called "a lark" they were not compromising themselves or others. In this however they were mistaken, for a bend in the town hedge commanded a view of the place where they stood, mixed up with Khame's men under Mogomotsi. It is possible these young men expected to see some brilliant exploits performed by the young chiefs at the head of their men. Instead of this Khame and Khamane retired to the mountain, and had evidently no intention of making any aggressive movement on the town. The men in the town were content with shots fired at long ranges, and from carefully selected shelter. After some four hours the excitement of the noisy commencement died away in the minds of the young Englishmen. The whole thing was now pronounced "slow," and they began to bethink themselves of their position as "neutrals" in a Bechuana town. A bullet which almost grazed one of their faces was of considerable weight at this stage of their discussions. It was evident they were in "a mess." How were they to get out of it? The curiosity of the youngest had not been yet fully gratified, so he volunteered to remain in charge of the waggons. The others resolved to make for my house. As soon as they left their shelter they were fired at, but they marched at more than "double-quick" time, and escaped unhurt. They made their appearance at my house about ten o'clock, and gave me an account of their adventure. I was very sorry that they had fired; and their present position, while it provoked a smile, had also its grave aspect. I readily tendered all the protection in my power, although, as I explained to them, I was not at that time aware what my own treatment was to be at the hands of Sekhome. Two other traders, who were not mixed up with the disturbance in any way, came up to my house and returned to their waggons without accident, although one of them was fired at. My own premises enjoyed perfect immunity. As some of the natives fire rather widely, a few stray bullets were to be expected, considering our proximity to the scene of conflict. One of these was picked up in my cattle-pen. The traders now removed their goods to the neighbourhood of my house. Although those who had broken neutrality were hooted at, they were no longer treated as enemies, but were also allowed to remove their property without much annoyance. In the afternoon my attention was attracted to an old man who, having got within range of the guns, sat for some hours under the shelter of a hedge. I went over to him and offered him food and shelter in my house. But he preferred to go his own way, although so weak and exhausted, perhaps partly with fear, that he could not rise without help.

The firing was continued on Saturday, but not with the steadiness of the previous day. When Sunday dawned, I had a sad prospect before me. Almost all my congregation were on the mountain, and the town was occupied by those who were opposed to my work as a missionary. At the usual hour for our morning service, I went to the town, and was directed to where Sekhome sat. He was surrounded by thirty or forty lingaka (sorcerers) and head men, all armed. He received me with unusual cheerfulness, calling for chairs to be brought for me and for those who accompanied me. "He has brought his books," said one. "Whom is he to teach to-day?" asked another. There seemed to be considerable curiosity to hear what I should say to Sekhome in such circumstances. The people crowded the place where the chief sat, and others listened outside the hedge. I returned the chief's warm greeting, and then explained that I had come to see him to express my great sorrow for what was taking place in the town. I was not altogether one of his people; but I had so much knowledge of the Bamangwato, and sympathy for them, that I was very sorry to see the town in its present condition.

Sekhome replied, "It was the fault of those on the mountain; his children were disobedient."

I did not hesitate to express my admiration of Khame's conduct, so far as it was known to me; and said there was not another chief in Bechuana-land who had such obedient sons. I could see from the faces of the people that I had their approbation in this remark. This was probably perceived by Sekhome also; for instead of continuing to find fault with them, or with the Word of God, he said that now, if he could only compass the death of Tshukuru, he would give up the quarrel, and his children might come back. I now intimated my wish to go up to preach to those who were on the mountain. Pointing to my New Testament and hymn-book, I said, "These are my weapons; you need not fear allowing me to go." The chief at once agreed, and the head men, with more or less readiness, expressed their consent.

The firing had now ceased from the town; and there had been none from the mountain this morning. On ascending the steep mountain-path, I found Khamo and Khamane on the summit, surrounded by their followers. All were glad to see me. Every one came to the service except the sentries, who were placed along the brow of the mountain. I explained to them some of the lessons and comforts of Christianity, and encouraged them to seek peace by every means except by forsaking the service of God. I found the young men evincing an admirable spirit, and bitterly regretting the position in which they were placed. "Our days of peace and happiness are over," they said; "for our father will never again believe himself safe in our hands, after driving us from the town." I could see also that there were heterogeneous elements among their followers, some of them being merely on the mountain on account of personal fear of Sekhome, such a commotion being a time for settling all old reckonings of enmity and revenge in a heathen town. After the service I was asked to visit a person of this description, an old sorcerer, who had been formerly a friend and accomplice of the chief. He had been shot through the knee on Friday. He lingered for some days, but afterwards died of the wound. Khame now explained to me that he intended to retire to a stronghold on the mountain at some distance from the town, and that he would engage in no offensive movement against his father. He said that Sekhome had informed Macheng of the position of affairs, and he himself had sent a messenger for the same purpose to Sechele. Khame hoped that one or other of these chiefs would interfere in his behalf. In the meantime he was determined to wait the issue with patience, and trust in God.

For six weeks the town of the Bamangwato was divided, and the men were daily under arms. On six Sundays I ascended the mountain fastness, and preached to those who had been driven from the town. I also took charge of property which had been left in the hands of Khame and other combatants by English hunters and traders. Sekhome was agreeable to this arrangement; so I removed from the town native produce and European goods, the owners of which were absent. I felt convinced that my position as a man of peace was strengthened when I was able to remove valuable goods in presence of both parties, and store them on my own premises. And so, with reference to cattle, I received both from Khame and from some of Sekhome's men oxen belonging to Englishmen which I placed at a post with my own.

At the first convenient opportunity I conducted to Sekhome and his head men the Englishman who had been seen firing, in order, if possible, to assist him out of his false position. Sekhome received him somewhat curtly; but I could see there was to be no serious difficulty. I began by saying that "this was the man who had taken refuge in my house; if he had done wrong, let those speak whom he had wronged, and let not evil thoughts be hidden in men's hearts." Sekhome sent for a man whose wrist had received some splinters of a bullet which had first struck a neighbouring rock.

"This man," said Sekhome, "has been shot by Moshow (Mr. K—); none of Khame's people had small shot in their guns; this is blood drawn by an Englishman."

My companion was somewhat uneasy, but protested that he had not fired any small shot. I bethought me of a simple diversion in his favour, and said, "This certainly looks somewhat like small shot; but might it not have been the bits of a bullet which had struck against a rock? Before coming to any decision, I would suggest that the chief take a walk up as far as this Englishman's waggons, and he will there find numerous bullet-marks which may guide him in settling the question."

The chief's face lighted up: "Was there much damage done to the waggon?" he asked.

I replied that there was a great deal, but that what interested me was the similarity of the marks on the side of the waggon to those on the man's wrist.

So it was agreed that Moshow's case should stand over till the damage to the waggon was inspected. Next day Sekhome and his head men appeared, and I pointed out to him the marks I had referred to. The waggons had indeed sustained a good deal of damage, and would always bear the marks of the bullets. After inspecting them with evident satisfaction, Sekhome of his own accord said that Moshow was acquitted: the wounds on the waggon would atone for the wounds on the man's hand!

On the night of Sunday the 18th March, I was going the round of my premises before retiring to rest, when to my surprise I stumbled in the darkness on a number of armed men. "Why do you sit there in the dark?" I asked. They said they had been appointed by Sekhome to surround my house for the purpose of waylaying Mogomotsi and Khamane. Sekhome had heard that they were every night in my house. I gave them a message to Sekhome that it was not correct that any of those from the hill had visited my house; but that I was glad that he had sent men who would now see for themselves. I had this "black watch" every night round my house for several weeks. The circumstances attending its withdrawal were somewhat amusing. I usually came upon some of them every night, in snug corners, where they were frequently sound asleep. I roused a party of them one night, and warned them that if I found them asleep again I should take their guns from them and hand them over to Sekhome next morning in the kotla, and before all the Bamangwato! They never made their appearance again.

On Wednesday the 21st, I took Mrs. Mackenzie and the children about three miles in the waggon, for a few hours' quiet in the country; we raised a swing for the children, and all thoroughly enjoyed the change. A little before sunset we returned to our house. One of my children exclaimed on our way home, "Who are all these coming behind us?" Looking back, I saw that perhaps two hundred armed men were following us into the town. It seemed that when I left in the morning it was immediately taken for granted that my journey had something to do with the quarrel going on, and that I had probably an engagement to meet some of Khame's men in the country, in order to supply them with ammunition. Although we knew nothing of their proximity, we had been watched by all these armed men the whole day. Surely it must have been a rebuke to them to see that instead of having any warlike object whatever, we had come purely for the sake of recreation.

Sunday the 25th was a day of some excitement. Early in the morning Mr. B— made his appearance and very kindly took me aside, and informed me of certain rumours which he had heard in the town, and strongly advised me not to go up to the mountain. I had already heard—not the floating rumours, but that on which they were based—the decision of a secret meeting of Sekhome's head men, and the discussion which had then taken place. The meeting had been held in the court-yard of the chief's mother, whose opinion was always sought by Sekhome on occasions of difficulty.

"It seems to me that the Bamangwato men have become entirely changed now-a-days," said this old hag. "There is one insignificant white man who is stronger than the whole town of the Bamangwato. He owes Sekhome cows, being the wages of his men, and refuses to pay them. Had he done so in the olden time a true chief would have seized his whole herd. He takes the property of the white men, which ought to have been eaten up by the chief, and removes it to his own premises. He goes out in his waggon, or he rides out on horseback, and there is treason under every movement. Every Sunday he visits your sons, to strengthen them in that Word of God which has been their ruin. And yet you all seem to think of this little thing called a teacher, as if he had power in the town. What power can he have? Does he not go about unarmed? I am a woman, but I am this day ashamed of the men of the Bamangwato."

Several head men then proposed the expulsion of all the white men and the plundering of their goods. Pelutona proposed more extreme measures with reference to the missionary, and then, he said, no more would follow to trouble the town by teaching the Word of God.

Sekhome denied that he was afraid of the missionary; but said that no one must injure him. "The blame of having the missionary rests with me," said the chief, "for it was I who invited him to come and dwell in the town. No white man's blood must be shed in this town while I am chief. Did I not spare the Boers whom Sechele tempted me to kill? And shall I imitate Sekeletu, and injure those who have come as friends, and whom I myself have invited? But they must all leave till this quarrel is over, and the missionary must go also, for his presence strengthens my sons."

Such had been some of the opinions expressed at this secret council. My informant was a school-girl, whose mother was the servant of the mother of Sekhome, and was in attendance upon the assembled councillors. The old woman, who was not a Christian, found occasion to go home and to despatch her daughter to inform me of my danger. Through this act of genuine kindness I knew the cause of the evil rumours and threats of which Mr. B— now warned me. After considering everything, I decided to go down to Sekhome as usual, and ask his permission to ascend the mountain to preach, and if he positively refused, to return home.

For the first time, I was that Sunday hooted in the streets, and from behind hedges, where I could not see the speakers. I was accompanied by a young Englishman, who went with me on almost every journey to the mountains. When we reached the entrance to the kotla we met several parties of young men "dressed" for a public assembly. Some were spotted with white clay like tigers, others were striped like zebras, while every kind of fanciful head-dress was worn. A considerable gathering had already taken place at the kotla. While I was looking round for the chief, I was surprised by two old men, who suddenly approached me brandishing their spears, demanding at the same time, amid many imprecations and threats, that I should at once leave the town. They both foamed at the mouth with excitement and passion while they went on with their raving charges. After they had both said a good deal, and gesticulated with their spears to their hearts' content, I reminded them that I had the same right to be in the town as the rest of its inhabitants. My house had been built with the full approbation of Sekhome. It was for the chief to find fault with me, but it was not becoming in old men, who ought to be an example to others, to insult and threaten a defenceless man in the kotla. They now went and sat down, exhausted by their efforts, when a person whom I did not know came up to me, and encouraged me not to heed these people; I had to look to Sekhome only. Soon after the chief strode into the kotla, looking very gloomy and angry. He at first positively forbade my going up to the mountain to preach, but after a little expostulation and patient waiting he gruffly gave his consent. He probably intended to frighten me, for while I sat beside him he called a well-known factotum who performed a good deal of his dirty work, and he in turn went and whispered to a Matebele soldier, who was sitting at some distance, assegai in hand. When we rose to go this soldier went with us for no object of his own that I could discover. After walking with us some distance he suddenly turned back. Sekhome also asked which road I was to take. When I had finished the services on the mountain I found two companies of armed men waiting at the place I had mentioned to the chief. But it seemed to me that the men themselves were now more respectful than in the morning. It struck me as if there had been a trial of determination, and that I had gained the day. The chief had declared I was not to go up to the mountain again, but had yielded me permission in the end. He had promised to expel me from the town; he could not muster heart even to mention such a thing.

While on the mountain I learned the cause of the increased irritation on the part of Sekhome and his people. On Friday night Sekhome despatched two lingaka or sorcerers with a large quantity of charms and spells, and perhaps poisons, which they were to throw into the fountain supplying water for the young chiefs' party and their cattle. Before these men started on their nefarious errand, the most potent spells were applied to themselves by the chief and the other sorcerers. When all was completed, they were assured that there would be darkness wherever they went—the clouds of night would compass them so that no eye should behold them. But alas for charms and incantations! The young chiefs had sentries posted at the water, who instead of challenging the approaching wizards, allowed them to come close to the water, when they fired and shot the very man who carried the charms, which were found beside his lifeless body next morning. This was what had irritated the chief, who saw in this circumstance more than the death of a man: it was the proved inefficacy of their greatest charms and most solemn rites.

On returning to my house I found that the Englishmen on the station were unanimously of opinion that it would not be desirable for us to remain longer on the place while the disturbance was going on among the Bamangwato. They had made their own arrangements to leave, and had kindly offered my wife their assistance in the work of preparation in my absence, so that when I returned I should have the less to do. With the kindest intentions they also pictured to Mrs. Mackenzie in the strongest light the dangers of our position, and the open threats which were now used. But my wife viewed the matter very quietly, declining the proffered assistance until she should know that I had made up my mind to leave. My arrival was that day waited for with more than ordinary anxiety. In the evening, after our usual English service, the subject was fully discussed. I represented to those present that in the excited state of the people's feelings, to go away would be the signal for the pillage and destruction of the property of absent hunters and traders, as well as of the mission station. For my own part I should leave only when the chief plainly informed me that he could no longer afford me his protection. It was not to be expected, however, that temporary residents would have the same feelings as myself about leaving Shoshong, and accordingly three of the traders took their departure on the following Tuesday.

Towards myself the temper of the people gradually improved. I went up more frequently to the mountain, and sometimes as the bearer of messages from the one side to the other. One day I was standing on the brow of the hill, taking leave of the young chiefs, when a man approached from the gardens, and, kneeling behind an ant-hill, took aim at the group. As we were about 300 yards from him there was little danger. The man had evidently some difficulty in his own mind about firing while I was one of the party; for after a short time he retired into the shelter of the corn and sugar-cane in the garden. As soon as I left, however, he again approached, and fired upon those with whom I had been conversing. At the same place, a few days afterwards, a Dutch hunter and an English trader, who had obtained permission from the chief to visit those on the mountain, were fired upon by Sekhome's men under Ralitlari, his son. The Dutchman, who was well known in the town, was very indignant, and complained to Sekhome of the violation of his safe-conduct by his own son, but received no satisfaction.

CHAPTER. XXIII.

FLIGHT OF SEKHOME.

AFTER this unhappy strife had lasted a month, Sekhome made a desperate effort to bring it to a close. He resolved to ascend the mountain and besiege Khame's position, so as to cut off his supply of water. For this purpose he called in all the neighbouring Bakalahari, mustered all the Makalaka, and every available man in Shoshong. Khame and his people stood the siege for eight days. During this time their live stock got no water. Even for themselves they could only procure melons from the gardens in the night by eluding the vigilance of those who invested their position. I saw the oxen and the sheep and goats when they had been seven days without water. Their piteous lowing and bleating might have been heard at a considerable distance. It was evident that this state of things could not last long. Latterly I had been the bearer of milder messages than formerly from camp to camp. At the request of Khame I led over a horse to Sekhome, which had fallen into the hands of his sons' followers. The chief now professed to me that he had not come to fight; he had only come to beg Khame to come home again.

Khame first requested that a separate position in the town should be assigned to him and to all who were with him on the mountain. He said he knew that the customs of the Word of God were displeasing to his father, and therefore proposed that those who adopted them should be allowed to reside in a division of the town by themselves. Should enemies attack the town they would be found at their post, although they would not attend upon the constantly recurring heathen ceremonies. Sekhome, however, was too far-seeing to consent to this. Had he done so, in less than a year the majority of the young people would have deserted him. Khame's next message to Sekhome was that he would return to the town on condition that his father should retire first, and allow him to enter the town as a free person, and not as a captive. He protested that he had been unjustly driven from the town, and cruelly hunted on the mountain, whereas he had never attacked the town, and had himself shown no enmity to his father. Sekhome did not at first agree to this demand of his son, which would rob himself and his party of the honour of driving their captives before them into the town amid the plaudits of the assembled population. But at length an interview took place between Sekhome and Khame at the camp of the former, when Sekhome agreed to return to the town first, and that Khame should follow with his men some hours after. When the young chief made his appearance in the neighbourhood of the town the applause was not so great as had been given to Sekhome, but still many cheered him. The conquered party sat down at the entrance to the court-yard, and were there detained a long time before Sekhome condescended to "call" his son to approach him and occupy the place of honour. After this took place, the young chief's followers returned to their own homes, and the division in the town of the Bamangwato was outwardly healed. Some time after, in giving me an account of these things, Khame said his idea in stipulating that he should be allowed to re-enter the town at the head of his own men, was to show that he had done no wrong before he was expelled; and that, whilst willing to return, he adhered to the opinions on account of which he had been driven out.

But there were some men on the mountain for whom it was well known Sekhome had no quarter. If Khame was to return to the town, these men must flee. Chief of these was Tshukuru, whom Khamane agreed to accompany as a protector. Khame had received a letter from Sechele a few days before, in which he offered any of them a place of refuge so long as the anger of Sekhome lasted. In this epistle Tshukuru's name was specially mentioned. It was nevertheless feared that Sechele might not keep this promise in the case of a man who had thwarted him in some of his cherished schemes; but it was imagined that if he was accompanied by a son of Sekhome, and one who, like Sechele himself, professed to be a Christian, no act of violence would take place. In this, however, they were mistaken. In the middle of the first night after reaching Sechele's, a messenger came to the sleeping-place of the Bamangwato, and roused Tshukuru. He said that Khosilintsi, the brother of Sechele, desired a private interview with him; as there was to be a public assembly of the Bakwena on the following day, Khosilintsi wished beforehand to master all the details of the Bamangwato quarrel, so as to be able publicly to advocate the claims of the refugees. As Khosilintsi had always been his special friend, Tshukuru left his men without suspicion, and followed the messenger. After they had proceeded some distance in the dark, they were joined by a Matebele refugee, who was a confidential servant of Sechele, and who was now accompanied by a few armed men. In a little Tshukuru discovered from the nature of the path that they were no longer in the town. "What head man lives in the bushes?" said the heathen man, whose mind was familiar with all the schemes which chiefs resort to in such circumstances. "You have been ordered by Sechele to kill me. If so, I need go no further." While speaking he was speared by those who attended him. His body was never buried, but was eaten by the wolves.

Thus died Tshukuru, a scheming and ambitious man, whose aims in the town of the Bamangwato were of a character as selfish and unprincipled as those of Sekhome. Sechele owed Tshukuru a grudge, because he was as astute as himself, and had co-operated with him in the execution of certain schemes only in so far as was pleasing to himself, and not so far as Sechele would have desired. The assassination of Tshukuru is a dark blot on the name of Sechele. When the news reached Shoshong, the large division of the town of which Tshukuru was the head man joined in sounding the death-wail of the murdered man. "O where shall we find him? Who shall now provide for us? Who will take his place in the council, or the chase, or the field of battle? Where shall we find him?" And then followed the wild chorus, expressive of great anguish—"Yo—yo—yo!" the mourners falling on their faces, tearing their hair, and beating their breasts in the frenzy of their sorrow. This harrowing dirge was frequently heard in such a large town as Shoshong. Its loudness and its long duration indicated the high rank of the person who had passed away. Christianity causes the death-wail to cease. In Bechuana-land those who profess to be believers mourn over their dead with as much self-restraint as people now do in England, and with much less heathenish demonstration than was exhibited, after centuries of Christian teaching, in the Celtic lyk-wake.

But the commotions at Shoshong were not to end with the return of Khame to the town. A new source of trouble soon after appeared in the person of Macheng, the brother of Sekhome, and the legal chief of the Bamangwato.

Sekhome had made overtures to him when he found that the sympathies of the Bamangwato were with his sons. But as soon as he saw that he would be able himself to subdue all opposition, he tried to draw back, and to dissuade his brother from coming. But Macheng was not to be thus put off. He had been invited, and he resolutely ignored all subsequent messages of a different import. He made his appearance therefore at Shoshong in the month of May, at the head of those Bamangwato men who had fled with him some eight years before. He left the women and the children until he should find what his own reception was to be. When Macheng arrived, Khame informed me that it was quite possible he would now have to flee. He was aware that Macheng was pledged to put him to death. He had given this promise to Sekhome before he left Sechele's town. Khame was entirely ignorant as to what course he would take, now that he had arrived. But if I heard that he had suddenly left the town, I was to understand that he had done so in order to avoid assassination.

For many weeks after his arrival Macheng preserved the utmost reserve. He lived in great retirement, sleeping and eating only in the company of his own men. Sekhome introduced Macheng to the Bamangwato at a public assembly. He told the people that he had called home his brother from his exile, and that he was now their chief. The smooth-tongued and perhaps bewildered head men rose one after the other to praise Sekhome, and to greet Macheng.

At length Khame rose and spoke. Addressing himself to Macheng, he said :—"Khosi! (king), it would appear that I alone of all the Bamangwato am to speak unpleasant words to you this day. The Bamangwato say they are glad to see you here. I say I am not glad to see you. If Sekhome could not live with his own children, but drove them from the town, and shot at them, how is he to submit to be ruled by you?—how will he learn to obey? If I thought there would be peace in the town, I would say I was glad to see you; I say I am sorry you have come, because I know that only disorder and death can take place when two chiefs sit in one kotla." Turning to the people, he said, "I wish all the Bamangwato to know that I renounce all pretensions to the chieftainship of the Bamangwato. Here are two chiefs already; I refuse to be called the third, as some of you have mockingly styled me. My kingdom consists in my gun, my horses, and my waggon. If you will give me liberty to possess these as a private person, I renounce all concern in the politics of the town. Especially do I refuse to attend night meetings. When men sit together in the dark, and are afraid to hold their meeting in the daylight, they themselves confess that their deeds are evil. If you wish me to attend your meetings, they must be held in the daylight. I am sorry, Macheng, that I cannot give you a better welcome to the Bamangwato."

This was a marvellous speech to fall among double-tongued, reticent, and scheming men. What was to be done with a man whose delight seemed to be to destroy all crooked counsels, and put an end to the "botlale" (wisdom) on which the Bechuana head men plumed themselves? The common people, however, secretly applauded Khame, although they were afraid to do so openly.

A little before the assembly broke up, Macheng rose and said, "Many speeches have been made to-day, many words of welcome have been addressed to me. All these I have heard with the ear; one speech, and one only, has reached my heart, and that is the speech of Khame. I thank Khame for his speech."

Some time after this, Macheng had a private interview with Khame, when he asked for the young chief's confidence. He said his mind had been poisoned by the false statements which Sekhome had published throughout Bechuana-land concerning his sons. All the chiefs and people living at a distance believed these reports, and had recommended him at once to fulfil his promise on his arrival, and put the disobedient sons to death. "But since I arrived at Shoshong," continued Macheng, "I have seen and heard for myself. The people of the Word of God alone speak the truth. By all the rest I am met with fair speeches and deceit. Henceforth you may trust in me, as I will rely on you."

In the public court-yard some time after this, Macheng said to Sekhome, "You called me from the Bakwena to kill your rebellious sons. My heart refuses to do this. They are your sons, not mine; if you wish them to be killed, kill them yourself."

Thus the unnatural plot of Sekhome fell to the ground. Afraid lest his men should now desert him, Sekhome in his blandest manner proposed to Macheng that there should be only one public court-yard in the town, at which both Macheng and he should sit. Were they not brothers? They might quarrel if they had separate courts; but not if they had only one. Macheng, however, fully apprehended the drift of his brother's treacherous proposition; and insisted on laying out a kotla for himself, round which he and his friends could build. Sekhome was thus placed in a secondary position in the town; and Macheng was the acknowledged chief of the Bamangwato. Liberty to attend upon instruction was once more enjoyed. Macheng did not come to church himself, but he did not hinder his people from coming.

As Sekhome was no longer in a position to take undue

advantage of the concession which I was about to make, I resolved to put an end to the only ostensible grounds of dispute between him and me, and to pay his men whom I had hired, twelve months' wages for six months' work. I accordingly called Sekhome, and paid him his unreasonable demand. That night he paid me a visit, with only one attendant, after his old custom.

"Why did you quarrel with me, Sekhome?" I inquired. "You always knew that my heart was white towards you."

"It's all past now," said the ex-chief. "It was not on your own account that I quarrelled with you, but to further my plans against Tshukuru and my children."

No one who knew Sekhome ever expected that he would live quietly under Macheng. He was soon at his favourite work of hatching plots—holding those secret councils which had been denounced by his son, and dealing largely, as before, in charms and incantations. Most of the old men still favoured his cause. It was resolved that he should now rid himself of all his enemies at one blow. An assembly was to be called. Macheng and Khame, and all Sekhome's enemies, were to be left to take their places in the court-yard first. It would only remain for Sekhome and for his trusty followers to surround them, and at least make sure of the leaders.

Macheng, without suspicion, agreed to call the assembly. When the day arrived on which it was to take place, the followers of Macheng were about to fall into the trap. But Khame had been informed, by some secret friend, of the conspiracy, perhaps with the idea that he would himself keep back, and allow Macheng to fall into the snare. But Khame at once gave notice to Macheng, who ordered his men not to assemble in the public court-yard until Sekhome's adherents had first taken their places. Frustrated in the scheme which he had laid, Sekhome still thought it possible to accomplish the main object which he had in view,—the death of a few of his chief opponents. He therefore gave notice to his men that when he assaulted one of Macheng's men in the court-yard, this was to be the signal of a general attack upon them, and especially upon their leaders.

Sekhome accordingly advanced into the yard at the head of his men, and, striking one of Macheng's men, felled him to the ground. But his followers had not the courage to support this bold course in the face of those who were prepared to receive them. Or, perhaps, they saw an easier way out of their difficulty; for, closing round Sekhome, they advised him to flee! With only a single attendant, the chief now fled from the town, and took refuge in the mountain. The assembly was never held. When the chief struck the head man of Macheng, the people rose in a body, and went "every man to his own house."

That evening a solitary figure was observed descending the mountain near to my house. It was Sekhome. He could no longer trust his own people; he knew he could still trust the missionary. He seemed relieved when he entered the house. I had now a glorious opportunity of rewarding good for evil, and took advantage of it. I gave him refreshments, and he sat down at my fireside. We had a long conversation, in course of which I recalled to his mind an interview which I had had with him before he began to quarrel with his sons. From some remarks which he had then made to me, I was led to see that his mind was being poisoned against his eldest sons; and I took occasion most solemnly to warn him against being led away by designing men from loving and confiding in his own children. "Did I not assure you," I asked, "that Khame would never seek to supplant you as chief; but that if you turned against your own children, whom God had given to support and defend you, evil would inevitably overtake you? You forgot my words, and those whose advice you followed, and who urged you on to fight with your own sons, have this day forsaken you and cast you off. Notwithstanding all the bitter words which you have spoken, your best friends in Shoshong to-day are the sons whom you have so cruelly used." That night Sekhome fled with only three or four attendants. Not believing that Macheng would allow him to drive away his flocks and herds in peace, Sekhome hurried them into the tsetse, destroying them without any cause; for Macheng publicly announced that he would not interfere with the removal of cattle which were the private property of his brother. At present Sekhome is a refugee in the town of Mokhosi, a chief residing near Kolobeng.

To a writer of fiction it would be easy to construct a more telling story than that of this "house divided against itself." The vengeance of Heaven might be introduced as falling upon the persecutor. The disciples might be exhibited as dying resignedly for the sake of their Lord amid the scornful taunts of the heathen. In such a story we should be careful to keep the Christians separate from the heathen. But having to narrate facts and not to compose fiction, I have had to describe a struggle in which not more than half a dozen lost their lives, and these neither Christians nor leading persecutors. And I have had to relate that one of the chief difficulties and trials of the position of the "people of the Word of God," was that they were surrounded by some personal friends who were no friends of the new religion.

It will at least appear from this narrative, that our work at Shoshong was carried on for a considerable period under adverse circumstances. We were thankful, indeed, that we were not expelled and the buildings on the station destroyed. In the end, however, the missionary was the only public character who succeeded in keeping his place in the midst of so many plots and counter plots. By the blessing of God he was able to secure and to retain the confidence of the people. He came at length to be recognised as the friend of all and the enemy of none. He was defamed and persecuted by Sekhome, yet that chief was in reality his jealous guardian against the over-zealous enmity which he himself had excited. He restrained his people with the promise that he would expel the supposed evil-doer; but he could never summon up resolution to give "the teacher" his orders to depart from the town. Lest, however, evil might befall him, he tried to frighten him away. And when the chief's own day of calamity came, he had no hesitation in repairing to the missionary's house; he counted upon a kindly reception there. The Christian life and character were a new force in the town of the Bamangwato. It was a thing to be wondered at—perhaps admired. It was exhibited not only by the missionary, but by their own countrymen who had "entered the Word of God." The Christians had headed the attack on the Matebele, and in defence of their homes, but had refused supremacy in the town when it was to be obtained by parricide. When driven from their home, they had acted only in self-defence. When conquered and brought back to the town they remained steadfast to their principles. One explanation which they gave of this new kind of life was, that I was a potent wizard, and had cast my spells upon the young chiefs and the other Christians. Thank God, the spell was a higher and a purer one—the world-conquering spell of the love of Jesus Christ. They had seen the Lord Himself, and were seeking to serve Him. With all their failings and mistakes, the Christian party, and especially their leaders Khame and his brother Khamane, exhibited during this struggle a spirit which is worthy of the admiration of the Christian Church.[1]

[1] The following extract from a work which has not been translated into English, will show what impression these young chiefs produced on the mind of an educated gentleman and man of science. Dr. Fritsch paid a brief visit to Shoshong in 1865. "I am glad by my acquaintanceship with Khame to have had an opportunity of mentioning a black, whom I would under no circumstances be ashamed to call my friend. The simple, modest, and at the same time noble deportment of this chief's son, awoke a delightful feeling which till then I had never experienced in the company of black men. I could thereby convince myself that it was really not the colour that prejudiced me against the Ethiopian race. The other brother, Khamane, in acquiring knowledge, is said to distinguish himself still more by his intelligence; but he has not laid aside the prying curiosity of the Bechuanas, although he also contrasts strongly with the rest of his tribe." —*Drei Jahre in Süd Afrika,* von Gustav Fritsch (Breslau, 1868).

CHAPTER XXIV.

DISCOVERY OF GOLD—BUILDING OF THE CHURCH.

In 1867 gold was discovered on the Tatie river, on the road leading from Shoshong to the Matebele country. Mr. Mauch, a German traveller, who had for several years given his attention to the geology and mineralogy of the interior, was the first to observe that the quartz rocks in the neighbourhood of the Tatie river were auriferous. Next year the same gentleman also discovered gold in Mashona-land, some 300 miles north-east of Tatie. In both cases there were evidences that the mines had been previously worked. In Mashona-land the digging has been carried on recently by the Mashona, for the purpose of trading with the Portuguese on the east coast. But the mines at Tatie, so far as I could ascertain, have not been worked within the times of native tradition. Whether districts intervening between Tatie and Mashona-land are also auriferous, or what extent of territory in either of these districts yields the precious metal, is yet matter of speculation. Nor is this problem likely to be soon solved; for as soon as the Matebele found out the value of gold in the eyes of Europeans, they became so jealous of the movements of the traders and hunters in the country, that the latter could not pick up a stone without exciting hostile remark.

Iron, or, as the diggers call it, emery, is found with the gold at Tatie, and copper has also been dug up in that neighbourhood.

The discovery of gold at Tatie produced some excitement at Shoshong. While the specimens were being tested in the colony, and before we were fully assured that gold was really contained in the quartz, an envoy arrived from the Transvaal Government, specially empowered to treat with Moselekatse and Macheng with reference to the gold-yielding districts. The ambassador was in haste, and merely announced to Macheng in an informal manner the burden of his errand, and the request which he said he would make of the chief on his return from the Matebele country. In the meantime Macheng would have time to consider the proposal, which was simply that he would present the Transvaal Government with any claim which he might have in the gold-yielding country as chief of the Bamangwato. In return for this, the envoy said the Republic would pledge itself in any quarrel which might arise between the diggers and the Bamangwato to take the side of the latter, and to protect them from all "foreigners and bad people." Macheng is somewhat slow in his movements, mental and physical, but there seemed to be something like a smile on his face as he listened to this proposal. The envoy had no success with Moselekatse. The chief positively forbade the settlement of any white men in his dominions, without which, of course, digging gold would be impossible. And when the ambassador returned to Shoshong he was equally disappointed. Macheng had duly improved the time given him for reflection, and had written to the Governor at the Cape, who is also Her Majesty's High Commissioner in South Africa, requesting his advice, and offering to the English Government, on certain conditions, the supremacy in the gold region of Tatie.

To show what latitude of action the Transvaal Government allows itself, I may just add that this want of success on the part of their envoy had no effect whatever at head-quarters. It would seem indeed that the executive were too excited to wait the result of their own diplomacy. Or perhaps they felt already assured that their ambassador would be hailed as a deliverer and protector in every native town, and would return with the title-deeds of the supposed El Dorado in his waggon-chest. At any rate, they practically ignored both the ambassador and his mission, and issued in his absence a proclamation, in which the whole country was claimed to belong to the Republic, "from Moselekatse's first post" (the name of the place was not even known, or its locality) "to Lake Ngami, and from Lake Ngami southward to the Lang Bergen near Kuruman." This comprehensive proclamation introduced into the Republic some thirteen independent native tribes, none of which had ever been consulted in the matter!

I may just mention that the chief, Macheng, was not advised by me, either directly or indirectly, to write to the Governor at the Cape, offering to the English Government the possession of the gold-fields. I was indeed on the point of recommending this course, when the Dutch ambassador left; but knowing the native character, I judged that it was not my duty as a missionary to volunteer advice on the subject. I imagined that if I strongly advocated the claims of the English immediately after the good offices of the Dutch had been tendered, the chief might feel inclined to set me down along with the Dutchman, as a political and interested canvasser for my own Government. But there were numerous English-speaking travellers and hunters passing through Shoshong and residing in it, who had no hesitation in strongly recommending the chief to take this course. The history of California and Australia was related to Macheng, and extracts from the Cape and Natal newspapers were translated to him, reporting that hundreds of men were then on their way north to dig this wonderful tsipi (metal). One evening, while on my way to attend a case of sickness in the town, I was met by the chief at the head of a party of men. He said he had very particular business with me. We went to his house, and I found that he was anxious to write at once to the Governor, and wished me to act as his scribe. Now, although it was generally believed that the metal which had excited so much speculation was gold, yet at this time this rather important question had not been quite settled. I explained this to the chief, and said that I had no wish to be connected with what might afterwards bear the appearance of a hoax. I stipulated also that if I wrote for him, he must previously call a public assembly of the Bamangwato, and explain what he was doing to his head men, and obtain their consent to it. Macheng was opposed to this; but in the end yielded. His speech to the assembled councillors was not very complimentary to them. He declared he did not think their judgment of any consequence, but the missionary had wished them to be brought together. "Now, you grey-headed men," he said, "who speak of having lived at Seroe, and before whom we who are still young are almost afraid to open our mouths, yonder come the white men—hundreds in number. They come in waggons, on horseback, on foot. They come to dig the tsipi found at Tatie. What are we to do? That is the question before you to-day. Let us now see that you are wise as well as old. But speak out all that you have got to say, for the missionary is afraid of being afterwards blamed by the Bamangwato if he assist us in any course which is not approved by us all."

The head men were apparently at a loss what to say. One after another stood up and praised the chief, and said that no doubt what he proposed was the best. But at length one old man rose and exclaimed, "Bamangwato, have you thrown aside your spears before the enemy approaches? You, who have now guns, and dress like white men, will you not fire one shot for your country? This is surely very wonderful! In the olden time we fled or we fought, but to-day we are asked to open our arms to the enemy. Bamangwato! I say, Let us fight." The old man sat down amid the laughter of all present, for it was well known that for many years his combats had been in the council-room and not on the battle-field. Pelutona made the speech of the day. He said "the missionary did not wish to assist their chief without their knowledge and consent. They could not deny that they had given him cause to mistrust them." And then he went on to detail the sinister counsel which he himself had given during the dispute between Sekhome and Khame. "He was a big man, and would not eat his words; but of course all these disputes had passed, and the missionary was still there to befriend them; and he for one felt quite inclined to be guided by the chief in this matter. Were they not seeing things which their fathers had not dreamt of? Those who spoke of fighting were evidently fools."

The report arriving soon after this meeting that the nuggets had been duly tested in the colony, and had been pronounced to be gold, I embodied the views of the chief in a letter to Sir Philip Wodehouse, who was then Governor at the Cape. The answer of his Excellency was satisfactory to Macheng as far as it went. But it did not go far. The Governor was responsible to the Home Government, and it would seem to be a maxim in Downing Street that, whatever Power may hereafter be intimately allied with the advancing and predominating Anglo-Saxon race in Southern Africa, it shall not be England. The members of the Cape Parliament voted money to equip an exploring party to survey and report upon the newly discovered gold regions. But the executive at the Cape, or the Colonial Office in London, was not in the same mood as the Cape Parliament. Although the cost of the exploring expedition was to have been borne entirely by the colony, it was delayed for one reason after another, and finally given up.

The inhabitants of the Cape Colony and Natal were naturally much interested in this discovery. But the Tatie river and Mashona-land were too far from the coast to be visited by a "rush" of diggers. Were these districts but a hundred, as they are more than a thousand, miles from the southern coast, parties of diggers would, in a short period, have scattered themselves over an extensive territory, and "prospected" the localities which yield the precious metal. On the Tatie river no signal success has attended the efforts of exploring parties. In Australia, when gold was discovered, the process of disintegration had made great progress; and the gold was found near the surface on low-lying tracts of country. Poor people had thus a reasonable prospect of obtaining gold with only a digger's cradle. At the Tatie, the gold was found only in very small quantities in alluvial soil. It was still embedded in the rock; and to crush the quartz required some capital. A company, which has its head-office in London, carries on this work of quartz-crushing at Tatie, and I understand recent reports speak favourably of their success.

It is somewhat singular that the colony of Natal was a country lying waste at the time of its occupation by the English; although, of course, claimed by Tshaka who had destroyed its former inhabitants. The Free State also, before its occupation by Europeans, was described by early travellers as one wide wilderness, having in the districts beyond Griqua-land scarcely an inhabitant. Still farther north, Moselekatse swept what is now the Transvaal region of its Bechuana inhabitants before he in turn gave place to the Dutch. Now Mashona-land to the north-east of the Matebele has also been unfortunately depopulated by the forces of Moselekatse. It is perhaps the finest country in Southern Africa. The Mashona work the cotton which this region yields, and I have seen blankets and other cloths which they themselves have made from it. It is affirmed that the white quartz rock in which the gold is there found extends over a wide extent of country. Now as the colony of Natal is a check upon the heathenism of Kaffraria, confining it to the south, and localizing it, so would an English colony in Mashona-land have an equally beneficial effect upon the Matebele and other native races. And if Englishmen were once in numbers to the north of the restless Dutchmen, the latter would give up their search for the Land of Canaan, and be content with their present residences. In their northward movement they always complain of the increasing "uitlanders," or foreigners coming from the south. Let there be once Englishmen to the north of them, and their spirit of restlessness would be checked, and there would be the hope of a more speedy amalgamation of the races of Englishmen and Dutchmen in Southern Africa. A question of the first importance to the Europeans who have already advanced far northwards, is to obtain a sea-port nearer than either Natal or the Cape Colony. Were it possible to find such an outlet for the products of the country to the east of Mashona-land, the occupation of that devastated but beautiful country might not be far distant.

Early in 1867, I commenced to build a church at Shoshong, having secured the services of two bricklayers. In the absence of a more qualified workman, I undertook the wood work as my department. Macheng was kind enough to furnish me with two regiments of men to assist me in felling the timber. When I followed them to the forest I found they had cut down, according to my orders, some tall trees, but in their ignorance had afterwards destroyed the timber by dividing each tree into several pieces! They said they had done so for the convenience of those who would have to lift the trees into a waggon. I explained to them that they must leave the trees at their greatest length, and expressed my fear that we should not find a sufficient number long enough to span the new church. My assistants, who were chiefly old men, loudly expressed their disapprobation and incredulity. "Why cut such large trees? It was wrong to fell them with an axe. Hitherto they had always been burned down when a man wanted to clear a field for cultivation. After they were felled, it was evident that no human beings could ever lift them. Macheng and the missionary had laid their heads together to impose a burden on them to no purpose," etc. In the end I had to hire other men before a sufficient quantity of timber was cut down. In them I had more willing assistants; but the work of the backwoodsman was hard for such people. I encouraged them by slaughtering an ox for their use; and Khamane, who accompanied me to the forest, killed a giraffe. The tall and resinous tambootie tree, which I selected for beams and rafters, was easily split. The partially dressed logs we conveyed to Shoshong in waggons which were kindly lent me by both Europeans and natives. A pit-saw was next set to work, and after a few lessons two raw natives were able to use it, and sawed almost all the timber for the church. Macheng again assisted me by ordering two regiments of women to cut bundles of grass for thatch. The building, which holds some 500 people, was finished by the end of the year. There are no pews or forms;

the people bring their camp-stools, or sit on the ground as they are accustomed to do elsewhere. A pulpit was afterwards made for the church by Mr. T. Wood, who was one of the party of hunters whose sudden death from fever in Mashona-land has been mentioned in a former chapter. The Europeans trading at Shoshong, or annually passing the station, subscribed towards defraying the expense of building the church, and some of the natives also gave ostrich feathers and cattle, so that only a small share of the cost of the building fell upon the Missionary Society.

When the church was finished, I resolved to celebrate its opening in a manner which would give me at once an opportunity of publicly thanking Macheng for his assistance in procuring both wood and grass, and also of addressing the old men of the town, who, as a class, gave least attention to the preaching of the gospel. I thought I could copy a little from their own usages, and along with some instruction provide for them an entertainment such as they are accustomed to on occasions of rejoicing. Having consulted an "authority" on such matters, I found that my project would be entirely orthodox and agreeable from a native point of view. I accordingly gave the invitation to Macheng "to meet me with his people in the new church on Tuesday the 7th of January, to see the house which they had assisted me to build, to hear why it was built, and to partake of the ox with which I thanked them for their assistance."

Early on Tuesday morning the people began to assemble at the church. Each division of the town came headed by its chief. Heathen men with hoary heads, toothless and tottering with old age, came leaning on their staffs. Full-grown men—the haughty, the cunning, the fierce—came with those younger in years, of brighter eye and more hopeful mien. As to their clothing, the heathen dress admits of little variety. But many appeared dressed partly or wholly in European attire, and here there was variety enough. We had the usual members of the congregation, some of whom were neatly dressed. But sticklers for "the proprieties" would have been shocked to see a man moving in the crowd who considered himself well dressed, although wearing a shirt only; another with trousers only; a third with a black "swallow-tail," closely buttoned to the chin—the only piece of European clothing which the man wore; another with a soldier's red coat, overshadowed by an immense wide-awake hat, the rest of the dress being articles of heathen wear, etc. etc.

The church-doors were thrown open, and many strange remarks were made with reference to the building. One man said "What a splendid place to drink beer in!" another, "What a capital pen for sheep and goats!" and a third declared that with a few people inside they could defy the Matebele nation.

I observed an unwillingness on the part of some of the old men to enter the church. Thinking it arose only from superstitious feelings, I went out and persuaded them to go in. I learned afterwards that these dark-minded people had conceived that foul play was that day to be enacted by the Christians in revenge for their previous hardships and sufferings at the hands of the heathen. They could not believe that all had been forgiven; they could only measure other minds by their own. And so they had come ully prepared for the worst, and the hand which was concealed below their mantle grasped a large knife or dagger, which they hoped would stand them in good stead when "the people of the Word of God" rose on them, within the new church, and sought to take their lives. The unsuspecting confidence with which I spoke to these men, and invited and pressed them to enter the House of God, must surely have touched their treacherous and suspicious hearts. The simple address, the solemn prayer, followed by open-hearted hospitality, must surely have suggested to those heathen men that the thoughts of the Christians were not their thoughts.

I held no regular service in the church, for had I done so some would have said I got them to be present at it under false pretences. My short address was composed of thoughts which had been gathering in my mind for years, but which I never had an opportunity to deliver before such an audience. The attention of the people was thoroughly arrested during the whole of the time I was speaking. I concluded my part of the engagements of the morning by solemn prayer, and then called upon Macheng to speak, if he desired to do so. Knowing the caution and reticence of his race, I was not surprised that the chief declined to speak in such circumstances. We now adjourned to the vicinity of our kitchen, where Mrs. Mackenzie and the servants had had a busy time cooking the ox, which I had slaughtered as soon as I had received Macheng's acceptance of the invitation. The pots and dishes of all kinds, with the meat, I showed to Macheng, and requested him to divide their contents. A considerable quantity of sour milk, and a few camp-kettles full of tea, completed the bill of fare for this Bechuana breakfast-party. Tables and chairs, knives and forks, bread and vegetables, we were content to regard as superfluities, after-thoughts; the first and main thought was the beef, and to that attention was given. It was feared by one who did not wish to give a stingy entertainment that one ox would not be enough for so many guests, but my "authority" decided otherwise. He said the chief himself killed only one ox at a time; it would therefore be over-lavish in me to kill more. My "authority" was right.

Although no miracle was performed, every one seemed to get something; every one was pleased.

As the feast proceeded, it was announced to Macheng that a certain head man had been overlooked. What was to be done? The meat was gone—the sour milk had disappeared: but, happy thought! the tea remained. Handing the man a large quantity of tea, the chief said to him: "Drink, for there is no longer aught to eat. The tea was prepared at the same fire as the meat; it is therefore quite the same thing; drink, for tea is your part of the feast." The man quietly sat down with his camp-kettle of tea, and drank it all.

After the people had departed, Macheng, Khame, and Khamane sat down at our table to a part of the same ox—this time, however, eaten with knife and fork.

I have reason to believe that the best impression was produced on the people's minds by the doings of that morning. I learned afterwards that for days my address was the subject of remark in the kotla, the majority declaring that "the words" were unanswerable. A few inveterate heathens, however, said "they could see nothing in the words; they thought they had been called to church to assist in praying for rain, and not to listen to such strange doctrines." On the whole, the result of the meeting was that heathenism did not carry the high head that it was wont to do.

In order to follow up the good impression produced, I began a regular course of district visitation. I appeared every Wednesday evening accompanied by one or other of the leading members of the congregation, at the kotla of the head man of a division of the town, and requested him to call his people together in his court-yard to hear the Word of God. In general the head men were willing to do this. In every case they consented to do it, after some patient waiting. Many of them were averse to calling the women, who are not usually allowed to enter the court-yard. This point was also yielded; but the women, who saw the reluctance of their lords, sat down at the very entrance of the kotla. The little children ran about in all directions, sometimes planting themselves in open-mouthed wonder opposite the strange white man to whom all the grown-up people were listening. The majority of these Wednesday evening congregations were people who did not come to church. To them also was the gospel preached—"to every creature," was the Divine commission. Sometimes as many as three hundred came together; in smaller districts the audience would number some thirty or forty. One result of these district-meetings was to increase the number of those who desired to learn to read for themselves the Word of God.

CHAPTER XXV.

"BY LITTLE AND LITTLE."[1]

"Where the Greek saw barbarians, we see brethren; where the Greek saw heroes and demi-gods, we see our parents and ancestors; where the Greek saw nations (ἔθνη), we see mankind, toiling and suffering, separated by oceans, divided by language, and severed by national enmity,—yet evermore tending, under a divine control, towards the fulfilment of that inscrutable purpose for which the world was created, and man placed in it, bearing the image of God."—MAX MUELLER, "Comparative Mythology," *Oxford Essays*, 1856.

THE missionary in modern times has an advantage over his predecessors of a more ignorant age. Devoted servants of the Church of Rome braved every danger in their work, and secured from the ignorant heathen the homage which self-denial and purity of life will always call forth. But the monastic life was unreal and unattainable to the mass of men. The people gazed upon it with reverence from a distance. There was much in such a system to excite their homage and their awe; there was little for them to copy. The missions of the English churches have not yet reached the development of the Roman Catholic establishments. Whether or not a model Christian village would be the best missionary institution, is a question still before the churches. But at present the life of the missionary is such as can be copied by his flock. In the mission-house they can see a home like their own, only better kept, purer and sweeter. While the missionary busies himself with the men, his wife (if he is fortunate

[1] Exod. xxiii. 30.

enough to have one) teaches the women to sew and to cut out dresses, and prescribes simple medicines for themselves and their children when they are ill. If the missionary among the men has the strength and the wisdom of an elder brother, his wife secures the confidence and affection of the women, and, by her own example, influences them to a higher and a purer life. The life of the mission-house is attainable, and it is desirable, even in the eyes of the heathen. After being shown, at their own request, some of the rooms of our house, a party of the wives of petty chiefs at length broke out, addressing Mrs. Mackenzie: "Happy wife and happy mother! You have a 'kingdom' here of your own!"

I may here describe a Sunday at Shoshong. I began the day's services by conducting a Bible-class, which was composed of all who could read the New Testament, and of others who sat as auditors. A chapter or portion of Scripture was read in order every Sunday by those present, after which I questioned them on what they had been reading. I invited them also to put questions to me. By this means I found out what impression the Divine words of Scripture produced on minds whose past training and habits of thought had been so different from my own. I have been saddened by the vacant-minded pupil, who had no question to propound, and hardly an answer to give to the question asked by me. But I have been often gratified with a ready and intelligent answer, and sometimes with a question which evidenced considerable grasp of mind. The narrative parts of Scripture were always read with the greatest interest by the class; their estimate of actions and of characters passing before us was often put in a fresh and striking manner. I regarded my Bible-class as one of the most important engagements of the day. The morning service which followed lasted about an hour and a quarter.

In the afternoon it was my custom to go down to the chief's court-yard and hold service there. When the new church was being built I heard the complaint that the site was too far away from the town, and that I must not be surprised if many old people did not attend. This was stated by those who attended occasionally, and who I fancied were not sorry to have what seemed a tolerable excuse for not attending at all. I promised these people, however, that I should obviate all difficulties by bringing "the Word" to the public court-yard of the town on the Sunday afternoon. I had thus every week an opportunity of addressing both those who were halting between two opinions, and the heathen who were opposed to the new doctrine, but who would not always rise up and go away, although I have seen them occasionally do so. I had also most of those present who were at the morning service. We began by singing a hymn well known to the church-going part of my audience. The heathen have a keen sense of the ridiculous, and the name they sometimes give for hymn-singing, "go bokwalela" (to utter the death-cry), was not in some instances altogether undeserved. When hymns are well sung, however, they are much admired, and in the course of time both words and music are impressed on the minds of the uninstructed hearers. Instead of reading one passage of Scripture at this service, I selected a number of verses expressing what Christians most surely believe. The object I had before me was to help a stranger who might only hear me once to form some idea of the faith of the Christian as a whole, and also by the reiteration of those sublime truths every Sunday, the more deeply to impress them upon the minds of more frequent hearers. This form or lesson in Scripture's own language began at the beginning, narrating the Creation and the Fall. It then described the life and death and resurrection of Jesus Christ, and went forward to the time when every man shall give an account of himself to God. It contained the Ten Commandments, with our Saviour's own comments on some of them. The dreadful loss and ruin of the rebellious —of those who knew their Master's will and did it not— were revealed in the words of Him who is Himself to judge the quick and the dead. And the lesson abounded with declarations of God's love and His willingness to pardon; with the invitations of Jesus—words which strike even heathen as unique in their pathos; and with the Divine promise to bestow the Holy Spirit to sustain and to deliver all who desire to struggle with evil and to overcome it. These and other truths were repeated in the hearing of all who happened to be in the chief's court-yard at Shoshong on Sunday afternoon. So far as I am able to judge, such a selection of Scripture is productive of greater result in the enlightenment and edification of such a congregation than the reading of a chapter or part of one. I remembered the words of a wise and kind-hearted teacher, when encouraging us in our youth to commit passages of Scripture to memory,—"Boys, these are God's own words; it must be good for us all to have them in our minds. They will warn us of danger, sustain us in trial, cheer us and bless us in life and in death. Store these words in your memory, boys, and depend upon it before you are old men you will have often thanked me for directing your attention to them." The prophecy of my revered teacher has been abundantly verified in my own experience, and I have no doubt in that of others of his pupils. In the same way I argued that if God's own blessed words concerning Himself and concerning man were by repetition impressed upon the mind of the stranger, the unwilling listener, and even the professed opponent of

God's Word, as I met them in the public court-yard at Shoshong, beneficial results might follow, even in cases of which the preacher might never hear. Without entering into the question of their excellence under all circumstances, I thought I could see reason why good men, in earlier times and in rude ages, had adopted certain forms of service, inscribing also important scriptures upon the walls of the house of God. As the peasantry gathered round the church, some one would be found ambitious to show his superior learning, by spelling over to his companions the Ten Commandments or the Creed, or the words of Gospel which were plainly inscribed on the walls. And in the oft-repeated service the ignorant parishioners learned something of their true position in the sight of God. I did not however appoint any portion of the service to be audibly joined in by the heathen audience. I feared lest such responses, ignorantly made, should come to satisfy their minds, and detain them in a stagnant formality. As an agent of the London Missionary Society, I was perfectly at liberty to have introduced a liturgical form if I had chosen to do so. The short address which I gave in the kotla was usually in explanation of one or other of the texts which had been read in the form of service now described.

As soon as this service in the town was over, I hastened home, and found the Europeans who might be then at Shoshong waiting for me on the veranda. We had now a service in English in my parlour, not lasting longer than an hour. I had always great pleasure in this service, and kept it up regularly, however few might be present. It was usually attended by all the Europeans—people of all Christian Churches joining in our simple worship. The passing hunter, arriving on Friday or Saturday, made a point of coming up to the service in English on Sunday evening. The resident traders at Shoshong were exemplary in their attendance, being seldom absent. Old associations were revived; early and perhaps forgotten vows brought to remembrance. The Christian Church at this distant outpost of her army had words of comfort and strengthening, of warning and entreaty, to offer to her wandering children. In a place of safety, and beside certain certificates and other documents of personal interest and value, I treasure an address which was presented to me, along with a sum of money, by the members of this English congregation, on the occasion of my leaving for a time the station of Shoshong. There is no document in my possession on which I set greater store than this spontaneous and unexpected expression of affection and of respect from my fellow-countrymen and other English-speaking people in Bechuana-land. Fully assured of the affection of my Bamangwato congregation, and also of the confidence of the chief and others who remained attached to heathenism, I regarded the address referred to as an indication that I had not altogether failed in what I had always set before me as an object—to be the servant of all classes in the gospel of Christ, and to endeavour not to set class against class, or colour against colour, but to endeavour to unite all in the common service of God through Christ Jesus.

The work of the missionary has only been begun at Shoshong. I have not been in haste to enrol the professing Christians in the fellowship of a church. More than once I was on the point of doing so, when something occurred to deter me. It is true I never heard any at Shoshong express the same definite trust in the Church and its ordinances for salvation as expressed by Sechele. But the same doctrines which had been preached to the Bakwena had been inculcated also for a shorter period at Shoshong.

By delaying the organization of a Christian Church, I taught the disciples that their safety was from Jesus Christ, and through personal faith in Him, and not from the missionary or from the Church. I have reason to believe that this truth supported some of them in trying circumstances. I have been in the habit of thinking of a few—a very few—at Shoshong as sincere disciples of Jesus Christ. There are also there outer circles of hearers of the Word, whose lives are more or less affected by the teaching of the gospel. I hope that those who continued true to Christ in temptation and trial will form a good nucleus for that Church which I trust our Lord will graciously build among the Bamangwato.

But it may with truth be said that the mission has left its mark upon the whole community. This mark may not be so deep as we could wish, still it is visible. Many of the leading ideas of our faith are now tacitly received by all classes. After rain has fallen I have often heard old heathen men exclaim, "God has helped us with rain." Before, it would have been announced all over the town as the rain of one or other of the priests then known to be practising necromancy. If an English traveller were now to ask a priest if he had the power of making rain, he would in most cases reply in the negative. "God alone could make rain. He prayed to Him by the herbs and plants of the field, as his fathers had taught him; the white men were taught to pray from the books." The young men are not growing up with the old reverence for customs which have been already shorn of much of their mystery, and somewhat modernized. The old assumption of power on the part of the priests and sorcerers, which is still kept up by many, was more likely to evoke the reverence and the service of the ignorant people, than their more "liberal'" declaration that God is the source of power and blessing, and not they themselves.

A short time before I left Shoshong I was told that throughout the whole town of some thirty thousand inhabitants, there were now very few who did not pay a certain deference to the "Letsatsi ya Morimo"—the Day of God, as the Sunday is called by the Bamangwato. When we commenced our labours, there was no day of rest to lighten the dreary monotony of the Pagan life. During the few years of our residence and teaching, it would seem that a certain undefined impression was produced upon the community at large. When we came away, the bulk of the workers in the fields usually stayed at home on the Sunday. And even in the hunting-field, I was told, this day is observed with a certain amount of respect even by the heathen. It is interesting to note the crudeness of the ideas which animate such ignorant masses at an early stage in their history.

"We observed," said the women who work in the fields, "that if one of our number injured herself with her hoe, it was always on the Great Day; so we gave up working on that day."

"A man may hunt with success all the week," said a heathen man in my hearing; "but if he goes out to shoot on Sunday, he gets nothing for his trouble. He meets with a lion, or lames himself with a thorn, or his gun bursts."

Now, these ideas have not come from the missionaries. They were never threatened with such things if they broke the Sunday; but by teaching and example the missionary showed that he regarded it as a peculiar day, a day for religion and for God. As the people had their own recurring religious observances, and dances at the time of new moon, the idea of a day set apart for religion was not entirely new to them. At present they show outward respect to the Sunday for very much the same reason as they perform any of their old religious services—from fear of the consequences of the opposite course. It is safer to abstain from work on the Sunday. Out of the large number who go this length, only about three hundred come to church on the Sunday. They have moved a certain distance; and there they at present content themselves. But every act of reverence to the new religion is an act of treason to the old customs. As the power of the one increases in the minds of the people the influence of the other will lose its hold.

In the beginning of 1869, I attended a meeting of the missionaries in Bechuana-land, which was held at Kuruman. Two subjects of importance were discussed—the revision of the Sechuana Scriptures and the establishment of a seminary for the training of native ministers. It had been my intention to proceed as far as Cape Town with my two eldest children, who were old enough to be sent to school in this country. But the Directors of the Society thought that after working for ten unbroken years north of the Orange river, I ought to have a greater change than is implied in a visit to Cape Town per ox-waggon; and kindly invited me to accompany my family to England. This invitation reached me some six days after I left Shoshong. I did not return, but wrote to my friends there to inform them that my absence from the station would be for a longer period than I had anticipated when I left. The District Committee made arrangements that the "few sheep in the wilderness" should not be without a shepherd while I was in England. I have had two letters from Khamane since I came to this country, written by himself in his own language, in which he informs me that all the recognised members of the congregation continue to attend the weekly services; but the members of the "outer circle" had fallen off considerably in my absence. I am persuaded, however, that the new religion has taken such root at Shoshong, as that, with a supply of Christian literature, it would not readily disappear, even if left to itself.

My story of every-day life and work is now told.

The subject of the support and management of missions to the heathen is one which addresses the highest Christian thought and feeling. Neither the necessity for the work, nor the motives for engaging in it, appear to the man who is not thoroughly and deeply a Christian. It is not so with reference to benevolent efforts to Christianize and elevate the degraded at home. The fact is, moral evil, with its train of sorrow and suffering, in our own neighbourhood, becomes a nuisance and eyesore which men will seek to remove from the same motives that influence them to improve the drainage of the town. The good offices of many end here; and a sharp critic might question whether genuine benevolence or an elevated kind of selfishness had most to do with their beneficent actions. But "neither pray I for these alone," said our Lord; "neither care I for these only," says Christianity. The reeking and offensive hovels which you fear may contaminate your neighbourhood, call forth from the Saviour only the same compassion which He entertains for the rude skin-clad Pagan in his circular hut. Your Church may be insular, your creed and your sympathies may be contracted; His message and His blessing are for all men without distinction.

The past history of the Church teaches us that the lesson of expansion and aggression has been one which in other ages the Church has not readily learned. The Church has had several rallying-cries which have served to increase her followers, and inspire them with new zeal. But after a time the ardour of the devotion has subsided. The first cry was, "The Lord is risen." Beginning at Jerusalem, this cry emboldened the lips of the timid Galileans who uttered it, and ringing in the ears of the murderers of Jesus Christ, filled thousands with anguish and remorse, till the message of repentance through faith calmed the terror-stricken multitude, and Christianity was planted in the city where Christ himself was crucified; its Divine forgiveness and its historical credibility being attested in the fact that its first members were from among the murderers of its Founder.

After a time, however, this happy community in Jerusalem would seem to have been more concerned for the conserving and perfecting of its own corporate existence than for the propagation of the gospel. It was therefore taught by the finger of Providence that the Church had a higher aim than even the edification of her members; or rather that the highest Christian life of the members would be best developed by battling for their new-found faith rather than by luxuriating in it in the daily fellowship meetings in Jerusalem. The Church was compelled to remember the command of her Lord, to preach the gospel to every creature. The hand of persecution dispersed her members; and we are told that "they who were scattered abroad went everywhere preaching the Word."

A wild cry resounded through Europe in the eleventh and twelfth centuries that the tomb of the Saviour was in the hand of the Saracen. It was but an empty tomb; the Lord was no longer there, having risen. But it was the place where He had lain, and Christendom was up in arms to rescue the sacred spot. It was a misapprehended idea of Christianity to support its pretensions by brute force. But whilst both as to the end in view and the mode of attaining it, the Crusades exhibit the superstition and ignorance of a dark age, they surely teach us something more. According to the light which they possessed, the brave men who hastened to the East from every European court, conceived that they were devoting themselves to the high and noble service of Christ and His Church. Their blood flowed freely in Palestine, while the treasures and the prayers of loved ones at home followed and sustained the Christian warriors. He is blind who can see no unselfish heroism in the brave Crusader, and no pious liberality in the members of the Christian Church of that age.

"Justified by faith" was the cry of the Reformation. The dark wall of sacerdotalism between Christ and His disciple was removed. Personal accountability to God was preached to the people. But the dissenting Churches of the Reformation, cut up into isolated sections, either gagged or soothed to sleep by the kings and queens who were their foster parents, almost entirely lost one distinctive characteristic of the Church of Christ. Orthodox in creed—blameless in the life of the clergy—eminently beneficial in the country or the parish where their labours were carried on, the National Established Churches had no organization for aggressive effort on the heathenism of the world. The idea was not recognised in their constitution nor in their local names. It was perhaps enough that the Church of Rome had her propaganda, to insure that Protestant Churches should have none. Whatever may have been the reason, the Reformation was succeeded by a period of cold and rigid formalism, interrupted only by the persistent and despotic efforts of rulers to impress their own ideas on the Church of Christ—efforts which were welcomed or borne or bravely opposed.

"Personal devotion to a personal Saviour" may be said to have been the cry of the Methodist and Pietist movement which in the end of last century broke in upon the slumbering Christianity of the period. Personal accountability was now preached in a wider sense than at the Reformation. The old bottles could not contain the new wine. Dissent from dissenting Churches overflowed the land. Christian men who professed to take their laws of church-government from the New Testament, and who objected to both civil and ecclesiastical interference with their religious life, might be expected to exhibit, in connection with what were then held to be extreme views, a new phase of Christianity. Accordingly, we have the establishment of a Baptist Missionary Society, and the subscription of some thirteen pounds for the conversion of the heathen! We have the departure for India of him who will live in polite literature as the "consecrated cobbler," but in the history of the Church of Christ as Dr. William Carey, the eminent Oriental scholar and missionary. The London Missionary Society was formed at this time; and from the beginning was thoroughly catholic in its character and constitution. Missionary societies were also established in America and on the continent of Europe; and in a few years Churches which disagreed on almost every other question agreed in the necessity for evangelizing the world.

The Christian Church has always exhibited the highest types of character when fighting for some worthy and specific object. These local struggles, however, passed away, and with them too frequently the heroic type of character. But in the evangelization of Pagan lands, there is a vast object than which none could be worthier, as none is nearer to the heart of Christ Himself. "The gospel for every creature" must be the new rallying-cry of the Christian Church. In pursuing such an object, elevated types of Christianity may be expected to appear. This is more than rescuing an empty tomb from infidel hands. It is to rescue and restore the blurred and defiled and well-nigh obliterated image of God in His creature man. All honest industry may be service to God. But this is angels' work. It is to carry the blessed daylight of Christianity into benighted regions where human spirits are groping with nothing to lighten them but the *ignis fatuus* of superstition. It is to dispense the heavenly balm of Christ's gospel to souls sick unto death. It is to combine in one life the highest service of man with the service of God; to help and to sympathize with the struggling repentant spirit seeking after the light; and when the light has been found to rejoice with Heaven in its joy "over one sinner that repenteth."

Where then are the knights burning with enthusiasm to engage in this noblest crusade? What ducal house or lordly name is represented among the missionaries of the English churches? Will not the men and the women of an age which we affect to despise rise against their judges, and condemn them for their greater selfishness and love of ease?

Or is it that in modern times there is a return to the manner of early Christianity, and He who called the unlearned and the obscure to be His disciples and witnesses, whilst now receiving the homage of the titled and the wealthy, as at the beginning, still chooses for His evangelists in Pagan lands men from among men, so that the success may be attributed to the message itself, and not to the political or social influence of the messenger?

To evangelize Pagan lands then is not only *a* duty: it is *the* duty of the Church of Christ. It is the same error for a church to confine her energies to her own borders, and to exist for herself, as it is for the individual Christian to live upon his own inner frames and feelings; or to extract from

Christianity only that which pleases and soothes his own feelings and tastes.

It seems to me that at present, in every College or Hall of Theology, there might, with great advantage, be established a chair or lectureship for the benefit of young men qualifying themselves as ministers of the Gospel, and directing their attention, among other subjects, to the circumstances in which Christianity was embraced in the various countries in Europe; the history of the missions of the Church of Rome; the history of modern missions; the Pagan religions of mankind—their value, and their inadequacy. It ought to be taken for granted that from every such College young men will go forth as missionaries. Therefore, as at present in the last year of the curriculum attention is given to such subjects as will qualify the minister at home for his office, so would this lectureship give similar assistance to those intending to go abroad. Were all students to attend such a class in their last year, those who go abroad would be qualified to do so, and those who remain at home would be better fitted to understand and to explain to their congregations the nature of the work abroad.[1]

The work of aggressive Christianity ought to be earnestly brought before the attention of the children of Christian families. Children see the names of their parents in a list of subscriptions, or possibly hear their father speak as chairman of a missionary meeting; but beyond these things no mention is made of the subject; or perhaps the mother or the nurse assembles the very young children on the Sunday afternoon or evening, and tells them some strange

[1] Such a lectureship has been already established in connection with the Free Church of Scotland, and its chair is at present filled by the Rev. Dr. Duff, the distinguished missionary to India. For some years the last session of the students of the London Missionary Society has been spent in studies bearing on their future work, under the tuition of the Rev. Dr. Wardlaw, who also laboured many years in India.

story about missionaries abroad. I am afraid that boys in some cases are even discouraged from giving their attention to the service of the church either at home or abroad, and the argument is used to them that if they can only succeed in making enough money they can have more influence for good than if they become ministers or missionaries. This is certainly not what the father said when he stood on the missionary platform. He there declared that the work of the missionary was the noblest on earth, and urged young men to give their attention to it. It is not to be wondered at if after listening to such diverse advices, chilling doubt and suspicion on the most sacred subjects enter the mind of the young man, and he learns to sum up in a few words the maxims of his home and of the society in which he moves, "Money is the chief thing; therefore get money." Of all the representatives of Christian English homes who are to be found in all parts of the world, how many are Christian evangelists? This is not asked by way of disparaging the honest and honourable pursuits of commerce; nor underrating the service which commercial men can render to the cause of religion. But I ask,—Is it befitting the merciful and unselfish spirit of our Christianity, or its immense importance to mankind, that so much of our energy should be devoted to ourselves—so little to God and our fellow-men; so much effort put forth from deference to the wishes or maxims of friends or society—so little in obedience to the command or from regard to the strong desire of our Lord and Saviour?

To the Christian boy or young man who may have accompanied me thus far in my story, I shall address my concluding sentences. I remember it was pleasant to dream of the future while sitting listening to the music of the mountain stream, the eye meanwhile watching the ever changing clouds of the deep blue summer sky. By the winter fireside also I often mused of the coming years, and of the many-sidedness of human life, while forms and shapes appeared and disappeared in the glowing embers before me. To him who has reached those years of reverie and resolve let me address an honest heart-felt word :—If you have faith in your Saviour and a sound constitution ; if you have acquired or can obtain a liberal education ; if you are not particular about what you eat and drink, or the hardness or softness of the bed you sleep on ; if you believe that Christ is able and willing to do for all men what He has done for you—young man, leave the money-making to your brothers. Let there be at least one out of every family devoted to the church and to aggressive Christianity. Be a missionary—a preacher of the gospel among the heathen—a good soldier of Jesus Christ!

APPENDIX.

THE RACES OF SOUTHERN AFRICA.

SECTION I.—ANTIQUITIES AND TRADITIONS—STEREOTYPING TENDENCY OF SOUTH AFRICAN SUPERSTITION.

A PROMINENT place in the history of all nations is occupied by accounts of the numerous wars which they have waged. In Southern Africa those who have mingled with its rude races, find that there also every tribe has its own traditions of strifes and feuds, resulting in conquest or defeat. Within the memory of man, insignificant tribes have risen to importance through the ability of their chieftain or commander; whilst other clans, formerly of importance, have been entirely swept away, by the indiscriminate slaughter of the savage. Extermination has been in some instances avoided by speedy flight over a vast expanse of territory. Thus, in many cases, the same district of country has changed hands several times in recent years. I have never myself met with a tribe whose traditions did not point to another, and sometimes distant locality, as having been at a former period the residence of their ancestors. But whilst constant changes have been taking place amongst these uncultivated races, we have no literature in which to find their dreary record. Tradition sheds its uncertain light backwards for only a few generations, and then leaves us in the dark. Beyond this, a bare list of the names of chiefs is all that has been preserved in the various tribes. The Kaffirs living to the east of Cape Colony would seem to have given the greatest attention to genealogical questions. Some tribes among them reckon up eleven ancestors, others fourteen; whilst the oldest or parent tribe, the Abatembu or Tembookies, treasures in its memory as many as eighteen chiefs—taking us back, according to recent computation, to about A.D. 1400.[1]

To the passing traveller the country itself tells little of its past inhabitants. Here and there, however, such "marks" have been made on it as testify to the fact of its having had ancient occupants, and some of them apparently of greater force and talent than its present masters. In certain caves within the colony, drawings of animals, supposed to be the work of Bushmen, were discovered by the colonists at an early date, and are described by Barrow,[1] who saw them in 1797. "For accuracy of outline and correctness of the different parts," says Sir John, "worse drawings have passed through the engraver's hands." Considerable curiosity was excited among naturalists at the beginning of the present century, by the discovery among these drawings of the representation of an animal with one horn, which was supposed to be the unicorn of Scripture. This animal, which had the head and neck of a giraffe, whilst its horn was placed not on the middle but on the right side of its forehead, probably existed merely in the superstition of the Bushmen, as does a certain bird called *tlari* in the mythology of the Bechuanas.

Throughout the whole of Southern Africa, the huntsman and the naturalist, whose pursuits may lead them to visit the summits of the mountains, find on their most inaccessible heights the little stone walls or enclosures, usually forming part of a circle, which partially surrounded the dwellings of former inhabitants. But beyond informing us that man's hand placed them where they now are, these ancient fences—many of which are nearly hid by grass and creepers—tell us nothing more that is definite; for such enclosures are used more or less by all the South African tribes. At Lobatse, near to Sechele's Town, we find the ruins of a native town, all the walls of which are built of

[1] *The Past and Future of the Kafir Races.* By Rev. W. C. Holden. London, 1866.

[2] *Travels in the Interior of Southern Africa in the Years* 1797 *and* 1798. By John Barrow, Esq. London, 1801-4.

stone. It is laid out after the manner of a Bechuana town; each subdivision having the small courtyard and cattle-pen of its master. Every wall is a circle, or part of a circle. It would seem that no native of South Africa ever drew a straight line, until he learned to do so from Europeans. The workmanship of these walls is good; the "joints" are well broken; and other rules are attended to, known to those who build what is called in Scotland "a dry stane dyke." The Bechuanas living in the neighbourhood uniformly tell us that these walls are the ruins of a town formerly occupied by the Bangwaketse, a tribe of Bechuanas. If this is true, these people have sadly deteriorated as to their style of building, for not a single house in their present town is built of stone, not a single cattle-pen in the style of those at Lobatse.

On the bank of the Impakwe river, and in a district which, when I passed through it in 1863, was all but entirely stripped of human inhabitants, we have the remains of an ancient smelting-furnace, the walls of which are built in the same style of workmanship as those at Lobatse. Here, therefore, in a district which is now a wilderness, there must have formerly lived an industrious and semi-civilized community, probably the Mashona, who now reside to the east and north-east of the Matebele Zulus, and have had hitherto little intercourse with Englishmen.

Perhaps the most striking circumstance tending to throw light on the dark history of the country, is the discovery of ancient pits or mines, on the bank of the river Tatie, in which gold had been dug in some previous age. None of the present natives of the country had noticed these pits. When discovered by Europeans in 1867 they were nearly filled up again with the drifting sand; and in the case of one of them a large mopane tree was growing out of what had been once the mouth of a gold mine. In this connection I may mention, that when the stone walls of my kitchen at Shoshong had risen to some height, a native of the Makalaka tribe, after surveying them attentively, remarked to me that he had now a new thought concerning certain walls in his native country, which lay to the north-east. He said when he was a boy he had looked on them as he did on the mountains and the plains—as things which had always been where he beheld them; but since he had seen the stone walls built by white men, he had come to the conclusion that those in his native land must have been built by the same people. In a work which has recently come under my notice,[1] I find it asserted that white men had seen these or similar ruins in the district indicated by my servant. In the extensive region of the recent gold discoveries, we may hope to find more than usually abundant materials to instruct us as to the past history of the country. As soon as it became probable that the source of the Nile was farther south than either the Victoria or Albert Nyanza, learned people reminded us that Ptolemy was in possession of this knowledge, and that old Portuguese maps also contained it. And as soon as it became certain that ancient gold mines had been discovered on the east coast of Africa, we were reminded that Milton had written in the eleventh book of *Paradise Lost*—

"And Sofala, thought Ophir."

Some are even sanguine enough to prophesy that not only is gold likely to be obtained there in remunerative quantities, but that monuments of the past may be discovered which shall throw light upon the former owners of the mines, and possibly upon Scripture itself, showing where King Solomon procured at least some of the commodities mentioned in the Book of Kings; and where gold was usually obtained at the much earlier period when the Book of Job was written.

But these are sorry materials, even when taken together, to stand as the monuments of man's residence during the long past, between the district of the Zambese and the Cape of Good Hope. They are as unsatisfactory as are those illustrative of a similarly rude though happily less protracted age in the history of our own island—the age of the round "wattle-and-daub" hut, whose painted or well-greased

[1] *Ruined Cities of Zulu-land.* By Colonel Walmsley.

occupant lived chiefly by the chase, to which he sallied forth armed with bow and arrow.

The religion or superstition of a people has an immense and direct influence on their physical condition. Illustrations will at once occur from Christianity, Judaism, Mahometanism, Confucianism, and Brahminism. These religions have had direct and specific effects on their votaries, encouraging free thought, inquiry, and discovery, or stereotyping a social system, and causing it to descend unchanged for thousands of years. For instance, in China for the last 2000 years the sameness of the Chinaman's features has been equalled only by the changeless monotony of his religious and social life. Every one knows how the religious traditions of the past have divided and enthralled the population of India. Whilst there was more apparent variety than in China, there was also a much greater bondage, and a more rigidly defined monotony. The system of caste taught the Hindoo that he must be in everything the counterpart of his father, not in opinions merely, but as to status in society and profession or trade. With regard to the religion or superstition of Southern Africa travellers have told widely different tales. Some writers find more in the native customs than observation would warrant, when unassisted by the imagination. Others again cannot find language too strong to express their estimate of the brutishness of the people, and their utter want of religious thought and feeling. The truth of the matter would seem to be, that the most degraded have not ceased to be worshippers. Fetichism, or the trust in the power of fetiches or charms, is the form of religion most extensively followed in Southern Africa. This kind of superstition may appear so trivial to some that a recent English traveller passes it by as "hocus-pocus;" but we must not forget that whatever its nature it was all that stood between our own ancestors and the unseen, and indeed to this day is not obsolete in Europe or in England. Like the sacrifices offered to Pagan gods, or to spirits of the dead, the observances of fetichism are simpler and ruder attempts to appease or to please the unseen, to ward off evil and to bring good to the devotee. For the same reason that he offers a goat to his ancestors, the African priest will lift up a charm on the end of a pole in the court-yard of the town, or will wear on his own brow the claw of a tiger, or will burn a mark in his forehead with the charred end of a certain piece of wood. The earnest manner in which the ceremonies are performed, and the satisfaction which is expressed when all has been gone through according to rule, testify to the force of the sanction of that which is handed down from remote antiquity. In most of the tribes we find the ideas of ceremonial cleanness and uncleanness, as well as of sacrifice and of prayer to the spirits of departed chiefs. My present object is not to describe these ceremonies, but to draw attention to the fact that throughout Southern Africa there obtains, in connection with the religion or superstition of the people, the same devotion to the traditions of the past, and the same disinclination, on "religious" grounds, to give them up, which characterize the natives of India,—it being understood that the possession of a literature enables the Hindoo to develop the same ideas in a more intensified and subtle form. The existence of this feeling among the South African tribes renders it probable that, as in India, not only religion, but the whole social system, has been stereotyped for ages. This would seem to be placed beyond all doubt by the fact that the ancient Egyptian sculptures represent dresses and occupations and utensils such as may be seen in any native town in Southern Africa at the present day. There, as in India, a man may do only what his fathers have done, and wear what his fathers have worn. A Bushman has told me that it did not belong to him to plant or to keep live stock. His forefathers knew nothing but the game and the roots of the earth, which was to him a reason why he also should know no more. A Bechuana man, who wears his cincture in one way, is shocked with the Zulu, who wears it after another fashion, and with the Kaffir, who hardly wears anything at all; and his name for these tribes (Mapotoko) has reference to their not being, in his estimation, sufficiently clothed. The peaceful and industrious Makalaka told me that Morimo (God) had not given them cattle like the Bechuanas, but skill in agriculture: their corn was their cattle. The warlike Zulus and Kaffirs again point to their spears, and inform you that these are their cattle; and one of the proud titles of their chief is "Eater-by-force." It is probable that such tribal distinctions, such "division of labour" in the dreary Pagan life, have obtained from earliest times. Although all are ready enough after a time to adopt European weapons, and most of them to don European clothing, they show little desire to interchange either weapons or clothing among themselves.[1] Instead, therefore, of having to dig up an arrow-head or axe-head, or minutely examine the texture of some cloth found in an ancient grave, in order to form an idea of the ancestors of the present inhabitants of Southern Africa, we have but to describe the people and their mode of life when first met by Europeans.

In the case of the tillers of the soil, as well as those who practised the few rude arts of South African industry, self-interest would increase the attention which superstition demanded should be paid to the acquirement of these arts by the young. They received insight into their secrets as a semi-religious service. Magic and science were here, as elsewhere, closely blended. The young worker in iron, for instance, was taught that certain charms were as necessary to the process of smelting the ore or of forging the iron into hoes and spears, as were the charcoal and the bellows. And so potent were the spells which the iron-master used to protect the scene of his industry from intrusion and depredation that no uninitiated person thought it safe to approach. Thus useful knowledge, in a stereotyped form, was handed down from father to son, protected and sanctioned by a stereotyped superstition.

[1] Sir John Lubbock, in his *Prehistoric Man*, p. 421, has the statement that the Hottentots, of late years, not only used iron weapons, but even made such for themselves. On referring to Kolben, the authority quoted by Sir John, I have not been able to discover any passage which refers to the art as having been then recently introduced among the Hottentots.

SECTION II.—DIVISION OF NATIVES OF SOUTHERN AFRICA INTO TWO FAMILIES.

(*a*.) LANGUAGE.

The tribes of Southern Africa may be divided into two families. This division holds good as to language, many religious rites and social customs, as well as physical appearance. In the second family I omit the names of several tribes living between Natal and the Zambese, giving only those with whom I have come into personal contact. Those given in the first family exhaust the tribes belonging to this race of men in Southern Africa :—

First Family.	*Second Family.*
Bushmen.	Kaffirs.
Hottentots.	Zulus.
Korannas.	Fingoes.
Griquas.	Basutos.
	Bechuanas.
	Damaras.
	Makobas.
	Makalaka.
	Mashona.

The comparative study of the languages of Southern Africa will no doubt throw great light upon the past history of the country, especially as to the descent and commingling of the various tribes. At the same time it is true that the absence of a native literature, such as that of India or China, will considerably curtail the fulness of the information from this source. Missionaries have reduced to writing the languages of the people to whom they have gone as evangelists ; and recently these and other contributions to the philology of Southern Africa have been analysed and classified by Dr. Bleek, of Cape Town, in a work which is still in progress.[1]

Hottentot and Bushman Languages.

With reference to the Bushman language, no European

[1] *A Comparative Grammar of South African Languages.* In Progress. By Wilhelm H. J. Bleek, Ph.D. London, 1858 and 1869.

has yet thoroughly mastered it. But "it seems to be clear that its relationship to the Hottentot language is at least very remote. In fact the probability is that it will be found to belong to what may be called the genderless languages. Members of this class seem to exist in almost all other parts of the world, and they interrupt particularly the contiguity of sex-denoting languages in Northern Africa (Bornu, Mandenga, etc.); Europe (Basque, Hungarian, Finnian, etc.); Asia (Tartaric, Mongolian, Dravidian, etc.) They occupy also some portions of America, and the whole Australian continent."[1]

The Hottentot language, which is the best known of this division, belongs to the sex-denoting languages. It has a dual number. Its pronouns are formed from the derivative *suffixes* of the nouns. It has therefore more in common with the Egyptian, Semitic, and Aryan languages, than with any of the languages of the other inhabitants of Southern Africa. This fact was recently ascertained independently, and almost at the same time, by different scholars. We give as an illustration the declension of a single Hottentot noun as to gender and number :—

Singular.	khoi-*p*	man (husband).
Plural.	khoi-*gu*	men (husbands).
Dual.	khoi-*kha*	two men (husbands).
Singular.	khoi-*s*	woman.
Plural.	khoi-*ti*	women.
Singular.	khoi-*i*	person.
Plural.	khoi-*n*	people (persons).
Dual.	khoi-*ra*[2]	two persons (a man and a woman, or two women).

The following Hottentot sentences show how the *suffixes* do duty as pronouns :—

Si-da e-sa	khoi-*p*	ta khui,	'nam-*bi* da-ra.
Our handsome	man	does appear,	love *him* we do.

[1] *Comp. Grammar,* Introduction. [2] *Ibid.* Part ii. p. 120.

Si-da e-sa	khoi-*gu*	ra khui,	'nam-*gu*-da-ra.
Our handsome	men	do appear,	love *them* we do.
Si-da e-sa	tara-*s*	ta khui,	'nam-*si*-da-ra.
Our handsome	woman	does appear,	love *her* we do.
Si-da e-sa	tara-*ti*	ra khui,	'nam-*ti*-da-ra.[1]
Our handsome	women	do appear,	love *them* we do.

What Europeans know as "clicks," are to be found in all the languages of the Hottentot family. Three-fourths of the syllabic elements of the Hottentot language are said to begin with clicks. Judging from its effect on the ear, a still greater number obtain in the Bushman language. Clicks are not confined to this family, however. They are found in other African languages, as in Zulu and Kaffir, and a few words in Sesuto, and it is said in the Galla language of North Africa. In the Circassian language, according to Klaproth, they are also to be found; and in the language spoken in Guatemala.[2] However difficult it may be for European adults to acquire the proper pronunciation of these uncouth sounds, children of Europeans growing up in the country acquire the language perfectly. When travelling through the Bushman country to the north of Shoshong, one of my own children, who was then just at the age when every sound which is heard is imitated with greater or less success, was able to pronounce several of the Bushman clicks which he heard spoken by the guides at our camp fire.[3]

These languages have also a peculiarly jerky, monosyllabic, and uncouth effect, besides the clicks; and some of the words are pronounced as if the person were singing. And this abrupt variation of tone is necessary in order to

[1] *Comp. Grammar*, Part ii. [2] *Ibid.* p. 14.

[3] Two of these "clicks" are in constant use in England. Many people, when shocked or surprised, withdraw the point of the tongue suddenly from the shut teeth, and the result is a sound something like *t s* blended into one. In Zulu and in Hottentot this is a constantly recurring consonant. Then in certain districts drivers urge on their horses by a sound familiar to many, and which is made by the tongue at the side of the mouth. This is another consonant, which may occur at the beginning or the middle of a word, and is represented by *x* in Zulu.

speak the language intelligibly, because there are some words which are the same in sound, but are modified in meaning by the tone in which they are uttered. Thus a certain word in Koranna, if pronounced in a loud key, means *handkerchief;* the same word, three notes lower, means *the spot;* and four notes lower still, it stands for the adjective *dark.*[1] I have been much interested to find that there are also four "tones" in the Chinese language, and that the giving of the proper one, as in Koranna, is essential to the understanding of the sentence. Dr. Lockhart, who resided some years at Pekin, as medical missionary, supplies me with the following illustration. In Chinese, a certain word in the first tone means *to fly;* in the second tone, *to subsist;* in the third tone, *to swim;* and in the fourth tone, *to issue.* The necessity for "pitching" one's words in Chinese at the proper height will be apparent when it is seen how widely different is the meaning of the word in one tone from what it is in another. The Hottentots and Korannas have this peculiarity in their languages in common with the Chinese. We shall see that their physical appearance resembles the same people. Indeed, the Bushmen are frequently called Chinese by the Dutch colonists in correspondence which has been printed by order of the House of Commons.[1]

The Ba-ntu Family of Languages.

"The Kaffir language belongs to an extensive family of languages, which occupy (as far as our knowledge goes) the whole of the South African continent, extending, on the eastern side, from the Keiskama to the equator, and on the western side from 32° south to about 8° north latitude. Members of this family of languages, which we call the Ba-ntu family, are also spread over portions of Western Africa, as far as Sierra Leone, where the Bullom and Timneh languages are cousins to the Kaffir. They are here interspersed, particularly by members of the Gor

1 Sir G. Grey's Library, vol. i. Part i. p. 20.

2 Papers relative to Cape of Good Hope, Part i. p. 92.

family of languages (Fulah, Wolof, Ga, etc.), which belongs to the same class of languages as the Ba-ntu family, and forms together with it the African section of this class; whilst the Malay, Polynesian, and Papuan families are to be considered as members of the Oceanic section of the same class. It has been divided into three great branches, each branch comprising several languages which are as distinct from each other as perhaps English is from German, or French from Italian or Portuguese."[1]

The affinity between these languages, as well as the peculiarity of their formation of the plural by prefix changes, will appear from the following table, compiled from the Grammar already quoted, and giving the words "person" and "persons" as used in fourteen of the Ba-ntu family of languages. A reference to the map will show over what an extensive area they are spoken, from Kaffirland on the south-east to Fernando Po on the north-west.

Through the kindness of Rev. Dr. Turner, author of *Nineteen Years in Polynesia,* I am able to supply two specimens of the Oceanic Section of the Ba-ntu family :—

AFRICAN SECTION.

	Singular.	*Plural.*
English,	Person,	persons.
Name of Tribe.		
Kaffir,	u-*mu*-ntu,	a-*ba*-ntu.
Tekeza,	a-*mu*-no,	*va*-no.
Southern do.,	*mu*-nu,	*ba*-nu *va*nu.
Sechuana,	*Mo*-thu,	*ba*-thu.
Tette,	*Mu*-nttu or *Mu*ntto,	*Va*-nttu.
Makua,	*Mu*-ttu,	A-ttu.
Kihiau,	*Mu*-ndu,	*Va*-ndu.
Kikamba,	*Mu*-ndu,	*A*-ndu.
Kisambala,	*Mu*-ntu,	*wa*-ntu.
Kinika,	*Mu*-tu,	*A*-tu.
Kisuaheli,	*M*-tu,	*wa*-tu.
Otyiherero (Damara),	o-*mu*-ndu,	o-*va*-ndu.

[1] *Comp. Gram.* p. 2.

Name of Tribe.	*Singular.*	*Plural.*
Sindonga or Ovambo,	u-*m*-tu, . .	o-*a*-ntu.
Dikele, . .	*mu*-tyi, . .	*bo*-tyi.
Fernando Po, .	*bo*-tshu, . .	*bu*-tshu.

OCEANIC SECTION.

Central Polynesia, Samoa, .	*o le* tangata, .	*o* tangata.
Western Polynesia, Tanna, . .	*n'* aremama, .	aremama.

The Ba-ntu languages differ widely from those previously described. The Hottentot and Bushman languages are abrupt, and abound with consonants. The Ba-ntu languages, on the other hand, are rich in vowel sounds. The Sechuana may be said to be a euphonious and flowing language. All words end in a vowel as in Italian, or in the ringing *ng*, which is a combination occurring at the beginning as well as at the end of words, thus, *ngaka*, a priest or sorcerer; *ngo-ngo-rega*, to murmur. But the most remarkable characteristic of this family of languages is, that the pronouns are originally borrowed from the derivative *prefixes* of the nouns. The following examples will show the method of constructing a sentence in Sechuana :—

*Ba*thu *ba* tsile.
People have come.
*Ba*thu *ba* *ba*intle.
People (are) beautiful.
*Ba*thu *ba ba* tsileng *ba* *ba*intle.
People who have come (are) beautiful.
*Se*tlare *se se* tala *se* *se*intle.
(The) tree which is green (is) beautiful.

This is the same as if it were correct for us to say in English :—

*Pe*ople *pe* come, *for* people have come.

*Pe*ople *pe pe* come *pe* pleasant, *for* people who have come are pleasant.

*Go*vernment *go go* good, *for* a government which is good.

*Go*vernment *go go* good *go* necessary, *for* a government which is good is necessary.

The following sentence has already been given in the Hottentot language; I now present it in the language of one of the African and one of the Oceanic sections of the Ba-ntu family. The relation of the two latter as prefix-languages will appear, as well as their wide separation from the suffix-language of the Hottentot:—

ENGLISH.

Our handsome man appears; we love him.

Singular.

SECHUANA.

*Mo*nna	oa	rona	eo	o	mointle	oa bonala;	rea	*mo*	rata.
Man	of	us	who	is	handsome	he appears;	we	*him*	love.

SAMOAN.

Ua afio mai	*lo*	tatou	tangata	au lelei;	ʻua tatou	alofa	ia te ia.
There comes		our	man	handsome;	we	love	to him.

Plural.

SECHUANA.

*Ba*nna	ba	rona	ba ba	baintle	baa bonala;	rea	*ba*	rata.
Men	of	us	who are	handsome	they appear;	we	*them*	love.

SAMOAN.

Ua afifio mai	*o*	tatou	tangata	au lelei;	ua tatou	alolofa	ia te i latou.
There come		our	men	handsome;	we	love	to them.

Sechuana Pronouns.

The Prefix-particle is used as a pronoun—thus, *ba*thu kia *ba* bona: the people, I see them. Demonstrative Pronoun—*ba*thu *ba*uo: these people. Pronoun indicating distance—*ba*thu *ba*le: the people yonder. Separative Pronoun—*ba*thu *ba*he? which people?

PERSONAL PRONOUNS.

Nominative.				*Accusative.*			
ki,	I.	re,	we.	'na,	me.	re,	us.
u,	thou.	lo,	you.	gu,	you.	lo,	you.
o,	he *or* she.	ba,	they.	mo,	him *or* her.	ba,	them.

EMPHATIC PRONOUNS.

'na,	I *or* me.	rona,	we *or* us.
uena,	thou *or* thee.	lona,	you.
ena,	he *or* him; she *or* her.	bona,	they *or* them.

POSSESSIVE PRONOUNS.

oa me,	mine.	oa rona,	ours.
oa gago,	thine.	oa lona,	yours.
oa gague,	his, hers.	oa bona,	theirs.

Sechuana Numerals.

In counting, Bechuanas invariably begin with the little finger of the left hand: the thumb of the right is six, and the little finger of the right hand is ten.

ngwe	one	
peri	two	
taro	three	
nne	four	
tlano	five	
tataro	six	two threes.
shupa	seven	index.
sia menwana meberi . .	eight	fold down two fingers.
sia monwana mongwehela .	nine	fold down one finger.
leshume	ten	
leshume le coa ka ngwehela .	eleven	ten followed by one.
mashume a le mabere . .	twenty	tens which are two.

Instead of dividing the nouns according to ideas of sex, there are in this family of languages a number of *classes* of nouns, which form their plural by certain prefixes, according to fixed rules. The following are the classes in Sechuana:—

Singular.	*Plural.*
*mo*thu, person	*ba*thu, persons.
*mo*re, tree	*me*re, trees.
pitse, horse	*li*pitse, horses.
'ncha (intsha), dog . . .	*l*intsha, dogs.
khomo, ox	*li*khomo, oxen.
thuto, instruction . . .	*li*thuto, teachings.
noka, river	*li*noka, rivers.
ngaka, doctor	*li*ngaka, doctors.
*bo*gosi, kingdom, . . .	*ma*gosi, kingdoms.
*le*phui, dove	*ma*phui, doves.
*lo*selo, sieve	*li*tselo, sieves.
*se*tlare, tree	*li*tlare, trees.

Sechuana Verb.

The verb is very copious. I give only a few of the forms.

Go rata, to love.

	Pres.	*Imperfect.*	*Perfect.*	*Aorist.*
Active.	Kia rata.	Ka rata.	Ki ratile.	Ki le ka rata.
Passive.	Kia ratoa.	Ka ratoa.	Ki ratiloe.	Ki le ka ratoa.

Act. Participle. Morati, he who loves.
Pass. Participle. Moratoi, he who is loved.

Kia ratéla, I love for *or* on account of.
Kia ratisa, I cause to love.
Kia ratega, I become loved; am loveable.
Kia ithata, I love myself.

Participles. Morateri, moratisi, morategi, moithati.

(b.) Physical Appearance.

These two divisions of the tribes of Southern Africa differ from one another very markedly in physical appearance. Early writers were struck with the resemblance borne by members of the first class to the Chinese or Mongolian features. It was especially noticed that they were characterized by the same peculiarly set eyes. Their woolly hair was never abundant, but was dotted over their head like clumps of bushes scattered here and there on a barren knoll. Their colour varied from a pale or dirty white in some, to a dusky bronze colour in others, the majority being lighter in colour than many Chinamen, and some inhabitants of the South of Europe. The second division approach the Arab caste of feature in the Zulu and Kaffir, and the Negro type in the Makoba and the Damara. Their woolly hair is abundant; and the Makoba and Makalaka might be called hairy from the appearance of the breast and face of the men. The Griquas are a mixed people, and many of them are half-castes. On the mother's side they belong to one or other of the Hottentot tribes. The tallest men in the first family would be found amongst the Korannas; but they are slightly made, and apparently not possessed of much physical power. The finest men in the second family would no doubt be found amongst the Zulus and Kaffirs.

(c.) Religious and Social Customs, Mode of Building Houses and Laying out Towns.

Whilst there are many of the observances of Fetichism common to both these families, there are other customs which serve to distinguish them. Circumcision is practised by the second family, but is unknown in the first, some of whom practised exsection instead, whilst others pierced the cartilage of the nose, and inserted a small piece of wood. All the members of the second family are tillers of the soil, while agriculture was entirely unknown to the first family when they met with Europeans.

A custom which tends to disconnect the Hottentot family from the rest of the South African tribes, and at the

House of Bushmen.

House of Hottentots, Korannas, and Griquas.

House of Zulus.

House of Bechuanas.

same time unites them to Northern nations, may be mentioned here. We are taught that our English word "daughter" may be traced back to times when to be a *daughter* was to be the *milk-maid* of the family. In like manner the Hottentot and Koranna women are still the milkers of the cows. But among the Kaffirs and Bechuanas and other tribes of the Ba-ntu family, women are not allowed even to enter a cattle-pen while the cattle are in it. It is customary for the Bechuana women to mix cow-dung in the plaster which they use for the walls of their houses; but I have often seen them have to wait patiently until the cattle went to graze, when it was lawful for them to enter the pen to collect the cow-dung. Customs could not be more diametrically opposed than in this instance. In this connection the inscriptions on the walls of the caves in different parts of the country, described by Sir John Barrow, by Sir James Alexander, and others, assume a fresh significance. Is this the lingering remnant of the ancient northern custom which caused the history of the country to be inscribed upon the rocks? We find nothing similar among the Ba-ntu tribes.

The two families are readily distinguished by their different modes of house-building. The "house" of a Bushman in Cape Colony is thus described by Barrow:—"The horde or kraal consisted of five-and-twenty huts, each made of a small grass mat bent into a semicircle, and fastened down between two sticks—open before, but closed behind with a second mat. They were about three feet high and four feet wide, and the ground in the middle was dug out like the nest of an ostrich; a little grass strewed in this hollow served as their bed, in which they seemed to have lain coiled round in the manner of some quadrupeds."[1] This traveller might have added, in the manner of some bipeds also, when they are cold in bed!

Like the hut of the Bushman, that of the Hottentot and Koranna is without proper walls as distinct from the roof. It is constructed of mats, made of reeds or rushes, which are stretched over poles, so bent as to be of a dome shape

[1] Barrow, vol. i. p. 276.

at the top, while the house is of a circular form at the bottom. The door is a mat similar to those of which the house itself is made. When it became necessary for these pastoral people to remove to another locality with their flocks and herds, it was easy to untie the mats from the poles which constituted the skeleton of the hut, roll them up, and pack them on an ox or the women's heads. At the new station fresh poles were soon cut and bent into position, the mats spread over, and the shepherd was as much at home as before.

It is worthy of observation, that in Bechuana-land the Bushman does not attempt the rush or mat house, as he did in the Cape Colony. As in the latter place he imitated the houses of his pastoral neighbours, so in Bechuana-land, and in districts where reeds and rushes abound, he imitates the house of the Bechuanas. His ordinary hut is usually constructed of withered branches of a suitable length, the ends of which are rested against the stem of a tree; a quantity of loose grass is thrown over for a roof, with, it may be, the raw hide of an antelope to keep everything in its place. But it is when you come upon one of their little villages in Bechuana-land that you see what seems to be the highest architectural effort of the Bushman. The result is "metlagana," the hunting or garden huts of the Bechuanas, which are, in point of fact, the roofs of Bechuana houses without the walls. When travelling, I have seen expert Makalaka raise a house of this description, and thatch it so as to keep out the rain, in a few minutes.

The Zulus and the Bechuanas build walls of wattle and clay, with roofs of grass, the house being round in shape. The Zulu hut is lower than that of the Bechuanas, and the doorway, if possible, lower and narrower. The Zulus make a wicker-work door for their house; the Bechuanas use a board, which, as they have no saw, they obtain by dressing down a large tree with their little adzes and axes. The grass thatch is not stitched to the rafters, but secured by cords of bark arranged obliquely over it, like the straw rope binding over the thatch of a corn-rick. The houses of some tribes of Bechuanas have two walls, the roof extending over both. The space between these walls—to which there is more than one entrance, is used as a sleeping-place in summer, as well as for noon-day repose. There are cabins within the United Kingdom—or they have very recently been removed—which are certainly less comfortable in every point of view than a well-built Bechuana hut.

The character and disposition of the different tribes are exemplified by the manner in which they lay out their towns. In a Hottentot or Koranna town, the houses are in the middle, surrounded by the cattle enclosure. The latter is now usually dispensed with, since lions have disappeared from their neighbourhood, and their cattle, which are very tame, form an irregular belt round their houses. A Zulu town, on the other hand, is built round the cattle-pen. The listless Korannas are surrounded by their cattle; the warlike Zulus surround, that they may the better defend and retain that which they have probably taken by force. In the laying out of the towns of the Basutos, Bechuanas, Mashonas, and Makalakas we find an approach to a higher civilisation, in the subdivision of property—the recognition of individual rights, and the adaptation of the town to the pursuit of the peaceful arts of rude industry. Whilst there is the great cattle-pen close to the public courtyard of the town, each subdivision has its own head man, its own pen for cattle, and fold for sheep and goats. We leave the three South African towns to point their own moral. Despotism is to be found in the garrison-town of the Zulu, where private property is all but unknown, where war is constantly waged, and secret assassination common. "Liberty, equality, and fraternity" —after a certain fashion—were to be found in the insecure villages of the pastoral Korannas and Namaquas, who were without chief, or public assembly, or government; where all property was of course private; and where drinking milk and basking in the sun were the only engagements of the day. Reverence for authority, with the assertion of individual rights, are to be found in the more happily constituted Bechuana and Mashona communities, where the power of the chief, being modified by the voice of the people, is sufficient to preserve cohesion and order, without altogether discouraging or repressing private enterprise or industry.

(*d.*) Dress and Weapons of War.

It would not be interesting, nor is it at all necessary, to particularize the tribal fashion or dress of the different nations of Southern Africa. The following description includes them all:—A cincture or cinctures round the loins, of various shapes, of greater or less dimensions, and more or less ornamented with shells or metal, or, in recent times, with beads; a head-dress which might be only a feather, or a flower, or a string of beads, or it might be a cap made of the striped zebra's skin, or of the warm fur of the jackal or wild cat; the large mantle or kaross, worn as a blanket in the night, and in winter during the day also, made of the dressed fur skins already referred to, or of the skin of the ox or antelope; with the small mantle in general use among Bechuanas as an ordinary article of clothing. These are the articles of dress worn by the uncivilized inhabitants of Southern Africa, and have been so, with unimportant changes, from earliest times. Some tribes, such as the Mashona, prefer clothing made by themselves from the cotton which grows in their country, to skin clothing as worn farther south. But the majority of the tribes found it easier to dress the skins of the animals killed by them in the chase, or caught in the hopo. The Bechuanas dress the skins very creditably; patch the bullet or spear holes, so that they cannot be detected, and dye the inside with the bark of a plant which makes it of a red colour. Upon examination of their work, a furrier in this country told me he could make no improvement on it. The abundance of the game supplies articles of clothing, not only to the aborigines but to many of the Dutch settlers and poorer colonists in remote districts at the present day, and Barrow mentions that at the end of last century the Dutch colonists wore little else than skin clothing.

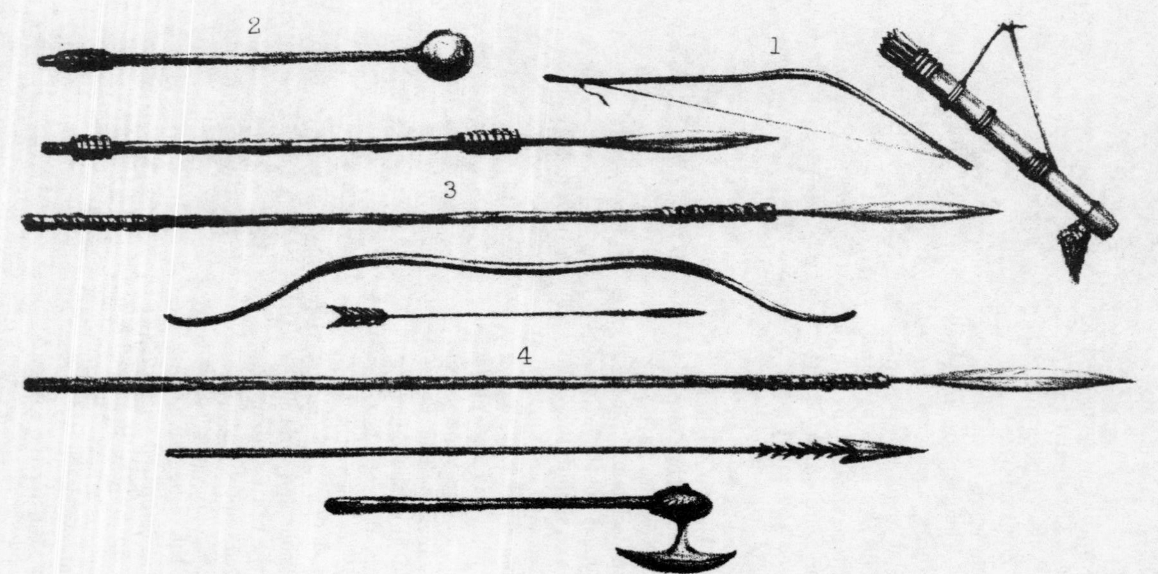

No. 1, Bushman. No. 2, Matebele. No. 3, Mashona. No. 4, Bechuana.

The warlike weapons of the present, and no doubt of the long past, are similar to those used by many other barbarous nations. The strongest and most warlike tribes, such as the Zulus and Kaffirs, use the shortest weapons, showing that they were in the habit of coming to close quarters in war. Their spears have short handles, and the Zulus never throw them, but sometimes in the heat of an engagement break off the wooden part, that they may use the blade as a knife or dagger. With a sword which was only fifteen inches long the Romans conquered the world; and in Southern Africa the men with the short weapon possessed the finest parts of the country. An immense shield of cow-hide is carried by the Zulus to war; a smaller one is used in their own country even in time of peace. The "knob-kerie," like the shillelah in Ireland, is chiefly used in time of peace to settle disputes, "in a friendly way." Next we have the spears and battle-axes of the less warlike Bechuanas and Basutos, the former of which they are accustomed to throw, whilst they trust to the chaka or battle-axe should they come to close quarters. The chiefs and head men are sometimes provided with a spear, barbed so profusely that it cannot at once be withdrawn from the body which it has pierced. Whilst the wounded man seeks to extract this cruel weapon, he is put to death by his assailant. The Bechuana shield is smaller than the war-shield of the Zulus; and those of the chiefs are so cut and carved as to leave very little to protect the wearer. Lastly, we have the bows and arrows, used, strange to say, at the two extremes of South African society—by the industrious and semi-civilized Mashonas, and by the Bushman, the restless, roving child of the desert—the furthest removed, not by stupidity, but by tradition, habit, and liking, from a settled and civilized mode of life. But what the diminutive weapon of the Bushman loses in force, as compared with that of the Mashona, is more than made up by the deadly poison which he places on the point of his arrow. He needs but to see that the arrow has entered the body of the antelope, to feel sure of his prize. But for the custom of rubbing their arrows with a paste in which is mixed up the poison extracted from the fangs of snakes, from several plants, and it is said from a certain deposit in the clefts of rocks in the Cape Colony—the Bushmen would probably have been exterminated by their native neighbours. Having reached the confines of the southern part of the continent, they lived as roving banditti, and in their inaccessible retreats managed to "hold their own" among their neighbours. It was reserved for the gun to cope with and to overcome the poisoned arrow. It is sad that the process should have been so much a war of extermination.

SECTION III.—POSSIBLE PHYSICAL EFFECTS OF CLIMATE AND FOOD ON BUSHMEN AND OTHER TRIBES.

THERE are physical differences between members of the same tribe which would seem to be referable to the outward conditions under which they exist. For instance, the Bushmen who formerly inhabited part of what is now the Cape Colony, were a much shorter race than those still to be found in Bechuana-land. Early travellers describe the Bushman as often under five feet in height.[1] Those about Kuruman are a degree taller than this; while the Masarwa or Bushmen belonging to Sechele and the tribes in his neighbourhood, approach the average height of the Makalahari or Bechuana vassals of these tribes, who also live in the open country, and are subject to many hardships in common with the Bushmen. In the country between Shoshong and the Zambese there is a tribe of Bushmen called Madenassana, who are as remarkable for their tallness and stalwart appearance as were the tribes in the colony for their shortness of stature. Their features, their language, their mode of life, their state of vassalage, all betoken them to be Bushmen. And yet finer men than some of them I have not seen anywhere in Southern Africa.

[1] In a Bushman kraal of some twenty-five huts, inhabited by perhaps 150 people, the tallest man measured by Barrow, in 1797, was 4 feet 9 inches in height; the tallest woman 4 feet 4 inches, and one woman who had borne several children, was only 3 feet 9 inches in height.

Whilst they have bows and arrows, they employ spears also, in the hunt, which are remarkably heavy and formidable. When I passed through their country, I found that they were not only able to supply their own wants by hunting, but also to provide meat for the Makalaka in their neighbourhood, who gave them corn in exchange. The other Bushmen belonging to the Bamangwato, and scattered over the country as far north as the Zambese, are not so tall as the Madenassana, but on the other hand, I have neither seen nor heard of any among them so short as the Bushman of the colony. Their average height is a little under that of the Makalahari and Makhurutse, their companions in vassalage in Bechuana-land, whilst many individuals might be found amongst them as tall and as powerful as could be shown from among their neighbours.

Again, the Bushmen of the Cape Colony and the southern part of Bechuana-land are a degree lighter in colour than those of their own tribe living farther north. In the same way the southern tribes of Bechuanas,—the Batlaping, Batlware, and others,—are lighter in colour and shorter in stature than those living in the northern part of the same country, such as the Bamangwato. The country of the Batlaping is more arid and devoid of moisture than is the country of the Bamangwato. Then the Bamangwato reside in a less humid country than that of the Bamapela to the north-east or the Makoba and Mashubea on the north-west. The last-mentioned tribes are all darker than the Bamangwato. The Bamangwato themselves separated about one hundred years ago, a portion of the tribe settling at the Lake Ngami, whilst the remainder took up their abode on the range of mountains on which their present town of Shoshong is placed. It is my opinion, after having visited the lake, that if twenty or thirty Bamangwato from Shoshong were drawn at random and placed alongside the same number of Batowana or Bamangwato from the lake, a stranger would be able to distinguish the latter by the greater darkness of their complexion. Thus it would seem that the further you recede from heat and moisture in Southern Africa, the lighter is the complexion, the more scanty the hair, until you come to the light-coloured Hottentot and Bushman of the Cape Colony, the scattered "dots" of woolly hair on whose head suggest that if the process had only gone a little further, we should have found men without any hair on their heads at all.

But these are not the only differences which would seem to be traceable to physical causes. Where there is moisture there is abundant vegetation, and the country is clothed with trees and shrubs which afford delightful shade to the inhabitants. The opposite of this is the case in the arid plain, where the traveller has no shelter but the "shadow of a great rock" in the "weary land." The natives of the tree-bearing countries have large full eyes, the eyelids and eyebrows being usually not wrinkled or compressed; the more arid the country the smaller the eyes of the inhabitants, and the more compressed and "puckered" the parts surrounding the eye. For instance, the Makoba on the Zouga river have usually large mild eyes, which are almost equalled by those of the Makalaka. Coming southward to the drier district of Shoshong, we find the eyes of the Bamangwato a degree smaller. In the still more arid district of Kuruman, the Batlaping have smaller eyes still; and if we go farther south into districts completely treeless, we find among the Korannas, Hottentots, and Bushmen, the smallest eyes in the country.

Lastly, where there is moisture in Southern Africa there is usually plenty of food, which, of course, has an important effect in the development of the physical frame. Receding southward from heat and moisture and plenty, we come to those who have had to struggle at increasing odds to obtain a subsistence. Passing the Makalahari and the Bushmen of Bechuana-land, and coming to the former Bushmen of the Cape Colony, we find that where the struggle was greatest, there the physical deterioration was greatest also. We are accustomed to believe that the difficulties connected with human existence amid the mists and fogs and colds of these northern European latitudes, have in themselves led to the development of a higher manhood than is to be found where these outward difficulties are not so great. This is true, however, only up to a certain point; beyond that, difficulties from their vastness would seem to cease to have a stimulating influence. The difficulties connected with life in England and in Germany may have helped to develop in the inhabitants of these countries greater energy and patience than are possessed by the Italian or the Spaniard. But where instead of the mists and fogs of our own island man has to face the snow and frost and darkness of the arctic regions, he wraps himself in his furs, eats his tallow, and lives the life of a Laplander.

Deterioration would thus seem to be at least suggested by what we know of the past history of the Bushmen. If it is granted that they travelled southward, and if the bulk of their tribes gave place to those who were stronger than themselves rather than remain as their vassals, then, if we institute a comparison between those who did remain as vassals in Bechuana-land, and those who removed into the more inhospitable country of the Cape Colony, the difference between them would seem to be fairly traceable to their different outward circumstances. Driven into a region where they had, all naked as they were, to contend with snow in winter—with the withering glare of an African sun every day in a treeless region,—now over-fed with meat, now scattered over the plain, digging with their curious sticks the innutritious and indigestible bulbs and roots, whose effects on the system could only have been injurious, while in the meantime allaying the pangs of hunger: in these distressing circumstances we seem to have an adequate reason for the deterioration of the Bushmen in the colony, as compared with those in Bechuana-land. And certainly their mode of life, viewed by itself, was such as would have told injuriously in the course of time upon the strongest European constitution.[1]

[1] The Dutch colonists have not undergone much change during their sojourn in the Cape Colony. Those who were originally dark-complexioned, are now of the colour of the inhabitants of Southern Europe. Light-complexioned people are usually ruddier than in Holland. Excessive corpulence in both men and women is the chief distinguishing physical

In concluding this review of the South African races, the tribal peculiarities of the people might be summed up as follows:—The Bushmen, whose only domestic animal is the dog, and who neither till the soil nor possess flocks or herds, are the most diminutive physically; the most acute in their senses; the most fickle and uncertain in their disposition and movements; the most careless and reckless of consequences. The Makalaka, who live chiefly by tilling the soil, are the most clumsy in their appearance and movements; the most peaceful in their disposition; and the most respectful to their women. A Makalaka man swears by his mother, not by his father, as do the other tribes. Amongst those who possess flocks and herds, and at the same time till the soil, the Zulus and Kaffirs are the most warlike of all the tribes; while the Bechuanas and Mashonas are the most advanced in civilisation.

characteristic of the Dutch in South Africa. The country which was so inhospitable to the Bushman who trusted solely to its spontaneous bounty, has become a pleasant home for the man of intelligence and resource, who cultivates the soil, shields himself from the elements by rearing a comfortable residence, and whose clothing and part of whose food come from distant quarters of the globe. That the Cape Colony is conducive to the health of Europeans is shown by the following figures taken from the Census of 1865. In a total population of 496,381, there were—

People who were 55 years of age and under 70 .	19,152
" " 70 " " 100 .	6,102
" " above 100 . . .	63

THE CONTACT OF EUROPEANS WITH THE NATIVES OF SOUTHERN AFRICA.

It is the custom for even educated persons to include "all these Africans" and "all these black people" in some sweeping statement, as if what is true of one tribe were true of all. Whatever may be the case with reference to the coloured inhabitants of America or Australia, this does not hold good when spoken of the natives of Southern Africa, any more than of the inhabitants of Europe or Asia. I have described the marked differences which prevail among the natives of Southern Africa as to language, habits, and customs. These are still further brought out, if we consult the past history of their contact with Europeans. Differing from one another in traditions and habits, their contact with Europeans has led in each case to a different result, which has had an evident connection with the peculiar character and habits of the tribe. To illustrate this, I proceed to give a very brief sketch of the contact of Europeans with Bushmen, Hottentots, Kaffirs, and Bechuanas.

Bushmen.

The Bosjesmans (Bushes-men) were the sworn enemies of all the other South African tribes, before the white man appeared on the scene. They were not swept away by the pastoral Hottentots and the pastoral and agricultural Kaffirs and Bechuanas, simply because their poisoned arrows and mountain fastnesses were sufficient to baffle such foes. But the Dutchmen shot them down as vermin. Barrow relates that when on the frontier, "a Boer being asked, in the Secretary's office, if the savages were numerous or troublesome on the road, replied that he had only shot four, with as much composure and indifference as if he had been speaking of four partridges." The same author says he heard one colonist boast of having destroyed with his own hand nearly three hundred of these unfortunate wretches. I do not wish to be understood to say that Dutchmen have been exceptionally impatient and bloodthirsty. The "Bushes-men" of America and of Australia (differing in personal appearance, but the same in habit and custom) have been killed off-hand in the same way. The reward of "twenty dollars apiece for Indian scalps with ears on," was offered only a few years ago by the Coloradan capital.[1] But according to the published records of the Cape Colony, English vengeance in South Africa was not quite so swift or so heavy as that of the Dutch. Between the years 1786-1795, under the Dutch Government, there were, Bushmen killed, 2480; made prisoners, 654; giving a proportion of nearly 4 killed to 1 taken prisoner. Under the English Government between 1813 and 1824, there were, Bushmen killed, 97; made prisoners, 280; giving a proportion of 1 killed to 3 taken prisoners.[2]

We sometimes hear people on platforms and elsewhere

[1] *Greater Britain*, i. 130.

[2] I obtain these figures from the following Table, which is formed from Reports and Records at Graaff Reinet, transmitted to Government in March 1836:—

	Killed.	Prisoners.	Proportion of Killed to Prisoners.
Last ten years of Government of Dutch East India Company, 1786 to 1795, ...	2480	654	4 to 1
English and Batavian Governments, 1795 to 1806, . .	367	252	3 to 2
English Government, 1813 to 1824, from Parl. Papers, p. 56, ...	97	280	1 to 3

See Report of Committee to the Subscribers to the Fund for Printing and Publishing Documentary Evidence relative to the Intercourse of the Colonists and Cape Government with the Native Tribes, by Hon. H. Cloete, LL.D., and Lieutenant-Colonel Bird, late Colonial Secretary, p. 5.

talking of the white men as a grand advancing army, before which the blacks melt away. Now there is truth in this, as to Bushes-men—that is, the men who have lived exclusively upon what Nature spontaneously yields, without domesticated animals and without agriculture. But even with reference to them, there seems to me an air of mystery thrown over this matter which is quite unnecessary. A rifle bullet, well aimed, puts as abrupt an end to the life of the philosopher as to that of the Bushes-man. There is nothing mysterious, nothing poetical, about a war of extermination. Nor is there anything dreadful or hopeless, considered by itself, in the determined position assumed by these wild men, which is simply that they will live and die in the customs of their forefathers. This is just the position of the Hindoo and of thousands of Englishmen. The Hindoo refuses to change one iota as to food or clothing or daily habit. Fortunately for him the aims and pursuits of his Western masters do not directly interfere with this resolve. If, however, Englishmen in India had some commercial object in preventing the eating of curry and rice in that country, and in insisting that all Hindoos should live on beef, and if, when the Hindoos persisted in stealing rice rather than change their food, they were shot down and exterminated, we should have something like what has taken place in the history of all Bushes-men. The white man destroys their hereditary food, and suddenly renders their traditional mode of life impossible. The wild beasts perish before the gun, and the country is cut up into farm-lots and sites for towns. The Bushes-men become as it were strangers in their own country. They look for the game; they find only sheep and cattle. They look for roots and berries; they find that the old familiar spots have been turned over by the plough, and they see instead the corn of the white man waving in the summer breeze. But as they have always lived on what they find in the open country, they will do so still. They seize sheep and cattle, and, fleeing into the wilderness, slaughter and make merry. For them they see no other way of living. The owner of the stolen animals at first expostulates, and offers food if the Bushes-man will work, or he shows him a patch of ground, and invites him to begin life as a cultivator of the soil. He might as well ask a Hindoo to apprentice himself to a butcher; or an English squire, all his life accustomed to his gun and his hounds, but whom sudden ruin has overtaken, to escape from starvation by hiring himself to the neighbouring owner of the cotton-mill at so much per week. Such alternatives would in each case be scornfully rejected. Did not God, or Brumha, or Morimo, or the Great Spirit, appoint them their lot in life? Other men might live on a narrow farm allotment, or butcher cows, or assist spinning-jennies. They prefer to die rather than forsake family traditions and customs. "What then is to be done?" asks the white man, leaning on his rifle. "Leave the country, and the game will return," is the ready solution of the son of the desert. But just as it seems necessary to the Bushes-man to live on game and roots only, so it appears quite indispensable to the sheep-farmer that he should remain in that country and graze his flocks on those plains, and nowhere else. Still it is always with great compunction and misgiving that the European Christian man shoots down the first sheep-stealer with his own hand. He hears a voice saying to him, "Thou shalt not kill." "Whatsoever ye would that men should do unto you, do ye even so unto them." "How much is a man better than a sheep?" But on the frontier a callous spirit soon takes possession of a man. Once blood has been drawn, to shed it becomes easier every day. At first the Christian colonist thought his fine estate would be dearly bought, if bought with blood. But by and bye the Bushes-man is ranked with the snakes and the wild beasts, and the jungle in which he lives—all are to be swept away. A little longer, and fanaticism comes to his assistance, and assures him it is his duty to shoot down a doomed race; and extremely clever men encourage him by professing to show that he is obeying a great "law of Nature" in displacing an inferior race.[1] I have endeavoured to explain that the reason

[1] This taking upon ourselves the working out of the "decrees of Pro-

for extermination in the Bushes-man is simply the plain one, not peculiar to himself, that he wishes to stick to the customs of his forefathers. The reason that Dutchmen have been the executioners of a race in Southern Africa was certainly not that they hated the Bushes-men more than did the Kaffirs and Hottentots, but that they possessed a better weapon. As a matter of fact, however, there was no imperative necessity for their extermination; for Kaffirs and Hottentots had been able to practise agriculture, and graze their flocks and herds within sight of those mountain ranges, out of which they were unable to dislodge the Bushes-men. And if this was possible, to these comparatively unprotected tribes, how much more might the well-armed Dutchman have done so? Agàin, this extermination was unnecessary, for as soon as the English appeared, the death-rate suddenly decreased. Thus it would seem that men kill men wantonly, because it is easy to do so, and because it brings *a* settlement of a difficulty. What if it is not *the* settlement? What if it was not the will of God that these degraded men should be shot down? Can we think of our Saviour as approving of such slaughter? Shall we tell HIM some story about a "doomed race," or an "inferior race"? At any rate it is a fact, that when, in His providence, He permitted men to appear in Africa, able to exterminate the Bushes-man, it was a people who, while they carried the gun, possessed also the New Testament.

vidence" or the "laws of Nature," has been exemplified in the manner of the persecution of the Jews by Christendom, and, before the late war, in the plainly-expressed reasoning of learned and reverend advocates of slavery in the Southern States of America. In our own land there are certain classes who prey upon the weak members of society, and most effectually destroy them. Ought not the keeper of the gin-palace and the keepers of other nameless houses to inscribe above their doors, "For the fulfilment of the decree of Providence and the law of Nature, in the destruction of the weaklings of society"? And ought not the English vessel which carries opium to China to hoist a flag with the inscription, "Fulfiller of Divine Decrees and Laws of Nature" in the destruction of the inferior race of Chinese?

Hottentots.

In one of the first letters which I sent home from the Cape Colony, I made the assertion that "the Hottentot race was fast dying out," and again, that "drink was exterminating the Hottentots." So far as I can recollect, my grounds for writing this was simply that some one whom I thought worthy of confidence had told me so. I saw a great deal of drunkenness among these people, which I regarded as an attestation of the truth of the statement. I find that others have had the same vague idea. Nothing could be more incorrect than this assertion, at least since the time the colony came into the hands of the English. Under the Dutch sway, indeed, judging from such evidence as I have been able to obtain, there would seem to have been no increase among the Hottentots. In 1666, Commander Wagenaar estimated the fighting men of one of the Hottentot tribes only (the Saldaniers) at about 3000, which would probably give a total population of 15,000. This was the largest tribe of Hottentots then known to the Dutch, but there were several smaller ones. After the lapse of some hundred and thirty years of Dutch rule from the time of Wagenaar, the total Hottentot population of the colony was estimated by Sir John Barrow at not more than 15,000. The following are Barrow's figures:[1]—

Population of Cape Colony:—

Christians, ...	21,746
Slaves, ...	25,754
Hottentots, ...	14,447
Total, .	61,947

The Hottentots were never absolutely reduced by the Dutch to the condition of slaves. Overtures in this direction had indeed been made by some of the farmers, before the advent of English rule, but their desires had not been fulfilled. But if not slaves, the Hottentots were

[1] Barrow, vol. ii. p. 378.

far from being free men. They occupied a position somewhat similar to the serfs and villeins of other countries. They could not be bought or sold, and, according to law, were permitted to claim their freedom when twenty-five years of age. But other laws existed which nullified this liberty. It was enacted by the Dutch Government that if a Hottentot child received a piece of meat from the colonist, that act constituted it also a vassal until it should be twenty-five years of age.[1] Thus, when the parents were twenty-five years of age, their children were all in bondage, which practically bound the Hottentot to his Dutch master for life. And should he insist on leaving, there was a law by which he could be arrested as a "vagrant Hottentot." There was no political cohesion among the Hottentots; and little opposition was shown by them to the Dutch. Had the latter continued to govern the colony it is probable that the former would, in the course of time, have passed away, and we should have thought of them as "having given place to a superior race." But the advent of the English Government, and of Christian instruction, produced a phenomenon among the Hottentots as marked as that to which we called attention in the case of the Bushmen. Those who were decreasing under Dutch rule began to increase under the sway of the English. Regarding Barrow's figures as being at any rate near the truth, we find that the Hottentot population of the colony doubled itself in the first thirty years of English rule. It was reported to Sir T. F. Buxton's committee of the House of Commons, in 1836, that the Hottentots then numbered some 32,000. Taking this estimate as approximately correct, it will be seen that a steady increase continued during the next thirty years. In 1865, the first elaborate census of the population of the Cape Colony was taken. From the information then collected, tables were formed, showing, with other important information, the sex, age, and race of the mixed inhabitants. The races are given under the divisions of "European," "Hottentot," Kaffir," and "other." Under the "Hottentot" column, I find

[1] Barrow, vol. i. p. 146.

the following figures, which do not include British Kaffraria, or what is now the divisions of King William's Town and East London :—

Western Division of Colony, . .	52,637
Eastern „ . .	28,961
Total Hottentot population in 1865,	81,598

I do not profess to explain the cause of the decrease of the Hottentot population under Dutch rule. I do not find that many Hottentots were killed in open warfare. Disease, indeed, carried away more than the Dutch killed in battle. We are told that soon after the occupation of the Cape by the Dutch the Hottentots were "very much diminished, and melted away" by "a sickness" among them. The small-pox also committed fearful and repeated ravages during the period of the Dutch supremacy. But this leaves the question unsolved, for both small-pox and typhus fever, which may have been the "sickness" referred to by Wagenaar, have ravaged the colony since it came into the hands of the English. This much seems to be clear, that a race which was decreasing in a state of serfdom, increases in a state of freedom; and that contact with Europeans, under English government, and with Christian training, has not been prejudicial to the Hottentot race. In connection with this increase of the Hottentot population, it must be mentioned that living as they do in the midst of Europeans and Kaffirs in colonial villages and farms, such connections have been formed as that the present Hottentot population is probably an abler and stronger race than were their ancestors. A Hottentot woman, while affecting to despise a Kaffir, usually prefers a European suitor to a man of her own nation. Such unions are not often sanctioned by marriage, but nevertheless frequently continue during the life of one of the parties. When they are broken, it is almost always by the desertion of the European man, and not by the unfaithfulness of the Hottentot woman.

Kaffirs.

But if the Hottentot race is not now dying out, but increasing, much less is the Kaffir family likely to "melt away" or "give place" to other races. Whatever our platform rhetorician may say, inexorable facts are against this supposition. While the Dutch from the south were mysteriously dealing with the Hottentots, a black army was advancing upon the same people from the north-east. The first mention of the Kaffirs in the Dutch colonial records represents them as having then (1688) driven the Hottentots as far south as the Great Fish River. In 1702 the first fight took place between Kaffirs and Europeans—the latter being forty-five in number, with an equal number of Hottentots. The Dutch were ostensibly on a trading trip, but powder and lead would seem to have been the commodity in which they chiefly dealt. In 1737 there was still a considerable tract of country between the Dutch settlers and the Kaffirs, which was inhabited by the Gonaqua Hottentots. At this time the hunting-field of the Dutchmen was at Sunday river; the Gonaquas lay to the east of the Fish river; while the town of the Amaxosa Kaffirs was five days' journey beyond the Gonaquas, and to the east. We learn thus minutely the position of the races at this early period from a paper written by Secretary Tulbagh, and signed at Cape Town in 1737 by two survivors of Heupenaar's party, who crossed the country from Natal to the Cape Colony.[1] In 1778 the two aggressive races had between them "eaten up" the Gonaquas, and now made their first treaty, recognising the Fish river as a boundary between one another. And now for years we have the spectacle of two races dashing against one another in hostile attitude. The law of the European society in Southern Africa was aggressive, but not more so than that of the Kaffir tribes, which was simply, as far and as often as they could, to "eat up" all their neighbours, black or white. The scene of this combat changed from time to time, like the ebb and

1 *Remarks on Publication of Cape Records.* By a Member of late Committee. P. 48.

flow of the tide. In the rich Zuurveldt, where the town of Grahamstown now stands, it seemed at one time as if the two races were to live together in peace and friendship. "Their flocks grazed on the same hills, and their herdsmen smoked together out of the same pipes." But, like an overflowing caldron, Kaffir-land, convulsed with internal feuds, poured its people into the Zuurveldt in 1789, from which they dislodged the Dutch, and followed them westward, until in 1797 Barrow found a large tribe of dusky emigrants on the banks of the Sunday river, and some had advanced as far westward as the borders of Swellendam. In 1811, the colony being now under the English Government, the black wave was rolled back again, some 20,000 Kaffirs being, wisely or unwisely, compelled to recross the Fish river. This was followed by an invasion of the colony by the Kaffirs in 1817. When peace was concluded in 1819, the country between the Fish river and the Keiskama was declared by the English to be a neutral territory, which was to be unoccupied except by military posts. This stipulation, however, was relaxed, and Gaika and other chiefs were allowed to settle there as a favour. In 1829 it was held that Makomo, the son of Gaika, had forfeited his claim to this privilege by attacking a small neighbouring tribe, and pursuing them within the colonial boundary. The Kaffirs were therefore again driven eastward beyond the Keiskama; and again, in 1834, was this succeeded by an invasion of the colony. However much we may regret the costly Kaffir wars of 1846 and 1851,—especially if we believe that the settlement of Sir B. Durham in 1835 would have prevented them, had it been carried into practice,—it would seem, on the other hand, simply impossible to have entirely avoided fighting, when warlike Kaffirs came into contact with scattered and pastoral colonists. If we consider what may be called the normal state of Kaffir society, of which they sing in their dances, and to which young men are encouraged to look forward when they are circumcised, it is evident that peaceful colonists could not possibly exist in their neighbourhood. As they drove the Hottentots before them, and robbed them of their cattle, so would they have treated the Europeans had they been able. The degree of latitude in which the two races met would have nothing to do with the matter. They might have a river, or a wide "neutral territory" between them, but they would certainly meet in combat, and stand or fall according to their ability to fight. In point of fact, the country, which was sometimes the ostensible cause of quarrel, belonged as much to the Europeans as to the Kaffirs—both races having only recently made their appearance in it, dispossessing its former Hottentot inhabitants. And with reference to the future, it is evident that if peace is to be permanent, the Kaffir idea of life and society must be changed or rendered impossible. Surrounded on all sides by Europeans, every Kaffir town occupied by missionaries, the downfall of this lawless and bloody feudalism is inevitable. And surely no South African Jacobite will be so sentimental as to shed a single tear when it passes away.

In 1857 the colony was again invaded by the Kaffirs, but this time they came not singing their war-song and anticipating victory. They made their appearance at the doors of the colonists emaciated and starving, humbly craving for a little food. The Kaffirs believe in the visions of certain prophets or oracles who arise among them from time to time. In the war of 1817-19, they were led by Makanna, and in 1850 by Umlanjeni, both of whom professed to have supernatural powers. In 1857, Umhlakaza gave forth a message which stirred the whole Kaffir people, and in which cunning and fanaticism would seem to have been strangely blended. He said that "in a certain subterranean cave in Kreli's country, there were innumerable fat cattle, which the Kaffirs might possess, but only after they had entirely destroyed their present flocks and herds, as well as the corn and other food which they had stored. Inducements were held forth that ten cattle would be restored for every one killed; that the ancestors of their nation would soon appear in person; that the white men were to be driven into the sea, and that then the Kaffir nation was to settle down and enjoy the land."

This prophecy had no doubt a deep and heathenish political meaning. It was evidently thought that if the Kaffirs had absolutely no food whatever in their own country, for themselves or for their families, and if they were led at once against the white people, they would fight as they had never done before. The sufferings of helpless old people and young children, necessarily involved in carrying out such a scheme, were not taken into account by this dreadful prophet, and those who shared with him his secrets and his counsels. But the scheme, which seems to have been well planned as a whole, utterly failed in the carrying out of its details. Had all promptly obeyed the commands of the prophet, slain their cattle and destroyed their corn and marched at once into the colony, no one can tell what the result would have been. But the chiefs did not all obey. The Fingoes and several Kaffir chiefs, who were more or less influenced by Christianity, openly expressed their disbelief in the oracle, and refused to destroy their cattle. Others professed their belief in the prophet, and wished it to be understood that they had obeyed his command, having, however, spared some of their cattle and a quantity of their corn. As the prophet insisted that everything should be destroyed, a difficulty arose, through the hesitancy and wavering of some. No general movement could take place. In the meantime those who had wildly and unquestioningly obeyed the command, giving their herds to the wolves and vultures to eat, and scattering their corn to rot on the ground, were themselves now famishing. In vain the wily chief Makomo endeavoured to strengthen the power of the prophet by declaring that he too had seen some of their Kaffir ancestors, and had spoken to them; the hesitating ones were not to be convinced. And so this scheme of vengeance and of conquest became a complete failure, and an awful calamity to the Kaffirs themselves. Many died of starvation, and some 30,000 were saved from death by the food which they obtained from their former enemies in the colony.

When we think of the inhabitants of the Cape Colony, we are accustomed to think of the Europeans who have at different times emigrated thither. But they are not the only emigrants there. As it has been impossible to arrest the northward and eastward spread of the white men, so has the attempt to stem the southward and westward progress of the Kaffirs been a complete failure. Swept more than once out of the colony by the English, the number of Kaffirs within its boundary, in 1865, and not including British Kaffraria, was 100,536.

These figures show that the Kaffir people themselves desire to be freed from the blind and despotic sway of chief and witch-doctor. If this were not the case, they might at once return to their own tribes, as no restraint is placed upon them. No doubt secret messages from the chiefs could be conveyed to the colony, and this has indeed taken place. But their long-dreaded power is waning every year, and while the presence of commissioners in Kaffirand is likely to put a stop to evil counsels, the scattered condition of the people must also discourage the chief from attempting to organize war-parties.

Bechuanas.

While the Dutch and English have been filling up the colony from the south, and the Kaffirs have poured in from the east, another immigration has been going on from the north. Every colonial village, every agricultural and pastoral district, contains a number of servants who come from Bechuana-land. Even on the sea-board you meet with them. In sequestered glens you find little colonies together. In the Census which we have quoted they are included under the head "other natives," of whom there are 132,655. Most of them do not intend to return northward. They prefer the colony on the whole. If the traveller in certain districts of Bechuana-land sometimes feels inclined to exclaim "Where are the people?" the answer is, I think, on the whole, a very satisfactory one. They have deserted the Pagan towns, and are helping the white man in the colony, by such service as they can render, to rear Christian homesteads and busy villages, where but a few years ago the solitary Bushman stalked the gnu and the springbok. It is to be hoped their masters and their masters' Christian overseers do not forget those pushing emigrants. It is to be hoped that in many cases they receive Christian instruction, which will make them better qualified either to reside in a civilized country, or to return to the land of their fathers. While tribes are being broken up in the north, sometimes as the indirect result of the labours of Christian missionaries, and their members are spreading themselves southward, working for their bread and paying for what they possess, the white men are looking northward, entering those partially disorganized countries, and gradually assuming in them the position which their greater ability as compared with natives enables them to sustain. For just as the black emigrant in the colony does not don civilisation in a day, or find himself all at once in possession of a waggon, or a shop, or a villa at Green Point or Mowbray, so it is not to be supposed that the white men beyond the colony will suddenly become divested of their energy and skill and civilisation. The one goes south and falls into the position of a servant, and finds masters and pay for his service. The other travels northward in the power and resource of the educated European, and gradually the management of things slips out of the hands of natives and of ignorant frontier-born men, and the "uitlander" (foreigner) finds himself in a position of trust and responsibility.

But it seems to me evident that the parties who are thus coalescing ought not to have among themselves the whole settlement of their quarrels on the border land. In this case, the strong would infallibly oppress the weak, and justice suffer and miscarry. For if it is hard for one race to be all at once energetic and industrious in an entirely changed state of society, it is perhaps even more difficult for the man of energy to be merciful and considerate, or even just, at all times, to those whom he is elbowing out of the way. While, then, it is for the black man to try to be "up to the mark" as to energy and perseverance, it is for the European to prove himself a Christian by repressing impatience in his dealings with men who are 1800 years behind his native land in thought and attainment. But if a third party is to be called in, it is evident that it must be one whom the white man will respect, and whose award he will obey. The Christian man, who wishes well to Europeans and to Africans, could desire no more than that, with Christianity to elevate, there should be a strong and just government to protect, to restrain, and, if necessary, to punish. For all colours and races let there be "a fair field and no favour," and may God's mercy be over all!

I have been much interested to find that Sir Charles Wentworth Dilke recommends, for the preservation of the remaining Red Indians, the very process which is now taking place, in God's providence, in Southern Africa. "Hitherto the whites have pushed back the Indians westwards; if they would preserve the remnant from starvation they must bring them east, away from Western men, and Western hunting-grounds, and let them intermingle with the whites, living, farming, along with them, intermarrying if possible."[1] In Southern Africa, and without the interference of any one, the restless, the powerful, and skilful are passing northwards; the comparatively weak and ignorant are emigrating southward, and there finding a peaceful home.

[1] *Greater Britain*, vol. i. p. 130.